Spiritualism and the Foundations of C. G. Jung's Psychology

Spiritualism and the Foundations of C. G. Jung's Psychology

F. X. Charet

State University of New York Press

Published by
State University of New York Press, Albany

© 1993   State University of New York

Printed in the United States of America

For information, address State University of New York
Press, State University Plaza, Albany, NY 12246

Production by Christine M. Lynch
Marketing by Dana E. Yanulavich

Library of Congress Cataloging-in-Publication Data

Charet, F. X., 1949–
        Spiritualism and the foundations of C. G. Jung's psychology /
F. X. Charet.
        p.   cm.
        Includes bibliographical references and index.
        ISBN 0–7914–1093–5 — ISBN 0–7914–1094–3 (pbk.)
        1. Jung, C. G. (Carl Gustav), 1875–1961. 2. Spiritualism.
I. Title.
BF109.J8C43   1993
150.19'54—dc20
                                                                    91–23521
                                                                    CIP

10 9 8 7 6 5 4 3 2 1

for
my children

Contents

Acknowledgments

This book was written under trying personal circumstances and largely in isolation from academic exchange and community.

Nevertheless, in writing this work I have incurred a number of debts. My greatest debts are to those closest to me. To all those family and friends who offered me their support and encouragement I offer my thanks. I would especially like to thank Tara Devi Menon for her loyalty and love. Most of all I owe to my children who, through the good times and the bad times, have filled my life immeasurably with their lives. This book is for them.

"*...a creative man has no choice. He may come across his supreme task almost accidentally. But once the issue is joined, his task proves to be at the same time intimately related to his most personal conflicts, to his superior selective perception, and to the stubborness of his one-way will: he must court sickness, failure, or insanity, in order to test the alternative whether the established world will crush him, or whether he will disestablish a sector of this world's outworn fundaments and make place for a new one.*"[1]

Preface

In recent years there has been a steadily increasing interest in C. G. Jung's psychology. His writings containing his psychological theories and observations have become more widely known, discussed, and written about both inside and outside of academic circles. In addition, Jung's followers have created a small but growing literature on the subject of his psychology and its myriad applications that sustains a dedicated coterie of practitioners, readers, and fellow travellers. Some of this literature and, more particularly, the works of Jung himself have attracted the attention of scholars. A good deal of this attention has found expression in publications devoted to Jung's ideas on religion and has come from individuals working in the area of religious studies. But, it is equally important to observe, the bulk of this scholarship is concerned with Jung's ties to, and criticisms of, traditional religion, and Christianity in particular.

There is every justification for continuing to author works on Jung and Christianity, especially in the light of Jung's own interest in the subject, which intensified as he became older. An almost equally legitimate case could be made for encouraging further studies on Jung and other religions, especially Eastern religions. At the same time it is often overlooked that Jung's interest in Christianity and Eastern religions was somewhat heterodox. His views on Christianity, while extremely interesting, were not formulated as a consequence of aligning himself with any of the Christian theological movements of the twentieth century, Catholic or Protestant. Jung was not a theologian, and it is difficult to imagine that his psychology could ever be completely reconciled with Christian theology. And even if Jung had more in common with some forms of Protestant theology, interest in his psychology is marginal among Protestant theologians who these days seem to be more concerned with politics. Jung had much to say about Christianity, and much of it is important, but it was said by someone who was, as he himself realized, *extra ecclesiam*.

Jung's interest in Eastern religions, on the other hand, largely took the form of forewords to, and commentaries on, such works as D. T. Suzuki's *Introduction to Zen Buddhism, The I Ching, The Tibetan Book of the Dead, The Tibetan Book of the Great Liberation,* and *The Secret of the Golden Flower.* While these books are Eastern, it is arguable that, in the second half of the twentieth century, they have had more influence in the West. It is also true that these works were more widely read than any Christian theological work, Catholic or Protestant. For example the *I Ching,* an archaic book of Chinese divination that most publishers initially judged to be too obscure to deserve translation, had by the early eighties, sales of one-half million hardcover copies. It was a new generation of pilgrims that were purchasing these books and along with them the writings of Carl Gustav Jung and his followers.

In these circles, outside of academia, Jung has become downright popular. He is linked to a host of quasi-religious movements, and his name is conjured up to justify any number of assertions and opinions. In fact, he is regarded by some as one of the harbingers of a New Age consciousness, an exemplary being who would not tolerate the traditional division between religion and science, and who united these in his own life and in the grandeur of his psychology.

Indeed, Jung's life and psychology stand together as the accomplishment of a remarkable and complex man. But the reality and significance of Jung's achievement demand to be understood and not simply praised. Understanding Jung is in its preliminary stages. In what follows I have attempted to contribute toward this understanding by investigating the early sources of some of Jung's ideas that have been found by many to be so appealing. To do so I have had to stray from the beaten path of traditional religion in order to track down one of the more unusual, and more deeply personal, religious influences in Jung's early life, namely Spiritualism. And, to anticipate doubts about the relevance of such an influence, I beg my readers, for a time, to suspend their disbelief.

Montreal, Autumn 1991

F. X. Charet

Notes

1. Erik H. Erikson, *Insight and Reponsibility* (New York: W. W. Norton, 1964), 22–23.

Introduction

The following essay is a study in the background of C. G. Jung's psychology focusing specifically on one of the important religious influences in his early life, namely Spiritualism.[1] In what follows I have given the term *Spiritualism* a rather wide latitude though, I hope, I have not moved too far from the definition I will provide in chapter 1. While in this study I use the term *Spiritualism* to mean a belief in the communication between the living and the dead, I also mean by it the various experiences and ideas that became attached to this belief. I should also like to make clear that I am neither advocating such a belief nor claiming that Jung definitely and consistently held to such a belief throughout his life. Instead, I will argue that Spiritualism became an important factor in Jung's early life and thought and contributed significantly to the foundations upon which he built his psychology.

In addition, what follows is also an essay in the psychology of religion, from within the field of religious studies.[2] As a discipline, Religious Studies recognizes religious phenomena as a category of human experience that can be subjected to study by various methods.[3] The method I am using is mainly a psychologically informed historical method, which I have applied in an endeavour to establish the influence of Spiritualism in the life and thought of C. G. Jung.

The specific area in the psychology of religion that I have focused on is the extent to which religious experiences have influenced thinkers in the sciences.[4] In particular, I believe such studies of distinguished psychologists could contribute to a greater understanding of the part religious experiences and beliefs play in the formulations of theories of the human person.[5] The following essay attempts just this by focusing on one school of psychology, by studying one particular religious influence in the life of its founder. The implication of my study of the influence of Spiritualism on Jung is that the religious dimension may, to some extent, be foundational and determinative in the formation of scientific theories in the lives of certain important individual thinkers.

In the field of religious studies, Carl Gustav Jung (1875–1961) is regarded as one of the towering figures of the twentieth century.[6] His works on religion, a subject central to his thinking as a whole, certainly belong in the twentieth century.[7] Nevertheless, Jung was born and came to maturity in the late nineteenth century, a period of his early life that has been largely left unexamined by both his followers and detractors.[8] Paradoxically, Jung's early life is left unstudied even by those who openly declare the importance of recovering the background of his psychology for an understanding of his later work. C. A. Meier provides a good example of this attitude which he clearly demonstrates in his textbook on Jung's psychology. His opening paragraph reads as follows:

> Only gods are born miraculously full-grown from trees, mountains or the head of Zeus. Every science possesses its own phylogeny and ontology, just as it possesses its own postulates and its own conclusions. We epigones are therefore only deceiving ourselves if we disregard the position of a school or doctrine in the history of thought or the personal history and development of its founder. If we do so, our assimilation of our subject will remain, as it were, at the epiphenomenal level.[9]

Yet Meier himself begins his presentation of Jung's psychology with the latter's *Studies in World Association* (1904–1909), most of which were undertaken when Jung was already in his thirties, completely ignoring a full discussion of his earlier life and work.[10]

It seems clear that the early years of Jung's life and thought presents difficulties for both friend and foe of his psychology. The paucity of data on Jung's early life certainly accounts for some of the problems in attempting a historical reconstruction of this period. Another factor, and an uncomfortable one for many, is the extent to which religion intrudes itself upon the events of Jung's early life. In fact, it could be argued that a preoccupation with religious matters and religious experiences characterize much of Jung's early life and thought. In the intellectual climate of the twentieth century this embarrassing fact attracts not only psychological, but psychopathological explanations of Jung's early experiences.[11] Paul Vitz accurately characterizes this attitude, albeit in traditional terms, when he states:

> Indeed, religion is now the only remaining seriously threatening, even taboo topic. The possibility of having uncon-

scious desires for one's mother, murderous hatred for
one's father, homosexual desires—all these have become
accepted, even expected. But as for unconscious desires for
God and an unconscious desire for salvation, these possibilities are today (at least for most intellectuals) still inadmis-
sible.[12]

Apart from simplifying the exceedingly difficult problem of
analyzing and interpreting religious experience, reducing Jung's
religious experiences and concerns to psychopathology also avoids
the question of the extent to which it disengages his early life from
the context within which it occurred. Unless, of course, it is argued
by way of a *reductio ad absurdum* that the broader preoccupation
with religion as an institutional and social reality, the emphasis on
religious experience, and the consequent emergence of such movements as Spiritualism in the nineteenth century are all indications
of mass psychopathology. A more balanced view, it seems to me,
would be to try to distinguish the pathological elements from those
which demonstrate purposiveness, healing, and a drive toward
greater consciousness. Jung's preoccupation with religion was not
something endemic to him alone but part of a much wider preoccupation with religion as an institutional, social, and psychological
reality in the nineteenth century. It is to this period of European
history and to the religious concerns Europeans had that we must
turn to understand the wider context within which to situate
Jung's early religious experiences.

The second half of the nineteenth century into which Jung was
born was a period in Western European history during which material progress became the measurement of success, with the clergy
and philosophers becoming increasingly displaced by scientists as
figures of authority.[13] So assured did the progress of science appear,
and so easily had this been read in terms of the overthrowing of
long-held religious doctrines, that in some minds even the Christian
church seemed threatened. Liberal theologians, caught between a
commitment to the old and the need to live with the new, attempted
to disengage from Christianity the miraculous and all that contra-
dicted what was scientifically defined as natural law. As a result, for
many Protestant thinkers religion was either defined exclusively in
terms of feeling or turned into a nondogmatic, moral, and ethical
system, both unimpeded by the difficulties science presented.[14]

So shaken were other religious believers by the dilemma science and positivism presented in the late nineteenth century that

they retreated into an outdated conservatism or pathetically avoided any discussion of the issue whatsoever.[15] Critical historical studies focused on the life of Jesus to determine how much he was a product of his environment. For many intellectuals these lives of Jesus and other attempts at higher criticism resulted inevitably in their renouncing belief in the finality of dogmatic judgments and the transcendental base they rested upon.[16] As Owen Chadwick has lucidly observed:

> Educated Europeans in the third quarter of the nineteenth century still looked towards the altar of God, for all that evolution could say. But they stumbled. This change was not just a change for the theologian. It was a change in the religious understanding or attitude of religious men.
>
> So indefinable a change may be described, provisionally, as an extension of the area of intellectual agnosticism within the realm of religion, even for religious men, especially for religious men.[17]

The consensus of opinion about the religious dilemma of late nineteenth-century Western Europe has achieved the status of a truism which one historian has expressed as follows: "The intellectual confusion of the age resulted in great part from the schism between theology and science, and a number of ardent minds set themselves to seek a reconciliation that would make man 'whole' again."[18]

True as this characterization might be, the fact is that such a schism and the attempts at reconciliation that followed, remained somewhat obscure to the general population.[19] Addressing the issue of the conflict between theology and science in a scholarly fashion produced few concrete and acceptable answers to the religious crises many ordinary persons dimly perceived. This debate remained an intellectual luxury, however much it was conducted in earnest, that was reserved for the select few. The emerging concerns expressed in nineteenth-century European literature suggest that many looked elsewhere than to traditional religion, liberal or conservative, to express their deep uncertainties. Nor did they turn to science.

It would seem, in spite of the often repeated but mistaken assumptions about the early nineteenth-century origins of the industrial age, little of its dominant energy actually influenced the literature of the times.[20] Instead, early nineteenth-century European society appears to have been considerably shaken by the disillusionment resulting from the collapse of the quest for a perfect, rational society. Rather than offering clues about the emerging industrial age, the literature actually mirrors very poignantly the weariness caused by the reality of this failure. Whatever prophetic intimations the literature contains, it points to something other than the engines of industry.

What form an important part of early nineteenth-century European literature are idealized novels and fantasy-haunted writers whose defiance of the world was stronger in emotion than reason. These works and their authors succeeded in "knitting a million readers in a vicarious kinship with those superb and tragic rebels, from Faust to Manfred, who defied and scorned the world's incomprehension."[21] By the second quarter of the nineteenth century the dominant literary themes expressed a preoccupation with "the emotional, the imaginative, the supersensuous, and the supernatural."[22] Toward the end of the century, free expression of one's thoughts and sensations became an accepted technique in literature where it produced "The interior monologue, the stream of consciousness' novel, the search for new symbols and for a unique personal vocabulary, revealing the growing absorption of the newer writers with inner states of thought and feeling."[23]

The natural outcome of this self-preoccupation was to personify the inner world by resorting to the literary device of the double, whose modern origins hark back to the time of Mesmer.[24] An early occurrence of the double is to be found in Goethe, where in his *Faust* (1808), Mephisto is Faust's *doppelgänger*. But, it is really only in E. T. A. Hoffmann (1776–1822) that we find the beginning of the identification of this literary device with mental states that will find a place in the later nineteenth-century psychiatric casebook.[25] One of Hoffmann's own primary sources was G. H. von Schubert's *Die Symbolik des Traumes* (1814) which in one place declares:

> The lower organs of the human body...are sensitive to spiritual influences from without, but may transmit the guidance of either higher or lower spirit worlds: so that the contradictory voice we hear within us counselling us to thoughts and deeds incompatible with those of our normal personality emanates from our 'conscience' which may express either the good or bad principles of our minds.[26]

In *Die Elixiere des Teufels* (1816) and *Der Doppelgänger* (1825) Hoffmann utilizes such emerging psychological ideas to confirm the identification of the double as duplicated self and the unconscious as second self.[27] Hoffmann's works foreshadowed an important trend in later nineteenth-century literature, which enshrined these ideas in stories and characters that are often a curious mixture of medical science and religion.[28]

If we view Jung's psychology in the light of these nineteenth-century trends we may perceive loose connections and similar ideas. I believe the similarity is more profound and bears closer examination. Like any modern thinker, Jung had to contend with the values and assumptions of those who preceded him. Nevertheless, it is my opinion that Jung's psychology is less reactionary than is generally assumed. The alienation he constantly complained about testifies not only to the deep uncertainties he shared with others, when the culture within which he lived disintegrated into what is now called a "pluralistic society," but also to the originality of some of his ideas.[29]

Jung grew up in historic Basel and had a deep and profound sense of history, which he often felt was thrust upon him and which he could not shrug off. His various attempts to unburden himself were unsuccessful, and he felt condemned to explain the past, beginning with his own life and then with the life of mankind as a collectivity. In this journey from the personal to the collective, Jung believed he uncovered unconscious processes that were fundamentally religious in nature. Jung enshrined this truth in his life and writing, ever anticipating that the future would vindicate him. This has not yet happened, and in some ways this truth seems so incongruous with certain streams of twentieth-century Western thought that it may be of some merit to inquire a little deeper into the immediate background and context out of which it has come.

Jung was aware of the nineteenth-century medical background out of which his psychology emerged.[30] In addition, he claimed that his own philosophical foundations lay in the eighteenth century, where the figure of Immanuel Kant (1724–1804) loomed large and whose basic premise concerning the limits of human knowledge Jung claimed as his own.[31] To this could be added the influence of Schopenhauer (1788–1860), whom Jung called his "great find" when he was a student.[32] In some ways, Jung's concept of individuation is prefigured in the writings of Schleiermacher (1768–1834).[33] Goethe (1749–1832), too, exercised a considerable fascination over Jung.[34] Carl Gustav Carus (1789–1869) and von Hartmann (1842–1906) are often looked upon as Jung's predecessors.[35]

The old university town of Basel, where Jung grew up, had an atmosphere heavy with nineteenth-century thinkers. The figure of Nietzsche (1844–1900) still cast a shadow over Basel University when Jung was a student there. Some years later Jung would lecture on *Thus Spake Zarathustra* producing, in its unpublished form, a ten-volume commentary.[36] Ignaz Paul Troxler (1780–1866) taught philosophy in Basel and had a theory about the center of the personality similar to Jung's ideas of the Self.[37] One of Jung's closest friends, Albert Oeri, was a nephew of the renowned cultural historian Jacob Burckhardt (1818–97). Jung would later equate his concept of the archetype with Burckhardt's primordial ideas.[38] J. J. Bachofen (1815–87), whom Jung passed now and then on the street, was another resident and professor at Basel University. It has been pointed out that his ideas on matriarchy find their psychological counterpart in Jung's concept of the "anima."[39]

Many of these influences are important, and some may even be crucial in any attempt at reconstructing the background of Jung's thought. No doubt there are others as well, all of which need to be examined in greater detail.[40] But, if we follow Jung's own account as found in his autobiography, we can only conclude that most of these influences, with the possible exception of Goethe, are indirect and occur later in his life. It is at the earlier stages in his life that Jung located the beginnings of what he termed "my encounters with the 'other' reality, my bouts with the unconscious."[41] Most of the formal influences to which I have alluded tell only part of the story and do not, by themselves, explain the early development of Jung's ideas. There is another influence which I believe has a more direct bearing on the background and early history of Jung's psychological theories. I will briefly outline this influence, which I term "Spiritualism," and in the coming chapters I argue how Spiritualism acted as a prism in Jung's early life, refracting some of those other, more formal, influences in a very specific way.

In chapter 1, I sketch the social and medical history of mesmerism, hypnotism, and Spiritualism in the nineteenth century. The phenomenon of trance, which is common to all three, is the chief focus of this chapter. The data emerging from individuals in the trance state often took the form of autonomous personalities. This was interpreted in two ways: (1) by neurologists and psychiatrists as subconscious formations and evidence of individual pathology, and (2) by certain persons in society as evidence of communication with the dead and therefore proof of a spiritual world.

There is little in this chapter that is original or controversial. I am largely indebted to Henri Ellenberger's *Discovery of the Unconscious* and the other sources I cite for the material presented.

In chapter 2, I focus in particular on Jung's early life and his ancestral background to demonstrate the extent of the influence of Spiritualism on him. I also contrast Jung's paternal and maternal background as the more personalized dimension of the conflict between Christianity and Spiritualism in Jung's early life. In addition, I suggest in this chapter that Jung's own early life is the source for his remarks about the general psychology of childhood. The material I base my arguments upon in this chapter is drawn largely from the autobiographical and biographical sources I indicate. None of these are controversial with the exception of Stephanie Zumstein-Preiswerk's *C. G. Jungs Medium*,[42] which I address in detail in my remarks on the sources to chapter 5.

In chapter 3, I outline the primary sources upon which Jung, during his university years, based his intellectual response to Spiritualism. The most important sources for Jung were certain works by the philosophers Kant and Schopenhauer. In this chapter I provide evidence that both Kant and Schopenhauer were preoccupied with the subject of Spiritualism. In addition, I argue that certain precritical writings of Kant on Spiritualism, as interpreted by Schopenhauer, provided Jung with the philosophical foundations upon which he would build his psychological understanding of Spiritualism. The sources I use in this chapter, chiefly Kant's *Dreams of a Spirit-Seer* (1766), and Schopenhauer's *Essay on Spirit Seeing* (1851), are not particularly controversial, though they are largely overlooked. The significance of the material I will present on Kant and Schopenhauer as a source for Jung's early ideas on the psychology of Spiritualism has not been previously studied, as far as I am aware.

In chapter 4, I examine the student lectures Jung gave in the 1890s in order to demonstrate the extent to which he used Kant and Schopenhauer to subject Spiritualism to a philosophical analysis. I also indicate there is evidence in these lectures that Jung was moving from philosophy to psychiatry, completing the foundation upon which he would build his psychological understanding of Spiritualism. The sources I have drawn upon for this chapter are Jung's recently published *Zofingia Lectures*.[43] Henri Ellenberger first brought these lectures to the attention of scholars when he presented an outline of their contents as described in a relatively unknown article written by Jung's fellow student, Gustav Steiner.[44] Jung himself never mentioned these lectures, nor was it known that he had kept a copy of them. A complete manuscript of these lectures surfaced when Jung's heirs made them available for a memorial exhibition marking the centenary of Jung's birth in 1975. They were subsequently published in 1983.[45] The importance of *The Zofingia Lectures* is recognized, but they have not been subjected to careful study.[46] The analysis of these lectures in chapter 4 is independent and breaks new ground.

In chapter 5, I focus on Jung's medical dissertation, *On the Psychology and Pathology of So-Called Occult Phenomena* (1902),[47] which is a psychological study of a medium observed during the course of a number of séances. Specifically, I will argue that the dissertation is an important document indicating the merging of certain personal and professional factors in Jung's early life. The medium, who appears to have been in love with Jung, was his cousin; the séances involved Jung's family and were set in his own home. These facts add an emotional quality to Jung's dissertation that clarifies certain points, the most important of which is the element of self-analysis, an outcome of Jung's identification with his cousin, the medium.

Professionally, Jung moved in the direction of formulating a psychiatric theory that posited the medium's spirits were subconscious personalities that anticipated the future development of her personality. The profound effect of Kant and Schopenhauer is evident in Jung's move from a spiritualistic view of the phenomenon of the séance to a more clearly psychiatric explanation. Nevertheless, Jung made reference to the fact that an exclusively psychiatric explanation may not account for all of the phenomena observed.

The chief sources for this chapter are Jung's dissertation, *On the Psychology and Pathology of So-Called Occult Phenomena*, and Stephanie Zumstein-Preiswerk's *C. G. Jungs Medium*. I have also made use of an article by William Goodheart.[48] The first, Jung's dissertation, has never been studied in detail, another testimony to the fact that Jung's early work has been left unexamined. Zumstein-Preiswerk's study of Jung's cousin, the medium Helene Preiswerk, has known a certain amount of criticism. James Hillman, in a somewhat ambiguous review article, has called the work a "semifictionalized biographical sketch" and yet goes on to disclose the important details Zumstein-Preiswerk adds to an understanding of this period of Jung's life.[49] What draws Hillman's greatest criticism is Zumstein-Preiswerk's allegation that Jung's and Helene's relationship was a repressed love story.[50] Barbara Hannah and Marie-Louise von Franz also make depreciating statements

about Zumstein-Preiswerk's attempts to turn Helene into a hero-
ine, but do not offer specific details.[51] Aniela Jaffé has accepted the
chronology of the séances as reconstructed by Zumstein-Preiswerk,
as well as certain other details that are in contradiction to statements made by Jung.[52] She does not, however, acknowledge Zumstein-Preiswerk as her source! Henri Ellenberger, in a recent article, has accepted the substance of Zumstein-Preiswerk's account of
Jung and Helene, including the allegations of suppressed love.[53]
Gerhard Wehr, Jung's most recent biographer has also accepted
Zumstein-Preiswerk's chronology of the séances.[54]

The third source, the article I referred to by William Goodheart, focuses on the place of intimacy, sexuality, repression, and
reaction in the making of Jung's dissertation on Helene. Goodheart
draws on Zumstein-Preiswerk's study to reveal the personal factors
that determined Jung's behavior and attitude toward Helene and
her spiritualistic revelations. In Goodheart's opinion, Jung's concept of the autonomous psyche, which emerged from the dissertation, originated,

> as a protective, partly adaptive, partly defensive measure
> and intellectual construct with which he isolated himself,
> and walled himself and Helly off from each other, in order
> to avoid the enormous and nearly impossible demands and
> responsibilities which an acknowledgement of the real
> cause-and-effect interactional relationship between himself
> and Helly would have placed on him, and on those about
> him, at that time in his life.[55]

Goodheart's article has provoked strong reaction and caused a
heated debate among Jungians.[56] In my opinion, what is important
about Goodheart's allegations is that they call attention to personal
factors that surround Jung's dissertation. I do not believe, as Goodheart seems to, that these bipersonal factors are solely determinative of Jung's view about the autonomy of the archetypal unconscious. Nevertheless, they are important and I argue that their
unresolved erotic nature figured in Jung's attraction to the psychological theories of Sigmund Freud.

In chapter 6, I address the part that spiritualistic phenomena
and their interpretation played in the relationship between Jung
and Freud. I present evidence to indicate that this subject is important in understanding the association and subsequent break
between Jung and Freud. During his psychoanalytic years, Jung

maintained an interest in Spiritualism. He was also seeking some comprehensive psychological method and model to provide him with a more secure and scientifically credible understanding of its manifestations. To some extent, Freud's psychoanalytic theories provided Jung the method and model. On a more personal level, the sexual nature of Freud's theories also provided Jung with a framework within which to fit the unintegrated erotic elements in his relationship with Helene Preiswerk that surfaced in his dissertation.

Jung demanded, over the course of his relationship with Freud, that psychoanalysis broaden its theoretical base to enable it to bring within its confines the spiritualistic phenomena that could not be explained solely in terms of sexuality. To some degree, as a consequence of Jung's interest, Freud took up the study of mediumistic phenomena or what he called "occultism." In the end, I argue that the break between Jung and Freud was influenced by the fact that Freud, unlike Jung, was not prepared to seriously consider spiritualistic data as raw material upon which to build a psychology.

The sources for this chapter are not particularly controversial. The most important item is the published correspondence between Jung and Freud, which documents their relationship.[57] Freud's interest in what he called "occult phenomena" is known, but has not received the attention it deserves.[58] The significance of the interpretation of spiritualistic or occult phenomena in the Freud/ Jung conflict has been studied in even less detail.[59]

In chapter 7, I focus on the period in Jung's life from near the end of his rift with Freud in 1912 up until 1920. This is the time during which Jung experienced severe dissociation, which necessitated a self-analysis. Both of these, in turn, moved Jung away from Freud and provided him the *prima materia* of his later psychology. What characterized Jung's severe dissociation was that it was often accompanied by the surfacing of certain memories of early traumatic experiences that became implicated in his personal relationships with Freud, Toni Wolff, and others. When these experiences were subjected to a Freudian analysis, disturbing and problematical sexual factors were laid bare. Jung recoiled from such a personal and subjective interpretation. The resulting tension was resolved with the occurrence of unusual phenomena identical to the spiritualistic phenomena produced by mediums. The most significant manifestation of this was the haunting of Jung's house by spirits and his subsequent writing of the *Septem Sermones ad Mortuos* (1916). In these sermons are contained, in exotic gnostic lan-

guage, virtually all of Jung's developed ideas: the problem of opposites, the archetypes, individuation, and so on. The sermons, I
argue, also express the ever existing tension between Jung's maternal Spiritualism and paternal Christianity.

I will also show that, as a consequence of constructing his
model of the psyche out of the experiences he had, Jung felt it necessary to address the subject of the possible independent existence
of spirits. Initially, in 1919, Jung subsumed spirits under the psychological category of complexes. At the same time, he made a distinction between the personal complex and the impersonal complex. The first he related to the subjective world of the individual;
the second he claimed was a more collective representation. The
former he would still designate "complex," the latter he would term
"archetype."

The main sources for this chapter are the autobiographical
and biographical materials to which I have already referred.[60] In
addition to these there are two sources, the first of which is Jung's
Septem Sermones ad Mortuos.[61] When this work first came to public
attention it was controversial.[62] Since the publication of the full
text of the *Septem Sermones ad Mortuos* a number of studies have
emerged mainly concerned with the extent to which the sermons
are an early embodiment of Jung's later ideas.[63] My own view is
that the importance of the *Septem Sermones ad Mortuos* as an
early expression of the basic elements of Jung's later psychology
has been generally underestimated.[64]

The second source is Jung's essay "The Psychological Foundations of Belief in Spirits" (1919).[65] This is not a controversial essay,
nor has it been the subject of detailed study. I draw on this particular essay because of its pertinence to the subject which forms the
central concern of the present study, namely that Spiritualism was
a major influence in the life and thought of C. G. Jung.

In the concluding chapter I recapitulate the main features of
my argument that Jung was significantly influenced by Spiritualism during the early period of his life. In addition, I suggest a specific relation between Jung's later views on spirits and his concept
of the archetype. I will also provide evidence from Jung's own
remarks to indicate he remained ambiguous about the reality of
spirits. Finally, I shall end with some observations about the significance of the material uncovered for an understanding of the impact
religious experience has had on Jung's psychological theory.

The chief sources I will draw upon for the concluding chapter
are Jung's essays "On the Nature of the Psyche" (1954)[66] and "Syn-

chronicity: An Acasual Connecting Principle" (1955).[67] These works represent Jung's excursion into the abstract area of the instinctual and spiritual ground of the psyche, the relativity of time, space, and causality, and the reality of the afterlife. These essays have attracted the attention of Jungians but, until recently, were largely overlooked by outsiders.[68] In these essays are to be found Jung's most profound reflections on the nature of reality, many of which have a direct bearing on the ideas and beliefs that make up Spiritualism.

Notes

1. The *Oxford English Dictionary* states that in the early 1850s the term *Spiritualism* began to be defined as "The belief that the spirits of the dead can hold communication with the living, or make their presence known to them in some way, esp. through a 'medium'; the system of doctrines or practices founded on this belief." *Webster's Third New International Dictionary* defines *Spiritualism* in a similar way as "a: a belief that departed spirits hold intercourse with mortals usu. through a medium by means of rapping and other physical phenomena or during abnormal mental states (as trances) b: the doctrines and practices of spiritualists." There is an enormous literature on Spiritualism but little of it is scholarly and critical. As a belief, Spiritualism is found at all levels of culture. As a loose religious movement, Spiritualism is a nineteenth-century phenomenon that started in America and spread to Europe and beyond. Most students of modern Spiritualism agree that its beginnings can be dated from the experiences of the Fox sisters in New York State, in 1848; see Frank Podmore, *Modern Spiritualism*, vol. 1 (London: Methuen & Co., 1902), 179 et seq.; Howard Kerr, *Mediums, and Spirit-Rappers, and Roaring Radicals* (Urbana: University of Illinois Press, 1972), 3 et seq. Spiritualism began as a religion of experience, and its central belief that spirits could communicate with the living was not expressed initially in any systematic manner. This is less so today; see J. Stillson Judah, *The History and Philosophy of the Metaphysical Movements in America* (Philadelphia: The Westminster Press, 1967), 63–91. As far as I am aware, no one has studied the influence of Spiritualism in the life and thought of Jung. Joan D. Koss, "Symbolic Transformations in Traditional Healing Rituals," *Journal of Analytical Psychology* 31 (1986): 341–55, has pointed to the striking parallels between Jungian psychology and Spiritualism, but she seems unaware of the historical influences.

2. For a history of the discipline of Religious Studies, see Eric J. Sharpe, *Comparative Religion: A History* (London: Duckworth, 1975); chapters 5 and 9 are specifically concerned with the psychology of religion. For a recent survey of the psychology of religion; see David M. Wulff, "Psy-

chological Approaches," in Frank Whaling, ed., *Contemporary Approaches to the Study of Religion*, vol. 2, *The Social Sciences* (Berlin: Mouton, 1985), 21–88; and his comprehensive *Psychology of Religion: Classic and Contemporary Views* (New York: John Wiley & Sons, 1991).

3. See, for example, Jacques Waardenburg, ed., *Classical Approaches to the Study of Religion*, 2 vols. (The Hague: Mouton, 1973–74); Frank Whaling, ed., *Contemporary Approaches to the Study of Religion*, 2 vols. (Berlin: Mouton, 1983–85); and the collection in Mircea Eliade and Joseph M. Kitagawa, eds., *The History of Religions: Essays in Methodology* (Chicago: The University of Chicago Press, 1959). The influential Mircea Eliade and others have argued for the irreducibility of the sacred as a methodological criterion in Religious Studies, but not without provoking controversy; see, e.g., Daniel Pals, "Reductionism and Belief: An Appraisal of Recent Attacks on the Doctrine of Irreducible Religion," *Journal of Religion* 66 (1986): 18–36. In many respects my study will show that this was one of the issues with which Jung contended when he moved toward creating a general psychology. It is also interesting to note that Jung is often thought to have influenced Eliade; see Mac Linsott Ricketts, "The Nature and Extent of Eliade's 'Jungianism'," *Union Seminary Quarterly Review* 25 (1970): 211–34. I personally agree with Pals when he states (29–30): "The question of whether Eliade (or anyone else) has 'proved' religion irreducible seems to be badly framed. If it is true, as it seems to me, that such a thesis acts at a high level of abstraction as a kind of disciplinary axiom, directing our attention to a certain aspect of the world and life, then it certainly will not be provable—or refutable—in any simple way.... Like biology's claim to be autonomous over against the reductions of chemistry and physics, it will have to prove itself over a long run by the quality of its fruits." As Ninian Smart has put it in his *Concept and Empathy*, ed. Donald Wiebe (New York: New York University Press, 1986), 206, "Religious Studies is neither the Queen of the Sciences nor the Knave of Arts; but it is one of the foci of the humanities and social sciences."

4. Most studies which have influenced the psychology of religion are of individuals explicitly identified as religious, e.g., Augustine, Luther, Gandhi. In addition, the emphasis is usually on uncovering the psychological origins of their religious beliefs, as in the classic study, Erik H. Erikson, *Young Man Luther* (London: Faber & Faber, 1958). This work, of course, is part of a larger controversial enterprise named Psychohistory; see William J. Gilmore's introduction to *Psychohistorical Inquiry: A Comprehensive Research Bibliography* (New York: Garland, 1984), xi–xxx; and William McKinley Runyan, "The Psychobiography Debate: An Analytical Review," *Review of Personality and Social Psychology* 3 (1982): 225–53. When studies have moved away from exclusively psychological models of analysis and incorporated a more literary, and even theological, form of analysis, the emphasis is still on individuals who are recognizably reli-

gious in the traditional sense of the term; see the collection in Frank E. Reynolds and Donald Capps, eds., *The Biographical Process: Studies in the History and Psychology of Religion* (The Hague: Mouton, 1976); John D. Barbour, "Character and Characterization in Religious Autobiography," *Journal of the American Academy of Religion* 55 (1987): 307–27; and James Wm. McClendon, *Biography as Theology*, (Nashville: Abingdon, 1974). As far as I am aware, there are very few works that have examined in detail the impact of religion on contemporary scientists, and none that I know of by anyone working in the area of the psychology of religion. In order to conduct such studies it is imperative that religion be understood in a broader, more comprehensive way.

5. Sigmund Freud has been much better served in this regard than Jung, though there is the sticky question of separating the specifically religious from the cultural features of his Jewishness; see, for example, David Bakan, *Sigmund Freud and the Jewish Mystical Tradition* (Princeton, N.J.: Van Nostrand, 1958), which claims a direct religious influence; Marthe Robert, *From Oedipus to Moses* (New York: Doubleday, 1976), claims psychoanalysis was born out of the tension between Freud's Jewish identity and secular culture; Justin Miller, "Interpretations of Freud's Jewishness 1924–1974," *Journal of the History of the Behavioral Sciences* 17 (1981): 357–74, examines the various claims about Freud's Judaism and ends up doubting the impact of religion on Freud was very significant. Dennis B. Klein, *Jewish Origins of the Psychoanalytic Movement* (Chicago: University of Chicago Press, 1985) has added his views which have been countered by Peter Gay, *A Godless Jew* (New Haven: Yale University Press, 1987), who minimizes any religious influences. Recently, the question has once again been reopened in favor of the influence of the religious elements of Freud's Jewishness; see William McGrath, "How Jewish Was Freud?" *The New York Review of Books* (Dec. 5, 1991): 27–31. In a different vein, Paul C. Vitz, *Sigmund Freud's Christian Unconscious* (New York: The Guildford Press, 1988), argues suggestively, but not entirely convincingly, that since his childhood Freud had an unconscious attraction to Christianity, which he never quite got over. Erwin R. Wallace, "Freud's Mysticism and its Psychodynamic Determinants," *Bulletin of the Menninger Clinic* 42 (1978): 203–22, moves the discussion to religion as a more broadly understood phenomenon and maintains Freud suppressed his own religious inclinations. I might mention two other brief attempts to indicate the influence of religious experience on a psychologist: George Windholz, "Pavlov's Religious Orientation," *Journal for the Scientific Study of Religion* 25 (1986): 320–27, which is quite sketchy and largely limited to showing Pavlov, though an atheist, was not so negative about religion because he was raised in a religious household. The second study is Paul Creelan, "Watson as Mythmaker: The Millenarian Sources of Watson's Behaviorism," *Journal for the Scientific Study of Religion* 24 (1985): 194–216, which argues persuasively that the father of behaviorism was profoundly influenced by fundamentalist Christianity.

Watson's perfect society engineered by a rewards and punishment technique, Creelan shows, is rooted in the world of Protestant dispensational millinarianism.

6. There is no one work which studies Jung's impact on religious studies, but see Sharpe, 203–19; and the works cited in James W. Heisig, "Jung and Theology: A Bibliographical Essay," *Spring* (1973): 204–55; and Harold Coward, *Jung and Eastern Thought* (Albany: State University of New York Press, 1985).

7. Several of these works from 1928 to 1954 are in C. G. Jung, *Collected Works*, vol. 11, *Psychology and Religion: West and East* (Princeton, N.J.: Princeton University Press, 1969). It is arguable that no single volume of Jung's works covers the subject of religion, which is so prominent in his thinking.

8. The history of Jung's early life is found in the various biographies on him. None is definitive. Those written by Jungians are interesting and informative but often somewhat hagiographical, e.g., Barbara Hannah, *Jung: His Life and Work* (New York: G. P. Putnam's Sons, 1976). Marie-Louise von Franz, *C. G. Jung: His Myth in Our Time* (London: Hodder and Stroughton, 1975), is certainly the best portrait of Jung's intellectual development written by a Jungian. But von Franz, as with the others, tells us little about Jung's early life that is not available in his own autobiography, *Memories, Dreams, Reflections,* ed. Aniela Jaffé (New York: Vintage, 1973) (hereafter *MDR*). Paul J. Stern, *C. G. Jung: The Haunted Prophet* (New York: George Braziller, 1976) is a critical biography which suffers chiefly because its author seems to find it unnecessary to substantiate and properly document many of his statements. Vincent Brome, *Jung: Man and Myth* (London: Macmillan, 1978); and Gerhard Wehr, *Jung: A Biography* (Boston: Shambala, 1987), are recent general biographies, but they add little to the known details about Jung's early life. Peter Homans, *Jung in Context* (Chicago: The University of Chicago Press, 1979); Robert D. Stolorow and George E. Atwood, *Faces in a Cloud: Subjectivity in Personality Theory* (New York: Jason Aronson, 1979), 73–109; and John E. Gedo, *Portraits of the Artist* (New York: The Guilford Press, 1983), 229–72, are recent attempts at a psychological study of Jung, but again the details of Jung's early life and thought are sketchy. The most satisfactory overall portrait of Jung, and the only one that demonstrates a definite concern with investigating his early life and thought, is Henri F. Ellenberger, *The Discovery of the Unconscious* (New York: Basic Books, 1970), 657–748. Ellenberger, however, is a historian of psychiatry and not directly interested in the religious influences in Jung's early life. While Homans (35), has drawn attention to this latter omission, he himself, in his attempt to contextualize Jung, has failed to uncover the historical significance of Spiritualism, reading instead (116), "a modality best described as 'personal-mystical-narcissistic.'"

9. C. A. Meier, *The Psychology of C. G. Jung*, vol. 1, *The Uncon-scious in Its Empirical Manifestations* (Boston: Sigo Press, 1984), ix.

10. Ibid., 65 et seq. Jung's works on word association are gathered together in his *Collected Works*, vol. 2, *Experimental Researches* (Princeton, N.J.: Princeton University Press, 1973). As Laurens van der Post, *Jung and the Story of Our Time* (New York: Pantheon Books, 1975), 70–71, has remarked: "All of us…have been proscribed in our valuations by a lack of knowledge of the younger Jung, and even his most loyal and deserving followers tend still to ignore the urgent need there is to go back to his earlier points of departure so that what his inspired and swift intuitive vision uncovered, relatively in passing, can be consolidated and expanded. It is of the utmost importance to realise that most current interpretations are of the older Jung and his work in its most mature form. However true, they remain somewhat partial."

11. Jung's early experiences are revealed publicly for the first time in his autobiography. Aniela Jaffé, who edited this work, records Jung's hesitation to reveal these details about himself and his insistence they not be published in his lifetime, *MDR*, viii. Gerhard Adler, a leading student of Jung's, states in his "The Memoirs of C. G. Jung," *Spring* (1964): 139–40, "I had thought I knew him fairly well: but when I read *Memories, Dreams, Reflections* it was a profound shock.… And it becomes evident from the autobiography that many of the discoveries and formulations of Jung's later life can be traced back to the early experiences of this most remarkable child.… This child's mind was shaped by thoughts about the nature of God, of Truth and Eternity,…[and] the confrontation with…the dark God; by gazing into the abysses of doubt and guilt connected with these independent thoughts." Curiously, these comments are left out of a substantially identical review Adler did for the *Journal of Analytical Psychology* 8 (1963): 173–175. Ernest Harms, who also knew Jung, writes in his "Review of *Memories, Dreams, and Reflections*," *American Journal of Psychotherapy* 19 (1965): 153, "Those familiar with the scientific work of Carl Gustav Jung and, even more so, those who knew him personally, are bound to respond with surprise to a reading of this volume of personal…autobiography." He adds, "Some of Jung's enemies, driven by pathologic hatred, have tried to use this book as a proof that Jung had been a psychopath, and even a schizophrenic from childhood." Nevertheless, Michael Fordham, a child psychiatrist and one of the editors of Jung's *Collected Works*, and surely no enemy of Jung, in a very revealing disclosure states in his "Memories and Thoughts About C. G. Jung," *Journal of Analytical Psychology* 20 (1975): 109: "After reading the first version of the chapters on childhood in that volume [*MDR*], he [Jung] asked me what I thought, so I said he had been a schizophrenic child, with strong obsessional defenses, and that had he been brought to me I should have said that the prognosis was good, but that I should have recommended analysis—He did not contest my blunt

statement." Eric Fromm, in his scathing review of Jung's autobiography, "C. G. Jung: Prophet of the Unconscious," *Scientific American* 209 (1963): 283–90, argues that Jung's psychology and "opportunism" are tragically rooted in the pathological defensiveness that goes back to his childhood. D. W. Winnicott in his "Review of *Memories, Dreams, Reflections*," *The International Journal of Psycho-Analysis* 45 (1964): 450, states that Jung's early life "gives us a picture of childhood schizophrenia." Naomi R. Goldenberg, "Looking at Jung Looking at Himself: A Psychoanalytic Rereading of *Memories, Dreams, Reflections*" in her *Returning Words to Flesh: Feminism Psychoanalysis and the Resurrection of the Body* (Boston: Beacon Press, 1990), 116–45, claims Jung's religious ideas have their source in the psychopathological fantasies of his childhood.

12. Vitz, 94.

13. Geoffrey Bruun, *Nineteenth-Century European Civilization 1815–1914*, (London: Oxford University Press, 1959), 122. For a detailed older history of this struggle, see Andrew D. White, *A History of the Warfare of Science with Theology in Christendom* (1896)(New York: George Braziller, 1955).

14. See Stephen Neill, *The Interpretation of the New Testament 1861–1961* (London: Oxford University Press, 1964); and the comprehensive study by Claude Welch, *Protestant Thought in the Nineteenth Century*, 2 vols. (New Haven: Yale University Press, 1972–85).

15. Alan Richardson, *History: Sacred and Profane* (London: S. C. M. Press, 1964), 118–24. Jung saw his father, the Reverend Paul Jung, as one of these pathetic figures, *MDR*, 90 et seq.

16. Albert Schweitzer, *The Quest of the Historical Jesus* (1906) (London: A. & C. Black, 1964) catalogues these attempts.

17. Owen Chadwick, *The Secularization of the European Mind in the Nineteenth Century* (Cambridge: Cambridge University Press, 1975), 184.

18. Bruun, 191.

19. Ibid., 182, points out how the language of science had already become "a script that only a small company of initiates could decipher."

20. Ibid., 29. See, for example, the literary and historical anthology, Hermann Glaser, ed., *The German Mind of the 19th Century* (New York: Continuum, 1981).

21. Bruun, 33.

22. Ibid., 69–70.

23. Ibid., 193.

24. Ralf Tymms, *Doubles in Literary Psychology* (Cambridge: Bowes & Bowes, 1949), 26. I will discuss Mesmer's theories in chapter 1.

25. Tymms, 23, 34 et seq.

26. Ibid., citing von Schubert, 60. See also Ellenberger, *Discovery,* 205–6.

27. Tymms, 43; Ellenberger, *Discovery,* 159–60; and the suggestive article John Kerr, *"The Devil's Elixers,* Jung's 'Theology' and the Dissolution of Freud's 'Poisoning Complex,'" *Psychoanalytic Review* 75 (1988): 1–33.

28. See, e.g., Jeremy Hawthorn, *Multiple Personality and the Disintegration of Literary Character* (London: Edward Arnold, 1983). I shall offer a few examples of this in chapter 1.

29. H. Stuart Hughes, *Consciousness and Society* (New York: Vintage Books, 1977), 160, claims Jung's "critics are on firm ground in calling him a 'reactionary.'" Nevertheless, it is becoming increasingly clear that the originality and significance of Jung's psychology is more evident when it is applied to matters religious, a subject even Hughes reluctantly admits (155–60) Jung knew a great deal about.

30. *MDR,* 112. This is also obvious in the medical literature Jung surveyed in his early writings. I will briefly outline some of the influences nineteenth-century neurology and psychiatry had on Jung in chapter 1.

31. Stephanie de Voogd has examined and rejected the accuracy of Jung's claim to being a Kantian in "C. G. Jung: Psychologist of the Future 'Philosopher' of the Past," *Spring* (1977): 175–82; and again in more detail, in "Fantasy Versus Fiction: Jung's Kantianism Appraised," in Renos K. Papadopoulos and Grahman S. Saayman, eds., *Jung in Modern Perspective* (Hounslow, Middlesex: Wildwood House, 1984), 204–28. T. David Brent, "Jung's Debt to Kant: The Transcendental Method and the Structure of Jung's Psychology" (Ph.D. dissertation, University of Chicago, 1977), has argued, in detail, in favor of Jung's Kantianism. I will refrain from commenting on this, as I will discuss Kant's influence on Jung from a rather different angle in chapter 3.

32. *MDR,* 69. James L. Jarret has pointed out certain similarities Jung shared with Schopenhauer in his "Schopenhauer and Jung," *Spring* (1981): 193–204. I will discuss the influence of Schopenhauer on Jung in chapter 3.

33. Ellenberger, *Discovery,* 729. Schleiermacher apparently received Jung's paternal grandfather into Protestantism; see C. G. Jung, *Letters 2: 1951–1961,* ed. Gerhard Adler and Aniela Jaffé (Princeton, N.J.: Princeton

University Press, 1975), 115, where Jung remarks that Schleiermacher is "one of my spiritual ancestors."

34. Jung discovered *Faust* when he was young and more than half-believed Goethe was his great-grandfather; *MDR*, 35 n. 1, 60, 87.

35. Ellenberger, *Discovery*, 729.

36. Jung gave these seminars during 1934–39; see his *Collected Works*, vol. 19, *General Bibliography*, comp. Lisa Ress (Princeton, N.J.: Princeton University Press, 1979), 213; and now in C. G. Jung, *Nietzsche's Zarathustra*, ed. James L. Jarrett, 2 vols. (Princeton, N.J.: Princeton University Press, 1988).

37. Ellenberger, *Discovery*, 206–7.

38. Philip Wolff-Windegg, "C. G. Jung—Bachofen, Burckhardt, and Basel," *Spring* (1976): 137–47. Jung made the equation between Burckhardt's primordial idea and the archetype in his *Collected Works*, vol. 6, *Psychological Types* (1921) (Princeton, N.J.: Princeton University Press, 1971), 377.

39. Wolff-Windegg, 137; Ellenberger, *Discovery*, 729–30. As far as I know, Jung did not draw this parallel. His library does contain a number of works by Bachofen including *Das Mutterrecht* (1897); see *C. G. Jung Bibliothek: Katalog* (hereafter *Katalog*) (Kusnacht-Zurich: 1967), 8.

40. I will refer to some of the current research on Jung in the course of this study. I might point out that there is a noticeable lack of any comprehensive study of Jung and nineteenth-century Protestantism.

41. *MDR*, 5.

42. Stephanie Zumstein-Preiswerk, *C. G. Jungs Medium* (Munich: Kindler Verlag, 1975).

43. C. G. Jung, *Collected Works*, suppl. vol. A, *The Zofingia Lectures*. (Princeton, N.J.: Princeton University Press, 1983).

44. Ellenberger, *Discovery*, 665, 687–89, basing his comments on Gustav Steiner, "Erinnerungen an Carl Gustav Jung." *Basler Stadtbuch* (1965): 117–63. Steiner was a fellow student of Jung's at Basel University; see Jung's letter to Steiner in *Jung: Letters 2: 1951–1961*, 406–7.

45. William McGuire's editorial note to *The Zofingia Lectures*, v–vi.

46. Marie-Louise von Franz's introduction to *The Zofingia Lectures*, xiii.

47. In C. G. Jung, *Collected Works*, vol. 1, *Psychiatric Studies* (Princeton, N.J.: Princeton University Press, 1970): 3–88.

48. William B. Goodheart, "C. G. Jung's First 'Patient,'" *Journal of Analytical Psychology* 29 (1984): 1–34.

49. James Hillman, "Some Early Background to Jung's Ideas: Notes on *C. G. Jung's Medium* by Stephanie Zumstein-Preiswerk," *Spring* (1976): 123, 123–36. I shall refer to many of these details in chapter 5.

50. Ibid., 131.

51. Hannah, *Jung,* 71 n. i; von Franz's introduction to *The Zofingia Lectures,* xviii, where she is critical and yet cites Zumstein-Preiswerk as a source for "more details concerning Jung's early studies of a medium."

52. Aniela Jaffé, *C. G. Jung: Word and Image* (Princeton, N.J.: Princeton University Press, 1979): 28–35. In addition to accepting Zumstein-Preiswerk's chronology of the séances in contradiction to Jung (*MDR,* 104–7), Jaffé, 32, also states Jung met Helene two or three times after the séances and that she died at thirty, again contradicting Jung (*MDR,* 107).

53. Ellenberger, "Carl Gustav Jung: His Historical Setting," in Hertha Riese, ed., *Historical Explorations in Medicine and Psychiatry* (New York: Springer, 1978), 147–49.

54. Wehr, 68–75.

55. Goodheart, "Jung's First 'Patient'," 34.

56. See James Hillman and Paul Kugler, "The Autonomous Psyche: A Communication to Goodheart from the Bi-Personal Field of Paul Kugler and James Hillman," *Spring* (1985):141–161; and, "Comments," *Spring* (1985): 161–85, featuring Goodheart, Beebe, Bosnak, Buresch, Gaumond, Giegerich, Guggenbühl-Craig, Haule, McCurdy, Samuels, and Barbara Stevens; and Gregory M. Vogt, "The Kugler/Hillman/ Goodheart Drama," *Spring* (1986): 156–61. A. Plaut, a Jungian analyst and former editor of the journal in which Goodheart's article was published, called its publication in his "Letter to the Editors," *International Journal of Psycho-Analysis* 69 (1988): 552, "A courageous editorial decision the like of which I have not come across before." The psychoanalyst Robert S. Wallerstein in "One Psychoanalysis or Many?" *International Journal of Psycho-Analysis* 69 (1988): 13, has also commented favorably on Goodheart's paper, provoking the latter to further clarifications of his views on Jung in "Letter to the Editors," *International Journal of Psycho-Analysis* 70 (1989): 545–49.

57. Sigmund Freud and C. G. Jung, *The Freud/Jung Letters,* ed. William McGuire (Princeton, N.J.: Princeton University Press, 1974)(hereafter *The Freud/Jung Letters*). These letters have been widely reviewed. The Freud/Jung relationship has been the subject of full length studies, i.e., K. R. Eissler, *Psychologische Aspekte Des Briefwechsels Zwischen Freud und Jung* (Stuttgart: Fromann-Holzboog, 1982); Robert S. Steele,

Freud and Jung: Conflicts of Interpretation (London: Routledge & Kegan Paul, 1982); George B. Hogenson, *Jung's Struggle with Freud* (Notre Dame: University of Notre Dame Press, 1983); Linda Donn, *Freud and Jung: Years of Friendship, Years of Loss* (New York: Charles Scribner's Sons, 1988); and Duane Schultz, *Intimate Friends, Dangerous Rivals* (Los Angeles: Jeremy P. Tarcher, 1990).

58. Ernest Jones, *The Life and Work of Sigmund Freud*, vol. 3 (New York: Basic Books, 1957), 375–407, because of Freud's ambiguity on the subject, is full of interesting details but shies away from offering any final interpretation. Christian Moreau, *Freud et l'occultisme* (Toulouse: Edouard Privat, 1976) is the most complete study and argues against Jones's view in favor of a view that would see Freud's interest in occultism as far-reaching but in harmony with the rest of his thinking.

59. Nandor Fodor, *Freud, Jung and Occultism* (New Hyde Park, N.Y.: University Books, 1971) is an interesting collection of studies but not a systematic examination of the place of spiritualistic phenomena in the Freud/Jung conflict.

60. See n. 8 in this chapter.

61. The early history of the *Septem Sermones ad Mortuos* is not entirely clear. In *MDR*, 189–92, Jung simply stated this work was written in three evenings and gives the year as 1916. Stephan A. Hoeller, *The Gnostic Jung and the Seven Sermons to the Dead* (Wheaton, Ill.: The Theosophical Publishing House, 1982), 7, claims the work was written sometime between December 15, 1916 and February 16, 1917. The latter date is too late as Jung was already sending out copies as early as January 19, 1917; see Jung, *Letters 1: 1906–1950*, 33–34. An English edition was privately printed for Jung in 1925 by the London publishers Stuart and Watkins.

62. *Septem Sermones ad Mortuos* was brought to public attention by Martin Buber in an article (February 1952) in which he accuses Jung of being a Gnostic; see Martin Buber, *Eclipse of God* (New York: Harper & Row, 1952), 78–92, 133–37; and Edward C. Whitmont, "Prefatory Remarks to Jung's 'Reply to Buber,'" *Spring* (1973): 188–95. Jung responded publicly (May 1952) denying Buber's allegation that he was a Gnostic and calling the *Septem Sermones* "a sin of my youth" adding that "In this poem I expressed a number of psychological *aperçus* in 'Gnostic' style...," in C. G. Jung, "Religion and Psychology: A Reply to Martin Buber," in *Collected Works*, vol. 18, *The Symbolic Life* (Princeton, N.J.: Princeton University Press, 1976), 663–64. Gilles Quispel, "C. G. Jung and die Gnosis," *Eranos Jahrbuch* (1968): 277–98, has compared Jung's *Septem Sermones* very positively with earlier forms of Gnosis.

63. The full text of the *Septem Sermones* was first published as an appendix to the German edition of Jung's autobiography *Erinnerungen,*

Träume, Gedanken (Zurich: Rascher, 1961). The first English translation of Jung's memoirs excluded the *Septem Sermones*. This omission was remedied in subsequent English editions; see C. G. Jung, *General Bibliography*, 54–5, 93–4, 96. There are very few studies of Jung's *Septem Sermones*, i.e., Judith Hubback, "VII Sermones Ad Mortuos," *Journal of Analytical Psychology* 11 (1966): 95–111; Quispel; James W. Heisig, "The VII Sermones: Play and Theory," *Spring* (1972): 206–18; Hoeller; and E. M. Brenner, "Gnosticism and Psychology: Jung's *Septem Sermones ad Mortuos*," *Journal of Analytical Psychology* 35 (1990): 397–419.

64. This may be due in some measure to the introductory remarks to the *Septem Sermones* by Aniela Jaffé (*MDR*, 378), where she implies that Jung himself regretted he had composed the work. Von Franz, *Jung: His Myth in Our Time*, 121 n.82, states that Jaffé has misrepresented Jung's own views on the matter. According to her, Jung regretted only the publication of the *Septem Sermones* and not the conceptions they contained. Both are agreed that the *Septem Sermones* contain elements of Jung's later thought.

65. C. G. Jung, "The Psychological Foundations of Belief in Spirits" (1919, rev. 1948) in *Collected Works*, vol. 8, *The Structure and Dynamics of the Psyche* (Princeton, N.J.: Princeton University Press, 1969), 301–18.

66. C. G. Jung, "On the Nature of the Psyche" (1946; rev. 1954), in *The Structure and Dynamics of the Psyche*, 159–234.

67. C. G. Jung, "Synchronicity: An Acausal Connecting Principle" (1952; rev. 1955), in *The Structure and Dynamics of the Psyche*, 419–519.

68. On the subject of synchronicity, see Robert Aziz, *C. G. Jung's Psychology of Religion and Synchronicity* (Albany: State University of New York Press, 1990). F. David Peat, *Synchronicity: The Bridge Between Matter and Mind* (Toronto: Bantam Books, 1987) is a recent work on the subject by a New Age physicist.

Part 1

The Background

Chapter 1

Mesmerism, Hypnotism, and Spiritualism in the Nineteenth Century

Important antecedents of Jung's psychology lie in nineteenth-century psychiatry and in the earlier forms of psychosomatic medicine whose roots are in the eighteenth century. European psychiatry in the nineteenth century sought to subsume under its evolving categories of understanding all of those illnesses which could not be exclusively explained by physical medicine. There emerged from this process certain insights into human behavior that pushed psychiatrists to make statements about general psychology. Delimiting the normal from the abnormal became exceedingly problematical. The result was the differentiation of mental states and the establishment of psychiatric classification. In the nineteenth century, the development of methods of treatment modified and augmented these classifications.[1] But psychiatrists also encountered evidence of unusual psychological processes that escaped easy analysis and categorization. The phenomenon of the hypnotic trance and the spontaneous manifestations of mediums were important examples of this difficulty.

The data that emerged from the hypnotic trance and the spontaneous somnambulism of the medium indicated certain psychological processes that escaped conscious control. Moreover, these processes frequently appeared as a group of psychological fragments which gathered together in a personified form and occasionally suggested a capacity that surpassed that of the conscious mind. On a popular level these "personalities" were interpreted as indications of communication with a spiritual world. The psychiatric view, in general, accepted as factual the autonomy and even the personification of these subconscious formations but preferred to read them as evidence of a pathological state. It is at this point that Jung, as a young psychiatrist, entered the debate. For certain personal and professional reasons, which I shall outline in the forth-

27

coming chapters, the vital question for Jung became: Are such autonomous psychical processes as found in Spiritualism necessarily always pathological? When Jung later provided a negative answer to this question, he moved away from psychiatry to create a general psychology with transpersonal dimensions. The background of his question and the answer he provided lies in the nineteenth century with the intertwining of mesmerism, hypnotism, and Spiritualism.[2]

Henri Ellenberger has recently traced the beginnings of dynamic psychiatry to 1775, one hundred years prior to the birth of Carl Jung. The decisive event he refers to was the clash between the physician Franz Anton Mesmer (1734–1815) and the Catholic exorcist Reverend Johann Joseph Gassner (1727–79). The latter was cast as the traditional man of God plying his trade as healer in the name of established religion; the former, a child of the Enlightenment supported by the spirit of the times. The importance of this encounter was that Mesmer could bring about and dispel at will various symptoms through what he called "animal magnetism," thus duplicating the results of Gassner. This demonstrated the existence of a method of healing that required no ties to formal religion, satisfying the demands of the then emerging modern world.[3]

Gassner died a few years after this event and was soon forgotten, but Mesmer's reputation increased. In spite of this, little is known of his early life other than that he was born into a Catholic family in the western region of Lake Constance, Switzerland, not far from where Carl Jung was born almost a century and a half later. At an early age Mesmer was taken in hand by the local Catholic hierarchy and sent to school in the hope that he would become a priest. In his late teens he entered the Jesuit theological schools of Dillingen and Ingolstadt where he studied theology, philosophy, and science.[4] At this point there is a gap in Mesmer's life—a fact which has given rise to some speculation as to his whereabouts. What is certain is that he left his homeland and distanced himself from his religion, both of which he returned to half a century later.[5]

In 1759 Mesmer enrolled in Law at the University of Vienna. The following year he changed to medicine entering the Old Vienna Medical School, one of the outstanding progressive schools of the day.[6] Six years later, in 1766, Mesmer completed the required dissertation and published it under the title *Dissertatio physico-medica de planetarum influxu*. This work was only forty-eight pages in length and is heavily indebted to an earlier work of Richard Mead.[7]

In a letter written later Mesmer described what he set out to claim
in this work:

> that these great celestial bodies [the planets] act on our
> globe in general...like great magnets...[and] produce an
> effect on the human body which is analogous to the way in
> which they affect the tides, the different seas, and the
> entire atmosphere.[8]

While Mesmer's description of his dissertation may sound
rather unusual, it, nevertheless, is rooted in a Newtonian model of
the universe. Even his borrowing from Mead who has been called
"the hard-headed empirical Englishman of the iatromechanical
school," suggests Mesmer was a child of the Enlightenment.[9] At the
same time, Mesmer represents a direct link with earlier thinkers
such as Paracelsus (1493–1541). And if, finally, his method of healing was somewhat inadequate, he does mark the dividing line
between pre-scientific and scientific methods of the study and
application of what was later called "hypnotism."

As conceived by Mesmer, animal magnetism as a method of
healing can be briefly summarized under four basic principles: (1) a
subtle physical fluid fills the universe and forms a connecting
medium between the human being, the earth, and the heavenly
bodies as well as between one person and another; (2) disease origi-
nates from the unequal distribution of this fluid in the human
body, and recovery is achieved when equilibrium is restored; (3)
with the help of certain techniques, this fluid can be channeled,
stored, and conveyed to other persons; (4) in this manner crises can
be provoked in patients and diseases cured.[10] In spite of Mesmer's
insistence on basing his theory upon a fluid, his chief contribution
to psychiatry was to demonstrate that the cures he effected
through animal magnetism were primarily due to the systematic
application of the power of suggestion based on the interpersonal
relationship between himself and his patients. His method, therefore, is an important precursor to modern psychotherapy.[11]

Mesmer was popular among his patients and became somewhat of a celebrity. At the same time he alienated other medical
practitioners because of his unorthodox methods and his success in
treating various patients. In the end he felt obliged to leave Vienna
as a consequence and moved to Paris in 1778. Magnetism and the
theory of magnetic fluid upon which it is based became his *idée fixe*.
The inability to tolerate equals and the tenacity with which he

clung to his theories were his undoing. He finally brought condemnation upon himself and his method by scientific colleagues in a
series of special medical commissions, the first one presided over by
Benjamin Franklin in 1784.[12]

Despite his unshakable belief in the existence of magnetic
fluid, Mesmer seems to have been forced to retreat more and more
from the practical consequences of his theory. By the 1780s he had
given up the use of magnets in treatment, replacing it by his *baquet*
with its iron bars, water, and metal shavings. This device bore a
strong resemblance to the contraptions used in electric therapy at
that time and with which Mesmer may have shared certain basic
assumptions.[13] The strange phenomena surfacing from patients in
trance states caused him, in 1781, to mention "a sixth sense" in his
Précis Historique, and, in 1799, in *Mémoire,* to regard this "sixth
sense" as clairvoyant.[14] In fact, the latter work so removes itself
from Mesmer's earlier position that it has been called "a treatise on
the occult sciences."[15] But this work was written some years after
Mesmer had left Paris to live in semiobscurity in Switzerland, far
from the din he had been so instrumental in creating.[16] In the end,
it is probably an accurate assessment of Mesmer to state he was
not a man of theory but an explorer: "his French disciples took care
of the system-building."[17]

If mesmerism lost its leader in 1785 as a result of Mesmer
leaving Paris, his discoveries did not perish with him but went
through a number of successive developments chiefly in France and
Germany. His earlier followers can be divided into three groups: (1)
the fluidists who held to the original idea that there was a physical
fluid underlying the phenomena of magnetism; (2) the animists
who believed that magnetism was a psychological phenomenon; (3)
a smaller number who took an intermediate position and held that
the fluid was directed by the will.[18]

In France the spread of mesmerism was interrupted by the
revolution of 1789, but by 1812 Mesmer's teachings attracted a new
group of admirers.[19] This later group of Mesmer's followers
explored the subject of trance states in a more scientific and empirical manner, documenting such "magnetic conditions" as dual personality, the influence of mind over body, and the possibility of cur-
ing diseases through suggestion. But, in the end, their efforts to
make mesmerism acceptable to the scientific authorities failed
chiefly because instead of concentrating on the elementary manifestations of the trance state, they chose to demonstrate their ideas
with reference to the extraordinary phenomena produced.[20]

The German mesmerists took a different course and showed their interests to be more philosophical in nature. This was chiefly because of the romanticist attraction to seeking universal truths. They perceived in Mesmer's magnetic fluid the justification for the notion that the universe was a living organism. Mesmer's idea, emphasized by his disciple Puységur (1751–1825), of a "sixth sense" in the magnetic fluid which endowed humans in trance with prophetic ability, moved the Germans to conclude this would enable the human mind to communicate with the World Soul.[21]

In the course of their experiments with various subjects, the mesmerists realized that certain ones were more susceptible to somnambulistic states than others. As Ellenberger has pointed out, the French sought these "as auxiliary subjects for medical practice," whereas the Germans "utilized them in an audacious attempt at experimental metaphysics."[22] Among these extraordinary subjects who aroused a great deal of interest in Germany was Friederike Hauffe (1801–29). It was claimed that while in a trance she could foretell future events and receive messages from spirits about various matters. The movement of physical objects was also said to have taken place in her presence. She went on to reveal a cosmological system of "magnetic circles," which consisted of "seven sun circles" and "one life circle." This was apparently a symbolical representation of spiritual conditions.[23] Frau Hauffe's system is not unlike that revealed by the medium who was the subject of Jung's dissertation, as we shall see later.

Frau Hauffe created quite a sensation and was visited by philosophers such as Görres, Baader, Schelling, G. von Schubert, Eschenmayer, and the theologians David Strauss and Schleiermacher who came repeatedly to see her and discuss her revelations.[24] The physician Justinus Kerner (1786–1862), Mesmer's first biographer, published a work on her, *Die Seherin von Prevorst,* in 1829 shortly after her death.[25] He had taken her into his house and was partly successful in treating her psychosomatic illness with a mixture of exorcism and magnetism. He recorded in detail what took place during her trance states as well as the progression of her cure. It has been stated that his was the first monograph devoted to an individual in the field of dynamic psychiatry.[26]

Kerner's study created quite a stir and was read even in Moscow, indicating how widespread was the interest in the subject of somnambulism.[27] One of the results of its popularity was to encourage the publication of similar reports as well as what may be the first periodicals devoted to psychical research, *Blätter von Pre-*

vorst (1831) and *Magikon* (1840).[28] Nevertheless, after 1850, under the impact of positivism and scientific rationalism, there was a rapid decline in the influence of mesmerism upon the French and German intelligentsia. This resulted in mesmerism being abandoned to street demonstrators and amateurs who made practical use of the occult beliefs to which many widely adhered. This popular use of mesmerism also occurred in America but unlike in Europe, not as the direct result of having been abandoned by physicians and metaphysicians.

As early as 1784, mesmerism was a topic that was introduced into the highest levels of American society by the Marquis de Lafayette in a letter he wrote to George Washington.[29] Lafayette was a member of Mesmer's Société de L'Harmonie Universelle and sought permission from its founder to communicate its teachings.[30] Mesmer himself wrote to Washington on June 16, 1784 confirming that Lafayette could speak on his behalf, which he did before the American Philosophical Society and elsewhere, yet met with little success.[31] As Robert Fuller has jocularly remarked: "It was to be a few more years before this magnetic fluid, ostensibly present throughout nature, would successfully cross the Atlantic."[32]

When mesmerism did cross the ocean it came in a number of guises, one a Frenchman, Charles Poyen, a self-proclaimed "Professor of Animal Magnetism," who embarked on a lecture tour across New England in 1836.[33] Like his French mentor, Mesmer's disciple Puységur, he focused more on the phenomena resulting from the somnambulist state than on the theory of a magnetic fluid.[34] His meetings had the character of religious revivals and, coupled with his talent for presenting mesmerism as a science, he could appeal to utopian yearnings and confidentially prophesy that this new teaching was destined to make America "the most perfect nation on earth."[35] After sowing the seed of his new gospel in the New World, Poyen returned to France in 1839.[36]

The same year Poyen left for Europe an Englishman, Robert Collyer, arrived in America. He began a lecture tour spreading mesmerism along the Atlantic seaboard. Collyer was critical of American medical practices and presented mesmerism as a phenomenon on the leading edge of science.[37] The influence of Poyen and Collyer generated a widespread interest in mesmerism. In contrast to Europe, where it attracted the upper class, mesmerism was to have its impact in America on the lives of a large middle class.[38] And again unlike in Europe, despite its use by a few medical practitioners during the decade 1840–50, no school of mesmerism was established in America. This effectively left it to others to introduce the practice of inducing trances and other phenomena which provided all the necessary ingredients for the making of a movement known as Spiritualism.[39]

Spiritualism has been defined by Frank Podmore in his history of the movement as:

> a system which in one aspect is a religious faith, in another claims to represent a new department of natural science— is based on the interpretation of certain obscure facts as indicating the agency of the spirits of dead men and women.[40]

The rise of the loose system of beliefs and claims known as modern Spiritualism has often been explained as one of the religious responses to a time of crisis and uncertainty in various sectors of nineteenth-century Western society. Historians have usually argued that population shifts, the breakdown of formal religion, a lack of a developed theology of the dead among Protestants, accompanied by the rise of rationalism and rigid industrialization, were major factors. True as these explanations might be, the fact remains that modern Spiritualism has not received the attention it deserves from historians of religion.[41] Modern Spiritualism is a nineteenth-century phenomenon which, because it is based on the possibility of communication between the dead and the living through the agency of a medium, is directly dependent on the phenomenon of trance. It is on this crucial point that the histories of both mesmerism and Spiritualism overlap and influence one another.[42]

As the spread of mesmerism increased, the idea of magnetism reached a popular audience, and a number of Mesmer's disciples fell into wild speculation believing that what had been discovered amounted to a new revelation. Individuals in trance had shown peculiar abilities and some had even claimed to be in touch with other personalities while in this state. It is not difficult to see how the next step to believing these personalities were spirits was, for some, not such a hard one to take. As Freud once shrewdly observed on the matter of telepathy, "Dans ces cas pareils, ce n'est que le premier pas qui coûte."[43] What was once Mesmer's *baquet* around which subjects sat with joined hands now became the closed circle of spiritualistic séances.[44]

The phenomenon of mesmeric trance was known in America from about 1836 onwards but no conspicuous school that endured

seems to have been founded. Any physicians who concerned themselves with the matter appear not to have subjected it to careful
investigation or to have imposed their views on others. Instead, it
was a topic served to the general population by itinerant preachers,
lecturers, and healers. Everyone seems to have become involved:
clergymen, lawyers, politicians, lay persons of every sort, even
farmers, as we shall see. Indeed, it has been called America's "first
popular psychology."[45] Moreover, if the so-called scientific methods
of Mesmer and some of his followers were seriously questioned and
even thought to be discredited by the savants of Europe who
adhered to more rigorous procedures, they were not wasted on the
American public who, fired by such discoveries as the telegraph,
were willing to believe that almost anything was possible, even
communication between this world and the next.[46]

This optimism also concealed a more menacing intuition
about science and human life. As James Webb has remarked:

> As the tide of rationalism and the new science rose higher,
> as the sense of collective insecurity waxed, men turned to
> the ultimate consolation of the immortality of souls. They
> could shout in the face of the bogey Darwin that they knew
> they were more than the outcome of a biological process,
> that they too had "scientific proof"—and that theirs was of
> the reality of the after-life. Death, the shadow at the backs
> of every generation, had in the 19th century to be met by
> many people face to face.[47]

This attitude was taken not only by the unlettered but by a number
of serious scientific thinkers as in the example of A. R. Wallace
(1823–1913), codiscoverer of the theory of evolution.[48] In America,
mesmerism and Spiritualism were often not distinguished from
one another. This is evident from the number of adherents to mesmerism who later became spiritualists—that is to say until 1848
when there occurred, in the words of Henri Ellenberger: "a seemingly trivial incident [which] became the starting point for a psychological epidemic of unexpected amplitude—the rise and spread
of Spiritism."[49]

It is now generally agreed that Spiritualism as a movement
arose in the northeastern United States and, while indebted to Mesmer's ideas, this was the fertile soil upon which these ideas had to
fall in order to grow into a force to be reckoned with before being
exported back to Europe. As one student of the subject has stated:

> To a large extent it [Spiritualism] grew out of the Mesmeric
> movement, and the motley collection of ideas which had
> fastened themselves to Mesmer were drawn along in the
> baggage. It was also connected closely with the millenarian
> expectations of the mid-century, both in social and religious
> terms. This legacy Spiritualism inherited from its time and
> its place of origin. Like the most contemporary American
> adventist movements, Spiritualism originated in the
> 'burned-over' district.... In the 'burned-over' district, suc-
> cessive waves of disoriented immigrants joined those who
> had felt the impact of Revivalist preachers to create a con-
> fusion of doubt and belief.[50]

From its rather innocuous beginnings on March 31, 1848, in
the bedroom of an American Methodist farmer, J. D. Fox, in western
New York State, Spiritualism as a movement was born. The following is a summary of what occurred: In March 31, 1848 the Fox family were disturbed by inexplicable noises. The two Fox daughters,
aged 12 and 15, began to make snapping noises and received a
response by hearing a rap in reply. They established a form of communication and in a series of questions discovered they were in contact with the spirit of someone who had once lived.[51] The next day a
crowd gathered and the news circulated. Halls were rented at the
direction of the spirits, lectures given, and the phenomenon of Spiritualism spread like a brush fire. By 1853 ten spiritualist periodicals
had been established. Two years later it was claimed there were 2.5
million spiritualists and four years after, in 1859, a Catholic convention put the number at 11 million.[52] While these figures may be
somewhat inflated, they testify to the popular perception that the
spread of the spiritualist movement had been extensive. Perhaps
because of the manner in which Spiritualism spread, and its lack of
organizational structure, exact estimates will remain impossible to
calculate. As Janet Oppenheim has pointed out:

> Spiritualistic prowess often spread among the members of a
> single family, for mediumship was catching, it would seem,
> and certainly the power of suggestion and example must
> have played a substantial part in the rapid multiplication of
> private mediums during the second half of the nineteenth
> century. Many of them, however, somewhat in awe of their
> abilities, shunned publicity, and it is impossible to compute
> with any precision the number of people, of all ages and

social strata, who became convinced spiritualists without ever venturing beyond their domestic séances.[53]

By 1852 Spiritualism had crossed the Atlantic, invading England and shortly afterwards spreading to continental Europe. Jung's grandfather, C. G. Jung, mentions its occurrence in Germany in an entry to his diary dated April 11, 1853. In it he states:

> Today one can read in the...newspaper...of table-turning in Bremen. The process is the following, that a chain is formed...and the participants are separated from one another by a foot. Their clothes should not touch.... Everyone places their hands on the table.... With the small finger everyone touches the small finger of the one beside them.... There is still nonsense in the world.[54]

Spiritualism originally was a loose movement which did not organize into a sect nor demand a commitment of faith from its followers, let alone present itself in creedal formulas or in a systematic theology. Rather, for the most part it attracted people who were sick and tired of such things. Instead, it aligned itself with the popular conception of science, and, indeed, its *lingua franca* was drawn primarily from popular tracts on empirical science. For spiritualists there was no war between science and religion, but they did fear that science would become increasingly materialistic if it were not utilized to explore the more elevated realms which, it was held, were not discontinuous with matter but rather a higher, more evolved form of matter. From about 1850, the leaders of Spiritualism adhered to four basic principles: (1) a rejection of supernaturalism which maintained that the spirit world was discontinuous with the material world; (2) that natural law was inviolable; (3) a reliance on objectively established facts and not on vague subjective inner states; (4) a belief in the progressive development of knowledge. In short, Spiritualism sought not only to liberalize religion but to liberalize science as well.[55]

The reaction to Spiritualism on the part of the Christian churches was mixed and among the clergy generally negative, as it was clearly perceived that any consorting with Spiritualism would compromise the moral and religious authority of Christianity. This was especially threatening in the late nineteenth century as Christianity itself was undergoing an identity crisis. Spiritualists themselves seem to have been of two minds about Christianity: some were willing to mix it with their Spiritualism, others were not. Moreover, as Janet Oppenheim has sagely remarked:

> This categorization of pro- and anti-Christian spiritualism is valid enough, as far as it goes, but like so many attempts to classify elusive attitudes, it merely highlights the black and white, leaving obscure the shades of gray.[56]

Generally, spiritualists had an aversion to Christian orthodoxies with their various insistence on perceiving the deity as trinity, the Calvinistic doctrine of predestination, the vicarious atonement wrought by the crucifixion, final judgment, and especially the belief in an eternal hell. Heaven, spiritualists held, was but the continuation of the present life, and Jesus Christ was really a highly evolved being who had progressed to a higher state. God, instead of being personalized, was thought of as the force that pervaded all of life on this plane and on higher planes. Morality too was not something that could be dictated in creedal formulas and enforced by the whispers and penances of an army of clerics, but a question of personal development and self-realization. Needless to say, the extent to which any of the above was added to, or subtracted from, depended on the religious orientation, or lack of it, of individual spiritualists on either side of the mean. What all spiritualists did agree upon was in describing themselves as empiricists and claiming that the truths they believed in had been established by direct experience in the form of communication with deceased women and men through the agency of a medium.

While most continental European spiritualists followed in the footsteps of their mesmeric predecessors and inherited the use of the various paraphernalia of the séance from their British and American brethren, their own contribution to Spiritualism was to be in the realm of doctrine. Specifically, the continental European contribution to Spiritualism is to be found in the doctrine of reincarnation propounded by a Frenchman known as Allan Kardec (1804–69). In *Le Livre des Espirits* (1856), which became the textbook of continental European Spiritualism, Kardec proposed a theory of reincarnation. The basis for this new doctrine allegedly came to him during séances with a medium who was in contact with a number of spirits, including that of Mesmer. This doctrine of reincarnation met opposition from Anglo-American spiritualists, but emerges as one of the central items of continental European séances, including the ones that were the subject of Carl Jung's dissertation.[57]

The spread of Spiritualism in continental Europe brought to the fore a number of remarkable mediums who exhibited what seemed to be extraordinary psychic abilities. In addition to the usual table turning, there were reports of spirits manifesting themselves, photographs of them, levitations, and so on. All of this attracted a good deal of attention, and a number of serious but insufficiently critical studies were made of the mediums and the phenomena they produced. One early example was the study by Maximilian Perty, Professor of Philosophy, University of Berne, Switzerland. In *Die mystischen Erscheinungen der menschlichen Natur* (1861) he described the phenomena produced by mediums, attributing them to the unconscious exercise of occult powers in the organism. To account for these powers Perty was forced to assume the existence of planetary spirits with whom the medium entered into communication.[58] In the end, this theory amounted to a somewhat spiritualized version of the theory Mesmer proposed one hundred years earlier. Gradually other studies emerged which were more critical and less speculative and whose authors were chiefly concerned to surmise there must be a connection between the observed phenomena and the personalities of the mediums.

Until the 1860s the scientific communities in England and America almost universally rejected or ignored the claims of Spiritualism and expressed no interest in subjecting them to careful study. After this period, and for the next two decades, the topic of Spiritualism would exercise a considerable fascination over a number of leading scientists, even succeeding in converting a few of them, as in the example of W. Crookes.[59] What attracted scientists to Spiritualism was the assertion by its adherents that its claims were open to scientific investigation. In view of the fact that science was just beginning to be professionalized, the debate over the scientific status of Spiritualism became entangled in the debate among scientists as to who among them were really amateurs and who were professionals.[60] For some scientists, Spiritualism seemed to allow them, as S. E. D. Shortt maintains,

> on the one hand, ostensibly to retain the empirical canons of their professional identity, while on the other, to reject the stark materialism to which many of their colleagues had succumbed.[61]

By the early 1870s this kind of support was adding scientific credibility to the claims of Spiritualism.[62]

The only professional group which seemed able to remain aloof and critical were physicians. Already in 1851 three physicians from the University of Buffalo had pronounced a negative judgment on the spiritualistic phenomena of the Fox sisters.[63] In 1853, Dr. Edward C. Rogers of Boston argued that the medium's ability had to do with an abnormal nervous constitution and not with spirits. The extraordinary phenomena produced while the medium was in trance he attributed to "unconscious cerebration."[64] Mediumship came to be looked upon by the medical profession as some sort of illness of a neurological and psychiatric order. Those specializing in these fields of medicine assumed center stage in the energetic debate that ensued on the subject of Spiritualism.[65] In general these physicians sought to disengage spiritualist claims from the trance and other phenomena exhibited by mediums. They did this by dismissing outright the more outlandish claims and interpreted the others in neurophysiological and psychological terms. As one scholar has stated,

> The neuroscientists were claiming epistomological sovereignty over a specific area of human experience to the exclusion of metaphysical or theological rivals. Science and religion, they believed, were separate realms of knowledge. Spiritualists, in attempting to employ science to prove their religion, were guilty of replacing faith with materialism.[66]

In the more strictly scientific circles of Europe there was a slightly different and more immediate consequence of the rise of Spiritualism. Mesmerism, which had fallen into disrepute from 1860 to 1880, now reappeared as an acceptable subject of discussion in its rehabilitated form known as hypnotism.[67] This period also marks the rivalry between the two French medical centers of Salpêtrière and Nancy with regard to the correct interpretation of the hypnotic state. Salpêtrière, under the leadership of Jean-Martin Charcot (1825–93), interpreted hypnosis to be "a physiological condition very different from sleep...that could occur only in individuals predisposed to hysteria, and could not be used for therapeutic purposes."[68] On February 13, 1882 Charcot, the most distinguished neurologist of his day, delivered a paper on hypnotism before L'Académie des Sciences in Paris. It was, reportedly, a *tour de force* and brought the subject of hypnotism back into medical circles, ironically, before the very institution that had condemned it before when it was known as "mesmerism."[69] In contrast to Charcot and the Salpêtrière school, the Nancy school under the leadership of Hippolyte Bernheim (1840–1919) had quietly experimented with hypnotism. Bernheim understood the hypnotic trance as "merely a sleep, produced by suggestion, with therapeutic implications."[70]

The debate between the two schools attracted a good deal of public attention and created a stir in the medical and popular press.[71] If the medical community had forgotten that hypnotism was simply mesmerism under an assumed name, the general public did not and, coupled with the widespread impact of Spiritualism, there was a waiting audience for any news on the subject. Such news came in the form of a murder trial which took place in Paris, in 1890, during which a woman accomplice claimed, as her defence, that she acted under posthypnotic suggestion.[72]

The trial attracted wide attention and made even more public the debate over hypnotism conducted for years by the two French schools of Salpêtrière and Nancy. In fact, members of the two schools became directly involved in the proceedings by presenting themselves as expert witnesses, effectively making the guilt or innocence of the accused the means of finally settling the debate.[73] Sensational claims were made for the powers of hypnosis which fired the public imagination and disturbed the French authorities.[74] In the end not only was the accused found guilty, partially vindicating the Salpêtrière school, but new laws were eventually introduced to prevent public demonstrations of hypnotism by street practitioners.[75] The consequences for hypnotism were similar to those which occurred for Spiritualism: the medical profession came to place hypnotism under its control and subject to its laws of explanation and interpretation.[76]

Another consequence of the rivalry between the two French schools was to encourage researchers to apply more rigorous methods in the study of the trance state, thereby removing it from the so-called occult complexities in which it had become entangled.[77] Psychiatrists such as the Austrian Richard Krafft-Ebing (1840–1902), whose *Lehrbuch der Psychiatrie auf klinischer Grundlage* (1890) was instrumental in Jung's decision to choose psychiatry as his profession, were drawn into the study of hypnotism.[78] Auguste Forel (1848–1931) studied hypnotism under Bernheim at Nancy and applied it to both his patients and staff in the Burghölzli Mental Hospital in Zurich.[79] Eugen Bleuler (1857–1939), who succeeded Forel as director of the Burghölzli, underwent hypnosis himself and encouraged its usage in the hypnotism clinic that had been established.[80] Jung, who joined the Burghölzli in 1900, was placed in charge of this clinic.[81]

As a student, Sigmund Freud (1856–1939) had observed a public demonstration by the well-known stage hypnotist Hansen. Freud became convinced of its authenticity and may have seen Josef Breuer (1842–1925) use it when he was in his twenties and attempted it himself in 1885.[82] However, its full impact upon him was only obvious when he returned from studying with Charcot in 1886.[83] At the end of the following year Freud devoted himself to the study of hypnotism and shortly afterwards embarked on the translation of Bernheim's *De la suggestion et de ses applications à la thérapeutique* (1886) which was accompanied by a preface and published in 1888.[84] Freud seems to have been rapidly disillusioned with the use of hypnosis and never became adept in its practice.[85] He contacted Forel, whose book on hypnotism he was reviewing at the time. Through him Freud was able to arrange to spend some time with Bernheim in order to improve his technique.[86] While retaining an interest in the theory of hypnosis, Freud allegedly abandoned its use after ten years of practice in 1896 and considered it as a prelude to the psychoanalytic technique. However, there is a possibility that he may have taken it up again in the 1920s.[87]

Other physicians continued to pursue the study of the trance state, selecting unusual subjects who were particularly susceptible to hypnotic suggestion. Increasingly it had become obvious that while the hypnotic state and the self-induced trance of the medium had much in common, it was the latter that offered the more spontaneous and original subject matter. In the 1880s Charcot, who had amassed a large collection of rare works on witchcraft and possession, addressed this topic in a lecture, "Spiritualism and Hysteria."[88] Wilhelm Wundt (1832–1920), the founder of experimental psychology, participated in séances and wrote on the subject.[89] Pierre Janet (1859–1947), with whom Jung later studied in Paris, Fredric Myers (1843–1901) and the Society of Psychical Research in England, William James (1842–1910) in America, and others were attracted by the bizarre demonstrations of mediums and published extensively on the subject.[90]

Not all of these investigators were of the same mind about the subject of mediumistic phenomena. The development of the neurosciences and the emerging detailed classification of pathological states seemed, when fraud was ruled out, to give those among scientists who were positivists all the explanation they needed. The manifestation of secondary personalities in individuals under hypnosis or at séances was interpreted as evidence that the personality when weakened had a tendency to dissociate and form alternate

personalities. The appearance of spirits in séances was considered
to be but exaggerated and pathological examples of hysterical dissociation which occurred in milder forms of psychiatric disorder. As
a result it was precisely the phenomena of multiple personality
that fused pathology, hypnosis, and Spiritualism in the minds of
numerous investigators and became the focus of great interest and
controversy.[91]

Other investigators, largely those of the societies of psychical
research in America and Britain, concurred with their positivistic
colleagues on the subject of the pathology of multiple personality
with one important caveat, that the pathology was only one aspect
of the phenomenology of multiple personality. Another part of the
spectrum of multiple personality, it was claimed, might indicate a
consciousness capable of paranormal perception and even evidence
of the possibility of postmortem survival. To a great extent, these
psychical researchers were motivated by the same impetus that
gave rise to the phenomena of Spiritualism: a desire to keep science
open to the religious dimension and not to dismiss it as otiose or to
subject it to the reductionism of positivism.[92]

Conversations with spirits, automatic writing, crystal balls,
gazing into mirrors to divine the future, and similar practices were
investigated with a great deal of seriousness. While certain phenomena emerged which presented problems for these investigators,
it was generally concluded that these various "arts" brought to
light subconscious material of the individual subject. This conclusion did not compel any of these pioneers to attempt to synthesize
all the material in a bid to explain such phenomena and present an
enduring model of the psyche. Instead, this was to be the great
achievement of the following generation of which Freud's and
Jung's psychological systems are notable examples.

Following the emergence of psychoanalysis at the beginning
of the present century, multiple personality as a psychological phenomenon gradually lost its separate classification and became
absorbed into a general classification as a form of dissociative hysteria. The conceptual shift from dissociation leading to multiple
personality to defense leading to repression was, by 1912, complete. In that year Freud sent a paper to the Society for Psychical
Research in Britain in which he criticized the idea of multiple personality as a misnomer because it implied consciousness within
the unconscious. A better explanation of such phenomena, Freud
maintained, was to regard it as a "shifting of consciousness,—that
function—or whatever it be—oscillating between two different psy-

chical complexes which become conscious and unconscious in alternation."[93]

Jung, while indebted to Freud, in the end held views on multiple personality that were more in harmony with those of Janet and another largely forgotten authority on mediums, the Swiss psychologist Theodore Flournoy (1854–1920).[94] In particular pride of place must be given to the latter's *Des Indes à la planète Mars: Etude sur un cas de somnambulisme avec glossolalie* (1900). The significance of this work is that it was, and remains, the most thorough and detailed study of a medium from a psychological point of view. It was the result of five years of observation and many more years of experience examining the products of mediumistic trance. The following is a brief history of its contents: The medium was a woman of thirty. She would fall spontaneously into trance exhibiting changes in her personality and re-enacting scenes from her former lives. In the first cycle of these lives she was a 15th century Hindu princess; in the second she was Marie Antoinette; in the third she was an inhabitant of Mars. Flournoy was able to show the medium borrowed most of these details from a book she read as a child. He interpreted as romances of the subliminal imagination these and other "revelations." He held they were based on forgotten memories and wish fulfillments all of which was constructed upon a reversion of the personality to different stages of her earlier life. The guiding spirit, Flournoy claimed, was in fact the emerging subconscious personality of the medium.[95]

Flournoy's work came to serve as the model for most studies of mediums which followed, including the one Jung published as his medical dissertation, *On the Psychology and Pathology of So-Called Occult Phenomena* (1902), which will be examined in a later chapter. In particular it was Flournoy's positive psychological approach to his subject that was to exercise considerable influence over Jung and depth-psychology in general. As Ellenberger has remarked: "It was a great step forward for dynamic psychiatry when Flournoy at the end of the nineteenth century, followed soon by C. G. Jung, undertook a systematic investigation of mediums."[96] In the course of Jung's professional career as a psychiatrist, his views of mediumistic phenomena and multiple personality became somewhat more complex. The development of these views, which is the chief subject of this study, will be examined in upcoming chapters.

In addition to surveying the impact of Spiritualism on psychiatry and psychology, it is also important to understand its influence on the general populace. An important source of this influence

is to be found in the literature of the time, which frequently shows
a concern with the subject of the double. Spiritualism was to add to
this legacy of the double as it made its mark on the literary products of the second half of the nineteenth century.

Mesmerism had influenced European literature and fostered
the idea of the double especially in the works of E. T. A. Hoffmann.
After Hoffmann's death in 1822, the influence of Mesmerism seems
to have subsided, caused by, in the words of one scholar:

> The contaminating effect of occultism, which remained in
> popular esteem; both doctrines [mesmerism and occultism]
> emerged in a general reputation of being undistinguishably
> obscure cults of the supernatural, and the scientific charac-
> ter of the theories of animal magnetism was, to a great
> extent, lost.[97]

What is being referred to here as the "occultism which remained in
popular esteem" and which replaced mesmerism, is most probably
evidence of the influx of Spiritualism which seemed to grow quite
naturally out of mesmerism and to follow in its wake.

The advent of Spiritualism in Europe produced a flood of literature either written by spirits or purported to have come from the
beyond. These were usually dictated through a medium who acted
as a channel. Automatic writing became popular and even such literary figures as Victor Hugo (1802–85) were involved in séances. In
this instance, Hugo's son, Charles, acted as the medium and illustrious men such as Aeschylus and Shakespeare dictated fine
French poetry to him which resembled Hugo's own.[98] Hugo himself
was alleged to have put in an appearance seven years after his
death as the spirit-control of the medium Flournoy studied.[99] The
French astronomer Camille Flammarion (1842–1925) wrote *Les
Habitants de l'autre monde* in the early 1860s, revealing, among
other things, a book of Genesis supposedly dictated to him by
another illustrious man, Galileo. While skeptical at first, he too
succumbed to a belief in the existence of spirits.[100] Several mediums
themselves wrote literary productions which were purported to
have been delivered to them by spirits and which, in some cases,
were of an unexpectedly high level.[101] One of the most publicized
examples of this was the completion by an American medium of an
unfinished work by Charles Dickens (1812–70). The manner, style,
and peculiarities of Dickens were so evident in the work that many
were convinced it originated in Dickens himself. Flournoy pointed

out that the unfinished portion of this work has been found and bears no resemblance to the "newly finished novel of Dickens."[102]

In addition to automatic writing was the slightly later occurrence of automatic drawing. The French dramatist Victorien Sardou (1831–1908), in whose plays Sarah Bernhardt made her triumphant return to the Paris stage, attracted attention with his drawing that allegedly depicted houses owned by Zoroaster and Mozart on the planet Jupiter.[103] Jules Bois, who was well acquainted with Charcot, had even advanced the theory that the Symbolist school of art, which began in the 1890s, was largely indebted to mediumistic drawings for its style.[104]

Hypnotism was hardly distinguished from either mesmerism or Spiritualism, as is evident in a prayerful remark by Christina Rossetti (1830–94):

> Please God, I will have nothing to do with spiritualism, whether it be imposture or a black art; or with mesmerism, lest it clog my free will; or with hypnotism, lest wilful self-surrender becomes my road to evil choice.[105]

The basic plot of most novels that took up the subject of hypnotism was the misuse by cunning individuals of their ability to induce hypnotic states in potentially profitable and desirable victims. In De Maupassant's *Le Horla* (1887) he has the victim remark upon realizing he has been hypnotized:

> Someone possesses my soul and governs it. Someone directs all my actions, all my movements, all my thoughts. I myself am nothing but a terrified, enslaved spectator of the things which I am accomplishing.[106]

From 1880 on these novels become increasingly "psychological" and the subject of multiple personality assumes the status of a literary genre. The high point of this style was Stevenson's *The Strange Case of Dr. Jekyll and Mr. Hyde* published in 1886.[107] It is also interesting to note that the chief character in this novel was a physician. In Stevenson's work and in others which followed we find not so much a departed spirit taking possession of another person but rather the personality of the victim comes under the influence of another part of themselves. After having been influenced by mesmerism, Spiritualism, and hypnotism, literature came under the sway of depth-psychology whose chief representatives were

Freud and Jung and whose ideas about the unconscious became popularized, providing material for the new psychological novels of the twentieth century.

In briefly outlining the background and setting of the nineteenth-century phenomenon of the trance state and its psychology, I have attempted to demonstrate the role of Spiritualism in this history by situating it in context of the time. Jung unquestionably came under the influence of the profession of psychiatry with which he associated himself and stands in a long line of investigators into the more unusual dimensions of the human psyche. His psychology grew out of the contending factions that existed in nineteenth-century European psychiatry. As a young psychiatrist he concerned himself with the psychopathology of mental disorder. The history of research into this area in the nineteenth century devoted a great deal of time to the subject of trance states and their pathology. The question of the origin of these unconscious processes and their relation to the personality as a whole assumed great importance. A significant portion of the population of both America and Europe was willing to tolerate as religiously and scientifically acceptable the possibility that mediums in trance could have access to transpersonal states and mediate the communication between the living and the dead. The medical view as represented by neurology and psychiatry argued, for the most part, that these processes were abnormal and indicated a dissociation of personality which would split off into personified fragments. Jung's own contention, as we shall see, was that the psychiatric model provided a basis for understanding the psychology of these unconscious processes. Nevertheless, he was unwilling to capitulate completely to a reduction of these processes to pathology.

In the chapters that follow I will also suggest that Jung's contact with these unusual dimensions of the human psyche came not only from the formal scientific efforts that preceded him but also from the more immediate influence of Spiritualism on the populace of Europe which, it would seem, was rather extensive in the late nineteenth century. For this reason I have sketched some of the important points of contact between mesmerism, Spiritualism, and hypnotism. In the next chapter I will show how Spiritualism, and the ideas associated with it, are evident in the lives of Jung's immediate ancestors, and in his own early life, in order to determine what influence this may have had on his later psychological theories. As will become clear in the course of the subsequent chapters, I will argue that Jung's later unwillingness to capitulate to a reduction of spiritualistic phenomena to pathology had to do not only with a need to update inherited psychiatric theories but with a series of his own early experiences which, in contrast, were deeply entangled in the phenomenon of Spiritualism.

Notes

1. The German psychiatrist Emil Kraepelin (1856–1926), attempted the most comprehensive psychiatric nosology and systematization in the nineteenth century. Whether mental disorders have largely been determined by, and expressed in terms of, social variables is a subject that is increasingly attracting contemporary historians of psychiatric medicine. Two recent examples focusing on the modern period are George Frederick Drinka, *The Birth of Neurosis* (New York: Simon and Schuster, 1984); and the excellent "case-study," Jan Goldstein, *Console and Classify: The French Psychiatric Profession in the Nineteenth Century* (Cambridge: Cambridge University Press, 1987).

2. Jung shared this background, as well as an interest in seeing psychology as a vehicle for spiritual values, with a number of slightly older contemporaries: William James in America and especially the leaders of the Society for Psychical Research in Britain. On the latter, see J. P. Williams, "Psychical Research and Psychiatry in Late Victorian Britain: Trance as Ecstacy or Trance as Insanity," in W. F. Bynum, et al. eds., *The Anatomy of Madness: Essays in the History of Psychiatry*, vol. 1, *People and Ideas* (London: Tavistock Publications, 1985), 233–54. While Williams mentions (248) Janet and Freud as offering theories of "altered consciousness...more definitely psychiatric, carrying a strong implication of pathology," he makes no mention of Jung's far more positive assessment of the same phenomena.

3. Ellenberger, *Discovery*, 53–57. For a favorable account of Gassner, see Francis J. Schaefer, "Gassner, Johann Joseph," in Charles G. Herbermann, ed., *The Catholic Encyclopedia*, vol. 6 (New York: Robert Appleton, 1907–14), 392.

4. Vincent Buranelli, *The Wizard From Vienna: Franz Anton Mesmer* (New York: Coward, McCann & Geohegan, 1975), 27–31.

5. Ibid., 31, 199–204. Some have speculated Mesmer was associated with secret societies just prior to 1759; see Ellenberger, *Discovery*, 58.

6. Buranelli, 31–34.

7. Frank A. Pattie, "Mesmer's Medical Dissertation and its Debt to Mead's *De Imperio Solis ac Lunae*," *Journal of the History of Medicine and Allied Sciences* 11 (1956): 275–87. Mesmer's dissertation is in Franz Anton Mesmer, *Mesmerism: A Translation of the Original Scientific and Medical*

Writings of F. A. Mesmer, ed. George Block (Los Altos, Calif.: William Kaufmann, 1980), 3–20.

8. Letter to A. M. Unzer, Doctor of Medicine (1775) in Mesmer, 25.

9. Pattie, 286–87.

10. Ellenberger, *Discovery,* 62, slightly modified, summarizing Mesmer's *Mémoire sur la découverte du magnétisme animal* (Paris, 1779). In this seemingly naive idea of a "universal fluid" there lies the still unsolved problem of the precise relationship between psyche and soma; see Leon Chertok, "Relation and Influence," *American Journal of Clinical Hypnosis* 29 (1986): 13–22.

11. Ellenberger, *Discovery,* 484, remarks that Bruer's Anna O. case, which was so important to Freud, is analogous to the cases of magnetic illnesses.

12. Buranelli, 89 et seq., 157–67; Robert Darnton, *Mesmerism and the End of the Enlightenment in France* (Cambridge, Mass.: Harvard University Press, 1968), 62–64. Franklin may have been privately less negative about mesmerism than the report of the commission he headed indicates. Its conclusions were exacerbated by the effects mesmerism might have had on public morality, which the private report the commission sent to the King and the police clearly highlights; see Kevin M. McConkey and Campbell Perry, "Benjamin Franklin and Mesmerism," *The International Journal of Clinical and Experimental Hypnosis* 33 (1985): 122–30.

13. Robert Darnton, "Mesmer, Franz Anton," in Charles Coulston Gillispie, ed., *Dictionary of Scientific Biography,* vol. 9 (New York: Charles Scribner's Sons, 1974), 326; Geoffrey Sutton, "Electric Medicine and Mesmerism," *Isis* 72 (1981): 375–92. Sutton has pointed out that often what passed for science among the socially sanctioned intelligentsia was as much determined by class and rank as by the strict canons of scientific method and evidence. He offers as an example the condemnation of Mesmer and the electrical healer Nicolas-Philippe Le Dru and the recognition of P. J. C. Mauduyt de la Verenne, appointed by the French Royal Society of Medicine to investigate electric cures, all of whom shared basic assumptions about magnetism, electricity, and healing.

14. Mesmer, 135, 120 et seq.

15. Buranelli, 189.

16. Ibid., 199 et seq.

17. Darnton, *Mesmerism,* 14.

18. Ellenberger, *Discovery,* 75.

19. Ibid.; Darnton, *Mesmerism*, on the political dimensions of mesmerism leading up to the French Revolution.

20. Ellenberger, *Discovery*, 77.

21. Ibid., 78.

22. Ibid.

23. Ibid., 80. Nandor Fodor, *Encyclopedia of Psychic Science* (1934), s.v. "Hauffe, Frau Frederica" (reprint, New Hyde Park, N.Y.: University Books, 1966), 160, states that the Seeress was bedridden from the time of her marriage in 1819 and given to convulsions and visions which she occasionally set down in elaborate geometrical designs.

24. Ellenberger, *Discovery*, 81.

25. Jung had a copy of *Die Seherin von Prevorst* (1892 ed.) as well as the following works of Kerner's: *Die Somnambülem Tische* (1853); *Kleksographien* (1857); and *Briefwechsel mit seinen Freunden*, 2 vols. (1897), indicating his interest in Kerner's studies of mediumistic phenomena; see *Katalog*, 41.

26. Ellenberger, *Discovery*, 81; Podmore, vol. 1, 99, mentions that Kerner had already treated two remarkable somnambules magnetically and published an account of this in 1826, the same year Frau Hauffe turned up at his door.

27. George Florovsky, *Ways of Russian Theology*, vol. 1 (Belmont, Mass.: Norland Press, 1979), 205; also Thomas E. Berry, *Spiritualism in Tzarist Society and Literature* (Baltimore, Md.: Edgar Allen Poe Society, 1985). Kerner's *Die Seherin von Prevorst*, first published in 1829, went through three enlarged editions in 1832, 1838, and 1846; see Fodor, *Encyclopedia of Psychic Science*, s.v. "Kerner, Dr. Justinus," 189.

28. Ellenberger, *Discovery*, 81.

29. Robert C. Fuller, *Mesmerism and the American Cure of Souls* (Philadelphia: University of Pennsylvania Press, 1982), 16; Buranelli, 154–55.

30. Darnton, *Mesmerism*, 75, 180 et seq.; Buranelli, 143–79.

31. Buranelli, 154–56. Fuller, 17, states that Lafayette never received permission to spread Mesmer's teachings. This seems incorrect, given the letter Buranelli cites.

32. Fuller, 17.

33. Ibid.

34. Ibid., 18.

35. Ibid, 21 citing Charles Poyen, *Progress of Animal Magnetism in New England* (Boston: Weeks, Jordon and Co., 1837), 55.

36. Fuller, 26.

37. Ibid., 26–29.

38. Ibid., 30.

39. Podmore, vol. 1, 154 et seq. There does seem to have been an early interest in mesmerism among physicians and other professionals which was expressed in the formation of active and organized societies, one among Franco-Americans in New Orleans with close ties to France, but these faded quickly; see William C. Wester, "The Phreno-Magnetic Society of Cincinnati—1842," *The American Journal of Clinical Hypnosis* 18 (1976): 277–81; and Wallace K. Tomlinson and J. John Perret, "Mesmerism in New Orleans: 1845–1861," *The American Journal of Clinical Hypnosis* 18 (1975): 1–5.

40. Podmore, vol. 1, xi.

41. The best overall survey of nineteenth-century Spiritualism remains Podmore's two volume study. Modern Spiritualism has also attracted sociologists and anthropologists, e.g., Geoffrey K. Nelson, *Spiritualism and Society* (London: Routledge & Kegan Paul, 1969); V. Skultans *Intimacy and Ritual: A Study of Spiritualism, Mediums and Groups* (London: Routledge & Kegan Paul, 1974). A good recent study of nineteenth-century American Spiritualism is by historian R. Laurence Moore, *In Search of White Crows* (New York: Oxford University Press, 1977). Moore (5–7) has cautioned against an excessively sociological approach to modern Spiritualism. He claims the historical record of nineteenth-century Spiritualism is complex and has not been adequately studied and emphasizes that Spiritualism and the subsequent development of psychical research have provided many Americans with an acceptable solution to the problem of reconciling religious and scientific interests. Janet Oppenheim has written the most comprehensive study of the rise of Spiritualism and psychical research in Britain in *The Other World: Spiritualism and Psychical Research in England, 1850–1914* (Cambridge: Cambridge University Press, 1985).

42. I have assumed a direct influence of mesmerism on the rise and development of Spiritualism, albeit complicated by the enmeshed relationship of religion and science in the nineteenth century which is by no means completely understood. Nelson, 45, 55–58, mentions the possibility of the influence of African ideas of possession as well as North American Indian Shamanism and guardian-spirit beliefs. I am not aware of any studies sup-

porting such speculation though it is not impossible that some detailed area studies could demonstrate the validity of such a hypothesis as Logie Barrow, *Independent Spirits: Spiritualism and English Plebians 1850–1910* (London: Routledge & Kegan Paul, 1986), 1–2, seems to suggest. The question remains as to the significance such evidence would have on any attempt to explain the rise and spread of Spiritualism on the massive scale which occurred in the late nineteenth century.

43. Jones, vol. 3, 380 et seq.

44. Edwin G. Boring, *A History of Experimental Psychology* (New York: Appleton-Century-Crofts, 1957), 117, 122–23, suggests that Mesmer's séance is the ancestor of the spiritualistic séance.

45. Fuller, x; Podmore, vol. 1, 154 et seq., gives a good summary.

46. Ellenberger, *Discovery*, 83. There was even an American weekly called *Spiritual Telegraph* (1852–60); see Fodor, *Encyclopedia of Psychic Science*, s.v. "Spiritual Telegraph." In fact the telegraph was a favorite electrical image for long distant communication widely used by spiritualists, and proof that what once was considered impossible could be accomplished through science (Moore, 22).

47. James Webb, *The Occult Underground* (La Salle, Ill.: Open Court, 1974), 43–44.

48. Malcolm Jay Kottler, "Alfred Russel Wallace, the Origin of Man, and Spiritualism." *Isis* 65 (1974): 145–92.

49. Ellenberger, *Discovery*, 83.

50. Webb, *Occult Underground,* 44. There is a good deal of speculation as to why the "burned-over district" of northeastern United States has been the region where a number of revivals and new religious movements began. Detailed area studies are Whitney R. Cross, *The Burned-Over District: The Social and Intellectual History of Enthusiastic Religion in Western New York, 1800–1850* (Ithaca: Cornell University Press, 1950); and Paul E. Johnson, *A Shopkeeper's Millennium: Society and Revivals in Rochester, New York, 1815–1837* (New York: Hill and Wang, 1978).

51. Summarizing Podmore, vol. 1, 179 et seq. Alan Gauld, *The Founders of Psychical Research* (New York: Schocken, 1968), 3 et seq., discusses some of the problems in reconstructing the event. Spiritualistic phenomena had already been observed in Europe and in America some years before, but as a movement Spiritualism seems to have begun in the U.S., in 1848. Anthony A. Walsh in "A Note on the Origin of 'Modern' Spiritualism," *Journal of the History of Medicine and Allied Sciences* 28 (1973): 167–71, has claimed that Dr. J. S. Grimes's mesmeristic gatherings and his association with Andrew Jackson Davis mark the beginning of Spiritu-

alism a few years prior to 1848. Robert W. Delp, "Andrew Jackson Davis: Prophet of American Spiritualism," *The Journal of American History* 59 (1967): 43–56, had earlier drawn attention to Davis's career; and Podmore, vol. 1, 154–76, did so long before, in 1902. While Davis is perhaps the chief architect of spiritualistic philosophy, it is generally agreed that Spiritualism as a movement dates from the experiences of the Fox sisters in 1848; see Kerr, *Mediums, and Spirit-Rappers, and Roaring Radicals*, 3–21; Moore, 7–8. A recent reconstruction of the event citing the earliest accounts is Rossell Hope Robbins, "The Rochester Rappings," *Dalhousie Review* 45 (1965): 153–64; see also Ernest Isaacs, "The Fox Sisters and American Spiritualism," in Howard Kerr and Charles L. Crow, eds., *The Occult in America: New Historical Perspectives* (Urbana: University of Illinois Press, 1983), 79–110.

52. Gauld, 29.

53. Oppenheim, 9. It is also important to note that the majority of mediums were women. This was part of a broader struggle to change the social and religious roles available to women in the nineteenth century; see Moore, 102–29; Mary Farrell Bednarowski, "Outside the Mainstream: Women's Religion and Women Religious Leaders in Nineteenth-Century America," *Journal of the American Academy of Religion* 48 (1980): 207–31; and Alex Owen, *The Darkened Room: Women, Power and Spiritualism in Late Victorian England* (Philadelphia: University of Pennsylvania Press, 1990).

54. Cited in Zumstein-Preiswerk, 114–15. See Podmore, vol. 2, for the transatlantic spread of Spiritualism.

55. Moore, xiii, chapter 1, and especially page 19 for the four basic principles of Spiritualism. Spiritualist churches did appear by the end of the 1850s but these were often merely meeting halls. When the gatherings were more traditionally religious in form these were among spiritualists who remained nominally Christian and even they were accused of focusing on spirit communications instead of the worship of God; see Moore, 46. Spiritualism later became organized into a number of conflicting sects; see Judah, 63–91.

56. Oppenheim, 67. On the subject of Spiritualism and Christianity, especially Anglicans and Protestants, see Moore, 40–69, and Oppenheim, 63–110. The official Roman Catholic position on Spiritualism was more intransigent than those of the Anglican and Protestant churches. It sought to separate the medical from the superstitious and the demonic in mesmerism, hypnotism, and Spiritualism, see Edward A. Pace, "Spiritism," in *The Catholic Encyclopedia*, vol. 14 (New York: Robert Appleton, 1907–14), 221; Joseph Lapponi, *Hypnotism and Spiritualism: A Critical and Medical Study*, 2nd ed. (New York: Longmans, Green, and Co., 1907); Lapponi was the chief physician of Pope Leo XIII and Pope Pius X. See also William J.

Gormley, *Medical Hypnosis: Historical Introduction to Its Morality in the Light of Papal, Theological and Medical Teaching* (Washington, D.C.: Catholic University of America Press, 1961). There, of course, remains the pertinent question of whether the Catholic population reflected in their behavior the directives that came from the Vatican.

57. Kardec's *Le Livre des Espirits* went through more than twenty editions and became extremely popular, selling by the tens of thousands, see Podmore, vol. 2, 161, 168; and Fodor, *Encyclopedia of Psychic Sciences*, s.v. "Kardec, Allan." Kardec's brand of Spiritualism became so popular it was exported to South America where, in 1957, the Brazilian government issued a stamp in his honour to commemorate the first centenary of Spiritualism. The doctrine of reincarnation has spread to contemporary spiritualist circles, creating a certain amount of dissension; see Judah, 72–74. Jung had a German edition (1891) of Kardec's *Le Livre des Mediums* (1864) in his library; see *Katalog*, 39. I will discuss Jung's dissertation in chapter 5. Jung himself seemed favorably disposed toward the belief in reincarnation; see *MDR*, 317 et seq.

58. I am following the summary of Podmore, vol. 2, 162. Jung had a copy of Perty's *Die mystischen*, as well as the earlier *Ueber die Seele* (1856); see *Katalog*, 57.

59. William Crookes (1832–1919) was a distinguished physicist. Late in life Jung recalled that he was an early influence in his study of Spiritualism, *MDR*, 99. His library contains Crookes's *Der Spiritualismus und die Wissenschaft* (1884); see *Katalog*, 17. Some of Crookes's colleagues thought that he was gullible. He has even been accused of fraud as a consequence of being romantically entangled with the chief subject of his investigations, the medium Florence Cook; see Oppenheim, 16 et seq.

60. For an overview, see Frank M. Turner, "The Victorian Conflict between Science and Religion: A Professional Dimension," *Isis* 69 (1978): 356–76; and, more specifically addressed to the subject of Spiritualism, Jon Palfreman, "Between Skepticism and Credulity: A Study of Victorian Scientific Attitudes to Modern Spiritualism," in Roy Wallis, ed., *On the Margins of Science: The Social Construction of Rejected Knowledge*, Sociological Review Monograph no. 27, (Keele, Staffordshire: University of Keele Press, 1979), 201–36.

61. S. E. D. Shortt, "Physicians and Psychics: The Anglo-American Medical Response to Spiritualism, 1870–1890," *Journal of the History of Medicine and Allied Sciences* 39 (1984): 342.

62. Ibid., 343.

63. Podmore, vol. 1, 184 et seq.

64. Shortt, 343. The term *unconscious cerebration* comes from W. B.

Carpenter, an authority on the brain and nervous system in late nine-teenth-century Britain. He was also a relentless foe of Spiritualism, which he attacked at every opportunity; see Oppenheim, 241 et seq. Jung had a copy of Carpenter's *Principles of Mental Physiology* (1891 ed.) which was a standard text for many years; see *Katalog*, 14.

65. Shortt, 344 et seq.; and Edward M. Brown, "Neurology and Spir-itualism in the 1870s," *Bulletin of the History of Medicine* 57 (1983): 563–77. Given the fact that most mediums were women, the attitude of the medical establishment toward the "weaker sex" is important; see, for example, Ilza Veith, *Hysteria: The History of a Disease* (Chicago: The Uni-versity of Chicago Press, 1965), 199 et seq.; Carroll Smith-Rosenberg, "The Hysterical Woman: Sex Roles and Role Conflict in 19th-Century America," *Social Research* 39 (1972): 652–78; Owen, *Darkened Room*, 139–67.

66. Shortt, 349. The opening lines of George M. Beard's "The Psy-chology of Spiritism," *The North American Review* 129 (1879): 65–80, are a good example of this view. He states (65), "Modern spiritism is an attempt to apply the inductive method to religion; to make faith scientific; to con-firm the longings of the heart by the evidence of the senses. In thus sub-mitting spiritism to the inductive method its friends forgot that to prove a religion would be to kill it—to transfer it from the emotions, where it belongs, to the intellect, where it can find no home." Beard, a physician, was no friend of Spiritualism and called it a delusion (66). For a vignette of Beard, including his own neurotic reaction as a consequence of choosing between science and religion, see Drinka, 184–97. Some American physi-cians also claimed the practice of "spirit rapping" would lead to insanity when individuals turned away from traditional Christian belief; see Nor-man Dain, *Concepts of Insanity in the United States, 1789–1865* (New Brunswick, N.J.: Rutgers University Press, 1964), 236 n. 40, 257 n. 34.

67. Ellenberger, *Discovery*, 85 et seq.

68. Ibid., 751. The Salpêtrière, an enormous Parisian women's hos-pital, was one of the most important neurological and psychiatric centers in the late nineteenth century; see Mark S. Micale, "The Salpêtrière in the Age of Charcot: An Institutional Perspective on Medical History in the Late Nineteenth Century," *Journal of Contemporary History* 20 (1985): 703–31.

69. Ellenberger, 750. Equally as ironic is the fact that Charcot's biographer, Georges S. Guillain, has alleged in *J. M. Charcot 1825–1893: His Life and Work*, ed. and trans. Pearce Bailey (New York: Paul B. Hoe-ber, 1959), 174, "Charcot personally never hypnotized a single patient, never checked the experiments and, as a result, was not aware of their inadequacies or of the reasons of their eventual errors." This allegation has stirred up controversy; see J. C. Tomlinson and W. Haymaker, "Jean-Mar-tin Charcot (1825–93)," *American Medical Association Archives of Neurol-*

ogy and Psychiatry 77 (1957): 44–48; and Jerome M. Schneck, "Jean-Martin Charcot and the History of Experimental Hypnosis," *Journal of the History of Medicine and Allied Sciences* 16 (1961): 297–305.

70. Ellenberger, *Discovery*, 751.

71. Robert G. Hillman, "A Scientific Study of Mystery: The Role of the Medical and Popular Press in the Nancy-Salpêtrière Controversy on Hypnotism," *Bulletin of the History of Medicine* 39 (1965): 163–82.

72. Ruth Harris, "Murder Under Hypnosis," *Psychological Medicine* 15 (1985): 477.

73. Ibid., 477 et seq..

74. Ibid., 486.

75. Ibid., 495.

76. Ibid., 497 et seq.

77. James Webb, *The Occult Establishment* (La Salle, Ill.: Open Court, 1976), 352–53.

78. Ellenberger, *Discovery*, 88; *MDR*, 108. Jung also had a copy of Krafft-Ebing's *Eine experimentelle Studie auf dem Gebiete des Hypnotismus* (1893); see *Katalog*, 43.

79. Ellenberger, *Discovery*, 88. Jung claimed he had discussed the subject of hypnosis with Forel when he was a young psychiatrist; see E. A. Bennet, *Meetings with Jung* (London: The Anchor Press, 1982), 41.

80. Ellenberger, *Discovery*, 116; E. A. Bennet, *C. G. Jung* (London: Barrie & Rockliff, 1961), 21 et seq.

81. Ibid., 22.

82. James Strachey's editorial comments in Sigmund Freud, "Papers on Hypnotism and Suggestion" (1888–92), in *Standard Edition*, vol. 1, *Pre-Psycho-Analytic Publications and Unpublished Drafts* (London: The Hogarth Press, 1966), 64; Jones, vol. 1, 235. In a postcard (Feb. 3, 1880) to Eduard Silberstein Freud declines to attend one of Hansen's demonstrations and admonishes his friend to be skeptical when doing so. It may be that Freud did attend another demonstration by Hansen, and became convinced of the authenticity of the hypnotic trance; see *The Letters of Sigmund Freud to Eduard Silberstein 1871–1881*, ed. Walter Boehlich (Cambridge, Mass.: Harvard University Press, 1990), 177.

83. Strachey's editorial comments in Freud's "Papers on Hypnotism and Suggestion," 64.

84. Ibid., 65, 73–75.

85. Ibid., 66.

86. Ibid., 65.

87. Melvin A. Gravitz and Manuel I. Gerton, "Freud and Hypnosis: Report of Post-Rejection Use," *Journal of the History of the Behavioral Sciences* 17 (1981): 68–74, outline the account of a stage hypnotist who claimed to have worked for Freud in the 1920s. Later these authors, in their "Polgar as Freud's Hypnotist? Contrary Evidence," *The American Journal of Clinical Hypnosis* 24 (1982): 272–76, seem to have retracted their former arguments that favored the hypnotist's account In this they seem to be following an earlier discussion they had initially overlooked: Jerome M. Schneck, "Freud's 'Medical Hypnotist'," *The American Journal of Clinical Hypnosis* 19 (1976): 80–81. Schneck questioned the hypnotist's claims based on letters from Ernest Jones and Anna Freud. O. L. Zangwill, "Freud on Hypnosis," in Richard L. Gregory, ed., *The Oxford Companion to the Mind* (New York: Oxford University Press, 1987), 275–76, has recently argued for Freud's renewed interest in hypnosis, in the 1920s, from the internal evidence of his writings.

88. Ellenberger, *Discovery*, 95. Charcot's lecture is in his *Clinical Lectures on Diseases of the Nervous System*, vol. 3 (London: The New Sydenham Society, 1889), 198–206. While Charcot may have taken an interest in earlier religious documents, he was certainly at odds with traditional religion and very much a positivist; see Jan Goldstein, "The Hysteria Diagnosis and the Politics of Anticlericalism in Late Nineteenth-Century France," *Journal of Modern History* 54 (1982): 209–39. Nevertheless, at the end of his life Charcot wrote an essay, "The Faith-Cure," *The New Review* 6 (1893): 18–31, which indicates a change in his views and suggests that he may have come to be a proponent of psychophysical parallelism. A. R. G. Owen, *Hysteria, Hypnosis and Healing: The Work of J.-M. Charcot* (London: Dennis Dobson, 1971), 213, has even suggested that experiments in psychical research were conducted at the Salpêtrière during Charcot's last years.

89. On Wilhelm Wundt as "the first psychologist," see Boring, 316–47. Wundt's negative views on Spiritualism are found in his "Spiritualism as a Scientific Question," *The Popular Science Monthly* (1879), 577–93; see also the editor's remarks, 700–02; and Marilyn E. Marshall and Russell A. Wendt, "Wilhelm Wundt, Spiritism, and the Assumptions of Science," in W. G. Bringmann and R. D. Tweney, eds., *Wundt Studies: A Centennial Collection* (Toronto: C. J. Hogrefe, 1980), 158–75.

90. Janet's interest in Spiritualism and psychical research has been documented in Ellenberger, *Discovery*, 84, 338, 348, 360, 398–99. Jung studied with Janet in Paris in 1902; see Jung, *Letters 1: 1906–1950*, 210.

On Myers, see Gauld, 38–44, 89–104. For William James, see his *Essays on Psychical Research* (Cambridge, Mass.: Harvard University Press, 1986).

91. Ellenberger, *Discovery*, 131 et seq., 176 n. 54, has outlined the phenomena of multiple personality, its classification, and the literature on the subject. See also Jacques M. Quen, ed., *Split Minds/Split Brains: Historical and Current Perspectives* (New York: New York Univeristy Press, 1986).

92. Moore, 133–84; Oppenheim, 236–66; Williams.

93. Sigmund Freud, "A Note on the Unconscious in Psychoanalysis," (1912) in *Standard Edition*, vol. 12, *The Case of Schreber Papers on Technique and Other Works* (London: The Hogarth Press, 1958), 263. Jones, vol. 3, 274–78, gives the background of this development in Freud's thinking. Ellenberger, *Discovery*, 141, points out that after 1910 there was little interest in the phenomenon of multiple personality. For an overview of the literature and the recent appearance of cases of multiple personality, see Myron Boor and Philip M. Coons, "A Comprehensive Bibliography of Literature Pertaining to Multiple Personality," *Psychological Reports* 53 (1983): 295–310.

94. Janet's influence on Jung has been investigated by John R. Haule, "Archetype and Integration: Exploring the Janetian Roots of Analytical Psychology," *Journal of Analytical Psychology* 28 (1983): 253–67; and in his "From Somnambulism to the Archetypes: The French Roots of Jung's Split with Freud," *The Psychoanalytic Review* 71 (1984): 635–59. On Flournoy and Jung, see James Witzig, "Theodore Flournoy—A Friend Indeed," *Journal of Analytical Psychology* 27 (1982): 131–48. On the recent interest in multiple personality and Jung's psychology, see R. Noll, "Multiple Personality, Dissociation, and C. G. Jung's Complex Theory," *Journal of Analytical Psychology* 34 (1989): 253–370.

95. Summarizing Ellenberger, *Discovery*, 315 et seq.

96. Ibid., 121.

97. Tymms, 72.

98. Ellenberger, *Discovery*, 163.

99. Fodor, *Encyclopedia of Psychic Science*, s.v. "Hugo, Victor."

100. Ibid., s.v. "Flammarion, Camille."

101. Ellenberger, *Discovery*, 163.

102. Theodore Flournoy, *Spiritism and Psychology* (New York: Harper & Brothers, 1911), 143–49. Dickens himself was quite interested in the subject of trance states; see Fred Kaplan, *Dickens and Mesmerism: The Hidden Springs of Fiction* (Princeton, N.J.: Princeton University Press, 1975).

103. Camille Flammarion, *Mysterious Psychic Forces* (Boston: Small, Maynard and Co., 1909), 25–26, and plates 2 and 3, which are reproductions of two of Sardou's somnabulistic drawings.

104. Ellenberger, *Discovery*, 164.

105. Cited in Russel M. and Clare R. Goldfarb, *Spiritualism and Nineteenth-Century Letters* (Rutherford, N.J.: Fairleigh Dickinson University Press, 1978), 118.

106. Cited by Ellenberger, 165.

107. Ellenberger, *Discovery*, 165 et seq.; and Peter B. Messent, ed., *Literature of the Occult: A Collection of Critical Essays* (Englewood Cliffs, N.J.: Prentice-Hall, 1981). For other examples into the twentieth century see Arnold M. Ludwig, "Hypnosis in Fiction," *The International Journal of Clinical and Experimental Hypnosis* 11 (1963): 71–80.

Chapter 2

Parental and Religious Conflict
in the Early Life of C. G. Jung

The influence of Spiritualism in Jung's early life is evident in the biographical details which are available. Jung himself first attempted to reconstruct the particulars of his early life following his traumatic break with Freud.[1] This reconstruction, in character with Jung's autobiography as a whole, is almost exclusively concerned with his own inner thoughts, feelings, and experiences. Many of these seem to have been of an unusual nature and, as I will show, are bound up with his parents, extended family, and ancestors. The insights Jung gained from his retrospective view of his childhood experiences, which he kept from public view, he later incorporated into his psychology. And while he never systematically developed a child psychology, he appears to have perceived childhood very much in the light of his own early life.[2]

In order to elucidate the role Spiritualism had in Jung's early life, it is necessary to assemble a number of biographical details. These details are important because they indicate a certain tension in Jung which will become a constant presence in his attempt to understand and interpret Spiritualism. This tension first manifests itself in Jung's early experience of the conflict between his parents and their families, which Jung seems to have gradually internalized. The result was to cause a split in him that it was the burden of his life to try to heal. The role Spiritualism played in this split in the early years of Jung's life will be the focus of this chapter.

In Jung's autobiography, *Memories, Dreams, Reflections*, published posthumously in 1961, he revealed publicly for the first time the remarkable experiences he had undergone during his long and rich life. In this work it becomes clear that Jung's psychology is deeply connected with his personal life, even though the external details of that life are largely excluded from the account. Jung was at first reluctant to write of his life, having a distaste for revealing himself publicly. Aniela Jaffé, the editor of his autobiography, prodded him to reveal details on external events but to no avail.[3] In much the same vein he wrote to his publisher:

> I regret that my biography, as I envisage it, is in many respects unlike other biographies. It is utterly impossible for me, without expressing value judgments, to remember the millions of personal details and then to have such a conceit of them in retrospect as to tell them again in all seriousness. I know there are people who live in their own biography during their lifetime and act as though they were already in a book. For me life was something that had to be lived and not talked about.[4]

Jung regarded the external details of his life as uneventful, even accidental, and granted meaning and substance only to his inner experiences.[5] The reason for this he himself concluded, is that:

> In the end the only events in my life worth telling are those when the imperishable world irrupted into this transitory one. This is why I speak chiefly of inner experiences, amongst which I include my dreams and visions. These form the *prima materia* of my scientific work.[6]

It is clear Jung considered his writings to have flowed from his inner life. The books he wrote, he often remarked, were a matter of fate. And in the introduction to his autobiography he is quoted as stating: "My life has been in a sense the quintessence of what I have written, not the other way around."[7]

While Jung's account of his creative life is highly subjective, he is also concerned with establishing links and parallels with the objective world, to give, as it were, a historical foundation for his psychology.[8] Yet, the overwhelming impression is that Jungian Psychology is stamped through and through by its founder's personality. As Vincent Brome, in a recent biographical study of Jung, has put it:

> There was a sense in which Jung's model of the human psyche converted autobiography into psychotherapy. He had experienced every detail of his model, and it was as if he had elevated an elaborate process of self-analysis into abstract theory convinced that it had universal application.[9]

If we follow the process of Jung's self-analysis we can see the general soundness of this conclusion.

Jung's break with Freud in 1913 not only put him into a state of severe disorientation but signaled in himself the beginnings of what he later termed "the process of individuation."[10] It was on December 12, 1913 that Jung resolved to take the decisive step and drop deep into a world of fantasy, visions, and dreams.[11] The experiences he was to undergo were so powerful they almost overwhelmed him and, more than once, he feared for his sanity. Several of these experiences were of an undeniably spiritualistic nature. Visions and ghostly figures populate these years and it is to a certain peasant tenacity and grip on life that Jung attributed the fact he was not overcome, a fate he claimed Nietzsche failed to escape.[12] Interspersed with these visions and the flood of fantasy figures, almost as though they had a power of attraction all their own, memories and experiences buried deep in the world of his childhood began to surface.[13] Jung's next step was to connect these fragments of his early life and fit them into a schema of development which would serve as the basic model for his theory of personality.

In a curious way Jung felt his later ideas were almost, if not in fact, experientially present in the early events he now recalled. I say curious, because in returning to the world of his childhood, he revisited not only a world in which occurred the first intimations of his own consciousness but also the world that bore the marks of having just been delivered from the womb of the unconscious, to Jung the mother and source of all psychical life. In a letter (July 29, 1939) to a psychotherapist Jung wrote:

> As a matter of fact we have actually known everything all along; for all these things are always there, only we are not there for them.... Even as a child I had alchemical insights which would sound much more astonishing.... Originally we were all born out of a world of wholeness and in the first years of life are still completely contained in it. There we have all knowledge without knowing it. Later we lose it, and call it progress when we remember it again.[14]

Indeed, in later life, Jung spoke about learning to be unconscious once again.[15] And we know from his autobiography that in his last years, long submerged images rose to the surface and he sensed their connection with his later writings.[16] Jung had, in principle, admitted as much publicly as far back as 1929 when he wrote:

"every psychology—my own included—has the character of a subjective confession."[17] It may well be, therefore, that it is not only to the obscure and often confusing literature of medieval and renaissance alchemy, philosophy, gnosticism, and a scattering of Greek thinkers, that we should turn to uncover the sources of Jung's psychology but also to the half-remembered/half-forgotten world of Jung's own childhood and early life.

In his study of the rise and development of depth-psychology, Ellenberger has stated: "Jung's most immediate sources were his own personality, his family, his ethnic background."[18] To Jung's Swiss background he attributes his

> practical bent that incited him, first, to bring his patients back to awareness and, then, to help them readjust themselves as much as possible to their social and traditional setting.[19]

We also know that Jung thought it necessary to have some knowledge of the national background in order to understand the individual. Jung clearly felt his Swiss background came to him through his own ancestors. As he once wrote:

> I have in my time been accused of "Swiss wooden-headedness."... I am perfectly content to let my psychological confession, my so-called "theories," be criticized as a product of Swiss wooden-headedness...as betraying the sinister influence of my theological and medical forebears.... I am proud of my subjective premises, I love the Swiss earth in them.[20]

This statement is characteristic of Jung's thinking, which reveals a decided inclination toward relating the personal to the collective. It is the individual who is to bear the burden of the collective traits and has the capacity to reflect them. Dr. Michael Fordham, a leading Jungian authority on children, goes even further and states:

> An important ingredient in Jung's thinking was his emphasis on individuality, and there is reason to suppose that periodically he thought of this as deriving from the collective unconscious, whose historical dimension was so important to him.[21]

All of this, of course, raises questions about the development of the personality in childhood and what part the culture, and especially the ancestors as vehicles of that culture, play in this development.

The bulk of Jung's writings are concerned with elucidating the archetypal background against which the experience of adult life should be understood. Very few of these writings are specifically concerned with children or with the life of childhood. And though he gave private seminars on children's dreams (1936–37), he was, in principle, against child analysis.[22] This is unusual because he thought the dreams of children contained much evidence for his theory of the collective unconscious.[23] But perhaps the chief reason Jung shied away from child analysis was his reluctance to allow profane hands to disturb the inner world of childhood. This is so despite his own severely disoriented early life, which Fordham has openly called schizophrenic.[24] Jung's wife, and the mother of five children, once told Fordham that Jung knew nothing about children and, turning to Jung, she said, "You know very well that you are not interested in people, but your theory of the collective unconscious."[25] It would be unfair to make too much out of this statement by Emma Jung, but there may be some truth in Fordham's contention that Jung idealized children, which Fordham sees to have been determined by personal factors—that is Jung's own childhood.[26] If this is in any way the case, then it must be concluded that what Jung assumed to be true about childhood in general more correctly applies to his own early life.

In his writings on the psychology of children, Jung placed a good deal of emphasis on the parents being the immediate source of childhood disorders. But it is important to recognize that, for Jung, the psyche was not a *tabula rasa* and therefore the constitution was considered decisive. As he himself put it: "in a family of several children only one of them will react to the unconscious of the parents with a marked degree of identity."[27] For the source of the ancestral influence on the individual, Jung goes back further than the parents and, bearing in mind Fordham's remarks about Jung deriving individuality from the collective unconscious, the following statement is significant:

> The psychology of "identity," which precedes ego-consciousness, indicates what the child is by virtue of his parents. But what he is as an individuality distinct from his parents can hardly be explained by the causal relationship to the parents. We ought rather to say that it is not so much the parents as their ancestors—the grandparents and great-grandparents—who are the true progenitors, and that

these explain the individuality of the children far more than the immediate and, so to speak, accidental parents. In the same way the true psychic individuality of the child is something new in respect of the parents and cannot be derived from their psyche. It is a combination of collective factors which are only potentially present in the parental psyche, and are sometimes wholly invisible. Not only the child's body, but his soul, too, proceeds from his ancestry, in as far as it is individually distinct from the collective psyche of mankind.[28]

In what follows it will become clear how autobiographical these assertions are.

In many ways it was very characteristic of Carl Jung to judge the new in terms of the old. His saturnine personality, as is so evident from his autobiography, had a deep respect for time and yet he was drawn to and pursued images into what he saw as the timeless world of the archetypes. He lived a full and rich life and yet lived in the present somewhat reluctantly. His own feelings and the thoughts that grew out of them are deeply linked with the past and, on a personal level, he connected them with his ancestors. Of these he wrote:

I feel very strongly that I am under the influence of things or questions which were left incomplete and unanswered by my parents and grandparents and more distant ancestors. It often seems as if there were an impersonal karma within a family, which is passed on from parents to children. It has always seemed to me that I had to answer questions which fate had posed to my forefathers, and which had not yet been answered, or as if I had to complete, or perhaps continue, things which previous ages had left unfinished.[29]

Jung enshrined his devotion to his ancestors in memorial stones and in the ceiling paintings of his family genealogy in Bollingen, his beloved country retreat on the shore of Zurich Lake.[30] In view of all of this, Jung's own family background may well be an important factor in an attempt to understand his own early experiences and his later thought.

On the paternal side of Jung's family there is a certain Carl Jung (d. 1654) who, Jung surmised, may have known the writings of the sixteenth-century alchemists Michael Maier and Gerhard

Dorn, but little is really known of him.[31] The first authenticated ancestor was Sigismund Jung (d. 1778) of Mainz, Germany. His son, Doctor Franz Jung (1759–1831), left Mainz for Manheim and during the Napoleonic campaigns was in charge of a military hospital.[32] Jung judged him to be an introvert, after he received photos of his portrait from a cousin.[33] But what chiefly interested Jung about this particular ancestor was the relationship between him and his wife Sophie Jung *née* Ziegler. The reason for this interest was an alleged family rumor that linked the great Goethe and Sophie in an affair, resulting in the birth of Jung's namesake grandfather, Carl Gustav Jung (1794–1864).[34] It is said that Jung was ambivalent with regard to the truth of this rumor, but in his correspondence with Freud he seemed to accept it as factual and refered to Goethe as his great-grandfather.[35] And as late as the end of 1959, Jung was once again preoccupied with Sophie Ziegler and wrote to his cousin about some letters of hers in his possession.[36] Nevertheless, Ernst Jung, son of the elder C. G. Jung, reports that this rumor was unfounded and was never mentioned by his father.[37] It is possible that the legend of Goethe as ancestor was born out of Jung's identification with his namesake grandfather and a defensive reaction on his own part against, as we shall see, the excessive influence of his mother and her side of the family, the Preiswerks. His encounter with Goethe's *Faust*, which he immediately identified with, and another encounter, between Goethe and a certain Marianne Jung, may have coalesced in his mind and jelled into the legend of Goethe as ancestor.[38]

Whether by blood or by temperament, Jung felt a kinship with Goethe. In particular it was Goethe's *Faust* that most impressed him.[39] He later admitted:

> *Faust* struck a cord in me and pierced me through in a way that I could not but regard as personal. Most of all, it awakened in me the problem of opposites.... Faust...encounters the dark side of his being, his sinister shadow, Mephistopheles.... My own inner contradictions appeared here in dramatized form; Goethe had written virtually a basic outline and pattern of my own conflicts and solutions. The dichotomy of Faust-Mephistopheles came together within myself into a single person, and I was that person.[40]

Faust was an early literary example of the theme of the double. And, as we shall see, Faust/Mephistopheles aptly characterized Jung's

own early self-image. In one way or another Jung wished to see his
Faustian inheritance having come to him through his so-called legendary grandfather, Carl Gustav Jung. The elder Jung had broken
with Catholicism and, under the influence of Schleiermacher,
became a Protestant, left Germany, and ended up as professor of
medicine in Basel. A rather dominating personality, the elder Carl
Jung was not without a social conscience and, among other achievements, established the Institute of Hope in Basel for emotionally disturbed children. In a lecture he made the following observation:

> In our age, when the attention of so many doctors is occu-
> pied with the psychic aspect of medical science...it would
> undoubtedly be greatly to the credit of any university to
> found an institution where it would be possible to study
> such cases objectively.... I am not thinking of the usual
> type of mental hospital...but of a hospital that would take
> patients of all kinds and endeavour to heal them by psychic
> methods.[41]

There can be no question but that the figure of Carl Gustav Jung
exerted a considerable influence on his grandson.[42]

Up to this point, Jung's paternal ancestors were men of science, physicians, and scholars. From them Jung felt he had inherited an inclination toward broad learning and the natural sciences.
His choice of medicine as a career seems only logical, in view of how
many of these ancestors were physicians. Against this background
Jung's father, Paul Jung, appears as a curious anomaly, and for
this reason his son was to judge him rather harshly.

The Reverend Paul Jung, a Protestant clergyman, was interested in Semitic languages as a student and completed a doctoral
dissertation on an Arabic version of the *Song of Songs* at Göttingen
University. Any academic ambitions he had were never realized.[43]
In general he gave the impression of being an unassuming man
whom, Jung claimed, harbored doubts about his Christian faith but
was never mature enough to face them, wasting his life in unnecessary and futile pursuits.[44] It is difficult to estimate the accuracy of
Jung's impressions, but the fact remains that they prejudiced his
image of his father until the end of his life. The apparent gap
between the legendary Carl Gustav Jung the elder and his
youngest son Paul is difficult to explain. It would appear, though,
that Jung may have exaggerated the status of his grandfather. It
has been suggested that he was somewhat of a more modest man

who suffered financially throughout his life and was often dependent on others to make ends meet. In addition, Paul Jung was so
pressed financially as the result of having next to no inheritance
that he had to go into the ministry to receive financial support.[45]
Further investigation into this matter may yet reveal that the legendary Carl Gustav Jung the elder might share in the responsibility for his own son's undoing. Jung tended to idealize his namesake
ancestor, perhaps giving him a status he never had, and contrasted
him sharply with his father. Ellenberger, for example, has pointed
out Paul Jung was held in high regard as the Protestant Chaplain
of the Friedmatt Mental Hospital in Basel, a possible source of
influence Jung never mentioned.[46]

When we turn to Jung's mother's side, we encounter a very
different type of family. It is from this side of the family that Jung
inherited his

> psychological intuition and his aptitude for parapsychologi-
> cal experiences [which] explain that other side of his teach-
> ing and therapy: the exploration of the collective uncon-
> scious and the world of archetypes.[47]

The earliest member of Jung's mother's family that is mentioned is
his grandfather Samuel Preiswerk (1799–1871), who was antistes
(or head) of the Protestant clergy of Basel. He was professor of Old
Testament Exegesis and Oriental Languages in the Evangelical
Theological Institution in Geneva, Switzerland, and a scholar of
Hebrew of some note.[48] He later taught Old Testament exegesis at
the University in Basel, composed hymns, and exercised considerable influence over the Basel clergy and an extended family.[49] But
he is chiefly remembered by his relatives for his highly visual experiences of the spirit world.

Samuel Preiswerk, after the death of his first wife, married
Augusta Faber (1805–65), the daughter of a Württemberg clergyman and Jung's grandmother. To the consternation of this second
wife, Samuel Preiswerk spent one day every week communicating
with the spirit of his first wife in his study.[50] Moreover, according to
family tradition, he had visions and conversed with different spirits.[51] Albert Oeri, a long time friend of Jung and resident of Basel,
agrees calling him "a visionary who often experienced entire dramatic scenes complete with ghost conversations."[52]

When Jung's mother was a girl, she was often given the task
of protecting her father Samuel from spirits. "She had to sit behind

him," Aniela Jaffé states, "when he was writing his sermons, because he could not bear "spirits" passing behind his back and disturbing him."[53] Jung said of him, "He was not only extremely learned but also poetically gifted. He was, however, a rather peculiar and original man who always believed himself to be surrounded with ghosts."[54] Jung's later diagnosis of grandfather Samuel was that he suffered from "waking hallucinations," at the same time dismissing this interpretation as a "mere word."[55] While Jung never knew his grandfather, he records an interesting experience he repeatedly had as a child that bears mentioning:

> When I was a little boy, I had a spinster aunt who lived in a nice old-fashioned house. It was full of beautiful old coloured engravings. Among them was a picture of my grandfather on my mother's side. He was a sort of bishop, and he was represented as coming out of his house and standing on a little terrace. There were handrails and stairs coming down from the terrace, and a footpath leading to the cathedral. He was in full regalia, standing there at the top of the terrace. Every Sunday morning I was allowed to pay a call on my aunt, and then I knelt on a chair and looked at that picture until grandfather came down the steps. And each time my aunt would say, "But, my dear, he doesn't walk, he is still standing there." But I knew I had seen him walking down.[56]

There is clear indication that Jung felt he had inherited from his grandfather a predisposition for having spiritualistic experiences and, in later life, he once remarked in a letter: "I have always suspected that my blessed grandfather laid a very strange egg into my mixture."[57]

Samuel's second wife, Jung's grandmother, Augusta Faber, was also endowed with unusual gifts. It was claimed that she had "second sight" and could see spirits. As Aniela Jaffé records:

> The family traced this back to an episode when, as a young girl, she lay for thirty-six hours in a state of catalepsy resembling death. Her gifts, however, could stand the test of a more rigorous judgment: she sometimes saw apparitions of persons unknown to her, but whose historical existence was later proved.[58]

Upon what Jaffé bases the last of these statements is not entirely clear, nor is it known whether Augusta Faber's claims were examined by anyone. But what is obvious is that she exhibited those characteristics that attracted physicians to the study of spontaneous somnambules, and, living until 1865, she falls into the period of the rise of Spiritualism. Not enough is known about her to make any direct connection to this movement, but she does fit the popular conception of a medium. In addition, it is said that several members of her family had parapsychological abilities.[59] Jung's eldest daughter, Agathe, had similar gifts, which he claimed she inherited from his maternal grandmother, Augusta Faber.[60]

Among the offspring of Samuel Preiswerk and Augusta Faber was Emilie, Jung's mother, born in 1848, coincidentally the very year that marks the birth of modern Spiritualism. She appears to have been no less gifted than both her parents with spiritualistic experiences and insights. Her ability to deal with spirits was widely recognized among her relations. Indeed, as Aniela Jaffé informs us: "She left behind a diary in which she noted down all the premonitions, "spookish" phenomena, and strange occurrences she had experienced."[61] Jung wrote of her that she was a somewhat difficult character with a dual personality. At times, we are told, she was very ordinary, and at other times she betrayed uncanny perception that could only be regarded as parapsychological.[62]

It is clear, therefore, that in considering the influence of Spiritualism on Jung's early life, the chief source was his mother's side of the family. It has already been pointed out that Jung felt he had inherited from his paternal side the necessary intellectual abilities to pursue the profession of a learned doctor. It was also from this side that he felt the responsibility for their "unanswered questions." In the end, it was the burden of Jung's life to feel in himself these two powerful inheritances, to be torn by them, and eventually to attempt to reconcile them in a rather unique system of psychology that still reveals the traces of both.

How and when Jung felt the tension between these two worlds is the subject of the chapters on his early life in his autobiography. It is obvious that what we have in Jung's account of his early life is a stylized, retrospective version of those pristine experiences which he sensed had a direct bearing on his later thought. There is more than a hint of this in the prologue of *Memories, Dreams, Reflections,* where he confessed:

> Thus it is that I have now undertaken, in my eighty-third year, to tell my personal myth. I can only make direct statements, only "tell stories." Whether or not the stories are

"true" is not the problem. The only question is whether what I tell is *my* fable, *my* truth.[63]

In describing "his story" Jung began by recalling the setting into which he was born. What might be called the atmosphere of his early years was pervaded with the reserve of Swiss Protestantism. Carl Jung was a pastor's son, and if the manse was one of the great breeding grounds of Swiss-German culture in the nineteenth century, it also sowed in some the seeds of rebellion against religious orthodoxy, or, as in the case of Nietzsche, against religion itself. Henri Ellenberger has pointed out:

> In Jung's case it seems that his religious and philosophical interests were awakened, but because he could not receive an answer that would satisfy him from his father, he turned his inquiry to other problems beyond the scope of traditional religion.[64]

This is precisely what seems to have occurred and is an important factor in Jung's later and more formal preoccupation with Spiritualism.

Many of the experiences of Jung's early childhood were forgotten or blocked out for several years and began to surface only when, after his break with Freud, he dredged up the memories of his early life. Even then Jung kept the knowledge of his early experiences to himself and was able to reveal them only when he was assured they would not be published until after his death.[65] Yet even this restriction did not entirely give him the security and calm he felt was necessary to be able to write about himself in a detached manner. As he stated:

> I have guarded this material all my life, and have never wanted it exposed to the world; for if it is assailed, I shall be affected even more than in the case of my other books. I do not know whether I shall be so far removed from this world that the arrows of criticism will no longer reach me and that I shall be able to bear the adverse reactions.... The 'autobiography' is my life, viewed in the light of the knowledge I have gained from my scientific endeavors. Both are one, and therefore this book makes great demands on people who do not know or cannot understand my scientific ideas. My life has been in a sense the quintessence of what

I have written, not the other way around.... Thus the 'autobiography' is merely the dot on the i.[66]

And yet Jung specifically requested that the autobiography—the dot on the i—be excluded from his *Collected Works*.[67] It may be that Jung's reticence about his autobiography had something to do with his inability to clearly integrate his early experiences into his otherwise comprehensive psychology. As he himself stated, "To this day, writing down my memories at the age of eighty-three, I have never fully unwound the tangle of my earlier memories."[68]

An event that Jung never included in the tangle of his earliest memories is the death of his elder brother, named after his father, Paul Jung. He was born in August 1873 and died soon after.[69] Little is mentioned of this event in any of the biographies of Jung, but it is difficult to imagine it had no effect on young Carl, who was born two years later. In fact, Jung seems to have had an inordinate preoccupation with death as a young child and possibly even inclinations toward suicide.[70] Jung associated his early insecurities with his parent's unhappy marriage: his mother took to her bed often and in one instance spent an extended period, in 1878, in a hospital in Basel. During this time Jung became ill and was looked after by one of his maternal aunts.[71] He later recalled, "At that time I also had vague fears at night. I would hear things walking about in the house."[72] The sources of these disturbing noises are not clear but are part of the dark foreboding and suffocating atmosphere of Jung's early life. Brooding, melancholic figures in top hats and black frock coats, weeping women, graves, and the ubiquitous smell of death are the images which make up the world of Jung's early memories.[73] Happiness was fleeting or simply elsewhere, a never-to-be-had land of dreams, like Uetliberg or Zurich.[74]

The specific figures which stand out in the depressive environment of Jung's childhood were an unhappy mother, who became overweight and much preoccupied with the spirit world, and a gentle but weak clergyman father, who seemed more like a woman than a man.[75] Indeed, the confusion of gender identity Jung had about his pastor father was extended to matters religious: Lord Jesus is represented as a hen in the first two lines of a prayer to shut out the fears of the night: "Spread out thy wings, Lord Jesus mild / And take to thee thy chick, thy child."[76] An even more disconcerting example Jung related in his memoirs:

> One hot summer day I was sitting alone...playing in the sand.... Looking up, I saw a figure in a strangely broad hat

and a long black garment coming down from the wood. It looked like a man wearing women's clothes. Slowly the figure drew nearer, and I could now see that it really was a man wearing a kind of black robe that reached to his feet. At the sight of him I was overcome with fear, which rapidly grew into deadly terror as the frightful recognition shot through my mind: "That is a Jesuit.".... Actually I had no idea what Jesuits were, but I was familiar with the word "Jesus" from my little prayer.[77]

At about the same time, when Jung was between three and four years old, he had a rather grotesque, surrealistic dream which etched itself into his memory for the rest of his life. In it we find the following images: a grave, an underground shrine, a frightening mother, and, most bizarre of all, an enormous phallus. Jung gave the following account of the dream:

In the dream I was in this meadow [near the vicarage]. Suddenly I discovered a dark, rectangular, stone-lined hole in the ground. I had never seen it before. I ran forward curiously and peered down into it. Then I saw a stone stairway leading down. Hesitantly and fearfully, I descended. At the bottom was a doorway with a round arch, closed off by a green curtain.... I pushed it aside. I saw before me in the dim light a rectangular chamber about thirty feet long. The ceiling was arched and of hewn stone. The floor was laid with flagstones, and in the center a red carpet ran from the entrance to a low platform. On this platform stood a...golden throne.... Something was standing on it which I thought at first was a tree trunk twelve to fifteen feet high and about one and a half to two feet thick. It was a huge thing.... It was made of skin and naked flesh, and on top there was something like a rounded head with no face and no hair. On the very top of the head was a single eye, gazing motionlessly upward....

The thing did not move, yet I had the feeling that it might at any moment crawl off the throne like a worm and creep toward me. I was paralyzed with terror. At that moment I heard from outside and above me my mother's voice. She called out, "Yes, just look at him. That is the man-eater!" That intensified my terror still more, and I awoke sweating and scared to death.[78]

This incredible phallus dream Jung later understood to have marked the beginnings of his intellectual life, an initiation into the secrets of the earth.[79] He did not associate its appearance with the disintegrating marriage of his parents. In fact, he shunned any explicit sexual interpretation, preferring a symbolic one even though he himself had written, "Where there is an undervaluation of sexuality the self is symbolized as a phallus."[80] The one detail about the dream that did perplex Jung he reported as follows:

> I could never make out whether my mother meant, "*That* is the man-eater." or, "That is the *man-eater*." In the first case she would have meant that not Lord Jesus or the Jesuit was the devourer of little children, but the phallus; in the second case that the "man-eater" in general was symbolized by the phallus, so that the dark Lord Jesus, the Jesuit, and the phallus were identical.[81]

This difficulty in interpretation reveals the tenuous nature of Jung's understanding of the dream: he was left in the lurch of the ambiguity, the resolution of which lay with his mother. In the final analysis, the phallus robbed men of their manhood, like Lord Jesus, a hen who devoured little chicks, or the Jesuit disguised in woman's clothes. And if it chose to rise from its quiescent state, young Carl would undoubtedly have been its next victim.

In 1879 the Jungs moved from Laufen to a small village, Klein-Hüningen, on the outskirts of Basel. The family took up residence in an eighteenth-century parsonage where they remained until 1896, the year of the Reverend Paul Jung's death. Jung had vivid recollections of this parsonage which would surface in memories and dreams much later in life.[82] The sense of foreboding and his intimations about the unconscious conspiracy over forbidden things accompanied Jung to his new home. Nudes in the Basel museum were forbidden, so were Catholic churches and exotic illustrations of Hindu deities. In Jung's mind these joined ranks with the priest in women's clothes and the incredible phallus.[83]

Jung later recalled games of turmoil and destruction, as well as an illness during which he saw, "a glowing blue circle about the size of the full moon, and inside it moved golden figures which I thought were angels."[84] He also had anxiety dreams and felt "the nocturnal atmosphere had begun to thicken."[85] Jung described this as follows:

All sorts of things were happening at night, things incomprehensible and alarming. My parents were sleeping apart.
I slept in my father's room. From the door to my mother's
room came frightening influences. At night Mother was
strange and mysterious. One night I saw coming from her
door a faintly luminous, indefinite figure whose head
detached itself from the neck and floated along in front of
it, in the air, like a little moon. Immediately another head
was produced and again detached itself. This process was
repeated six or seven times.[86]

Going to Church afforded Jung little comfort. He recalled
Christmas as joyous, but even this festival had a shadow cast over
it because Advent, "had to do with night, storms, and wind, and
also with the darkness of the house. There was something whisper-
ing, something queer going on."[87] The demands by his young peers
that he conform to schoolyard convention and participate in their
games and pranks only alienated him from himself and threatened
what little inner security he had.[88] Instead of capitulating, he
devised another pastime: tending a fire in the niche of a wall
behind the parsonage. Nearby a stone jutted out of the ground
which served him as a throne.[89] Soon afterwards he carved a small
two-inch-long figure resembling the frock-coated figures of his
childhood. He placed this figure, together with a small oblong
stone, into a pencil box and hid it in the attic of the eighteenth-century manse. Whenever he felt insecure he would visit this figure,
adding a tiny scroll each time.[90] The little black attired figure and
stone, like the Church, phallus, and Jesuit, was part of the secret
world of Jung's childhood. Of this he later recalled:

This possession of a secret had a very powerful formative
influence on my character; I consider it the essential factor
of my childhood. Similarly, I never told anyone about the
dream of the phallus; and the Jesuit, too, belonged to that
mysterious realm which I knew I must not talk about. The
little wooden figure with the stone was a first attempt, still
unconscious and childish, to give shape to the secret.[91]

Even at this time Jung continued to consciously feel he was a
Christian, but he was always daunted by the reality of his secret
world. Moreover, as he remarked of the Reverend Paul Jung: "my
father demonstrably knew nothing about these things."[92]

Jung's expanding experience of the outside world, brought about by his entry into the gymnasium in Basel, made him acutely aware of his parent's poverty and the ordinariness of their lives.[93] At school he found religion classes "unspeakably dull."[94] Privately, Jung began to formulate certain vague ideas about God, to whom he prayed and whom he viewed as quite independent of Jesus or the black-robed Jesuit.[95] Then there was the unwelcome event of the birth of his sister when he was nine which served, in his own mind, as the prelude to a significant experience.[96]

At noon, in the early summer of 1887, in the cathedral square of Basel, Jung was pushed by a schoolboy and bashed his head on the curb.[97] He conspired to manipulate this event by feigning illness so he could return to daydreaming, game playing or engage in the endless drawing of caricatures. Of the latter Jung remarked:

> Similar caricatures sometimes appear to me before falling asleep to this day, grinning masks that constantly move and change, among them familiar faces of people who soon afterward died.[98]

The shock of realizing that he was frittering away his life made Jung get a hold on himself and, through a series of attempts, to overcome what he later called "a neurosis."[99]

During the period of his "neurosis," Jung lost all memory of the little carved man and tiny phallus stone he had hidden in the attic. Having overcome his weakness, he returned to the gymnasium with a feeling he had emerged from a cloud and become truly himself.[100] And yet this self he had become, he realized in a fit of rage, was really two persons: one a young inexperienced boy, the other an older man with position and authority.[101] The latter figure he described as follows:

> This "other" was an old man who lived in the eighteenth century, wore buckled shoes and a white wig and went driving in a fly with high, concave rear wheels between which the box was suspended on springs and leather straps.[102]

Jung traced his associations to the eighteenth century to having seen a horse and carriage from this period as well as an old statuette of a Basel doctor.[103] He also made mention of his paternal grandfather, C. G. Jung, who, however, was born at the close of the eighteenth century. Late in life, in retrospect, he speculated that because of the dating, the figure of Goethe may have exercised a considerable influence over the production of his fantasy of the eighteenth-century.[104] Yet as a boy problems of chronology were of little concern to him, and Jung's cousins report that he claimed he was the favorite grandchild of C. G. Jung who had, in fact, died a decade before his grandson was born.[105] Indeed, he went even further and described his grandfather driving along the Wiese river in an old carriage on his way to see his grandson in Klein-Hüningen.[106] These visits, Jung is reported to have said, were frequent.[107]

In his memoirs Jung recorded another experience which was to be added to those secrets he had already stored in himself. One fine summer day in the cathedral square, the same setting in which his head injury occurred, he looked up at the cathedral bathed in glorious sunshine. Suddenly, he was overcome by a choking sensation and knew something terrible was looking to find expression in his mind. He resisted, sensing that whatever it was, it had to be of a sinister and blasphemous nature. It occurred to him that if he allowed himself to be the vehicle for the formulation of this dark thought, he might be committing the unforgivable sin, the sin against the Holy Ghost.[108]

Jung recalled making every effort to repress the disturbing thought that was seeking expression, but he kept involuntarily returning to the image of the cathedral. He wondered if his grandparents were responsible for this state of affairs.[109] Through a process of naive deduction he reasoned back even further and concluded that Adam and Eve might be implicated. At that point he found himself prepared to take the next distressful step and lay all responsibility at the feet of God.[110] With this conclusion Jung surrendered his resistance:

> I gathered all my courage, as though I were about to leap forthwith into hell-fire, and let the thought come. I saw before me the cathedral, the blue sky. God sits on His golden throne, high above the world—and from under the throne an enormous turd falls upon the sparkling new roof, shatters it, and breaks the walls of the cathedral asunder.[111]

This resulted in making Jung feel "an enormous, an indescribable relief."[112] He wept and pondered:

> That was what my father had not understood, I thought; he had failed to experience the will of God, had opposed it for

the best reasons and out of the deepest faith.... He had taken the Bible's commandments as his guide; he believed in God as the Bible prescribed and as his forefathers had taught him. But he did not know the immediate living God who stands, omnipotent and free, above His Bible and His Church, who calls upon man to partake of His freedom, and can force him to renounce his own views and convictions.... In His trial of human courage God refuses to abide by tradition, no matter how sacred.[113]

The result of Jung's experience, and his reflections upon it, made him conclude that God could indeed be terrible. As a consequence he felt that he had been honored with a glimpse into a dark and terrible secret which, for reasons he left unexamined, produced in him feelings of guilt and inferiority.[114]

It is remarkable that throughout Jung's account of the "cathedral experience" he made little mention of the devil. He explained this curious omission by stating that as a child he thought the devil was little more than God's "vicious watchdog."[115] And yet at the outset of the "cathedral experience" he did have troubling fears about committing the sin against the Holy Ghost. The specific nature of the sin against the Holy Ghost is to attribute evil origins to holy acts and is based on Gospel texts that deal with the denial of Jesus.[116] This latter concern is quite understandable in view of the fact that the entire "cathedral experience" points to Jung's later rejection of the Christian church, which he felt he accomplished by following the example and bidding of God, Himself. In the meantime the ambiguous figure of Jesus had come to be replaced by a God who was full of darkness and secret intentions. This God was linked in Jung's mind with the parade of those other secret figures and images that overshadowed his early life and will later emerge in his psychology as the personified collective unconscious, the archetype of the Self. Jung's increasingly evident dissent from Christianity becomes clearer in the subsequent discussions he had with his maternal uncles and with his father, all of whom were clergymen.[117]

The religious conversations, theological discussions, and sermons that were an ever-present reality in Jung's early life he found empty of meaning. None of them conveyed the reality of an encounter with the divine such as he knew from his "cathedral experience." He felt similarly about theological writings and even the Bible.[118] His mother recalled him being depressed during this period, but he later maintained that he was simply brooding over his stone: "I was but the sum of my emotions, and the Other in me was the timeless, imperishable stone."[119]

The doubts that Jung had about his father's religion became so deeply felt that he had an urge to help him, but he did not know how. All discussion between father and son deteriorated into irritating or angry exchanges. The Reverend Paul Jung maintained, "One ought not to think, but believe."[120] Jung would counter this by asserting to himself, "No, one must experience and know."[121] In addition to these heated arguments, Jung also had outbursts of violent rage at school. He felt he was being treated unfairly by both teachers and fellow students. At the same time he was plagued by feelings of guilt and inferiority. As he described it:

> Although I had not in reality done what I was accused of, I felt that I might have done it. I would even draw up a list of alibis in case I should be accused of something. I felt positively relieved when I had actually done something wrong. Then at least I knew what my guilty conscience was for.[122]

The consequences of such a dilemma for Jung were ominous, yet familiar:

> Somewhere deep in the background I always knew that I was two persons. One was the son of my parents, who went to school and was less intelligent, attentive, hard-working, decent, and clean than many other boys. The other was grown up—old, in fact—skeptical, mistrustful, remote from the world of men, but close to nature...and above all close to the night, to dreams, and to whatever "God" worked directly in him.[123]

Along with the division between inner and outer, this polarization took the form of ideas about God that were distinctly removed from Christianity. Jung felt that not only human beings but nature, too, the high mountains, lakes, trees, flowers, and animals were also expressions of God.[124] It was in his secondary personality that he perceived such things. For in personality No. 2, "nothing separated man from God; indeed, it was as though the human mind looked down upon Creation simultaneously with God."[125]

The tension that became more and more acute between the two sides of himself he did not interpret as an indication of a pathological disorder. As he remarked toward the end of his life:

The play and counterplay between personalities No. 1 and No. 2, which has run through my whole life, has nothing to do with a "split" or dissociation in the ordinary medical sense. On the contrary, it is played out in every individual. In my life No. 2 has been of prime importance.... He is a typical figure, but he is perceived only by the very few.[126]

With the increased awareness of his No. 2 personality, and its religious dimensions, Jung became doubtful about Christianity. In particular he grew more and more skeptical of his father's sermons about the "good" God and "Church gradually became a place of torment."[127] He began to understand that the traditional religion of his childhood was overtaken by the experiences he had had and he found no security or understanding in his father, who always sided with traditional religion against him. He took comfort in his No. 2 personality, who was alone with God, outside time itself, and belonged to the centuries.[128] The only person he imagined he could have shared these thoughts and experiences with was his mother:

> I could not talk with anyone about these things. I knew of no one to whom I might have communicated them except, possibly, my mother. She seemed to think along somewhat similar lines as myself.[129]

Even so, Jung claimed he remained alone with his thoughts.[130] What made him think he might have been able to communicate his thoughts and experiences to his mother is that he shared with her the propensity to split into two personalities. He described this in his mother as follows:

> She held all the conventional opinions a person was obliged to have, but then her unconscious personality would suddenly put in an appearance. That personality was unexpectedly powerful: a somber, imposing figure possessed of unassailable authority—and no bones about it. I was sure that she consisted of two personalities, one innocuous and human, the other uncanny. This other emerged only now and then, but each time it was unexpected and frightening.[131]

Jung remembered that the first time he sensed this division in his mother he was six years old.[132] In his memoirs he recalled vividly the dual nature of his mother:

There was an enormous difference between my mother's
two personalities. That was why as a child I often had anxiety dreams about her. By day she was a loving mother, but
at night she seemed uncanny. Then she was like one of
those seers who is at the same time a strange animal, like a
priestess in a bear's cave. Archaic and ruthless; ruthless as
truth and nature.[133]

And, Jung added, "I too have this archaic nature, and in me it is
linked with the gift...of seeing people and things as they are."[134] As an
example of this gift he reported an instance of how he knew all about
a man's life he had never met before adding, "In the course of my life
it has often happened to me that I suddenly knew something which I
really could not know at all."[135] Presumably Jung discussed such
unusual experiences with his mother, because a cousin who spent
the summer of 1890 with the Jung family reports she had many conversations with Jung and his mother about spiritualistic matters.[136]
    Though Jung was losing faith in Christianity he had little
choice but to submit to be instructed for confirmation and prepared
for communion.[137] This proved to be a profoundly disappointing
experience, as he recalled:

I had reached the pinnacle of religious initiation, had
expected something—I knew not what—to happen, and
nothing at all had happened.... [T]his ceremony contained
no trace of God—not for me, at any rate.[138]

The consequences for Jung were fatal:

I knew that I would never again be able to participate in
this ceremony. "Why, that is not religion at all," I thought.
"It is an absence of God; the church is a place I should not
go to. It is not life which is there, but death."
    I was seized with the most vehement pity for my father.
All at once I understood the tragedy of his profession and
his life. He was struggling with a death whose existence he
could not admit. An abyss had opened between him and
me, and I saw no possibility of ever bridging it, for it was
infinite in extent.[139]

Not only did the absence of any experience upon taking communion
shake Jung's Christian beliefs, but it loosened his ties to the world
around him as well. As he himself described it:

> My sense of union with the church and with the human
> world, so far as I knew it, was shattered.[140]

This only seemed to reinforce the reality of his inner secret. Brooding on his unfortunate circumstances led him to feel that he was an
outsider.[141]

What Jung's secret amounted to was that it had been revealed
to him by God Himself that He cared but little for His own church, as
was demonstrated when God dropped an enormous turd and shattered the cathedral. This vision of God raised in Jung's mind the
issue of the problem of evil. He concluded that God must be responsible for evil—a conclusion that is to be found in a more sophisticated
form in his later writings. What drove him to such lengths is hidden
away in his early experiences. Some were dreams, others were experiences of a visionary nature, all of them together drove a wedge
between him and Christianity. In his autobiography, he seems to
thread these together into a meaningful sequence of events, but how
many are left out or altered is impossible to say. What does stand
out, though, is the increasing part Jung's mother played and the
influence of what might be called her "night religion."[142]

Jung held that the forebodings of his childhood and the peculiar religious ideas that preoccupied him were the products of his
father's uncertainties and a reaction to the spirit of the age.[143] He
goes on to state categorically: "I never had the impression that
these influences emanated from my mother."[144] Yet, as a child, Jung
recalled that his mother had two personalities. And, as I have
pointed out in the previous chapter, among somnambules such a
dual personality was common and even a prerequisite. In Jung's
case it would seem that it was his mother and her two personalities
that pressed him into recognizing a similar, yet more disturbing,
division within himself.

There can be no doubt but that Jung felt the influence of his
mother's mysterious side, and this seems to have increased, the
more tragic a figure his father became in his eyes. As the figure of
his father and his religion diminished in stature and influence,
Jung came under the power of his mother and her "night religion,"
which appears to have been an expression of the wider phenomenon of Spiritualism. And, on an interior level, in direct pro-
portion to the extent the father figure dwindled, so arose in its
place the inner figure of Jung's own No. 2 personality. No. 2 had
separated from No. 1 personality and become:

an autonomous personality. I did not connect this with the idea of any definite individuality, such as a revenant might have, although with my rustic origins this possibility would not have seemed strange to me. In the country people believe in these things according to the circumstances: they are and they are not. The only distinct feature about this spirit was his historical character, his extension in time, or rather, his timelessness.... nor did I form any conception of his spatial existence.[145]

While Jung did associate his No. 2 personality with his grandfather, he also went on to write, *"Faust*...was the living equivalent of No. 2, and I was convinced that *he* was the answer which Goethe had given to his times."[146] No. 2 also had something to do with the creation of dreams and it is interesting to note that the nonspatial and timeless quality Jung associated with No. 2 he would later find characteristic of the dead.[147]

The period between Jung's fifteenth and eighteenth years was critical for him and marked by vehement discussions with his father which, in the end, were tedious and sterile.[148] These encounters only succeeded in making Jung believe that it was Christian theology that had alienated him and his father from one another. It also, he claimed, made him understand the deepest meaning of his earlier experiences which was: "God Himself has disavowed theology and the Church founded upon it."[149] Through this struggle with his father and the Christian religion, Jung's mother stood by him. Or, as he put it in his own words:

> My mother's "No. 2" offered me the strongest support in the conflict then beginning between paternal tradition and the strange, compensatory products which my unconscious had been stimulated to create.[150]

Here again Jung does not go the full distance in acknowledging the influence stemming from his "maternal tradition" and lays the emphasis instead on his "paternal tradition." While it is true that Jung was influenced by his ancestors on both sides, his mother was unquestionably the dominant influence in his early life. This expressed itself in his own deep division into No. 1 and No. 2 personalities as well as in the type of visionary experiences he underwent, most of them connected in some way with her. In the following chapters it will become clear why Jung shied away from giving his mother and her side of the family the importance which was their due. What will become equally clear is the extent to which Jung associated his experiences with Spiritualism, for which he sought a coherent explanation, laying the foundations of his later psychology.

Notes

1. *MDR*, 170 et seq.

2. Jung's psychology has largely ignored childhood. The few works in which he did discuss childhood are problematical and rather unsystematic. For example, his "Psychic Conflicts in a Child" (1909, rev. 1946), in *Collected Works*, vol. 17, *The Development of Personality* (New York: Pantheon Books, 1954), 1–35, is a short essay on his daughter Agathe; see *The Freud/Jung Letters*, 311. Freud remarked to Jung of this essay that he "regretted that the scientist did not entirely overcome the father" (*The Freud/Jung Letters*, 348). Jung, in another essay, "The Gifted Child" (1942), in *The Development of Personality*, 135–45, makes some general statements about childhood on the basis of his own early experiences. In the end Jung viewed the psychology of children as intimately bound up with the psychology of the parents and even grandparents; see Frances G. Wickes, *The Inner World of Childhood* (New York: Appleton-Century-Crofts, 1927). There is ample evidence that Jung did not explore the life of childhood in order to establish the precise causes of later psychiatric and psychological disorders. The difficulty this put some of his followers in led eventually to the establishment of a quasi-Jungian set of theories about early development. In order for this to have taken place, a great deal of clinical experience of childhood acquired by Freudians and Kleinians had to be recognized and accepted. While this may have placed some aspects of Jungian theory on a more secure foundation, some of Jung's later metapsychology has also been undermined. See especially the works of Michael Fordham, the leading Jungian authority on children, "Primary Self, Primary Narcissism and Related Concepts," *Journal of Analytical Psychology* 16 (1971): 168–87; and *Children as Individuals* (New York: G. P. Putnam's Sons, 1970); and James Astor, "A Conversation with Dr. Michael Fordham," *Journal of Child Psychotherapy* 14 (1988): 3–11. Fordham's other works are listed in Roger Hobdell, "A Bibliography of the Writings of Michael Fordham," *Journal of Analytical Psychology* 31 (1986): 307–15.

3. *MDR*, Editor's introduction, vii et seq.

4. Jung, *Letters 2: 1951–1961*, 452.

5. *MDR*, ix.

6. Ibid., 4.

7. Ibid., xii.

8. Ibid., 200 et seq.

9. Brome, 284.

10. Individuation, in Jung's psychology, is a process of psychological differentiation whereby the individual personality attains a completeness distinct from the general, collective psychology; see C. G. Jung, *Psychological Types*, 448 et seq.

11. *MDR*, 179.

12. Ibid., 189.

13. Ibid., 173 et seq.

14. Jung, *Letters 1: 1905–1950*, 274–75.

15. Aniela Jaffé, *The Myth of Meaning* (New York: G. P. Putnam's Sons, 1971), 149.

16. *MDR*, vi.

17. C. G. Jung, "Freud and Jung: Contrasts" (1929), in *Collected Works*, vol. 4, *Freud and Psychoanalysis* (Princeton, N.J. Princeton University Press, 1961), 336.

18. Ellenberger, *Discovery,* 727.

19. Ibid.

20. C. G. Jung, "A Rejoinder to Dr. Bally" (1934), in *Collected Works*, vol. 10, *Civilization in Transition,* 2nd. ed. (Princeton, N.J. Princeton University Press, 1970), 540.

21. Michael Fordham, "Maturation of a Child Within a Family," *Journal of Analytical Psychology* 22 (1977): 95.

22. C. G. Jung, "A Seminar with C. G. Jung: Comments on a Child's Dream" (1936–37), *Spring* (1974), 200–23; Hannah, 23 n.g., remarks that this seminar was based on dreams given Jung by adults from their own childhood recollections; Michael Fordham, "Memories and Thoughts about C. G. Jung," 109, mentions Jung's negative views of child analysis.

23. Fordham, "Memories and Thoughts of C. G. Jung," 109.

24. Ibid.

25. Ibid.

26. Ibid.

27. C. G. Jung, "Introduction to Wickes's *Analyse Der Kinderseele*" (1931), in *The Development of Personality*, 42.

28. Ibid., 44.

29. *MDR*, 233.

30. Ibid., 232.

31. Ibid., 233.

32. Aniela Jaffé, "Details About C. G. Jung's Family," *Spring* (1984): 35, 43.

33. Jung, *Letters 2: 1951–1961*, 527–28.

34. *MDR*, 35 et seq.

35. *The Freud/Jung Letters*, 384.

36. C. G. Jung, *Letters 2: 1951–1961*, 528.

37. Ernst Jung's introduction to the published edition of C. G. Jung's diary, *Aus den Tagebüchern meines Vaters* (Winterthur, 1910), cited by Zumstein-Preiswerk, 115.

38. Some of Jung's relatives claim they first heard that the elder C. G. Jung was the illegitimate offspring of Goethe and a certain Marianne Jung from Jung himself; see Zumstein-Preiswerk, 48–49. Goethe's well-known romance with Marianne Jung, whom he called "Demoiselle Jung" in his diary, began in 1814 when he was in his sixty-fifth year and she was about thirty. Marianne Jung was a talented "anima figure" with whom Goethe was infatuated in his later years and who figures as Suleika in *Westöstlicher Divan* (1819). There is no evidence to connect her with Jung's family because, as Richard Friedenthal, *Goethe: His Life and Times* (London: Weidenfeld and Nicholson, 1963), 436, has pointed out, "her origins are obscure; her father is unknown, the date of her birth doubtful, and even the name of Jung was a stage name taken by her mother, who played minor roles in the Vienna suburbs." Zumstein-Preiswerk, 116–17, speculates that when Jung realized the impossibility of the chronology—the elder C. G. Jung was born in 1794 when Marianne Jung was about ten years old—he substituted the name of Sophie Jung. Late in life Jung did allude to the possibility of confusion between Marianne Jung and Sophie Jung, but he does not attribute this to himself; see C. G. Jung, *Letters 2:1951–1961*, 528–29.

39. *MDR*, 235.

40. Ibid.

41. Hannah, 20, citing C. G. Jung, *Erinnerungen, Träume, Gedanken,* 404. Aniela Jaffé, "Details About C. G. Jung's Family." 36–39 gives a brief summary of the life of the elder C. G. Jung.

42. Ellenberger, *Discovery,* 661.

43. *MDR,* 91.

44. Ibid., 90 et seq.

45. Zumstein-Preiswerk, 114; Bennet, *C. G. Jung,* 14. Paul Jung had lost his mother when he was 13 and was 22 when his father died; see Jaffé, "Details About C. G. Jung's Family," 39.

46. Ellenberger, *Discovery,* 662, 738 n. 9, points out that Paul Jung was chaplain at the Friedmatt Mental Hospital during the years 1888–96. Jung himself entered the Medical School of Basel University in April 1895; see ibid., 665.

47. Ibid., 727.

48. James Mearns, "Preiswerk, Samuel," in J. Julian, ed., *A Dictionary of Hymnology* (rev. ed., 1907), vol. 2 (Reprint, New York: Dover, 1957), 907.

49. B. Pick, "Preiswerk, Samuel, Dr.," in J. M'Clintock et al., eds., *Cyclopedia of Biblical, Theological and Ecclesiastical Literature,* vol. 8, (New York: Harper and Brothers, 1879), 505. Jung cites one of his grandfather's hymns in *Collected Works,* vol. 5, *Symbols of Transformation* (1912) 2nd ed. (Princeton, N.J. Princeton University Press, 1967), 344.

50. Aniela Jaffé, "Details About C. G. Jung's Family," 40.

51. Ibid.

52. Albert Oeri, "Some Youthful Memories of C. G. Jung," *Spring* (1970), 185.

53. Aniela Jaffé, *From the Life and Work of C. G. Jung* (London: Hodder and Stoughton, 1971), 2.

54. Hannah, 22, citing Jung in conversation.

55. Jaffé, *From the Life and Work of C. G. Jung,* 2.

56. C. G. Jung, *The Tavistock Lectures,* (1935) in *The Symbolic Life,* 171 et seq.

57. Jung, *Letters 2: 1951–1961,* 132.

58. Jaffé, *From the Life and Work of C. G. Jung,* 2.

59. Ellenberger, *Discovery,* 661.

60. Jung, *Letters 1: 1905–1950*, 70; *MDR*, 190, 232. Ruth Bailey, a friend who looked after Jung in his later years, stated that he had a special understanding with his eldest daughter Agathe; see Glin Bennet, "Domestic Life with C. G. Jung: Taperecorded Conversations with Ruth Bailey," *Spring* (1986): 181.

61. Jaffé, *From the Life and Work of C. G. Jung*, 2.

62. *MDR*, 48 et seq.; Ellenberger, *Discovery*, 662.

63. *MDR*, 3.

64. Ellenberger, *Discovery*, 663.

65. *MDR*, viii.

66. Ibid., xii.

67. Ibid., ix.

68. Ibid., 27.

69. Brome, 28. Bennet, *C. G. Jung*, 9, states that there were two male children who died as infants prior to the birth of C. G. Jung.

70. *MDR*, 7, 9.

71. Ibid., 8.

72. Ibid., 9.

73. Ibid.

74. Ibid., 7.

75. Ibid., 8, 16.

76. Ibid., 9–10. For a somewhat different understanding of this prayer see Guenther Looser, "Jung's Childhood Prayer," *Spring* (1966): 76–80.

77. *MDR*, 10–11.

78. Ibid., 11–12.

79. Ibid., 15.

80. C. G. Jung, *Collected Works*, vol. 9ii, *Aion* (1951), 2nd ed. (Princeton, N.J. Princeton University Press, 1968), 226. David C. Noel, in "Veiled Kabir: C. G. Jung's Phallic Self-Image," *Spring* (1974): 224–42, has shown how central the image of the phallus was for Jung throughout his life. George R. Elder, "Phallus," in Mircea Eliade, ed., *The Encyclopedia of Religion*, vol. 11 (New York: Macmillan, 1987), 263–69, has outlined the

religious and symbolic significance of the phallus and cites Jung's experience as a modern example.

81. *MDR,* 12.

82. Ibid., 15–16. There is a nineteenth-century drawing of the parsonage in Jaffé, *Word and Image,* 16.

83. *MDR,* 16–17. Jung records that the sense of being forbidden,
which he associated with the Catholic Church, was reinforced when he
injured himself during an attempt to steal a look inside one. This was to
stay with him until, on a visit to Vienna, presumably to see Freud, he went
into St. Stephen's Cathedral.

84. Ibid., 18.

85. Ibid.

86. Ibid.

87. Ibid., 19.

88. Ibid.

89. Ibid., 20.

90. Ibid., 21.

91. Ibid., 22.

92. Ibid., 23.

93. Ibid., 24.

94. Ibid., 27.

95. Ibid.

96. Ibid., 25, 30.

97. Ibid., 30.

98. Ibid.

99. Ibid., 32.

100. Ibid., 32–33.

101. Ibid., 33.

102. Ibid., 34.

103. Ibid., 34–35.

104. Ibid., 35.

105. Zumstein-Preiswerk, 26.

106. Ibid., 116.

107. Ibid., 26.

108. *MDR*, 36.

109. Ibid., 37–38, where Jung mentioned his parents and grandparents as suspects in his search to explain the thoughts that were trying to overwhelm him. In Bennet, *C. G. Jung*, 16–17, the scene of Jung standing before the cathedral is stated to have been a dream, and Jung recalled trying to attribute the cause of the thoughts that followed to his parents and grandfathers.

110. *MDR*, 38–39.

111. Ibid., 39.

112. Ibid., 40.

113. Ibid.

114. Ibid., 41.

115. Ibid., 46.

116. Matt. 12:31–32; Mark 3:28–29; Luke 12:10.

117. *MDR*, 42.

118. Ibid.

119. Ibid.

120. Ibid., 43.

121. Ibid.

122. Ibid., 44.

123. Ibid., 44–45.

124. Ibid., 45.

125. Ibid.

126. Ibid.

127. Ibid.

128. Ibid., 48.

129. Ibid.

130. Ibid.

131. Ibid., 48–49.

132. Ibid., 49.

133. Ibid., 50.

134. Ibid.

135. Ibid., 51.

136. Zumstein-Preiswerk, 35–36.

137. *MDR*, 52–53.

138. Ibid., 54–55.

139. Ibid., 55.

140. Ibid., 56.

141. Ibid.

142. Jung defined "night religion" in "Mind and Earth" (1927), in *Civilization in Transition*, 33, as "the magical form of religion, the meaning and purpose of which is intercourse with the dark powers, devils, witches, magicians, and spirits."

143. *MDR*, 90.

144. Ibid.

145. Ibid.

146. Ibid., 87. I might also point out that the opening scene of *Faust* has Faust practicing necromancy, i.e. the conjuring up of the spirits of the dead, which he turns to in his boredom and desperation.

147. Ibid., 89, 304 et seq.

148. Ibid., 73, 91.

149. Ibid., 93.

150. Ibid., 90 et seq.

Part 2

The University Years

Chapter 3

Kant, Schopenhauer, and the
Philosophy of Spiritualism

The years leading up to and including the period of Jung's university studies (1895–1900) marked a turning point in his life and
opened up a new world drawing him both to philosophy and to the
natural sciences. During this period he discovered philosophy, especially the philosophy of Kant and Schopenhauer, and realized "that
while science opened the door to enormous quantities of knowledge,
it provided genuine insights very sparingly."[1] In his mind, religion
took on a much broader meaning and merged with philosophy, while
institutional religion was spoken about negatively. This shift in
Jung's thinking is evident in the student lectures he delivered in the
second half of the 1890s. These lectures will be examined in some
detail in the following chapter. But perhaps the most important
development during this time was that Jung discovered a psychological perspective from which he could examine the various psychic
phenomena he had encountered. The culmination of this development is evident in Jung's medical dissertation, which will also be
examined in a subsequent chapter. In order to fully appreciate the
development in Jung's thought during this period of his life it is necessary to reconstruct the philosophical basis upon which he built his
psychological understanding of Spiritualism. The latter will be the
chief subject of the succeeding chapters.

Jung's interest in philosophy had its beginnings in his religious preoccupations. In addition to the acrimonious disputes over
theological questions he had with his father, Jung engaged Christian theology on a number of other fronts as well. Dissatisfied with
his father's defensive theological stance, Jung searched for a more
independent and sophisticated theological interpretation of the
Christian message. He came upon A. E. Biedermann's *Christliche
Dogmatik* (1869).[2] What he grasped of its argument led him to be
suspicious that the Christian message was being served up yet

again, only this time in confusing and convoluted theological prose. As Jung himself put it:

> This weighty tome on dogmatics was nothing but fancy drivel; worse still, it was a fraud or a specimen of uncommon stupidity whose sole aim was to obscure the truth. I was disillusioned and even indignant, and once more seized with pity for my father, who had fallen victim to this mumbo-jumbo.[3]

The terrible truth that Biedermann's "weighty tome" had tried to obscure, according to Jung, was the answer to the burning question, "What were the reasons for suffering, imperfection, and evil?" In *Christliche Dogmatik*, Jung wrote, "I could find nothing."[4]

Disappointed by Biedermann's attempt to provide a persuasive theological rationale in favor of traditional religion, and influenced by *Faust* who was "a philosopher of sorts," Jung turned to philosophy.[5] In his father's library he found Krug's *General Dictionary of the Philosophical Sciences*. Jung was, once again, disappointed. This time the reason for his disappointment lay not only in the cursory way the problem of evil was addressed but in the intellectual fudging he perceived in Krug when it came to the subject of God.[6] Yet Jung's first encounter with philosophy brought home to him an important realization:

> all that about Lord Jesus was always suspect to me and I never really believed it, although it was impressed upon me far more than God.... Why have I come to take God for granted? Why do these philosophers pretend that God is an idea?...
>
> Suddenly I understood that God was, for me at least, one of the most certain and immediate of experiences.[7]

This realization, like the secrets of his childhood, made Jung feel estranged from those around him. Nevertheless, he reported:

> It never occurred to me that I might be crazy, for the light and darkness of God seemed to me facts that could be understood even though they oppressed my feelings.[8]

Jung's religious and philosophical preoccupations took him away from schoolwork, but he managed to maintain fairly good marks.[9] Once, Jung's preoccupations and his schoolwork coalesced when he was assigned an essay. He chose the subject "On the Meaning of *Faust*" and thrust himself into the project.[10] The result was good—too good, for the teacher accused him unfairly of plagiarism.[11] Jung reacted by expressing grief and rage which grew until they threatened to get out of control. A familiar calm came over him. Late in life Jung reflected upon this experience:

> Although at the time I doubtless saw no difference as yet between personalities No. 1 and No. 2, and still claimed the world of No. 2 as my own personal world, there was always, deep in the background, the feeling that something other than myself was involved. It was as though a breath of the great world of stars and endless space had touched me, or as if a spirit had invisibly entered the room—the spirit of one who had long been dead and yet was perpetually present in timelessness until far into the future. Denouements of this sort were wreathed with the halo of a numen.[12]

And, as if in recognition of the power of this aged spirit in Jung, some time after, his classmates dubbed him "Father Abraham."[13]

Nevertheless, from his sixteenth year Jung began to identify more and more with his No. 1 personality. His readings in philosophy indicated to him that his religious interests had historical analogues.[14] In particular, Jung mentioned being drawn to Pythagoras, Heraclitus, Empedocles, Plato and Meister Eckhart. The scholastics, and especially Thomas Aquinas, left him cold.[15] Of moderns, Jung regarded Hegel "with downright mistrust."[16] But in Schopenhauer Jung found a mentor whose writings in turn introduced him to Kant.[17] Kant would become for Jung his philosophical *point de départ* in his first attempts at creating a psychology.[18] In order to precisely understand the nature of the influence of Kant and Schopenhauer on Jung, it is important to turn to a number of other events that were occurring in his life at this time.

Jung's excursions into philosophy led him to become increasingly conscious of the division in himself. As he wrote reflecting back on this period of his life:

> The most painful thing of all was the frustration of my attempts to overcome the inner split in myself, my division into two worlds. Again and again events occurred which forced me out of my ordinary, everyday existence into the boundlessness of "God's world."[19]

This split also insinuated itself into the next dilemma Jung faced: the choice of a profession. As he stated:

> My interests drew me in different directions. On the one hand I was powerfully attracted by science, with its truths based on facts; on the other hand I was fascinated with everything to do with comparative religion.... At that time, of course, I did not realize how very much this choice of the most varied subjects corresponded to the nature of my inner dichotomy.[20]

One of Jung's uncles sensing his interest in religion tried to push him in the direction of theology.[21] On this score Jung's father was emphatic, "Be anything you like except a theologian," he is reported to have told his son.[22] Jung was able to assure his father that he had no intentions of becoming a theologian even though he "continued to waver between science and the humanities."[23]

Jung was left in the lurch of his dilemma for some time and he remained filled with conflicting inclinations. When he approached the time to enter university, he realized he would be able to extricate himself only by making a conscious choice between one of his two propensities. The problem, and the first indications of a solution, Jung formulated as follows:

> Schopenhauer and Christianity would not square with one another, for one thing; and for another, No. 1 wanted to free himself from the pressure or melancholy of No. 2.[24]

In the end, in 1895, Jung enrolled in the medical curriculum at the University of Basel.[25] Shortly afterwards he joined the Zofingia student fraternity, where he later delivered his first lectures.[26]

In the following year two occurrences were to have a significant impact upon Jung. His father, the Reverend Paul Jung, died in January 1896.[27] Jung's mother remarked of his father's untimely death in her No. 2 voice: "He died in time for you." By this she apparently meant he could have become a hindrance to her son.[28] These words affected Jung deeply, and about six weeks after his father's death he dreamt he had recovered and returned home. Two days later the dream was repeated.[29] Jung wrote about this dream: "It was an unforgettable experience, and it forced me for the first time to think about life after death."[30] At about the same time, Jung made a discovery which, he stated, "was to have great consequences."[31] In the library of a friend's father he came upon a book on the origins of Spiritualism written by a theologian. He found that the contents of the book described experiences he had encountered as a child. Of this he later wrote:

> I could not help seeing that the phenomena described in the book were in principle much the same as the stories I had heard again and again in the country since my earliest childhood. The material, without a doubt, was authentic.[32]

Jung realized that the unusual experiences he and his maternal relatives had undergone were identical to those found in Spiritualism. His discovery of the book on Spiritualism marks the beginning of the period during which Jung began to seriously evaluate the possibility of the existence of spirits. We can also surmise that his father's death had something to do with this.

Jung went on to read virtually all of the literature on Spiritualism that was available to him at the time.[33] A fellow student of Jung's recalled that these works shared the same shelf as his student books.[34] Jung later claimed that the observations of the spiritualists contained in these works were the first accounts he had read of objective psychic phenomena.[35] Most of his fellow students casually spoke of table-turning as a form of amusement.[36] Yet, during the first semester of 1895, one theological student gave a talk before the Zofingia student society in which he argued there may be some truth to the claims of Spiritualism.[37] Whether this talk had any influence upon Jung is not clear. In fact, Jung claimed his interest in Spiritualism was unusual and estranged him from his friends, who were incredulous about his enthusiasm. He wrote of them:

> I wondered at the sureness with which they could assert that things like ghosts and table-turning were impossible and therefore fraudulent, and on the other hand at the evidently anxious nature of their defensiveness. I, too, was not certain of the absolute reliability of the reports, but why, after all, should there not be ghosts? How did we know something was "impossible"? And, above all, what did the anxiety signify? For myself I found such possibilities extremely interesting and attractive. They added another dimension to my life; the world gained depth and background.[38]

While Jung claimed that his fellow students disapproved of the seriousness of his new interest in Spiritualism, his mother stood by him. Of this he wrote:

> My mother's No. 2 sympathized wholeheartedly with my enthusiasm, but everyone else I knew was distinctly discouraging.... I found this even with my closest friends. To them all this was far worse than my preoccupation with theology. I had the feeling that I had pushed to the brink of the world; what was of burning interest to me was null and void for others, and even a cause for dread.[39]

That Emilie Jung should have been supportive of her son's preoccupation and enthusiasm for Spiritualism is not at all surprising. Her own involvement and interest in spiritualistic phenomena has been pointed out in the previous chapter. Nevertheless, though her support may have been of considerable importance to Jung, it was more emotional than intellectual in nature. Jung now needed and sought to formulate an objective way of understanding spiritualistic phenomena. A theological perspective with its accompanying Christian biases offered little appeal for him. He turned instead to philosophy. As he stated in his own words:

> But the great question of whether these stories were physically true was not answered to my satisfaction. Nevertheless, it could be established that at all times and all over the world the same stories had been reported again and again. There must be some reason for this, and it could not possibly have been the predominance of the same religious conceptions everywhere, for that was obviously not the case. Rather it must be connected with the objective behaviour of the human psyche. But with regard to this cardinal question—the objective nature of the psyche—I could find out absolutely nothing, except what the philosophers said.[40]

During this period Jung's interest in philosophy was conditioned by his enthusiasm for Spiritualism. He sought in philosophy, as I will demonstrate, to clarify his own ideas and to provide himself a sound intellectual base from which to assess spiritualistic phenomena. As I previously stated, in Jung's excursions into philosophy he turned in particular to the writings of Kant and

Schopenhauer. That these authors should assume such a prominent position in Jung's encounter with philosophy is not at all
unusual, given his interest in Spiritualism. Liselotte Mosic has
pointed out that during the late nineteenth century, Spiritualism
attracted philosophers of rank. She states:

> Besides countless modifications of the old spiritistic theo-
> ries about psychic and extra-mundane forces a new kind of
> interpretation of paranormal phenomena began to emerge.
> This was derived from the Kantian theory that space and
> time have no reality, but are solely forms of our own per-
> ception. No less a figure than Schopenhauer deduced from
> this the possibility of clairvoyance.[41]

This idea of Schopenhauer's would find its way into Jung's thinking. Schopenhauer was, in fact, the first philosopher of note in
whom Jung took an interest. In his excursion into philosophy
Schopenhauer was, as Jung put it, "the great find."[42]

Schopenhauer (1788–1860) presented a highly individualistic,
pessimistic philosophy in his writings.[43] His somber view of the
world had Jung's undivided approval.[44] Much the same could be
said of Jung's reaction to Schopenhauer's *Essay on Spirit Seeing*.
But before the influence of this writing upon Jung is examined, it is
necessary to point out that it was through Schopenhauer that Jung
found his way to Kant (1724–1804). It became evident to him that
Schopenhauer's theory of knowledge derived from Kant. This realization, Jung claimed, is what drew him to the writings of Kant,
above all to his *Critique of Pure Reason* (1781).[45] In what follows I
will examine this claim of Jung's and argue that he was initially
influenced more by Kant's writings on Spiritualism than by the
Critique of Pure Reason. Moreover this influence continued
through into Schopenhauer's *Essay on Spirit Seeing*, eventually
making a major contribution to Jung's psychological perspective.

Jung repeatedly claimed that "epistemologically I take my
stand on Kant, which means that an assertion doesn't posit its
object."[46] In this statement Jung alluded to the Kantian distinction
between noumena and phenomena. The latter refers to the world of
appearances apprehended by the senses; the former, the result of
purely intellectual intuition, devoid of phenomenal attributes.[47]
Kant maintained that objects of the senses were not reality but
appearances. The basis for this claim rested on Kant's assertion
that space and time are not objective entities, but are simply *a pri-*

ori forms of human perception. All objects are perceived through space and time and therefore cannot be absolutely real. Unlike phenomena, noumena are realities, things-in-themselves, and not the result of a sensory process. It follows that human knowledge is possible only within the limits of the world of appearance; the world of noumena remains inaccessible to human reason. The former contains objects of knowledge, the latter, objects of belief. This distinction between phenomena and noumena is at the heart of Kant's *Critique of Pure Reason* and serves as the foundation for his theory of knowledge.[48]

Jung's claim to have shared this foundation with Kant deserves closer examination. For now, it is important to point out that Jung did not initially encounter Kant of the *Critiques* but Kant of the precritical period, before his theory of knowledge became formalized. Jung eventually found his way to the writings of the mature Kant. He did this via his interests in Spiritualism. This is not the chronology Jung presented, but if we examine Kant's writings on Spiritualism and Jung's student lectures, it becomes obvious that this is the case.

Sometime in the 1760s Kant took an interest in the Swedish seer Emanuel Swedenborg (1688–1772). Swedenborg was a student of science who had studied Sir Isaac Newton's writings.[49] By profession he was Assessor of the Royal College of Mines in Sweden. His initiation into spirit-seeing began with the dreams and visions he had in 1744.[50] Many of the works he subsequently wrote embody his experiences of the spirit world and the theological and dogmatic conclusions he drew from these experiences.[51]

In a letter, now dated to 1763, Kant wrote to a certain Fräulein von Knoblock that he had first heard of Swedenborg from a Danish officer who had formerly been his student.[52] The officer alleged that Swedenborg had demonstrated his parapsychological abilities to none other than the Queen of Sweden. Swedenborg claimed to have had a conversation with the Queen's dead brother and revealed a secret known only to the Queen.[53] This incident seems to have ignited Kant's interest in Swedenborg. He requested of an English friend who was in Sweden to interview Swedenborg. This friend reported to Kant two additional occurrences in which Swedenborg allegedly demonstrated his extraordinary gifts. The first concerns the widow of the Dutch ambassador to Sweden. A silversmith was demanding payment for a silver service he had sold to the ambassador. His widow was desperate to find the receipt and made inquires to Swedenborg. He duly contacted the husband's spirit and uncovered the receipt in a special compartment of a bureau.[54] One last occurrence Kant mentioned impressed him as the most convincing. This involved a fire that took place in Stockholm in 1759. Swedenborg was staying with a friend some fifty miles away during the time of the fire. He allegedly saw the fire in a vision and reported details of the damage that it caused and the precise time that the fire was extinguished. All of these details were confirmed in the news which was received in the days that followed.[55]

Kant's letter to Fräulein von Knoblock reflected his interest in, and attitude toward, spirit-seeing and parapsychology in general. In it he stated:

> So much is quite certain, that regardless of all tales about apparitions and visions concerning the world of spirits, the majority of which are probably known to me, I have always tended to make these conform to the rules of sound reason, and I have always been inclined to regard such tales quite skeptically. Not that such things are impossible, for how little we know about the nature of spirits? Yet, these instances have not been proved sufficiently. Furthermore, when we talk about their incomprehensible character, and their uselessness, we must take into account the many difficulties which arise due to the ease with which one can be deceived; I have, therefore, found it unnecessary in the past to worry much about such things or to allow myself to shiver and be scared by the dead in the darkness of a cemetery. Such was the position which I had adopted for a very long time until I came to know about Mr. Swedenborg.[56]

In particular Kant pointed to Swedenborg's vision of the fire which he wrote: "appear to me to possess the greatest authenticity, and as a proof it will eliminate the last possibility of doubt (concerning Swedenborg's extraordinary gift)."[57]

In fact, before encountering Swedenborg, Kant did not always find it more reasonable to incline to the negative side when encountering stories about apparitions and activities in the spirit world, as he stated. In an early work, *Universal Natural History and Theory of the Heavens* (1755), to which I will now turn, Kant inclined more to the positive than negative side.[58] I mention this work for two reasons: (1) it indicates that eight years prior to the letter to von Knoblock, Kant was speculating about those things-in-themselves he would call "noumena" in his later *Critique of Pure Reason* and (2) this work surfaces in Jung's medical dissertation, where it was the subject of some discussion.

In the neglected third part of *Universal Natural History*, Kant indulged in marvelously imaginative astronomical speculations. Robert Butts gives the following summary of its contents:

> Thus in his [Kant's] 1755 treatise on the nebular hypothesis we find references to "various classes of intelligent beings," "kinds of thinking natures," and to the various "habitations" of these "intelligent creatures." He writes about the dependence of the "spiritual faculties" of the various inhabitants of planets (all of the planets are inhabited) on grosser or finer, heavier or lighter, matter as determined by the "distance of these habitations from the sun." The inhabitants of Jupiter or Saturn belong to the "most exalted class of intelligent creatures. Their conception of time differs from ours; they are not subject to death in the same degree that we are." Man occupies a middle ground between these most excellent and the more imperfect grades of "thinking natures."[59]

Butts concludes with the following evaluation:

> The speculations in the third part of *Allgemeine Naturgeschichte* [*Universal Natural History*] are typical of the period and prove...that Kant was prepared at least seriously to entertain the possibility of the existence of different kinds of spiritual beings.[60]

Though such speculations about spiritual beings may have been typical, as Butts contends, few of Kant's contemporaries seem to have been aware that he indulged in them. This appears to have been the case for two reasons: (1) These speculations are hidden away in a work largely devoted to discussing the mechanistic framework of the universe and (2) the publisher of *Universal Natural History* went into bankruptcy, and nearly all copies were impounded until 1765 or 1766.[61]

In 1766 Kant published a book that Jung would repeatedly refer to, entitled *Dreams of a Spirit-Seer Explained by Dreams of Metaphysics*. The style of this book is casual and even confused. It would appear Kant somewhat reluctantly authored the work, which originally appeared anonymously.[62] As Butts pointed out, a contemporary of Kant's remarked "that the 'bantering profundity' of the writing makes it unclear whether Kant intended to ridicule metaphysics or to render spiritseeing believable."[63] Broad has summarized the contents as follows:

> The book begins with a preface, and the rest of it is divided into two parts. Part I, which is subdivided into four sections, may be described as an able and elaborate general discussion of the philosophical problems involved in the notion of a disembodied spirit, of a world of such spirits, and of the relations of body and soul in human individuals, and in claims by certain men to be in touch with the inhabitants of the spirit-world.... Part II is subdivided into three sections. The first of these repeats the three stories of Swedenborg's alleged feats of ostensibly supernormal cognition which were discussed in the letter [to Fräulein von Knoblock]. The second section contains an elaborate account of the doctrine as to the nature and laws of the spirit-world which Swedenborg professed to have derived by personal observation and from conversations with spirits.... The third section...is, roughly, that we should...not waste our time with either what metaphysics or what self-styled mediums claim to tell us about the spirit world.... [A]ny morally good man feels assured of human survival without recourse either to metaphysics or to alleged mediumistic evidence.[64]

It seems, given Kant's earlier letter to von Knoblock, which was more positive about Swedenborg, and his own speculations in *Universal Natural History*, what makes *Dream of a Spirit-Seer* ambiguous and confused is that in this work Kant is struggling with his own inclination to believe in the possibility of the existence of a spirit world. Kant admits as much in a letter to Moses Mendelssohn (April 8, 1766), where he states about *Dreams of a Spirit-Seer*:

> It is true that I hold certain convictions and beliefs of my own which I have not got the courage to profess in public, but in what I say I shall never state something that I don't believe....
> I admit that I had the greatest difficulty in finding a suitable method of expressing my thoughts on the subject without incurring the risk of being ridiculed. Then I

decided that the best way of forestalling any attacks of mockery directed against my person would be to mock at myself. This I did quite sincerely, for my mind was in a state of paradox.... I can't help suspecting that there was some truth in the stories mentioned, and the same applies to the principles of reason concerning them, regardless of the absurdity of the former and the incomprehensible character of the concepts, and all the concoctions surrounding them, which render them valueless.[65]

That this struggle finally pushed him in the direction of abrogating all metaphysical assertions as assertions made on the basis of reason is obvious only in his *Inaugural Dissertation* (1770) and complete in the *Critique of Pure Reason* (1781). As Butts, who has studied in detail Kant's writings from this period, remarks: "That Kant made a very serious analytic study of spiritualism some time between 1762–1770 now seems beyond dispute."[66]

In the 1890s Jung underwent a similar struggle with Spiritualism. His interest in Kant's effort, *Dreams of a Spirit-Seer*, reflected his own need to establish some *point de départ*, some solid perspective, from which to understand spiritualistic phenomena. Initially, one of the reasons Jung may have felt he was a Kantian was because he shared this dilemma with Kant. Nevertheless, Jung differed from Kant, as I will later argue, because the walls Kant erected between noumena and phenomena were, for Jung, at times transparent.[67] There were ideas expressed by Kant in *Dreams of a Spirit-Seer* which Jung, unlike Kant, would not relinquish. Instead, Jung modified some of these ideas in the light of his own experience and incorporated them into his psychology. I will now outline these ideas in more detail.

Broad has pointed out that Kant's notion of spirit is based on a theory of matter which he delineates in *Dreams of a Spirit-Seer*.[68] According to this theory, finite bodies consist of a number of simple substances. These substances are located in one space at one time. It follows that no two substances can occupy the same space at the same time. From this Kant concluded that any substance exerts a repulsive force on any other. This force increases as the distance between them is diminished beyond a certain critical amount.[69] Kant theorized that a macroscopic body consists of a limited number of microscopic fields of repulsive forces, each grouped around a point within the space a body occupies. Each point would have an intensity within a limited radius, increasing to infinite intensity as the distance from the point decreases toward zero.[70] On the basis of this assumption about matter, Kant defined spirit as a rational, nonmaterial substance which was not subject to the laws of repulsion. It could, therefore, occupy a given time and space simultaneously with a material substance.[71] Kant went on to identify spirit and soul and concluded that communication between spirit and body might be possible through inner states by a kind of telepathic rapport.[72] Broad summarizes Kant's argument about spirits as follows:

> (i) That, even in this life, each human soul is in close connection with the rest of the immaterial world, acts on it, and receives influences from it. But under normal conditions it is unaware of these actions and passions. (ii) That disembodied spirits have no conscious sense perception of the material world. For such a spirit is not connected with any particular organic body to form a person, and thus has no location in the material world and no bodily organs through which to perceive and act upon it. (iii) That disembodied spirits can influence and be influenced by souls which are animating human bodies, since these are of the same nature as they and stand in direct mutual relations with them. But disembodied spirits could not receive and assimilate those ideas in embodied souls which depend upon the body and its relations to the rest of the material world. Conversely, embodied souls could not receive and assimilate the intuitive cognitions which disembodied spirits have of themselves and of other immaterial entities. At best each party could receive such ideas from the other only in a *symbolic* form.[73]

Kant claimed to have examined the hypothesis that spirits exist and speculated about how this could possibly be explained in order to give a fair hearing to this point of view.

The next section of *Dreams of a Spirit-Seer* is concerned with whether the theory about spirits outlined by Kant could be proven by subjecting Swedenborg's experiences to a detailed study. In contrast to what he stated in his letter to von Knoblock, Kant came to a negative conclusion. Swedenborg's spiritualistic experiences were held up by Kant as the test case for the existence of spirits that could not bear the burden of his emerging theory of knowledge.[74] It was not, as Kant pointed out, that the existence of spirits was a log-

ical impossibility. It was simply that the alleged facts as data supporting an actual world of spirits were inadequate.[75]

On the basis of this conclusion, Kant indicated that an alternative reading of spiritualistic experiences would be to associate
them with mental disorders.[76] How much of an influence this
recourse to a psychiatric explanation had upon Jung is difficult to
estimate. Kant certainly expressed an interest in psychopathology,
but this is nowhere systematically presented in his works; it has to
be reconstructed from his writings as a whole.[77] It becomes quite
clear that in his later works Kant would see the assertion that the
supersensible was accessible to experience, as a form of fantasizing. Those who take the world of appearances to be a collection of
symbols sustaining a hidden world, he would charge with engaging
in fantasy. Fantasy, Kant would later assert, is either superstition
or madness.[78] It is quite clear that Jung would differ with Kant in
his understanding of fantasy. In fact, I will later argue that this is
the crucial difference between the mature Kant and Jung. In
Dreams of a Spirit-Seer, Kant is still willing to indulge in fantasy,
but, in the light of his later works, he does so in order to hold it
firmly in check so his theory of knowledge cannot be undermined.
Madness, Kant would argue, could be prevented by clarity of reasoning and moral behavior. Indulging in fantasy would threaten
the walls dividing noumena from phenomena; it was both dangerous and corrupting.[79]

In order to complete the Kantian sources Jung would draw on
in his student lectures, it is necessary to turn to one more work. In
contrast to the letter to Fräulein von Knoblock and *Dreams of a
Spirit-Seer*, this work is from a later period. As early as 1773–74
Kant taught a course the notes of which were later published as
Lectures on Rational Psychology. There is evidence that these lectures were still being given in 1788–89.[80] The spiritualist, Carl Du
Prel, published an edition of these lecture notes in 1889 under the
title *Immanuel Kants Vorlesungen über Psychologie*.[81] There are
two reasons why this work assumes some importance: (1) In these
lectures Kant seems to take a more favorable view of Swedenborg's
Spiritualism and (2) Jung possessed a copy of this work and cites it
in his student lectures. As Broad points out, the fact that Kant still
lectured on rational psychology eight years after he wrote the *Critique of Pure Reason* is significant.[82] Rational psychology, Broad
relates, was a system of allegedly *a priori* knowledge about spirits
and the soul which Kant had taken great pains to discredit in the
Critique of Pure Reason.[83]

In *Lectures on Rational Psychology* Kant referred to Swedenborg in a respectful manner. In fact he seemed to be outlining Swedenborg's doctrines about the spirit world in a favorable way. The
focus again was on the relation between the *mundus intelligibilis*
and the *mundus sensibilis*. This is another variation of Kant's
noumena and phenomena. It was Swedenborg's contention that all
spirits are in communion with one another, which fascinated Kant.
In his outline of Swedenborg's doctrines Kant stated:

> But we do not *see* each other to be in this communion,
> because we still possess a *sensible* form of intuition.... If
> now the hindrances to spiritual intuition are temporarily
> removed, we see each other in...the other world.... So the
> virtuous person does not *go* to Heaven, but is already in it
> here and now. But only after death will he see himself to be
> in this communion.[84]

Broad concludes that Kant's later *Lectures on Rational Psychology* indicate his opinion toward Swedenborg and Spiritualism
underwent a change.[85] In the light of Kant's more critical works he
makes the following observations about *Lectures on Rational Psychology*:

> Kant, in his more "unbuttoned" moments, took a not
> unfavourable view of certain features in Swedenborg's doc-
> trines which are compatible with (though they go beyond)
> his own account of the 'empirical' and the 'noumenal' self in
> the *Critique of Pure Reason* and the *Critique of Practical
> Reason*. His private opinion may have been that something
> like this part of Swedenborg's doctrine may well be true....
> But in his published professional contributions to philoso-
> phy he was not prepared to commit himself.... to anything
> beyond what he thought to be capable in principle of being
> proved.[86]

Robert Butts has also studied Kant's *Lectures on Rational
Psychology* as well as a number of additional sources which Broad
does not mention and in which Kant touched on the subject of spirits.[87] He argues for a greater consistency in Kant's thinking and
sees the *Lectures on Rational Psychology* as an attempt to come to
terms with such ideas. Eventually, Butts contends, Kant developed
his notion of the Central Nervous System. That is to say, Kant

would place such theorizing about the spirit world in a psychiatric context equating it with fantasy, which is either a form of mental weakness expressed as stupidity or out and out madness.[88]

Whether Kant's *Lectures on Rational Psychology* indicate he was of two minds about Spiritualism, as Broad contends, or perhaps are more consistent with the *Critiques* and other works, as Butts argues, is incidental to the discussion that will follow.[89] The relevance of Kant's *Lectures on Rational Psychology* insofar as Jung is concerned is that it allowed him to understand Kant in a particular way. This will become obvious in his student lectures and in his later writings.

In summary, it is evident that Spiritualism was a subject of burning interest for Kant. This is reflected in a number of his writings: (1) the letter to Fräulein von Knoblock (1763), in which he was favorably disposed to Swedenborg's Spiritualism; (2) *Dreams of a Spirit-Seer* (1766), an ambiguous work in which he discussed a philosophy of Spiritualism in detail, at the same time rejected Swedenborg's claims, and affected a psychiatric interpretation of Spiritualism; (3) the *Lectures on Rational Psychology* (1773–89) where he appears to be favorably disposed toward or, at the very least, neutral about the subject of Spiritualism. The relevance of these sources, I will argue in the following chapter, is that they influenced Jung's understanding of Spiritualism. As we shall see, not only did Jung draw on these writings of Kant in his student lectures, but they were the only ones to which he explicitly made reference.

The other philosopher whom Jung held in high regard is Schopenhauer. As I have already pointed out, it was through Schopenhauer that Jung found his way to Kant. And, in many respects, it was Schopenhauer who, basing himself on Kant, provided Jung with a critical framework within which to fit Spiritualism. This framework was psychological in nature, and in it Schopenhauer offered Jung an interpretation of human behavior which would prepare him for his encounter with Freud.

Kant had distinguished the noumenon, the unknowable thing-in-itself, from phenomena, that which is accessible to reason. Schopenhauer accepted this distinction and called the thing-in-itself, the will, and phenomena, representations. The will, according to Schopenhauer, was a blind, dynamic force which drove human beings and which could be equated with the unconscious.[90] This view is reflected in the title of Schopenhauer's major work *The World as Will and Representation* (1819). Jung cited this work in his student lectures along with Schopenhauer's *Essay on Spirit Seeing* (1851). It is in particular the latter work which provides an insight into the way in which Jung understood spiritualistic phenomena in the light of Kant's theory of knowledge.

Schopenhauer's *Essay on Spirit Seeing* is an attempt to subject the entire range of spiritualistic phenomena to philosophical scrutiny. His interest in, and knowledge of, spiritualistic phenomena was wide and penetrating. He was thoroughly aware of the practice of mesmerism and the various trance states this produced. In particular he focused on the deeper trance states which were accompanied by a splitting of the personality and produced various parapsychological phenomena. Schopenhauer took these phenomena as established fact. As he himself stated at the outset of *Essay on Spirit Seeing*: "Whoever at the present time doubts the facts of animal magnetism and its clairvoyance should be called not a skeptic but an ignoramus."[91]

Schopenhauer was aware of the phenomenon of rapport between the magnetizer and the magnetized subject.[92] He also recognized that the personality of the medium was the ultimate source of the spiritualistic phenomena produced.[93] And, in particular, he knew that apparitions were associated with the splitting of the medium's personality.[94] Schopenhauer argued that all previous attempts to explain these phenomena were spiritualistic. As such, they were subject to Kant's critique in *Dreams of a Spirit-Seer*.[95] By spiritualistic Schopenhauer understood the assumption that body and soul are distinct, and that:

> After the severance of the two that occurs at death, the soul, although immaterial, simple, and unextended, was still said to exist in space, thus to move, to go about, and moreover to act on bodies and their senses from without precisely as does a body and accordingly to manifest itself exactly like this. Here, of course, the condition is the same real presence in space which a body seen by us has.[96]

Schopenhauer continued making explicit the problem the spiritualistic hypothesis poses and why it must be rejected. He stated:

> All rational denials of spirit apparitions and also Kant's critical elucidation of the matter which constitutes the first or theoretical part of *Träume eines Geistersehers* [*Dreams of a Spirit-Seer*], apply to this utterly untenable *spiritualistic*

view of such apparitions. And so, that view, that assumption of an immaterial yet mobile substance, which moreover acts on bodies as does matter and consequently on their senses as well, has to be entirely given up so that a correct view of all the relevant phenomena may be reached.[97]

By referring back to Kant's discussion in the first part of *Dreams of a Spirit-Seer*, Schopenhauer makes clear the problem which the spiritualistic view of paranormal phenomena presents and thereby softens the ambiguity of the work. The problematical nature of the spiritualistic position on paranormal phenomena, according to Schopenhauer's understanding of Kant, is that spiritualists claimed spirits can manifest themselves directly in time and space. In Kant's language, the spiritualistic hypothesis about spirits confuses the noumenal with the phenomenal. In *Dreams of a Spirit-Seer*, Kant argued, in contrast to the spiritualistic position, that spirits might only be able to influence and be influenced through the souls that animate human bodies. This could be done, Kant inferred, only through some sort of telepathic rapport where, as C. D. Broad has stated, "each party could receive such ideas from the other only in a *symbolic* form."[98] Kant concluded that if spirits were things-in-themselves then they could never cross the barrier separating noumena from phenomena, because phenomena were the results of a sensory process of embodied beings conditioned *a priori* by time and space. If there was some sort of communication it was not direct, but could be made only through the embodied soul. Even then, Kant speculated, the embodied soul might not even be aware any communication was taking place.

Schopenhauer accepted the preceding interpretation as Kant's critique of the spiritualistic view of paranormal phenomena. He also accepted that there was overwhelming evidence of paranormal phenomena. The nature of these phenomena, such as knowledge of events from a distance and future events, indicated to Schopenhauer they were not conditioned by space and time. He concluded they were proof of the validity of Kant's distinction between noumena and phenomena. In *Essay on Spirit Seeing* he stated:

the phenomena that are here discussed [paranormal phenomena]...have as their specific characteristic...*actio in distans* and *passio a distante*. But in this way...they first afford a confirmation, as unexpected as it is certain and *factual*, of Kant's fundamental doctrine of the contrast between the phenomenon and the thing-in-itself and of the antithesis between the laws of both. Thus according to Kant, nature and her order are mere phenomenon. As the opposite thereof, we see all the facts that are here considered and can be called magical, rooted directly in the thing-in-itself and in the world of appearance giving rise to phenomena that can never be explained in accordance with the laws thereof. They were, therefore, rightly denied until the experience of hundreds of cases no longer allowed this. Not only Kant's philosophy, however, but mine also obtains on a closer investigation of the facts important corroboration, namely that in all these phenomena the *will* alone is the real agent, whereby it proclaims itself as the thing-in-itself.[99]

Schopenhauer went on to remark that though Kant demonstrated the distinction between the noumenal and the phenomenal, he finally gave up as insoluble the problem of how the one could possibly relate to the other.[100] This problem Schopenhauer attempted to address.

In *Essay on Spirit Seeing* Schopenhauer turned to what he called the "dream-organ" to demonstrate that the human being had a faculty of perception other than the senses. In dreams, he contended, images arose, impressed themselves on the mind, and spread out to the senses. This was the reverse of normal sensory perception.[101] For Schopenhauer, the dream-organ represented a mode of intuitive perception independent of the external impression on the senses. This dream-organ was also able to introduce impressions into the mind even when a person was awake—indicating, according to Schopenhauer, a capacity for intuitively representing objects.[102] Moreover these impressions (e.g. visual and auditory hallucinations), appeared to the perceiver to occupy time and space. As a result Schopenhauer concluded that impressions could arise from some internal source, and when they encountered the sensory faculties of the human being, they appeared as though conditioned by the qualities of phenomenal reality, namely time, space, and causality. In fact, though, their source was the noumenal. In language strikingly reminiscent of Jung's, Schopenhauer explained this process as follows:

> Just as sometimes two persons...dream the same dream... so *in wakefulness* the dream-organ of two...can enter the same activity, whereby a ghost...appears like a body. But

generally speaking, the difference between subjective and objective is at bottom not absolute, but always relative. For everything objective is again subjective in so far as it is still always conditioned by a subject in general, in fact exists really only in this.... We...imagine we have abolished the reality of a spirit apparition when we show that it was subjectively conditioned. But what weight can this argument have with the man who knows from Kant's doctrine how large a share the subjective conditions have in the appearance of the corporeal world? Thus that doctrine shows how this world, together with the space in which it exists, the time in which it moves, and the causality in which the essence of matter consists...is merely a product of the brain-functions,...brought into play by a stimulus in the nerves of the organs of sense, so that here we are left only with the question concerning the thing-in-itself. The *material* reality of bodies acting on our senses from without naturally belongs as little to the spirit apparition as to the dream through whose organ it is in fact perceived; and so, at all events, it can be called a waking dream...but at bottom, it does not in this way forfeit its reality.[103]

I cite what Schopenhauer stated after this passage because in what followed he presented his theory of will and representation.

Like the dream, it [the waking dream] is of course, a mere mental picture or representation and as such exists only in the knowing consciousness. But the same thing may be said of our real external world, for this too is...representation.... If we demand for it a further reality, then this is the question of the thing-in-itself.... But just as in any case the thing-in-itself which manifests...in the phenomenon of an external world is *toto genere* different therefrom, so by analogy may it be related to that which manifests itself in the spirit apparition; in fact, what reveals itself in both may perhaps be ultimately the same thing, namely *will*.[104]

Schopenhauer's speculations bear a striking resemblance to Jung's theory of archetypes.[105] He seems to have provided Jung with a clear philosophical foundation for his psychology and is largely responsible for determining the way in which Jung understood Kant's theory of knowledge. As with Kant's writings on Spiritualism, Schopenhauer's *Essay on Spirit Seeing* will surface in Jung's student lectures. Before I turn to these lectures, I would like to conclude Schopenhauer's argument by adding one or two points which seem also to have influenced Jung.

Schopenhauer claimed that the dream-organ could function while the person was asleep or awake and was the means by which inner impressions, rooted in the noumenal, could indirectly enter the phenomenal world. It logically follows that the dream-organ was operative in the somnambulistic states of the medium. The dream, the waking dream, and somnambulistic states were all activities of the dream-organ. In some respects this places Schopenhauer in tension with Kant, whose views on fantasies, or waking dreams, I mentioned earlier. Kant expressed himself critically when it came to the subject of fantasy. He held there were two kinds of fantasy: (1) the product of human weakness which manifests as superstition and (2) madness. In the end Kant's formal understanding of fantasy was, with the possible exception of his remarks in *Lectures on Rational Psychology*, psychiatric, in that he saw it as pathological and the result of the attempt to bridge the noumenal and the phenomenal. Schopenhauer appears in *Essay on Spirit Seeing* to view fantasy as primarily psychological, in that it revealed the dynamics of a process taking place between the will and the world of phenomena.

At the end of *Essay on Spirit Seeing*, Schopenhauer addressed the possibility of communication with the spirit of a dead person, as allegedly occurred during séances:

> as the result of the whole of my discussion so far are spirits seen through the dream-organ and in consequence of an influence that reaches the brain from within instead of the usual one through the senses from without.... Accordingly, although the spirit apparition is brought about by an internal influence that springs from the being-in-itself of things and hence by a magic influence on the organism...such an apparition is nevertheless perceived after the manner of objects that act on us from without.... Yet how can it be assumed that, during such transference and in such roundabout ways, an actual dialogue of statement and reply can take place, as is so often reported?...And so the way in which a dead man could obtain knowledge of living persons, in order to act on them in accordance therewith, is highly problematical.[106]

Schopenhauer does not deny the possibility that the dead can influence the world of the living but "such could take place only
extremely rarely and wholly by way of exception."[107] For the most
part an apparition "primarily and directly is nothing but a vision in
the brain of the spirit seer."[108] Schopenhauer seemed definite about
this fact, but just before he closed *Essay on Spirit Seeing* he added,
circumspectly:

> Finally, when explaining spirit apparitions, we might still
> refer to the fact that the difference between those who were
> formerly alive and those now alive is not absolute, but that
> one and the same will-to-live appears in both. In this way, a
> living man, going back far enough, might bring to light
> reminiscences that appear as the communications of one
> who is dead.[109]

To summarize: Kant's view of the distinction between the
unknowable noumena and phenomenal reality is the starting
point of his critique of all metaphysical postulations, including
those of the spiritualists. In his *Dreams of a Spirit-Seer* (1766), he
subjected the spiritualistic claim to be able to communicate with
spirits to a careful analysis. Though he expressed himself somewhat ambiguously in the end emerged with an argument that (1)
presented a consistent theory of spirits as things-in-themselves,
(2) subjected Swedenborg's spiritualistic claims to examination,
and rejected them, (3) suggested a greater focus on the phenomenal as an alternative to speculation that can never be confirmed
nor denied, and (4) offered a critique of spiritualism as fantasy,
which he concluded may be a psychiatric disorder of varying seriousness.

Schopenhauer for his part took up Kant's theory of knowledge
adding to it his own original contributions. In *Essay on Spirit Seeing* (1851) he interpreted Kant's theory about spirits as an argument which seeks not to deny the existence of spiritual reality but
to separate it from phenomenal reality in which the spiritualists
had entangled it. He then went on to propose a psychological
understanding of the process whereby a person could experience an
image arising out of the noumenal through an inner course and
entering the phenomenal world to be conditioned by all that characterized this world. Schopenhauer concluded that this process is
so subjective, and so entangled with the sensory faculties, that in
the final analysis it is primarily related to the individual through

whom such an experience occurs. He did not deny the possibility of spirits influencing living persons but surmised they could only do so through that person's neuropsychological faculties so conditioning this influence as to make it exceedingly difficult to separate the dead from the living.

An acquaintance with Jung's psychology would suggest certain similarities with the theories of Kant and Schopenhauer outlined in this chapter. When Jung's student lectures and medical dissertation are examined, it will become evident that more than just similarities are involved. The following chapters will demonstrate that Jung's psychological perspective on the subject of spirits and multiple personality has been greatly influenced by his encounters with the philosophical ideas on spirits of both Kant and Schopenhauer. The ideas that were beginning to take hold of Jung as the result of his encounter with Kant and Schopenhauer allowed him to free himself from the intellectual constraints of a naive Spiritualism and at the same time provided him a sound intellectual basis for its scientific interpretation. This reinterpretation would eventually take its final form as Jung's psychological theory of the archetypes.

Notes

1. *MDR*, 98.

2. Ibid., 56. Biedermann (1819–85) had been a Protestant pastor in Basel, then a professor at Zurich (1850–85). He was passionately involved in bringing about a union among the various factions of the Swiss Protestant Church. He was also a theologian of considerable stature and owed a great deal to Hegel, about whose philosophy he also retained some reservations. He sought to establish "a strictly scientific dogmatics—that is, a genuine historical science and a philosophical *Wissenschaft* with a definite metaphysics and a definite psychology of religion" (Welch, vol. 1, 162). Jung's characterization of Biedermann's theology is not entirely accurate: compare *MDR*, 56–59, and Welch, 160–67; and for an introduction to, and selections from, Biedermann's *Dogmatik*, see Claude Welch, ed., *God and Incarnation in Mid-Nineteenth Century German Theology* (New York: Oxford University Press, 1965), 287 et seq.

3. *MDR*, 59.

4. Ibid.

5. Ibid., 61.

6. Ibid., 61–62. Wilhelm T. Krug's *Allgemeines Handwörterbuch*

der philosophischen Wissenschaften, nebst ihrer Literatur und Geschichte, nach dem heutigen Standpuncte der Wissenschaft, 4 vols. 2nd ed. (1832–33) was, as the title and size suggest, a somewhat more substantial work than Jung implies; see William Gerber, "Philosophical Dictionaries and Encyclopedias," in Paul Edwards, ed., *The Encyclopedia of Philosophy,* vol. 6 (New York: Macmillan, 1967), 180. It is also interesting to note that Jung took issue with Krug, who succeeded Kant in the chair of philosophy at Königsberg, and whose Kantianism Jung claimed to have shared.

7. *MDR,* 62.

8. Ibid., 63.

9. Ibid., 64; see Jung's report card for April–July 1894 reproduced in Jaffé, *Word and Image,* 19.

10. *MDR,* 64; Brome, 56.

11. *MDR,* 64–65.

12. Ibid., 66.

13. Ibid.

14. Ibid., 68.

15. Ibid., 68–69.

16. Ibid., 69. This was the case in spite of the fact that Jung would later admit, "There is...a remarkable coincidence between certain tenets of Hegelian philosophy and my findings concerning the collective unconscious," see C. G. Jung, *Letters 2: 1951–1961,* 502.

17. *MDR,* 69 et seq.

18. I shall return to this subject in the pages that follow.

19. *MDR,* 72.

20. Ibid.

21. Ibid., 73.

22. Ibid., 75.

23. Ibid.

24. Ibid., 80.

25. William McGuire's editorial note to C. G. Jung, *The Zofingia Lectures,* v.

26. Ibid.

27. Ibid.

28. *MDR*, 96.

29. Ibid.

30. Ibid., 97.

31. Ibid., 98.

32. Ibid., 99.

33. Ibid., 99, where Jung mentions several names, among them Swedenborg, Zoellner, and Crookes. Steiner, 143, recalls Jung speaking of Mesmer, Lombroso, Kerner, Jung-Stilling, and unknown seers. Jung's library contains several nineteenth-century works on Spiritualism; see *Katalog*. Von Franz has also remarked "from his early youth he kept a watchful eye on parapsychological...phenomena reading more on these subjects than is perhaps evident in his works," in "The Library of C. G. Jung," *Spring* (1970), 192.

34. Steiner, 144.

35. *MDR*, 99.

36. Steiner, 131.

37. Ibid., 146.

38. *MDR*, 99.

39. Ibid., 100.

40. Ibid., 99.

41. Liselotte Moser, "Germany" in Eric J. Dingwall, ed., *Abnormal Hypnotic Phenomena*, vol. 2 (London: J. & A. Churchill, 1967), 177–78.

42. *MDR*, 69. Jung states (ibid., 70) that he studied philosophy from his seventeenth year (1892) until well into the period of his medical studies (1895–1900). Jung's library contains Schopenhauer's *Parerga und Paralipomena* (1891 edition; includes "Essay on Spirit Seeing"); *Uber den Satz vom Grunde*; *Ueber den Willen in der Natur*; *Die Grundprobleme der Ethik* (1891 edition); *Die Welt als Wille und Vorstellung* (1891 edition); see *Katalog*, 67.

43. Patrick Gardiner, *Schopenhauer* (Harmondsworth, Middlesex: Penguin, 1963), 11–32.

44. *MDR*, 69. Jung also wrote, ibid., that he was not convinced by Schopenhauer's solution of the blind "Will." In his 1925 seminar *Analytical Psychology*, ed., William McGuire (Princeton, N.J. Princeton University

Press, 1989), 4, Jung clarified this by stating that he disagreed with Schopenhauer's notion of the Will as formulated in his early writings but in Schopenhauer's later *Will in Nature* (1836) "he assumes that there is direction in the creating will, and this point of view I took as mine."

45. *MDR*, 70. Schopenhauer repeatedly referred to Kant in his writings, and though he took issue with him on certain matters, he claimed him as his mentor; see, e.g., Arthur Schopenhauer, *The World as Will and Representation* (1819, 3rd ed. 1859), trans. E. F. J. Payne, vol. 1 (Indian Hills, Colo.: The Falcon's Wing Press, 1958), 413–534. Often Jung referred to Kant in his Zofingia lectures, as I will point out in the following chapter, but not to his *Critique of Pure Reason*. Jung's library has the following works of Kant: *Allgemeine Naturgeschichte* (1884); *Kritik der praktischen Vernunft* (n.d.); *Kritik der Urteilskraft* (n.d.); *Macht des Gemüths* (1824); *Die Persönlichkeit als Einführung in das Werk* (n.d.); *Prolegomena zu einer jeden Metaphysik* (1888); see *Katalog*, 39. On the influence of Kant's later works on Jung, see Brent.

46. C. G. Jung, *Letters 1: 1905–1950*, 294. C. G. Jung, *Letters 2: 1951–1961*, 375–79, is a detailed discussion of what Jung meant by "Kantian." Brent, 75–83, has argued persuasively that there is far too much emphasis on Jung's use of Kantian epistemology and not enough on the extent of his debt to the whole corpus of Kant's works. While I accept Brent's strictures, I must argue on behalf of my own emphasis on Jung's debt to Kantian epistemology that I have attempted to extend the study of Jung's dependence on Kant to works Brent neglected to include in his otherwise informative dissertation.

47. Frederick Copleston, *A History of Philosophy*, vol. 6, pt. 2 *Kant* (New York: Image Books, 1960) 61–65, for this and what follows.

48. Ibid. Schopenhauer, in *The World as Will and Representation*, vol. 1, 417–18, claims "*Kant's greatest merit is the distinction of the phenomenon from the thing-in-itself*, based on the proof that between things and us there always stands the *intellect*, and that on this account they cannot be known according to what they may be in themselves." If, in place of *intellect*, we read *psyche*, we have Jung's later view exactly stated. The difference between intellect and psyche in this comparison is that Schopenhauer would not exactly attribute mind to the Will and Jung would of the unconscious. In this regard Jung claimed he was influenced by von Hartmann's emendation of Schopenhauer found in *Philosophy of the Unconscious* (1869); see C. G. Jung, *Analytical Psychology*, 5, where he stated: "My ideas of the unconscious, then, first became enlightened through Schopenhauer and Hartmann. Hartmann...living in a later period than Schopenhauer, formulates the latter's ideas in a more modern way.... In Schopenhauer's conception mind belongs to man alone and is not connected with the *Weltgrund* or *unbewusster Geist*. I held, following Hartmann, that our unconscious is not meaningless but contains a mind."

49. For this and the details that follow, see Sten Lindroth, "Sweden-borg, Emanuel," in Gillispie, ed., *Dictionary of Scientific Biography*, vol. 13, 178–81; and Inge Jonsson, "Swedenborg, Emanuel," in Paul Edwards, ed., *The Encyclopedia of Philosophy*, vol. 8, 48–51.

50. Jung seems to have maintained an interest in Swedenborg, because he added to his library a 1918 English edition of Swedenborg's *Journal of Dreams and Spiritual Experiences in the Year 1744*; see *Katalog*, 74.

51. In *MDR*, 99, Jung claimed he read seven volumes of Sweden-borg's writings. In addition to Swedenborg's *Journal*, Jung's library contains *Abrégé des ouvrages de Swedenborg* (1788); see *Katalog*, 74.

52. Kant's letter to Fraulein von Knoblock is in Immanuel Kant, *Dreams of a Spirit-Seer and Other Related Writings*, trans. John Manole-sco (New York: Vantage Press, 1969), 149–54. For the problems involved in dating this letter, see ibid, 177–82; C. D. Broad, "Immanuel Kant and Psychical Research," in *Religion, Philosophy and Psychical Research* (London: Routledge & Kegan Paul, 1953), 116–23.

53. Broad, 118; Kant, *Dreams of a Spirit-Seer*, 150.

54. Ibid, 151–52.

55. Ibid., 152–53. Kant incorrectly dated the fire 1756. For this and other difficulties with Kant's account, see Broad, 150 et seq.

56. Kant, *Dreams of a Spirit-Seer*, 149–50.

57. Ibid., 152.

58. Immanuel Kant, *Universal Natural History and Theory of the Heavens*, trans. Stanley L. Jaki (Edinburgh: Scottish Academic Press, 1981), 183–96; see also Robert E. Butts, *Kant and the Double Government Methodology* (Dordrecht: D. Reidel, 1984), 66.

59. Butts, 66.

60. Ibid., 67.

61. Ibid., 66 n. 5. See also Jaki's rather scathing introduction to his edition of Kant's *Universal Natural History*, 1–76, where he castigates Kant's interpreters for misrepresenting this work to the public as a work of science. He also points out that the infamous third part was expurgated from previous translations.

62. Butts, 76.

63. Ibid., 76 n. 12, citing the review of *Dreams of a Spirit-Seer* by Moses Mendelssohn in *Allgemeine deutsche Bibliothek* (1767). Ernst Cas-

sirer in *Kant's Life and Thought,* trans. James Haden (New Haven: Yale University Press, 1981), 78–79, seems to be in agreement with Mendelssohn when he comments of *Dreams of a Spirit-Seer,* "But in this paradoxical mixture of jest and earnestness, which was the decisive factor? Which was the author's true face and which the mask he had assumed?" W. H. Walsh, in his entry on Kant in Paul Edwards, ed., *The Encyclopedia of Philosophy,* vol. 4, 307, calls *Dreams of a Spirit-Seer,* "enigmatic."

64. Broad, 123–24.

65. Cited in Kant, *Dreams of a Spirit-Seer,* 155–56.

66. Butts, 86.

67. *MDR,* 355. Ben-Ami Scharfstein in *The Philosophers: Their Lives and the Nature of Their Thought* (New York: Oxford University Press, 1980), 391, has observed "there is a profound temperamental likeness between Kant and Jung, which belies the striking difference between the two. I am referring to the subtle balance in both of them between metaphysical restraint and belief."

68. Broad, 128.

69. Ibid., 128–29.

70. Ibid., 129.

71. Ibid., 130. Compare Jung's remarks in C. G. Jung, *Letters 2: 1951–1961,* 43–47.

72. Broad, 135.

73. Ibid., 137.

74. Butts, 64–78, 206–13.

75. Ibid., 208.

76. Ibid., 286.

77. Kant had already made a preliminary excursion into the area of mental illness in *Essays on the Diseases of the Mind* (1764), where he divided mental illnesses into two groups: (1) incapacity of the mind (retardation) and (2) disturbances of the mind. In the latter group he introduced a further subdivision: (a) distortions of concepts of experience (neurosis and hysteria), (b) disorders in judging concepts of experience (psychoses or madness) and (c) disorders affecting the whole faculty of reason concerning judgments (insanity). The visionaries and mystic dreamers, Kant classified as neurotics; see the extracts from Kant's essay in *Dreams of a Spirit-Seer,* 162, 164; Butts, 282–318, also examines other later sources.

78. Immanuel Kant, *Anthropology From a Pragmatic Point of View* (1798), trans. Victor Lyle Dowdell, rev. and ed. Hans H. Rudnick (Carbondale, Ill.: Southern Illinois University Press, 1978), 56 et seq.; Butts, 86, and the sources cited.

79. In a letter (1790) to Ludwig Borowski, Kant remarked: "I have the impression that the chief cause of the epidemic of the Supernatural is the rapidly growing fashion of reading all sorts of books. Thus, the craze for reading books is not merely the means and vehicle through which this evil is propagated, but the very germ and miasmic poison of this disease." Kant goes on in this same letter to make disparaging remarks about mesmerism and hypnotism. His chief criticism is that the practitioners of these arts use science to establish that something actually occurs, but deny science the power and authority of total explanation. As he put it, "Perhaps the persons who ask the questions do not realize that one may also study effects which are merely the result of their imagination, regardless of the fact that some one acts as observer and the other as the observed, and that such kind of laboratory experiments cannot truly be conducted as proper laboratory experiments," cited in *Dreams of a Spirit-Seer*, 160–61; see also Butts, 71 n. 8.

80. Broad, 148.

81. Ibid.

82. Ibid., 149.

83. Ibid.

84. Ibid 148–49 citing Kant's doctrines on rational psychology.

85. Broad, 149–50.

86. Ibid., 150.

87. Butts, 82–86, mentions *Metaphysik Herder/Nachträge Herder* (1765–66); *Metaphysik K* (1791–93); *Metaphysik Dohna* (1792–93), and other sources.

88. Butts, 282–318. For example, in 1798 Kant made the following claim in *Anthropology from a Pragmatic Point of View*, 17:

> To scrutinize the various acts of the imagination within me, when I call them forth, is indeed worth reflection, as well as necessary and useful for logic and metaphysics. But to wish to play the spy upon one's self, when those acts come to mind unsummoned and of their own accord (which happens through the play of the unpremeditatedly creative imagination), is to reverse the natural order of the cognitive powers, since then the rational elements do not take the lead (as they should) but instead follow behind. This

desire for self-investigation is either already a disease of the mind (hypochondria), or will lead to such a disease and ultimately to the madhouse. He who has a great deal to tell of inner experiences (for example, of grace, of temptations, etc.) may, in the course of his voyage to self-discovery have made his first landing only at Anticyra [a Greek town associated with insanity].

89. In this regard Kant may be remarkably like Freud, of whom Jones, vol. 3, 375, wrote: "Freud's attitude toward occultism is of peculiar interest to his biographer, since it illustrates better than any other theme the explanation of his genius.... In it we find throughout an exquisite oscillation between skepticism and credulity so striking that it is possible to quote just as many pieces of evidence in support of his doubt concerning occult beliefs as of his adherence to them."

90. Ellenberger, *Discovery*, 208.

91. Arthur Schopenhauer, "Essay on Spirit-Seeing" (1851), in *Parerga and Paralipomena*, trans. E. F. J. Payne, vol. 1 (Oxford: The Clarendon Press, 1974), 229.

92. Ibid., 263.

93. Ibid., 286.

94. Ibid.

95. Ibid., 229.

96. Ibid., 292.

97. Ibid.

98. Broad, 137. Kant repeats this assertion in his inaugural dissertation, *On the Form and Principles of the Sensible and Intelligible World* (1770), 2, 10, stating, "An *intuition* of intelligible objects [e.g. spiritual realities] is not given to man, but only a *symbolic knowledge*" (cited in Copleston, vol. 6, pt. 1, 229). Jung makes a similar remark when discussing the dissociability of the psyche in his "On the Nature of the Psyche," 175, where he stated, "the secondary subject does in fact have an effect upon ego-consciousness—indirectly or, as we say, 'symbolically'."

99. Schopenhauer, "Essay on Spirit Seeing," 266–67.

100. Ibid., 299.

101. Ibid., 229 et seq.

102. Ibid., 238–39.

103. Ibid., 298–99.

104. Ibid., 299.

105. I will discuss this in my conclusion.

106. Schopenhauer, "Essay on Spirit Seeing," 306–7.

107. Ibid., 308.

108. Ibid., 309.

109. Ibid.

Chapter 4

Spiritualism in Jung's Zofingia Lectures

From 1895 to 1900 Jung was a student in science and medicine at the University of Basel. In 1900 he chose to specialize in psychiatry and became attached to the Burghölzli clinic in Zurich.[1] While he was at university Jung developed a serious interest in Spiritualism and familiarized himself with the literature on the subject, as I pointed out in the previous chapter. In certain respects, these two interests, science as well as Spiritualism, reflect once again the division in Jung's own personality, which manifested itself when he was young. The origin of this division was the subject of an earlier chapter. During his university years Jung sought to reconcile these two interests, and, by implication, to heal the division within himself by bringing together science and Spiritualism. He did this in two ways: (1) he subjected Spiritualism to a philosophical analysis, drawing upon Kant and Schopenhauer and (2) he moved from philosophy to psychiatry, completing the foundation upon which he built a psychological understanding of Spiritualism. Jung's student lectures document the first part of this development and his medical dissertation, the second part. The development of Jung's psychological perspective as reflected in his student lectures will be the subject of this chapter.

Until the publication of Jung's student lectures not a great deal was previously known of the direction of Jung's thought during the years he attended university. In 1935 Albert Oeri, a fellow student and lifelong friend of Jung's, revealed that Jung had been a serious student and a member of the Zofingia student fraternity.[2] Jung had joined the Zofingia fraternity in the spring of 1895.[3] Most of his fellow students, both in the humanities and the sciences, expressed an attitude of open materialism. This attitude was evident in the student meetings.[4] Oeri mentions that Jung took issue with this materialism and often intellectually dominated the discussions by forcefully presenting his interests in Spiritualism. Oeri described how Jung asserted himself over his fellow students:

> This was possible—and I would not wish to conceal it—
> because he had courageously schooled himself, intensively
> studying occult literature, conducting parapsychological
> experiments, and finally standing by the convictions he
> derived therefrom.... He was appalled that the official sci-
> entific position of the day toward occult phenomena was
> simply to deny their existence, rather than to investigate
> and explain them. For this reason, spiritualists...about
> whose teachings he could speak for hours, became for him
> heroic martyrs of science. Among his friends and relatives
> he found participants for séances. I cannot say anything
> more detailed about them, for I was at the time so deeply
> involved in Kantian critique that I could not be drawn in
> myself. My psychic opposition would have neutralized the
> atmosphere.... It was really wonderful to let oneself be lec-
> tured to, as one sat with him in his room. His dear little
> Dachshund would look at me so earnestly, just as though
> he understood every word, and Jung did not fail to tell me
> how the sensitive animal would sometimes whimper
> piteously when occult forces were active in the house.[5]

It is interesting to note that Oeri felt his interests in "Kantian critique" prevented him from taking Jung's Spiritualism seriously.
This was obviously the mature Kant of the *Critique of Pure Reason*
and not the Kant whom Jung was initially familiar with from the
sources I outlined in the last chapter.

    In addition to Oeri's recollections, another source for this
period is Jung's autobiography, which briefly mentions his involvement in the Zofingia student association. Of this Jung wrote:

> In the fraternity meetings I gave several lectures on theo-
> logical and psychological subjects. We had many animated
> discussions.... We argued over Schopenhauer and Kant...
> and were interested in theology and philosophy.[6]

    At this time Jung also discovered the literature of Spiritual-
ism. As I pointed out in the last chapter Jung's interest in Spiritualism coincided with his father's death. The latter event certainly
must have added to Jung's anxiety and deepened his personal need

to explore the subject of Spiritualism. Formal religion offered Jung little support. Instead of going to church on Sundays, Jung studied Kant.[7] Schopenhauer's philosophy had already entered Jung's thinking. As he himself related:

> This philosophical development extended from my seventeenth year until well into the period of my medical studies. It brought about a revolutionary alteration of my attitude to the world and to life.... I also became noticeably more accessible and more communicative.... I felt firmer ground under my feet and even summoned up courage to speak openly of my ideas.[8]

Jung's encounter with Kant and Schopenhauer was of great personal significance. Early in life Jung had experienced a division within himself which he described as No. 1 and No. 2 personalities. It is evident in his autobiography that Jung's interest in science and philosophy became implicated in his attempt to overcome this inner division, of which he stated:

> No. 2 personality became more and more doubtful and distasteful to me.... I tried to extinguish No. 2, but could not succeed.... At school and in the presence of my friends I could forget him, and he also disappeared when I was studying science. But as soon as I was by myself,... Schopenhauer and Kant returned in full force, and with them the grandeur of "God's world."[9]

Jung found that philosophy could not reconcile his No. 1 and No. 2 personalities. In fact, the discovery of Kant and Schopenhauer intensified the division within him. "It was just at this time," Jung revealed, "that, out of the clash of opposites, the first systematic fantasy of my life was born."[10] Jung's fantasy consisted of a world in which he had his own castle, arsenal, and library. Inside the tower of the castle was a kind of laboratory in which, through an elaborate underground process, he made gold drawing from some substance in the air. This substance was some sort of spiritual essence.[11]

I mention this experience because it indicates that Jung resorted to fantasy in an effort to reconcile the tension he was experiencing between his No. 1 and No. 2 personalities. More precisely this conflict and the resulting fantasy revealed (1) that Jung found the split in himself intolerable and (2) that he could only overcome this by active fantasy. Jung seemed to have recognized his experience of No. 1 and No. 2 personalities and the irreconcilable split between them as evidence in his own person of the Kantian distinction between the phenomenal and the noumenal. Kant, as I pointed out in the previous chapter, would finally refuse to allow fantasy a valid mediating role between these two separate worlds. Instead, he came to view fantasy as ranging from mildly to severely pathological. By contrast Schopenhauer was more willing to grant fantasy an active and positive role in bridging the cleft between the knowable and the unknowable. Jung, for his part, would eventually develop a psychological perspective which would include both of these views and reconcile them.[12] In the meantime, it could be said, Jung's turning to Kant and Schopenhauer reflected his overwhelming concern to bring together his No. 1 and No. 2 personalities. He seems to have set about to accomplish this by entangling these parts of himself in science and Spiritualism, and in the problem of the phenomenal and the noumenal. In attempting to reconcile these he was, at bottom, trying to heal the split in himself. Oeri's observations about Jung's interests in Spiritualism provide circumstantial evidence of this attempt at reconciliation, which is confirmed and amplified by Jung's autobiography.

In addition to Oeri's observations and Jung's autobiographical reflections, there is another account of this period by Gustav Steiner, a fellow student of Jung's and a member of the Zofingia fraternity. Steiner recalled that Spiritualism and hypnotism were topics of debate in the Zofingia meetings.[13] Jung in particular, Steiner claims, was so enthusiastic about Spiritualism that he even sought out converts. Moreover, Steiner added, he was not above frightening his peers with hair-raising tales about ghosts.[14] Jung's proselytizing inclinations may have created some tension between himself and his fellow students, but this did not prevent him from addressing them on the subject of Spiritualism in the Zofingia meetings. Steiner, like Oeri, reports that Jung regaled him with stories about spiritualists.[15] He also recalls that Jung discussed Schopenhauer's *Essay on Spirit Seeing*.[16] His account agrees and adds to what Oeri and Jung himself have written. This material, combined with the outline of Kant and Schopenhauer in the last chapter, provides us with the necessary information with which to properly understand the ideas Jung expressed in *The Zofingia Lectures*.

The most important sources for the university years of Jung's

life are *The Zofingia Lectures* (1896–99) and his medical dissertation, *On the Psychology and Pathology of So-Called Occult Phenomena* (1902). The lectures which I will now consider are, in fact, the
earliest body of Jung's writings that have been published. Jung
joined the Zofingia fraternity along with four other medical students on May 18, 1895.[17] He remained inactive during the meetings
until he presented his first lecture, "The Border Zones of Exact Science," in November 1896. Six months later, in May 1897, he delivered another lecture, "Some Thoughts on Psychology." In the following winter semester 1897–98, Jung was elected chairman of the
Zofingia club and gave an "Inaugural Address." In the summer of
1898 he delivered his next lecture, "Thoughts on the Nature and
Value of Speculative Inquiry." Jung's last lecture, dated January
1899, is entitled "Thoughts on the Interpretation of Christianity,
with Reference to the Theory of Albrecht Ritschl."[18]

With the exception of the "Inaugural Address" (1897), these
lectures represent the intellectual preoccupation of Carl Jung, the
university medical student. The "Inaugural Address" is merely a
general rallying call to uphold noble ideals and values and, as
Marie Louise von Franz observes, is somewhat political in nature.[19]
The other four lectures show the same preoccupation with Spiritualism that Oeri and Steiner have already reported. They also
demonstrate Jung's attempt to come to terms with the problems,
addressed by both Kant and Schopenhauer, of the possible relation
between the phenomenal and the noumenal. Lastly, if we follow
Jung's own autobiographical disclosures, we can see in the more
formal discussions in these lectures that he was struggling to come
to terms with his own inner division.

In the first of *The Zofingia Lectures* which Jung entitled "The
Border Zones of Exact Science," he attacked contemporary natural
science for its materialistic assumptions and prejudices. In addition, Jung argued that scientific method should be strictly empirical and take into consideration nonmaterial reality in the formulation of theories. As he stated it:

> The critical examination of rational scientific claims leads
> us into an immaterial or metaphysical realm....
> The physical phenomena have been studied and
> threshed out down to the last detail. Metaphysical phenom-
> ena are virtually a closed book. Surely it would be valuable
> to inquire into properties other than those with which we
> have long been familiar.[20]

While Jung demanded that science extend its empirical
method into analyzing metaphysical data, he did not specify in his
lecture which data he had in mind. On this matter he appears to
have spoken in generalities. This oversight of Jung's has drawn the
following comment from von Franz:

> But what has he in mind as an alternative? ...He
> means...the possibility that an immaterial phenomenon
> might manifest materially, but he does not explain this fur-
> ther. The first lecture stops short here.[21]

In the recorded discussion that followed the lecture it becomes
clear what Jung had on his mind when he called for science to subject the metaphysical to empirical examination. In his exchange
with the other Zofingia members, as reported by a medical student,
Jung specifically referred to the phenomena of hypnotism and Spiritualism. He described hypnotism as "One of the most misunderstood transcendent virtues of the vital principle."[22] And Jung is
reported to have said that Spiritualism was "The science which
deals with the experimental research of these problems [of nonmaterial existences]."[23] In order to clarify his argument Jung became
even more explicit and stated that the actual purpose of his lecture
was "to show the connection of Spiritualism to the exact natural
sciences and its reasoning and not to state or reveal the essence of
Spiritualism."[24] There was a certain vagueness in Jung's lecture
which might explain why the editorial committee decided against
accepting it for publication.[25] It was only in the discussion that followed the lecture that Jung brought out into the open that he had
Spiritualism in mind when he called for science to analyze and
investigate the data of metaphysics. In addition, Jung drew a distinction between what could be empirically demonstrated about
Spiritualism and what he called "the essence of Spiritualism." This
distinction Jung has drawn deserves more comment.

In the light of the discussion about Kant and Schopenhauer in
the previous chapter, it is the distinction between the phenomenal
and the noumenal that Jung must have had in mind when he distinguished between the empirical facts and the essence of Spiritualism. If the role of Spiritualism and the Kantian distinctions Jung
mentioned in the discussions were not explicit in "The Border
Zones of Exact Science," they would be made so in the next lecture
he delivered six months later.

In May 1897 Jung gave his second Zofingia lecture, "Some

Thoughts on Psychology." The lecture is divided into four parts. In the first part, entitled "General Introduction," Jung gave a prosaic description of his intentions:

> to abandon the safe path laid out for us by esteemed science and accredited philosophy, to make our own independent raids into the realm of the unfathomable, chase the shadows of the night.[26]

In this part of the lecture Jung also cited three similar attempts to extend empirical science into the realm of the metaphysical. These three, according to Jung, were unimpeachable authorities "whose critical powers and keenness of judgment are beyond all question."[27] They were the theologian David Strauss, Schopenhauer, and Kant.[28]

David Strauss is mentioned by Jung because he had written a review of the life of the famous Seeress of Prevorst as presented by Justinus Kerner.[29] In his lecture Jung made reference to Strauss' study *Characteristiken und Kritiken* (1839) and cited his description of the seeress as follows:

> Her face, suffering but with noble and tender features, suffused with a celestial radiance;...her talk gentle, slow, solemn, musical almost like a recitative. Its content, rapturous emotions which drifted across her soul, now like soft and fluffy clouds, now like dark stormclouds, and then dissolved.... [Her] conversation with or about blessed or accursed spirits [was] conducted with such truth that we could have no doubt that we were truly in the presence of a prophetess who partook of communion with a higher world.[30]

This romantic description is evidence of how attractive the seeress appeared to Strauss. The reason Jung recorded this description was presumably to show how convinced Strauss was of the Seeress' demonstrations. It might also be pointed out that Jung, at this time, was conducting séances with a young woman he also found very attractive. In fact, the Seeress of Prevorst served as the model for Jung's medium.[31] Jung recorded the séances with this medium and made them the subject of his medical dissertation. This work will be examined in the next chapter. I mention these additional facts in this context to explain why Jung may have cited Strauss's description of the Seeress, which otherwise had little bearing on his argument in this lecture.

The second authority Jung referred to in his introduction to
"Some Thoughts on Psychology" is Schopenhauer. Specifically Jung
makes reference to Schopenhauer's opening remarks in *Essay on
Spirit Seeing* where he stated: "Nowadays anyone who doubts the
fact of animal magnetism and the clairvoyance it confers, must not
be called skeptical but ignorant."[32]

The third and final authority Jung invoked was Kant. Jung
cited both *Lectures on Rational Psychology* and *Dreams of a Spirit-
Seer*. I have outlined the contents of these two works in the last
chapter. In them Kant addressed himself to the subject of Spiritualism and it is for this reason that they are cited by Jung. He
quoted the following passage from Kant's *Lectures on Rational Psychology*:

> We can conceive of spirits only as problematic entities, i.e.,
> we can cite no a priori cause *to reject their existence....*
> Something can be admitted, on a problematical basis, pro-
> vided that it is quite clear that it is *possible*. We cannot
> demonstrate...that such spirits should exist, but neither
> can anyone disprove it.[33]

Without much comment Jung next turned to *Dreams of a Spirit-
seer* and cited Kant's confession contained in this work. It runs: "I
confess that I am strongly inclined to assert the existence of immaterial natures in the world, and to class my own soul among these
beings."[34] Jung immediately added two more quotations, both from
part 1 of *Dreams of a Spirit-Seer*. The first ends as follows:

> Accordingly it would be necessary to regard the human soul
> as already, in this present life, linked with two worlds of
> which, it being joined in personal union with a body, it
> clearly perceives only the material; whereas on the other
> hand, as a member of the spirit world, it receives the pure
> influences of immaterial natures and distributes these
> influences in turn, so that as soon as its union with the
> body has ended, nothing remains but the communion in
> which it continually dwells with spiritual natures, and
> which must reveal itself to consciousness as an object of
> clear contemplation.[35]

The last citation is introduced by Jung as indicating Kant's
"prophetic gaze far beyond his own age."[36] It runs:

it will be demonstrated in the future,...that even in this life the human soul dwells in an indissoluble communion with all the immaterial natures of the spirit world, alternatively affecting these natures and receiving from them impressions of which, in its human nature, it is not conscious *as long as all goes well.*[37]

These citations in the general introduction to Jung's second Zofingia lecture indicate the manner in which he understood both Schopenhauer and Kant. It seems quite clear that Jung perceived Kant's dilemma as emerging from the difficulties in trying to relate the phenomenal and the noumenal. These difficulties, Jung implied, were not insurmountable. In fact, Kant's prophetic gaze, Jung inferred, pointed to his own period and to the evidence coming from Spiritualism.

The second part of "Some Thoughts on Psychology" Jung entitled "Rational Psychology." I pointed out in the previous chapter that rational psychology was a system of allegedly *a priori* knowledge about spirits in general and the human soul in particular. In his *Lectures on rational psychology* Kant had spoken most positively about the possible existence of a spiritual world. I have already indicated that these lectures may be in tension with the ideas presented on the subject in his more formal works. Rational psychology, as Broad puts it, was a subject Kant "had taken great pain in the *Critique of Pure Reason* to explode as completely bogus."[38]

Jung opened this section of his lecture with a description of the emptiness which occurs when a person dies. The vividness of his description suggests he may have had in mind the memory of his father's death which he witnessed the previous year. He recalled this experience in his autobiography:

I could see that he was in the death agony.... Suddenly he stopped breathing. I waited and waited for the next breath. It did not come....
The following days were gloomy and painful.[39]

In his Zofingia lecture Jung offered a similar description:

The corpse is lying there cold and stiff...The entire organism is there, complete, ready to live, and yet it is dead and we know of no art to make it live again.[40]

Jung went on to argue in the same part of his lecture that the body must have housed some vital principle before death. This principle, he stated, cannot have been of a material nature because the body did not lose size or weight at death.[41] Jung pointed out that the location of this vital principle is problematic but should not be sought "within the consciousness, and most particularly not in the consciousness of the self, as Kant did."[42] In contrast, it is, according to Jung "more or less equivalent to the 'life force'.... It governs all...functions, including those of the brain."[43] Taking issue with Kant, Jung sided with Schopenhauer, quoting him as having stated, "Consciousness is the object of a transcendental idea,"[44] Jung then came out and boldly declared:

> Let us...assign to this transcendental subject the name of "soul." What do we mean by "soul"? *The soul is an intelligence independent of space and time.*[45]

Jung understood intelligence as purposeful acts. The body shows purpose, he stated, and so we could postulate that the soul is also intelligent. Jung, no doubt with Kant in mind, added, "If the law of causality did not possess an a priori status, this postulate would be proven."[46] Turning to the second part of his definition of the soul as independent of space and time Jung argued:

> The concepts of space and time are categories of the understanding and for this reason are not compelling with regard to the *Ding an sich* [thing-in-itself]. The soul eludes all sense perception and thus cannot constitute any form of material force. Only forces in material form constitute objects of perception. But within the categories of space and time, judgment is based on sense perceptions. Accordingly only forces in a material form can serve as objects of judgment, i.e., only forces in a material form move within the boundaries of space and time.[47]

> The soul does not represent a force in a material form, and thus there can be no judgment concerning it. But everything that cannot be judged subsists outside the concepts of space and time. Accordingly the soul is independent of space and time. Thus sufficient reason exists for us to postulate the immortality of the soul.[48]

In this part of his lecture Jung built on the idea of a vital principle which animated the body—a doctrine of the immortality of the soul. He argued along the lines presented in Kant's exposition of Spiritualism in part 1 of *Dreams of a Spirit-Seer,* which I summarized in the last chapter. Jung, having accepted the Kantian distinction between the phenomenal and the noumenal, identified the soul as a noumenon and therefore not subject to time, space, or causality. Jung completed his argument by granting the soul immortality and thereby made explicit his belief that the soul is a spirit.

In the third and longest part of the lecture "Some Thoughts on Psychology," Jung addressed himself to "empirical psychology." By empirical psychology he meant the systematic factual documentation of the soul's activities in the phenomenal world in order to support the theories of rational psychology.[49] Kant did not have access to this factual data, according to Jung, and so made such statements as the following in *Lectures on rational psychology*:

> We can say nothing more about these spirits, such as what a spirit can achieve separated from the body. They do not constitute objects perceptible to the external senses, and thus they do not exist in space. We can say nothing beyond this: if we did we would only be spinning idle fancies.[50]

Jung argued that the factual data subsequently available did not render Kant's epistemology obsolete. In fact, for Jung, it confirmed Kant's distinction between the phenomenal and the noumenal. What had been rendered obsolete, Jung insisted, were Kant's dogmatic teachings.[51] He did not clarify directly what he intended by this last statement. However, it can be inferred, on the basis of the material he presented, that Jung felt Kant's comments made him appear somewhat ambiguous about Spiritualism. He was prepared to exonerate Kant by arguing that he did not have all the facts at hand.[52] Indeed, Jung stated, "if Kant were alive today, he would undoubtedly be a spiritualist."[53] Jung mentioned that Kant gave Swedenborg an unbiased reading, but he passed over Kant's rejection of Swedenborg's claims.[54] Instead, he castigated those who used Kant to criticize Spiritualism, calling them "puerile epigones" and "fools."[55] He cited Schopenhauer in support of his comments, yet he failed to mention that Schopenhauer made a clear distinction between the spiritualists' conception of spirits and Kant's.[56]

In the last chapter I outlined the distinction Schopenhauer had made in *Essay on Spirit Seeing* between the basic assumptions of the spiritualists and those of Kant. The standpoint of Spiritualism, Schopenhauer said, is that the human person is made of *two substances*, a material body and an immaterial soul.[57] At death, Schopenhauer pointed out, the spiritualists claimed the soul, though immaterial, acted on other bodies and their senses from without, as though it itself was a body. Kant for his part, Schopenhauer went on to state, theorized that if there were spirits they were *not* subject to the *a priori* categories of cognition, namely time, space, and causality. Therefore, Schopenhauer concluded, spirits *could not be bodies* and so *could not* manifest and act as bodies. They could manifest *only* through an embodied soul which would clothe them with all the characteristics of phenomenal reality.[58] This difference between the spiritualists and Kant that Schopenhauer placed such emphasis on seemed to have been passed over by Jung. This is the more remarkable as it was made in *Essay on Spirit Seeing*, a work to which Jung repeatedly referred.[59]

After condemning the critics who used Kant to dismiss the claims of Spiritualism, Jung listed distinguished members of late nineteenth-century psychical research.[60] These illustrious individuals were used by Jung as a means of legitimizing the study of Spiritualism. Some of these persons have already appeared in the outline of Spiritualism I presented in chapter 1. Jung next turned on the clergy and police for spreading false rumors about Spiritualism and taking punitive action against its practitioners. Of them he wrote:

> Naturally the clergy make a great-to-do about the steady progress the devil of unbelief is making in the hearts of men, but this does not prevent them from mounting the pulpit and inveighing against the sin of spiritualism and stuffing people full of all sorts of old wives' tales about the spiritualists. Thus without realizing it the clergy are encouraging the general moral debacle, and the police, the guardians of the law, are contributing to the same end by prohibiting spiritualistic fraud.[61]

Having dealt with its critics and persecutors Jung presented what he considered to be the principal contribution and significance of Spiritualism. Spiritualism, he asserted, offered empirical proof of the existence of the soul. It did this in two ways: (1) by demonstrating the organizational activity of the soul as evident in the phenomena of "materialization" (by materialization Jung meant the actual manifestation of objects, limbs, etc., which he claimed were witnessed and photographed by reputable persons); (2) by offering proof of the fact that the soul is independent of space and time.[62] Hypnotism and telepathic phenomena, Jung claimed, were also proof of the existence of the soul because while in these states individuals displayed the ability to know things at a great distance or even in the future, which indicated a relativization of space and time.[63] Therefore, both materialization and extrasensory demonstrations were taken by Jung as evidence that there was a soul which was intelligent and not conditioned by space and time.

Jung concluded the final part of his lecture "Some Thoughts on Psychology" by claiming he had demonstrated that there was empirical proof for the existence of the soul. He went on to deplore the materialists who had ignored these facts and had gone astray and tried to lead others in the same direction. One day, he predicted, "They will build monuments to Schopenhauer."[64] In the meantime, Jung stated:

> we must institute a "revolution from above" by *forcing* morality on science and its exponents through certain transcendental truths, for after all, scientists have not hesitated to impose their skepticism and moral rootlessness on the world.[65]

Returning to religion, Jung argued, is not the way to combat materialism. "Nowadays the masses no longer want to believe," he stated, "They want to *know*."[66] Jung concluded his lecture with the following paragraph:

> The new empirical psychology furnishes us with data ideally designed to expand our knowledge of organic life and to deepen our views of the world. They enable us to glimpse nature's abyss, to gaze into an intelligible world where the eyes seek in vain for any shore or any limit. Nowhere do we feel as keenly as here that we are living at the boundary between two worlds. Our body formed from matter, our soul gazing toward the heights, are joined into a single living organism. We see our lives coming in contact with a higher order of being. The laws governing our mental universe grow pale before that light, emanating from the metaphysical order, which it is granted us to dimly divine. Man lives at the boundary between two worlds. He steps forth from the darkness of metaphysical being, shoots like a blazing

meteor through the phenomenal world, and then leaves it
again to pursue his course into infinity.[67]

There are a number of ideas that surfaced in "Some Thoughts
on Psychology" which later became so characteristic of Jung's out-
look that its importance can hardly be overstated. The source of
Jung's ideas and the direction of his thinking at this stage can be
summarized as follows: Firstly, it is quite clear that spiritualistic
phenomena served Jung as the primary source for the data he
called on to substantiate his idea of the reality of the soul. Sec-
ondly, he defined the soul in terms which are directly borrowed
from both Kant and Schopenhauer as expressed in their works on
Spiritualism. Thirdly, it is evident in these lectures that Jung was
struggling to formulate a psychological perspective that would be
intellectually credible and address certain questions that he formulated as the result of his own experiences.

In the summer of 1898 Jung delivered another lecture
"Thoughts on the Nature and Value of Speculative Inquiry." In contrast to the earlier lectures, this one is cast in the form of a lengthy
philosophical meditation. It would appear from the contents that
Jung had undergone a change in his thinking. There is no mention
of either Spiritualism or empirical psychology. The focus of Jung's
attention seems to be on certain philosophical ideas about the *Ding
an sich* (thing-in-itself) and the notion of causality. Jung also introduced a dynamic element into his interpretation of Kant upon
which I will comment. In addition, Jung advanced certain ideas
about unity and reconciliation in this chapter that, I suspect, had
mainly to do with his own inner feelings about himself.

Jung opened his lecture "Thoughts on the Nature and Value
of Speculative Inquiry" by emphasizing the limitations of external
success and happiness. As an alternative to those limitations he
asserted that the inner personality must be allowed to emerge.[68]
Jung then briefly touched on the Kantian categories and followed
Schopenhauer in reducing these to time, space, and causality.[69] He
called the *a priori* categories "judgments prior to experience" and
recognized:

> The mind cannot function without them, for there is no
> such thing as a mental image that does not unfold within
> the structure of time and space, and there is no such a
> thing as a thought process whose innermost nature is not
> causality.[70]

In this lecture Jung appeared to have taken Kant's epistemology much more seriously. But he did not go so far as to deny that the *Ding an sich*, the noumenal, can be by some means appropriated by phenomenal reality. Real experiences, Jung asserted, should be made the basis of knowledge.[71]

In his earlier "Some Thoughts on Psychology" Jung seemed to have inclined more toward a dualistic view of the human person. A person, Jung appears to have believed, consisted of a body and a soul. In that earlier lecture he maintained this dualism like the spiritualists in order to retain some conception of the spiritual. In attributing this dualism, without qualification, to Kant, he misread both Kant and Schopenhauer. In "Thoughts on the Nature and Value of Speculative Inquiry," he corrected this misunderstanding stating,

> At bottom, i.e., in itself, everything that exists,...moves within one and the same world: that which is unfathomably existent beneath the governance of an unknown final cause. The absolute realm is not divided into two distinct realms, the *Ding an sich* on the one hand and the phenomenal world on the other. All is One. A separation exists only in relation to us, because our sense organs are capable of perceiving only specific areas of the world-as-absolute.[72]

As Jung went on to observe, Kant left the problem of the noumenal unsolved. Schopenhauer, according to Jung, was the one philosopher who resuscitated this unsolved problem and interpreted the noumenal as the blind will.[73] The will was blind, Schopenhauer said, because the world was full of suffering. As Jung pointed out, this assigned "suffering a transcendental ground in the *Ding an sich*. Thus Schopenhauer's Will is blind because it has created a world full of suffering."[74] Jung countered Schopenhauer's pessimistic monism, not by denying his pessimism, but by rooting it in the dualism that he perceived to be at the heart of the "One World."

> On the other hand, if we take dualism as a basis—thereby failing to satisfy our striving for unity—we immediately possess an eminently sufficient reason for the suffering of the world. If we were to declare empiricism the only possible foundation of all speculative inquiry, then the dualistic world view would not seem so far off the mark.[75]

Jung saw a struggle in nature itself as expressing the clash of contending opposites:

> somewhere in the depths of nature there must be concealed something of unspeakable obtuseness, something that continually strives to suppress all independent activity and to paralyze every undertaking.[76]

This antagonism at the most primitive level, Jung claimed, is the root of dualism. "Here in inorganic nature ...," he stated, "is the place where that struggle begins that the philosophers term the suffering of the world."[77] Jung concluded: "Man's inner dualism is the direct continuation of the dualism of inorganic nature."[78]

Having traced this dualism from inorganic matter to the level of the human being, Jung claimed that all multiplicity is born out of the collision of opposites. On the basis of this he affirmed:

> the will to personality, to individuality, in the sense of the most radical diversity between an individual and everything else that exists, as the most radical diversification is consistent with the activity inherent to our nature, and thus the will to diversity is purposeful.[79]

Jung closed his philosophical meditation by observing that all religions, worthy of the name, are pessimistic and he ends with a quote from Nietzsche on the bitter/sweetness of life.[80]

There are a number of ideas in "Thoughts on the Nature and Value of Speculative Inquiry" which would find a permanent place in Jung's later psychology. The basic elements of the struggle between the unconscious and consciousness are evident in his discussion on dualism.[81] Spiritualism as a subject of interest seems to have moved into the background and speculation on the *Ding an sich* assumes the central place in the lecture. But, perhaps what can be perceived in this lecture, more obviously than in the previous two, is Jung's struggle with himself. The tone of the discussion which is evident in this lecture reflects Jung's personal involvement with the issues that emerged. Jung had managed to causally relate his inner division to the dualism in nature itself. His struggle with himself became part of the larger struggle to free consciousness from the unconscious. This emerging perspective must have provided him not only insight into his own conflict but meaning and purpose.

Jung gave his last lecture "Thoughts on the Interpretation of Christianity with Reference to the Theory of Albrecht Ritschl" before the Zofingia Club in January 1899. He opened his talk by observing that individuals such as Jesus Christ are not subject to historical analysis. The conventional view of the normal man can not be adequately used as a yardstick by which to judge such persons.[82] Jung went on to castigate theologians, and especially Ritschl, for attempting to rehabilitate Christianity and present it as a rational and ethical system. This removes the mystery, the involvement in the metaphysical and, above all, the inner experience of the believer. Christianity, Jung maintained, demands from those who believe in its message that they break from the world.[83]

The role as interpreter of religion assumed by Jung in this last lecture is one he would assume again and again.[84] The tone, certainty, and the insistence on inner experience would also become characteristic of Jung's writing on religion. What is also typical is his willingness to sit in judgment over theologians, clergy, and institutional religion.[85]

During the summer of 1899 Jung became inactive and resigned as president of the Zofingia Club. He returned as a member of the discussion group and spoke about himself as a kind of Faust and also about Swedenborg.[86] Jung became involved in one discussion following a lecture given by a theological student on theology and religion. In the course of the exchange, the theological student said that God could be experienced. Jung responded that he had never had such an experience. In fact, Jung claimed, modern psychology indicated there was an inner relation between religion and the sexual drive. The experience of God, Jung concluded, originated in the unconscious of the individual.[87] Häberlin, a philosophy student, entered the discussion and spoke of an all-good God. Jung responded that belief in such a God was not a universal experience.[88] The theological students who were present pointed out that Jung seemed to have changed his views from those he had expressed in earlier discussions. Jung admitted this change of mind. The exchange became heated, with each side assuming a rigid position, and a motion was put forward to end the debate. This was the last time Jung participated in a Zofingia Club meeting. After the state examination he left Basel for Zurich.[89]

Jung's last debate with the Zofingia theological students brings out and clarifies his own views of religious experience. He seems to have moved from the position of believing that God could be more or less directly experienced, to situating this experience within the unconscious and even to associating it with sexuality. If Schopenhauer's *Essay on Spirit Seeing* is recalled, this shift can more easily be explained. Schopenhauer made it very clear that any experience is conditioned by the *a priori* categories of time, space and causality. Direct experience of the thing-in-itself is impossible. Schopenhauer argued that such experiences may come from *within* and not from *without,* but the moment they surface into consciousness, they become subject to the conditions governing the sensory process. In Jung's later language, the God-image which arises out of the unconscious, is experienced and not God, as thing-in-itself.[90] That he moved even further in the Zofingia discussion and linked religion with sexuality may also be partly attributed to the influence of Schopenhauer.

Schopenhauer, in *The World as Will and Representation,* argued that the sexual instinct was one of the primary irrational forces of the will.[91] Moreover, he added:

> In keeping with all this is the important role played by the sex-relation in the world of mankind, where it is really the invisible central point of all action and conduct, and peeps up everywhere, in spite of all the veils thrown over it. It is the cause of war and the aim and object of peace, the basis of the serious and the aim of the joke, the inexhaustible source of wit, the key to all hints and allusions, and the meaning of all secret signs and suggestions, all unexpressed proposals, and all stolen glances; it is the daily thought and desire of the young and often of the old as well, the hourly thought of the unchaste, and the constantly recurring reverie of the chaste even against their will, the ever ready material for a joke, only because the profoundest seriousness lies at its root. This, however, is the piquant element and the jest of the world, that the principle concern of all men is pursued secretly and ostensibly ignored as much as possible. Indeed, we see it take its seat at every moment as the real and hereditary lord of the world....[92]

In addition, Jung by this time had begun to read the psychiatric literature which from 1880 to 1900 showed a preoccupation with sexual psychology and psychopathology.[93] Krafft-Ebing, whose *Textbook of Psychiatry* Jung used as a medical student, also wrote extensively on the psychopathology of sex.[94] Jung's experiences during the séances conducted at this time with his medium are further proof of the significance of sexuality in the beliefs and fantasies of individuals.[95] All of these influences must have produced in Jung the change revealed in the last Zofingia Club discussions. It could also be suggested that this interest in the relation between sexuality and religion played a role in preparing Jung for his encounter with Freud and his theories.

To summarize, Jung's *Zofingia Lectures* reveal the attitudes and intellectual concerns he had as a university student. These lectures also bring to light the development of Jung's thinking on the subject of Spiritualism. It seems that Jung was intensely preoccupied with Spiritualism and called for science to modify its claims in the light of spiritualistic phenomena. In order to grasp more clearly the nature of spiritualistic phenomena, Jung schooled himself in the literature on the subject. Part of this schooling involved reading certain works on Spiritualism by Kant and Schopenhauer. It became clear to Jung that the epistemological reservations regarding spiritualistic phenomena presented by these two philosophers formed a position with which he had to seriously come to terms. He gradually understood the limitations that Kant's theory of knowledge imposed upon metaphysical assertions. In the light of Kant and under the influence of Schopenhauer, Jung began to reinterpret Spiritualism. He eventually understood the dilemma caused by the Kantian distinction between the knowable phenomena and the unknowable noumena. Under Schopenhauer's guidance Jung situated the source of spiritualistic experiences within the individual and accepted the limitations to which these experiences would be subject when they entered phenomenal reality. This amounted to a shift in perspective for Jung from a metaphysical to a psychological understanding of Spiritualism. The transformation of the former into the latter would be completed and expressed in Jung's dissertation.

The development of Jung's thinking as revealed in *The Zofingia Lectures* involved more than a formal intellectual change. There are indications that the deep division and instability Jung experienced as a child did not cease but rather became implicated in his philosophical struggle with Spiritualism. Jung tried to reconcile this inner division by seeking to unite Spiritualism and science in what he termed "empirical psychology." This presented Jung with a serious problem which he temporarily overcame by eventually embracing the full implications of the Kantian distinction between phenomena and noumena. As Kant did before him, Jung was tempted to leave the problem as unsolved or, perhaps wording it more correctly, tempted to maintain that the solution itself was to turn away from the problem. Again, like Kant before him, Jung would turn to psychiatry to explain Spiritualism, only, as his medical dissertation makes clear, and unlike Kant, he would be deeply reluctant to reduce all the phenomena of Spiritualism to psychopathology.

Notes

1. *MDR*, 108–13.

2. Oeri, 186.

3. Steiner, 142.

4. Oeri, 187.

5. Ibid., 187–88.

6. *MDR*, 97.

7. Ibid., 101.

8. Ibid., 70–71.

9. Ibid., 74.

10. Ibid., 80.

11. Ibid., 81–82.

12. In particular, in the practice of active imagination as a technique of exploring the unconscious. I will discuss the significance of active imagination in the concluding chapter.

13. Steiner, 146–48.

14. Ibid., 144.

15. Ibid., 143.

16. Ibid.

17. Ibid., 142.

18. Jung, *The Zofingia Lectures*, ix.

19. Von Franz's introduction to *The Zofingia Lectures*, xix.

20. Jung, *The Zofingia Lectures*, 17, 19.

21. Von Franz's introduction to *The Zofingia Lectures*, xvii.

22. Steiner, 147.

23. Ibid.

24. Ibid.

25. Ellenberger, *Discovery,* 687.

26. Jung, *The Zofingia Lectures,* 23.

27. Ibid., 24.

28. Ibid., 24–25.

29. This famous medium and Strauss' visits to her were mentioned in chapter 1.

30. Jung, *The Zofingia Lectures,* 25.

31. C. G. Jung, *On the Psychology and Pathology of So-Called Occult Phenomena* (1902), in *Collected Works,* vol. 1, *Psychiatric Studies,* 2nd ed. (Princeton, N.J.: Princeton Univeristy Press, 1970), 36, 66, 87.

32. Jung, *The Zofingia Lectures,* 25, citing Shopenhauer's *Parerga und Paralipomena,* 243.

33. Jung, *The Zofingia Lectures,* 25, citing Kant's *Lectures on Rational Psychology.*

34. Jung, *The Zofingia Lectures,* 26, citing Kant's *Träume,* 14.

35. Jung, *The Zofingia Lectures,* 26, citing Kant's *Träume,* 20.

36. Jung, *The Zofingia Lectures,* 26.

37. Ibid., 26, citing Kant's *Träume,* 21.

38. Broad, 149.

39. *MDR,* 96.

40. Jung, *The Zofingia Lectures,* 29.

41. Ibid.

42. Ibid., 31.

43. Ibid.

44. Ibid.

45. Ibid.

46. Ibid.

47. Ibid., 31–32.

48. Ibid., 32.

49. Ibid., 38.

50. Ibid., 33, citing Kant.

51. Jung, *The Zofingia Lectures*, 33.

52. Ibid., 34.

53. Ibid.

54. Ibid.

55. Ibid.

56. Ibid.; see Schopenhauer, *Essay on Spirit Seeing*, 292.

57. Schopenhauer, *Essay on Spirit Seeing*, 292.

58. Ibid.

59. This may also be an indication that Jung had not as yet come to terms with the full implications of Kant of the later *Critiques*.

60. Jung, *The Zofingia Lectures*, 34–35, where he mentions Crookes, Wallace, Zöllner, DuPrel, Schiaparelli, Lombroso and others.

61. Ibid, 36.

62. Ibid., 38–39.

63. Ibid., 39–43.

64. Ibid., 44.

65. Ibid., 45.

66. Ibid., 46.

67. Ibid., 47.

68. Ibid., 61–65.

69. Ibid., 66.

70. Ibid.

71. Ibid., 68.

72. Ibid., 77.

73. Ibid., 78.

74. Ibid.

75. Ibid.

76. Ibid., 79.

77. Ibid., 83.

78. Ibid., 85.

79. Ibid., 86.

80. Ibid., 88.

81. See, e.g., C. G. Jung, *Collected Works,* vol. 7, *Two Essays on Analytical Psychology* (Princeton, N.J. Princeton University Press, 1966).

82. Jung, *The Zofingia Lectures,* 93–94.

83. Ibid., 97–111. See also Marilyn Nagy, "Self and Freedom in Jung's Lecture on Ritschl," *Journal of Analytical Psychology* 35 (1990): 443–57.

84. See, e.g., Jung's *Psychology and Religion.*

85. This inclination is especially evident later in his letters to clergymen, see C. G. Jung, *Letters 1: 1905–1950;* and *Letters 2: 1951–1961.*

86. Steiner, 159.

87. Ibid., 161.

88. Ibid., 162.

89. Ibid.

90. See the survey on the God-image in Jung's psychology by James W. Heisig, *Imago Dei* (Lewisburg: Bucknell University Press, 1979).

91. Arthur Schopenhauer, *The World as Will and Representation,* vol. 1, 329–30; vol. 2, 510–13.

92. Ibid., vol. 2, 513.

93. Ellenberger, *Discovery,* 291 et seq.

94. *MDR,* 108; Ellenberger, *Discovery,* 297–98.

95. Jung, *On the Psychology and Pathology of So-Called Occult Phenomena,* 69–70.

Chapter 5

Multiple Personality and Spiritualism in Jung's Medical Dissertation

Jung completed his medical studies at the University of Basel in 1900. He decided to specialize in psychiatry and went to Zurich to work under Eugene Bleuler, director of the Burghölzli clinic, an important psychiatric center in Europe, in the late nineteenth century. Bleuler and August Forel, the previous director, were particularly interested in hypnotism, the various phenomena the hypnotic trance produced, and how these could be related to the psychiatric understanding of the human personality.[1] Jung, prior to going to Zurich, had experimented with a medium and kept a detailed record of what had transpired during the séances that were conducted. At the Burghölzli he discovered a sympathetic audience for his interest in spiritualistic phenomena, and Bleuler encouraged him to organize his notes and subject them to a psychiatric analysis.[2] Jung did so and delivered his inaugural dissertation for his medical degree, *On the Psychology and Pathology of So-Called Occult Phenomena*, before the Faculty of Medicine, University of Zurich. It was subsequently published in 1902. The ideas Jung presented in this work, and the personal and professional significance they had for him, will be the focus of this chapter.

Jung's dissertation marked the end of his university studies and launched him into a career as a psychiatrist. As well, it is an important example of how certain personal and professional factors merged into a carefully thought out yet somewhat ambivalent work. In the light of Jung's earlier life and later intellectual development, the significance of his dissertation is that it expressed for the first time Jung's psychological perspective. This perspective had its origins in his early introverted broodings and received theoretical form when he encountered the philosophies of Kant and Schopenhauer. But it was only in psychiatry, and in the psychiatric concern with somnambulistic states and multiple personality,

149

that Jung found a suitable framework which he would modify and augment.

In his biography of Jung, Vincent Brome has succinctly described Jung's dissertation as an attempt to answer the following question: "Are psychic powers rationally explicable as special psychological states or are they powers of a different order?"[3] Though Jung preferred a psychological explanation of the medium's experiences, some of his remarks indicate he would not exclude the possibility of the paranormal. This makes the dissertation subtly ambivalent in places. Such ambiguity would become characteristic of Jung and does indicate that as a young psychiatrist he was not completely comfortable with a purely conventional psychological explanation of spiritualistic phenomena. I will return to this matter at a later point.

Henri Ellenberger, the noted historian of psychiatry, has highlighted the importance of Jung's dissertation for an understanding of his psychology by describing it as follows: "The germinal cell of Jung's analytic psychology is to be found in his discussions of the Zofingia Students Association and in his experiments with his young medium."[4] Later in life Jung seemed to have valued the latter in much the same way and stated of the séances he had observed:

> Just as the Breuer case…was decisive for Freud, so a decisive experience underlies my own views. Towards the end of my medical training I observed for a long period a case of somnambulism in a young girl. It became the theme of my doctor's dissertation. For one acquainted with my scientific writings it may not be without interest to compare this forty-year-old study with my later ideas.[5]

If we turn to the actual contents of the dissertation, it is evident that the focus of Jung's concerns was on the unusual states of mind which are found in the phenomenon of trance. He opened his dissertation with the following remarks:

> In that wide domain of psychopathic inferiority…we find scattered observations on certain rare states of consciousness as to whose meaning the authors are not yet agreed….
> It is, in fact, exceedingly difficult, and sometimes impossible, to distinguish these states from the various types of neurosis, but on the other hand certain features point

beyond pathological inferiority to something more than a merely analogical relationship with the phenomena of normal psychology, and even with the psychology of the supranormal, that of genius.[6]

And of those individuals who experience these rare states of consciousness Jung wrote:

> Persons with habitual hallucinations, and also those who are inspired, exhibit these states; they draw the attention of the crowd to themselves, now as poets or artists, now as saviours, prophets, or founders of new sects....
>
> In view of the—sometimes—great historical significance of such persons, it were much to be wished that we had enough scientific material to give us closer insight into the psychological development of their peculiarities.[7]

And, Jung concluded:

> These reflections have prompted me to publish some observations which will perhaps help to broaden our knowledge of the relations between hysterical twilight states and the problems of normal psychology.[8]

The subject of Jung's observations was a young female medium whom he reports he observed in the course of seven séances which began in 1899 when she was fifteen and a half and ended in 1900. She was, Jung stated, of a not particularly distinguished Basel Protestant family, several of whose members were eccentric and given to unusual visionary experiences.[9] The girl herself was a delicate, daydreaming type with no defined interests. And though she had visionary experiences as a young child, Jung assured his readers, "there were no abnormalities to be noticed...and especially no serious hysterical symptoms."[10] The séances, Jung added, began among her friends and relatives in July 1899 more as a form of amusement than out of serious intent. By the beginning of August the girl showed definite mediumistic abilities by falling into a trance and becoming a channel for dead relatives whose characters and idiosyncrasies were displayed so accurately that they made a vivid impression on those present.[11] Gradually she communicated, in grandiose and dramatic scenes, the concerns and nature of the other world.[12]

In the course of the séances one particular spirit emerged as the control spirit, and this was the late grandfather of the medium.[13] "The character of this personality," Jung commented, "was distinguished by a dry and tedious solemnity, rigorous conventionality, and sanctimonious piety (which does not accord at all with the historical reality)."[14] Among the other spirits who put in an appearance was one with the rather ostentatious-sounding name, Ulrich von Gerbenstein, who eventually threatened the integrity of the séances with his trivialities and flattery of the ladies present.[15] He was, as Jung described him, "a gossip, a wag, and an idler, a great admirer of the ladies, frivolous and extremely superficial."[16]

A much more serious personality also emerged who was named Ivenes and described as "a small but fully grown black-haired woman, of a markedly Jewish type, clothed in white garments, her head wrapped in a turban."[17] In sharp contrast to von Gerbenstein, she revealed herself to be "a serious, mature person, devout and right-minded, full of womanly tenderness and very modest, who always submits to the opinion of others."[18] At the same time Jung's medium made some rather extravagant claims on behalf of Ivenes about former lives she had lived: as various celebrated mediums, a woman seduced by Goethe, and other individuals as far back in time as the biblical King David.[19] Entangled with these previous incarnations were the former lives of those present at the séances, all woven together in a complex genealogy of family romances that amounted to a veritable *chronique scandaleuse,* complete with seductions, murders, and crimes of all kinds.[20]

Jung, in his dissertation, went on to state that after the family romances, in March 1900, a final revelation was received by the medium from the spirit world. He recorded this revelation in a chart showing how the cosmic forces were arranged in a configuration of seven circles. The medium added more inner and outer circles to this basic design and claimed they represented stages between matter and force with the primary force residing at the very center of the entire system. To each circle she gave a high-flown latinized name to which she added a history of how the primary force coupled with matter and gave birth to other spiritual forces.[21]

Jung stated that the most significant séances came to an end with the production of the medium's cosmological system.[22] Following this the sittings became stale and repetitious. Jung suspected that the medium was contriving her material and he soon withdrew. Six months later she was, apparently, caught cheating and accused of having hidden objects under her garments which she tossed into the air during the semidarkness of the séances. This discovery brought her career as a medium to an abrupt end. Subsequent reports, according to Jung, indicated that the girl did not engage in any further spiritualistic activities and showed no marked indications of abnormality.[23] In fact she developed a maturity of personality that allowed her to pursue a career in a large business.[24]

In his analysis of the case Jung pointed out that the myriad of spirits which appeared soon after the onset of the séances could be divided into two types: the "serio-religious" and the "gay-hilarious."[25] These spirits, he argued, are really two different subconscious personalities under the guise of a multiplicity of names.[26] Jung claimed that the spirits were modeled on significant persons with whom the medium had been emotionally and psychologically linked earlier in her life. He interpreted these spirits to be the medium's subconscious personalities which originated in repressed thoughts and feelings connected with persons she knew but that now began to lead independent existences of their own.[27] Of this Jung stated:

> The individualization of the subconscious is always a great step forward and has enormous suggestive influence on further development of the automatisms. The formation of unconscious personalities in our case must also be regarded in this light.[28]

Jung considered even more important the emergence of the figure named Ivenes. He identified Ivenes as the medium's secondary personality and called this spirit her "higher ego."[29] He was careful to add that this second personality should be distinguished from the pathological phenomena of multiple personality, and of this distinction he stated:

> Just as Ivenes is a continuation of the waking ego, so she carries over her whole conscious content into the waking state. This remarkable behaviour argues strongly against any analogy with cases of double consciousness.[30]

And as for the innumerable family romances, Jung concluded:

> We shall not be wrong if we seek the main cause of this curious clinical picture in her budding sexuality. From this

point of view the whole essence of Ivenes and her enormous family is nothing but a dream of sexual wish-fulfillment, which differs from the dream of a night only in that it is spread over months and years.[31]

At the same time Jung pointed out that Ivenes, understood psychologically as the medium's second personality, demonstrated the teleological nature of unconscious processes:

> The patient pours her own soul into the role of the Clair-voyante, seeking to create out of it an ideal of virtue and perfection; she anticipates her own future and embodies in Ivenes what she wishes to be in twenty years' time—the assured, influential, wise, gracious, pious lady.... the patient builds up a personality beyond herself. One cannot say that she deludes herself into the higher ideal state, rather she dreams herself into it.[32]

Jung concluded his analysis with some remarks on what he termed "heightened unconscious performance" or what might now be called the paranormal:

> As we know, occultism has claimed a special right to this field and has drawn premature conclusions from dubious observations. We are still very far indeed from being able to say anything conclusive, for up to the present our material is nothing like adequate....
> But in our case...there is no choice but to assume for the present a receptivity of the unconscious far exceeding that of the conscious mind.[33]

It is quite evident from this brief summary that several of Jung's later ideas are anticipated in *On the Psychology and Pathology of So-Called Occult Phenomena.* Chief among these is his theory of archetypes and what he called the "process of individuation." Nevertheless, the fact remains that the dissertation is largely a descriptive work and the reader is given very little indication of the degree to which Jung was personally involved in what he wrote. This stance is maintained whenever he referred to the work, from the early account of its contents in a seminar in 1925 to the summary he provided in his autobiography shortly before his death, in 1961.[34] If we inquire into the background of Jung's dissertation, the extent to which Jung was implicated in the material he subjected to a psychiatric analysis and the reasons why he was reluctant to publicly disclose this fact becomes very clear.

In chapter 2, I have already documented that several members of the maternal side of Jung's family had experienced phenomena of a spiritualistic nature. These events seem to have formed an important part of Jung's early background and to have had a noticeable effect upon him. In light of this, it is quite significant that the medium of Jung's dissertation, so-called S.W., was in fact his cousin Helene (Helly) Preiswerk, the daughter of his mother's brother. Though she was six years younger than Jung, she was, nevertheless, a childhood playmate.[35] Since Jung did not get to know any girls apart from his cousins until he was sixteen, we can assume that they may have been close.[36] Jung speculated that Helly's ability to fall into trance states may have been inherited from their mutual grandmother, Augusta Faber, to whom, as we have already seen, he traced his own eldest daughter's gift of "second sight."[37]

Jung kept a detailed diary of the séances he conducted with Helly. In his dissertation he stated that his medium cousin "was under my observation during the years 1899 and 1900."[38] The dates Jung offered presents certain problems. In fact, he seems to have altered the dates to disguise the participants, because it now appears that he was experimenting with Helly as early as 1895.[39] And five years prior, in 1890, it is reported that he had conversations on the subject of Spiritualism with his mother and Helly's sister.[40]

Indeed, it appears that it was Jung who had studied the method of "table-turning" and who decided to experiment seriously one evening in June 1895. Jung, his mother, and three of his cousins, including Helly, were present. They gathered around a table, placing a glass of water in the middle, and joined hands. The glass began to shake and the table to move. "We have an excellent medium among us," Jung is said to have remarked.[41] Helly went pale and broke the chain sinking back into her chair.[42] Such was the beginning of the séances.

The table Jung and the others gathered around later mysteriously cracked and a knife also shattered. These objects Jung's mother had inherited from her father, Samuel Preiswerk, the peculiar Basel clergyman who was given to ghostly visions and who was the grandfather of both Jung and Helly. Jung connected these two incidents with his young cousin, the medium. He stated that in the summer of 1898, while in the house with his mother and sister:

Suddenly there sounded a report like a pistol shot. I
jumped up and rushed into the room.... My mother...stam-
mered out "W-w-what's happened? It was right beside me!"
and stared at the table.... The table top had split from the
rim to beyond the center, and not along any joint; the split
ran right through the solid wood. I was thunderstruck.
How could such a thing happen? A table of solid walnut
that had dried out for seventy years—how could it split on
a summer day in the relatively high degree of humidity
characteristic of our climate?[43]

Two weeks later a similar incident occurred, only this time it
was a large bread knife that shattered. The following day, Jung
took the knife to a cutler and was told that the only way it could
have been broken in such a manner was if someone had done so
deliberately.[44] Jung kept the knife and later had it mounted.[45] In a
letter (November 27, 1934) to the well known parapsychologist, J.
B. Rhine, Jung claimed that his medium cousin had not been near
the house at the time, but that soon after, the séances began. He
also added:

She told me that she had vividly thought of these séances
just in those days when the explosions occurred. She could
produce quite noticeable raps in pieces of furniture and in
the walls. Some of those raps also happened during her
absence at a distance of about 4 km.[46]

It is difficult to ascertain the accuracy of Jung's dates and
some of the details. For instance, in his letter to Rhine, he reversed
the order of the explosions, claimed that the table was ninety years
old, and stated that he had nothing to do with the medium prior to
1898.[47] And, in his autobiography, he seems to be deliberately trying to give the impression that there was no connection between
Helly, his family, and himself by describing the entire matter in
"scientific" and "objective" language. However, what is now clear is
that the séances were a family affair which were attended by
Jung's relatives who, with the exception of Jung himself and possibly another young man, were all female.[48]

The control spirit who manifested in the séances was none
other than grandfather Samuel Preiswerk, who had once owned
both table and knife which had cracked and shattered.[49] The
séances, it now appears were conducted intermittently between the

years 1895 and 1899.[50] The parapsychological phenomena connected with them were, among others, precognitive dreams, spontaneous psycho-kinesis, xenoglossia, and, of course, trance states.[51]

Admitting publicly all of these facts may have proven to be too incriminating for Jung to have revealed them. Yet, there is a further dimension to the séances which is of interest in filling out the background and setting of Jung's dissertation and which may explain his concern to disguise certain facts. As I previously mentioned, Jung's paternal grandfather, C. G. Jung, while serving as a role model for him, may not have possessed quite so distinguished a status as Jung tried to portray. The dominant and undoubtedly more important side of the family was the Preiswerks. They were an old and distinguished Basel family of considerable number and significance.[52] It would appear that they took charge of Jung, his mother, and sister after the Reverend Paul Jung's death and were largely responsible for housing them and financing Jung's education.[53] Jung's reaction to the Preiswerk side of the family suggests he resented the authority and control they exercised over his life. The stories he heard in his youth may have revolved more around the Preiswerk ancestors than the Jungs. Jung seems to have become so disturbed by the influence and status of the Preiswerks that this may have played a part in his having believed Goethe was his paternal great-grandfather.[54]

The Preiswerk family appears to have been somewhat patronizing toward Jung and kept a close watch on his activities. One of his maternal uncles, hearing of the séances, had them stopped in 1897 as he was preparing Helly for confirmation that spring.[55] Jung resented this interruption and in the fall he insisted they continue. Jung, his mother, and the other participants had to conduct the séances in semisecrecy.[56] In addition, the influence Jung had over Helly seems to have disturbed some of the Preiswerks. This is evident in the negative reactions to Jung by Helly's mother and brother.[57] They suspected Helly had fallen in love with Jung and complained to Jung's mother. She defended her son's activities by stating that her father, Samuel Preiswerk, had dealings with spirits as well.[58] An uncle who was the senior family authority intervened and Helly was sent to France in October 1899. Her departure brought the séances to an abrupt end.[59]

The tragic fact which Jung claimed he only realized later, was that Helly fell in love with him.[60] The situation was impossible because they were first cousins. Perhaps because of this Jung seemed uncertain of how to respond and after the séances ended he withdrew into himself.[61] In October 1902, Jung visited Paris and contacted Helly. They met often and spoke briefly about the séances.[62] In the meantime, Jung had established a relationship with Emma Rauschenbach and married her in 1903. Shortly afterwards, in 1905, Jung had Helly make a dress for her.[63] Years later, after his wife's death, he had a dream she was wearing this same dress. Jung felt, "It was perhaps the most beautiful thing she had ever worn."[64] Helly never married. One proposal which came her way after she opened her own dressmaking shop in Basel, in the fall of 1903, was quickly withdrawn after her suitor read Jung's dissertation. He was apparently afraid Helly would bear him mentally defective children.[65]

In 1904, Jung's dissertation came to the attention of the senior members of the Preiswerk family. Predictably, they were extremely upset by what they found. They had not realized the actual extent of Helly's involvement in the séances. In particular, they were horrified over the sexual nature of Helly's communications and regret was expressed by everyone that they had financed Jung's education.[66] From then on a certain family taboo was placed on the subject of Helly and Jung.[67] Perhaps this is why Jung remarked that he felt the atmosphere of Basel to be somewhat suffocating.[68] However, it would appear that his own feelings for Helly were not entirely resolved, even after his marriage.[69]

Years later Jung claimed Helly died at the age of twenty-six and that shortly before her death her personality had disintegrated and ultimately returned to the state of a two-year-old child.[70] According to other of her relatives, Helly's personality did not deteriorate as Jung stated, and she died on November 13, 1911 of tuberculosis. She was buried two days later on what would have been her thirtieth birthday.[71] At the time of Helene Preiswerk's death Jung had four children. The next child he fathered was a girl (b. 1914) and she was named Helene.[72]

If we turn to the actual contents of Jung's dissertation we can see that he focused his interest on those unusual states of mind which are found in the mesmeric trance, in hypnotism, and in Spiritualism. For his interpretation of these phenomena Jung largely depended on certain prevalent nineteenth-century psychiatric theories of multiple personality and its accompanying disorder, which I reviewed in chapter 1. In particular, there is the obvious influence of Flournoy's work *Des Indes à la Planète Mars* (1900), though Jung did not subject his material to the same detailed examination. He did, however, draw the same conclusion and appears to be indebted to Flournoy for pointing the way. Flournoy concluded his study of the medium Helene Smith by interpreting the spirits with whom she was in communication, as subconscious personality complexes. Helly's personalities, Jung observed, demonstrated an independence and, at times, were taken as evidence of the teleological nature of psychological processes. We can see in this interpretation the seeds of Jung's later thinking about archetypes and their existence independent of the conscious mind.[73] From these general observations Jung pleaded for a more objective examination of individuals such as his cousin, the medium, who experienced such states. But equally important is Jung's personal involvement with Helly, which must have resulted in a certain identification of one with the other so that it may be no exaggeration at all to see certain signs of self-analysis at work in his dissertation.

We can see, beginning in Jung's own early life, that he had a predilection for unusual and paranormal experiences. Marie-Louise von Franz, a close friend and pupil of Jung, has remarked of him later in life: "Jung had to an extraordinary degree the gift of empathy, almost to the point of being mediumistic."[74] G. R. Hayer, another of Jung's pupils, concurs, likening his analytical technique to that of a medium. Hayer has stated of Jung that he had a "power of perception that could often be called mediumistic."[75] And of his method of dream interpretation, Hayer added:

> What appears after such interpretations to be logically arrived-at certainty (and which he readily offered as 'substantiation' in such cases) was at bottom frequently the result of such a highly intuitive inspiration that one cannot help calling it 'mediumistic.'[76]

In chapter 2, I pointed out that Jung understood his later ideas as linked by a chain of meaning to the unusual and bizarre experiences of his childhood. In his autobiography he noted of these experiences:

> I can only make direct statements, only "tell stories." Whether or not the stories are "true" is not the problem. The only question is whether what I tell is *my* fable, *my* truth.[77]

By way of comparison, the following is what Jung wrote of his cousin:

> Her whole development into a somnambulist, her innumer-
> able weird experiences, seemed to her entirely natural. She
> saw her whole past only in this light. Every in any way
> striking event from her earlier years stood in a clear and
> necessary relationship to her present situation.... She once
> said: "I do not know if what the spirits say and teach me is
> true, nor do I know if they really are the people they call
> themselves; but that my spirits exist is beyond question."[78]

In the light of Jung's later life and his attempt to seek connections
between his early experiences and his later work, the first of these
statements about his cousin may be easily applied to Jung himself.
The second is equally apposite in the light of his notion of "psychic
reality" and his later experiences.[79] But at this stage in his life it is
perhaps the personality traits and characteristics of his cousin that
stand out as being most similar to his own.

Jung claimed that Helly was painfully aware of the difference
between her nocturnal world and the crude reality of day, that she
led a double life with two personalities existing side by side.[80] It is
in this respect that Helly was most like her cousin Carl who, too,
experienced a gulf that separated his dream world from everyday
reality. This division can be clearly seen in Jung's No. 1 and No. 2
personalities.

In chapter 2, I indicated the problematic relationship between
Jung's parents and suggested that this was one of the causes for the
split Jung experienced in himself. Helly's parents were equally disturbed. Jung recorded that her father was an oddly original man
with bizarre ideas. Her mother, he stated, had "a congenital psychopathic inferiority often bordering on psychosis."[81] Furthermore,
Helly, like Jung, lost her father: she in September 1895 and he in
January 1896—the period that marks the beginning of the séances.[82]

In addition to her revelations of the spirit world, which were
largely taken up with run-of-the-mill spiritual advice, family
romances, and gossip, Helly added the notion of reincarnation and
expanded her already developed repertoire of characters. At one
point, she claimed to have been seduced by Goethe, an association
we can readily see as an attempt to identify herself with Jung's
great-grandmother, and thereby with Jung himself.[83] She also
claimed to be Jung's maternal grandmother, Augusta Faber, of
spiritualistic fame, and the wife of Samuel Preiswerk, hers and
Jung's grandfather. She added as well a complex genealogy that
extended further back, linking one incarnation with another in

almost karmic fashion and in which Jung, in his alleged former incarnations, figured prominently.[84]

In these "romances" there are two elements that stand out: (1) Helly appears to have shared with her cousin Carl the same inclination toward mythologizing the burdens of inheritance that we have seen in Jung's own concerns to identify with his grandfather and with Goethe and (2) she tried to rationalize the feelings of love and affection that were passing between herself and Jung by way of the "romances" she revealed in the séances. William Goodheart, one of the few analysts who have examined Jung's dissertation, claims that in these family mythologies and romances:

> Jung and Helly could play out their affection, their flirtation,...free from risk, free from living contact with each other, free from the agonies of interpersonal reality.[85]

He added that Jung's interpretation of these *histoires de famille* was, to some extent:

> born out of severe conflict both as an adaptively coping compromise and an isolating intellectual construction against the truths of an interpersonal reality which were sternly forbidden to his consciousness by the harsh repressiveness of the social-professional collective and its internalization and reinforcement within Jung's psyche.[86]

It is equally as likely that if the burdens of Jung's and Helly's inheritance came to the fore as the result of the conflicting emotions in their relationship, they may well have been set up for it by their own experience of the unresolved emotional conflict in the lives of their parents. Jung's father was unsuccessful in trying to resolve this conflict on some transpersonal level. Jung, for his part, would seem to have felt he accomplished what his father had failed to, by establishing the reality of the transpersonal dimensions of the psyche. He would later argue that this was indeed possible only because these transpersonal dimensions informed and supported the more personal and more transitory realities of an individual's life.[87]

In contrast to Jung's *Zofingia Lectures,* what is missing from his dissertation is the personal involvement with his material that is so evident when his earlier sympathy for Spiritualism was scarcely disguised. It is as though Jung's relationship with his cousin, that was impossible to live out in reality, the undercurrents

of which surfaced in the incestuous family romances, finally drove
a wedge between him and his family. As a result Jung seems to
have distanced himself from his personal involvement in his data
by internalising it, then subjecting it to a psychological analysis. Of
this he himself wrote:

> All in all, this was the one great experience which wiped
> out all my earlier philosophy and made it possible for me to
> achieve a psychological point of view. I had discovered some
> objective facts about the human psyche. Yet the nature of
> the experience was such that once again I was unable to
> speak of it. I knew no one to whom I could have told the
> whole story. Once more I had to lay aside an unfinished
> problem.[88]

On the whole, Jung's years as a medical student form a continuum with his past with regard to spiritualistic phenomena and
the family entanglements this involved. Jung left Basel and
assumed his position as an assistant at the Burghölzli mental hospital on December 10, 1900. In his dissertation, published in 1902,
he attempted to remove spiritualistic phenomena from the rather
confining and limited context of his family situation and provide a
more general and, he felt, critical basis from which he could eventually examine his own intimidating early experiences. In a sense
he had freed himself from his conflict, though he kept his own No. 2
personality alive by writing in his secret diary until he became
engaged to the wealthy Emma Rauschenbach in 1903.[89] This
engagement led him into marriage, financial security, and to establish a family of his own. He had, he thought, closed the door on his
early life.

Jung's *Zofingia Lectures* and the séances he conducted with
his cousin are events in his life which occurred simultaneously.
Together they reveal Jung's intense personal involvement with
Spiritualism and his attempts to intellectually come to terms with
this involvement. He turned at first to the philosophies of Kant and
Schopenhauer and then to psychiatric theory to find a basis upon
which to build an understanding of Spiritualism.

On a personal level Jung was driven to seek such an understanding because of his own unusual experiences. The division
these experiences caused in himself, and the resulting conflict,
became exceedingly threatening. Jung could not find security in
formal religion, because he had observed how Christianity had

failed his father. At first he looked to Spiritualism and felt this would provide him a solution by offering him a unified view of the world and thereby bringing together the divided parts of himself.

When, as a student, Jung encountered Kant and Schopenhauer, he realized the problematical nature of the spiritualistic position. As Kant did before him, and under the influence of Schopenhauer, Jung turned to a more psychological mode of understanding. Under the influence of Kant, Jung became aware that the division he sensed within himself was reflected in the Kantian distinction between phenomena and noumena. The problem of reconciling this division he at first disappointedly accepted as unsolvable. Yet, Schopenhauer speculated that it might be possible that these would come together in the embodied soul. Jung seems to have taken this view to heart and sought the proof of this theory in spiritualistic experiences. He also became aware, as Kant did before him, that experiences of this nature can also be pathological.

In psychiatry, Jung found descriptions of pathological disorders that were similar to spiritualistic experiences. Nevertheless, in his dissertation he tried to separate the pathology of Spiritualism from its other characteristics. He argued that these characteristics are indicative of an organized, purposive intentionality within the unconscious. Though he claimed to have retained the Kantian epistemology he received via Schopenhauer by reducing Spiritualism to psychology, he distinguished between its pathological and therapeutic characteristics. That these therapeutic characteristics suggested a consciousness independent of an ego, Jung took for granted. Whether he believed such a consciousness could ultimately originate in a disembodied state, he was not prepared to say.

Notes

1. Ellenberger, *Discovery,* 285–88.

2. Jaffé, *Word and Image,* 29.

3. Brome, 81.

4. Ellenberger, *Discovery,* 687.

5. C. G. Jung, "On the Psychology of the Unconscious" (1917 rev. ed. 1943), in *Two Essays on Analytical Psychology,* 118.

6. Jung, *On the Psychology and Pathology of So-Called Occult Phenomena,* (1902), 3–4.

7. Ibid., 16.

8. Ibid., 17.

9. Ibid.

10. Ibid., 18.

11. Ibid., 19.

12. Ibid., 19–20.

13. Ibid., 22, 28, 30.

14. Ibid., 31.

15. Ibid., 32.

16. Ibid.

17. Ibid., 33.

18. Ibid., 36.

19. Ibid., 36–37.

20. Ibid., 38–39.

21. Ibid., 39–42. Jung pointed out the possible influence of Immanuel Kant's *Universal Natural History and Theory of the Heavens* (1755), which he had discussed in her presence. It is interesting to note that the third part of this work is concerned with "the inhabitants of the stars." See Kant, *Universal Natural History and Theory of the Heavens*, 183–96.

22. Jung, *On the Psychology and Pathology of So-Called Occult Phenomena*, 43.

23. Ibid.

24. Ibid.

25. Ibid., 72–73.

26. Ibid., 73.

27. Ibid., 77–78.

28. Ibid., 53–54.

29. Ibid., 64.

30. Ibid., 65.

31. Ibid., 70.

32. Ibid., 66.

33. Ibid., 80.

34. Jung, *Analytical Psychology*, 3–6; *MDR*, 106–07.

35. Zumstein-Preiswerk, 13.

36. *MDR*, 76–80.

37. Jung, *On the Psychology and Pathology of So-Called Occult Phenomena*, 17, 70; *MDR*, 232.

38. Jung, *On the Psychology and Pathology of So-Called Occult Phenomena*, 17.

39. Zumstein-Preiswerk, 7.

40. Ibid., 35–36.

41. Ibid., 53.

42. Ibid.

43. *MDR*, 105.

44. Ibid., 105–6.

45. Jaffé, *From the Life and Work of Jung*, 123, where the author, Jung's secretary, states that Jung instructed her to mount the knife in the autumn of 1955; Jaffé, *Word and Image*, 32, reproduces a picture of the knife.

46. Jung, *Letters 1: 1905–1950*, 182.

47. Ibid., 181.

48. Jung, *On the Psychology and Pathology of So-Called Occult Phenomena*, 37, mentioned a man who often took part in the séances. Zumstein-Preiswerk, 85, claims Jung was the only male present at the séances and that the other young man did not really participate.

49. Zumstein-Preiswerk, 80.

50. Ibid., 53, 93. This chronology of the séances has now been accepted by most of Jung's followers, as I indicated in my discussion of the subject in the introduction.

51. James Hillman, "Some Early Background to Jung's Ideas: Notes on *C. G.Jung's Medium* by Stephanie Zumstein-Preiswerk," 127.

52. Zumstein-Preiswerk, 48–49.

53. Zumstein-Preiswerk, 62–63, points out that the Bottminger Mill the Jung family moved into after Paul Jung's death was provided by Eduard Preiswerk, Carl Jung's maternal uncle. In *MDR*, 97, Jung remarked negatively about his maternal relatives and claimed a paternal uncle loaned him money for his education. Zumstein-Preiswerk, 125 n. 61, claims that Jung received the money for his education from his maternal uncle, Eduard Preiswerk, and states that of Jung's four paternal uncles: one was not wealthy, two were dead, and the fourth was of uncertain character and had emigrated to America!

54. Zumstein-Preiswerk, 48–49.

55. Ibid., 64.

56. Ibid., 74.

57. Ibid., 37, 52.

58. Ibid., 90–91.

59. Ibid., 92, 95.

60. Jung, *Analytical Psychology*, 5, where he reported in 1925: "I know now that I overlooked the most important feature of the situation, namely my connection with it. The girl had of course fallen deeply in love with me, and of this I was fairly ignorant and quite ignorant of the part it played in her psychology."

61. Zumstein-Preiswerk, 99.

62. Ibid., 100, 102. Little is known of this period in Jung's life. He spent the winter semester of 1902–3 at the Salpêtrière with Pierre Janet, but apparently much of his time was taken up sightseeing; see Ellenberger, *Discovery*, 667–68.

63. Zumstein-Preiswerk, 106.

64. *MDR*, 296.

65. Zumstein-Preiswerk, 95–96, 104–5.

66. Ibid., 105–6.

67. Ibid., 13.

68. Charles Baudouin, *L'Oeuvre de jung*, (Paris: Payot, 1963), 23; *MDR*, 111; Hannah, 40 n.a.

69. I will return to this subject in the following chapter.

70. *MDR*, 107.

71. Zumstein-Preiswerk, 13, 101, 107.

72. Jaffé, *Word and Image*, 132–33.

73. See C. G. Jung, *Collected Works*, vol. 9i, *The Archetypes and the Collective Unconscious*, 2nd. ed. (Princeton, N.J.: Princeton University Press, 1969); and *Aion*. I will return to Jung's concept of archetype in chapter 8.

74. Von Franz, *C. G. Jung: His Myth in Our Time*, 19.

75. Wehr, 8, citing Gustav R. Hayer, "C. G. Jung: Ein Lebensbild," in *Aus meiner Werkstatt* (Munich, 1966), 166.

76. Wehr, 8, citing Hayer, 171 et seq.

77. *MDR*, 3.

78. Jung, *On the Psychology and Pathology of So-Called Occult Phenomena*, 23.

79. In his "Terry Lectures" (1937) Jung stated: "[An] idea is psychologically true inasmuch as it exists. Psychological existence is subjective in so far as an idea occurs in only one individual. But it is objective in so far as that idea is shared by a society...." in Jung, *Psychology and Religion*, 6.

80. Jung, *On the Psychology and Pathology of So-Called Occult Phenomena*, 24 et seq.

81. Ibid., 17.

82. Zumstein-Preiswerk, 57; Wehr, 57.

83. Jung, *On the Psychology and Pathology of So-Called Occult Phenomena*, 37.

84. Ibid., 36 et seq.

85. Goodheart, 14.

86. Ibid.

87. I will address this subject in the concluding chapter.

88. *MDR*, 107. J. Marvin Spiegelman in his "Psychology and the Occult," *Spring* (1976):107, has remarked on the move toward the "impersonal" in Jung's dissertation: "...I think the girl had fallen in love with Jung, and he seemed to have missed the personal connection with her. This is understandable for the young, scientific Jung, but gives us a hint as to what is ailing in the whole field of investigation of the occult. I see this as a lack of unification of the personal and the impersonal. Jung here lacked the knowledge and feeling to make a more adequate personal con-

nection with the medium, which he would have done as a psychotherapist later on. He was too scientific and impersonal. And the medium failed to be aware that her voices were personal. She was also too 'impersonal', but in a different way. Neither, of course, took up the problem of making a relationship with these voices or spirits, which the later Jung was to make the core of his life's work."

89. Jaffé, *Word and Image*, 26.

Part 3

The Psychoanalytic Years

Chapter 6

Jung, Freud, and the Conflict over Spiritualistic Phenomena

At the turn of the century Jung found himself housed along with other staff and patients in the Burghölzli mental hospital.[1] Affiliated with the University of Zurich, the Burghölzli admitted about two hundred patients per year, attended by a staff of four physicians and seventy-six nurses. Most of the patients were acute but prognostically hopeful cases.[2] The emphasis, therefore, was on treatment with a view toward eventual discharge. Under the direction of Eugene Bleuler the staff was encouraged to maintain close observation of the patients as part of the therapy.[3] Because of this and the fact that the Burghölzli was a university clinic, research and new forms of treatment were emphasized. As a consequence, Jung buried himself in psychiatric literature and kept abreast of current investigations. This stimulated him to conduct psychiatric studies of his patients and attempt the application of new theories of treatment.[4]

From 1902 to 1906 Jung investigated three areas, in particular: hysteria, word association, and dementia praecox (later known as schizophrenia).[5] He had brought definite ideas about psychology with him to the Burghölzli. His dissertation had demonstrated that the human soul could be scientifically studied and that split-off portions of the unconscious could form personalities that were not only pathological but personalities that could also be therapeutic.[6] In hysteria Jung now noted that the symptoms indicated one powerful unconscious complex related to an earlier psychological injury that could be cured if the patient would face this and assimilate its contents.[7] In his word association studies Jung was able to isolate more accurately the factors that formed complexes whether they were normal, accidental, or permanent.[8] In addition, his study of dementia praecox revealed that one or more of the fixed complexes could no longer be integrated into consciousness.[9]

On the more theoretical side Jung, at first, depended largely on Pierre Janet and Theodore Flournoy both of whom had investigated spiritualistic phenomena.[10] In 1902–03 Jung went to study under Janet, who taught at the Salpêtrière, in Paris.[11] He referred to Janet's theory of dissociation, but Janet's direct influence upon him does not extend much beyond 1907, though it may have contributed to Jung's break from Freud.[12] In his word association studies Jung identified the split-off portions of the unconscious, such as he had uncovered in his dissertation, with Ziehen's "emotionally loaded representation complexes."[13] Jung also thought he encountered similar phenomena in Freud's "traumatic reminiscences."[14]

In addition to these more scientific preoccupations Jung maintained an interest in Spiritualism. At Basel, in 1905, he delivered a lecture on spiritualistic phenomena which was published in the newspaper *Basler Nachrichten.*[15] In this lecture Jung remarked:

> The dual nature of spiritualism gives it an advantage over other religious movements: not only does it believe in certain articles of faith that are not susceptible of proof, but it bases its belief on a body of allegedly scientific, physical phenomena which are supposed to be of such a nature that they cannot be explained except by the activity of spirits. Because of its dual nature—on the one side a religious sect, on the other a scientific hypothesis—spiritualism touches upon widely differing areas of life that would seem to have nothing in common.[16]

In the same lecture he also outlined the theory of magnetism, the rise of Spiritualism, and the accompanying phenomena with which these movements were associated. He remarked on Schopenhauer's interest in Spiritualism as well as Swedenborg's "considerable influence on Kant."[17] Jung went on to inform his listeners that his interest in these phenomena was purely psychological, and for that reason he had kept "track of persons who are gifted as mediums."[18] Specifically, he investigated eight mediums who were accessible to him in Zurich, two of whom were clairvoyant.[19]

One of these investigations consisted of almost thirty sittings and was carried out over a period of six months.[20] Of these sittings Jung stated:

> The results are of purely psychological interest, and no physical or physiological novelties came to light. Every-

thing that may be considered a scientifically established fact belongs to the domain of the mental and cerebral processes and is fully explicable in terms of the laws already known to science.

All phenomena which the spiritualists claim as evidence of the activity of spirits are connected with the presence of certain persons, the mediums themselves. I was never able to observe happenings alleged to be "spiritual" in places or on occasions when no medium was present.[21]

He then compared mediums to hysterics and argued that there are autonomous unconscious processes which govern the medium's physical movements, producing such phenomena as table turning.[22] As far as the so-called clairvoyant abilities of the mediums, he claimed, "nothing that quite unquestionably exceeded the normal psychological capacities was observed."[23] While he was able to assure his listeners that there was nothing supernatural about the mediums studied, he also cautioned:

On the other hand, any unprejudiced investigator will readily admit that we do not stand today on the pinnacle of all wisdom, and that nature still has infinite possibilities up her sleeve which may be revealed in happier days to come....

So far as the miraculous reports in the literature are concerned, we should, for all our criticism, never lose sight of the limitations of our knowledge, otherwise something embarrassingly human might happen.[24]

This caution was also evident in Jung's dissertation, as I have pointed out. However, Jung, at this stage in his life, was prepared to side publicly with science, and in rather uncharacteristic enthusiasm for the experimental scientific method he concluded:

Nevertheless I believe that the present state of affairs gives us reason enough to wait quietly until more impressive physical phenomena put in an appearance. If, after making allowance for conscious and unconscious falsification, self-deception, prejudice, etc., we should still find something positive behind them, then the exact sciences will surely conquer this field by experiment and verification, as has happened in every other realm of human experience. That many spiritualists brag about their "science" and "scientific knowledge" is, of course, irritating nonsense. These people are lacking not only in criticism but in the most elementary knowledge of psychology. At bottom they do not want to be taught any better, but merely to go on believing—surely the naïvest of presumptions in view of our human failings.[25]

Jung's interest in mediums had the support of his chief, Bleuler. With his help Jung "set up a kind of laboratory for parapsychology in the Psychiatric Clinic at Burghölzli in 1904/5."[26] During this period Bleuler often attended séances with Jung.[27] It is evident that Jung's interest in spiritualistic phenomena had not subsided. He seems to have maintained this interest, though he sought to understand and explain such phenomena in purely psychological terms. This tendency first became manifest in Jung's dissertation and was reinforced by his studies in hysteria, word association, and dementia praecox. By identifying with an exclusively psychological position, Jung also prepared himself for his encounter with Freud. It is the role that their different interpretations of spiritualistic phenomena played in this encounter and final breakup that will highlight this chapter.

Jung first encountered Freud in the latter's German translation of Bernheim's *De la suggestion et de ses applications à la thérapeutique*, which appeared in 1888. Freud had written a lengthy preface to his translation recapitulating the controversy between the Nancy and Salpêtrière schools I outlined in chapter 1.[28] Jung recalled that his father read this work, and he may have read it himself when he was a student.[29] In 1901, at the request of Eugene Bleuler, Jung presented a summary of Freud's *On Dreams* (1901) to the staff of the Burghölzli.[30] The significance of this report, as Robert Steele has pointed out, is that it fails to explicitly mention Freud's central thesis that it is repressed infantile sexual wishes that are the cause of most dreams.[31] In *On the Psychology and Pathology of So-Called Occult Phenomena* (1902), Jung quoted Freud four times in passing and a few times in articles written from 1902 to 1905.[32] In his foreword to *The Psychology of Dementia Praecox* (1907), it is evident that Jung was aware of Freud's theory of sexuality, but he was unwilling to subscribe to it completely.[33] Apart from the occasional faltering and lack of clarity in the public presentation of his ideas, Jung would not markedly alter this position vis-à-vis Freud.[34] In March 1907, Jung visited Freud in Vienna and thereby sealed a friendship that had begun a year earlier when Jung sent him *Diagnostic Association Studies* (1906).[35]

When Freud and Jung met in Vienna in the late winter of 1907 they spoke for several hours.[36] Jung also attended the Wednesday meeting of the Vienna Society, where Freud read a draft of "Obsessive Actions and Religious Practices."[37] This was Freud's first incursion into the psychology of religion and set the stage for his later works on the subject.[38] The thrust of this lecture was, in Freud's words:

> to regard obsessional neurosis as a pathological counter-part of the formation of a religion, and to describe that neu-rosis as an individual religiosity and religion as a universal obsessional neurosis.[39]

Jung must have found Freud's point of view somewhat disturbing. In his first letter (March 31, 1907) to Freud after returning to Zurich he wrote: "Up till now I had a strong resistance to writing because until recently the complexes aroused in Vienna were still in an uproar."[40] At the end of the same letter Jung appears to have temporarily capitulated to Freud's theory of sexuality. He wrote: "I am no longer plagued by doubts as to the rightness of your theory. The last shreds were dispelled by my stay in Vienna."[41]

Jung later recalled of their first meeting that he was respect-ful of Freud's experience and stated, "What he said about his sex-ual theory impressed me."[42] But, he added:

> Above all, Freud's attitude toward the spirit seemed to me highly questionable. Whenever...an expression of spiritual-ity...came to light, he suspected it, and insinuated that it was repressed sexuality....
>
> I had a strong intuition that for him sexuality was a sort of *numinosum.*[43]

On the surface it appeared that Jung had now gained the nec-essary psychiatric knowledge and clinical experience to put his ear-lier spiritualistic experiences into some sort of perspective. I focused on the interpersonal relationship between Jung and his cousin the medium in the previous chapter, and I pointed out that the element of unlived or repressed sexuality seemed to have been an important factor in Jung's psychological interpretation. In Freud, Jung now encountered an emerging psychology that was dynamic and took human sexuality very seriously. As a conse-quence it must have offered Jung an insight into his own difficulties. In addition, Freud's personality made a great impression on him. "Freud was," Jung remarked later in life, "the first man of real importance I had encountered."[44] Nevertheless, while echoes of Freud's sexual theory occur here and there in Jung's writings during this period, though he tried, he was unable to accept the theory as a whole.[45] If Jung was impressed with Freud and his psychoanalytic theories, he would also press him to modify these theories in the light of spiritualistic phenomena.

For his part, Freud was reluctant to seriously consider any such modifications. His concerns and resistances can be seen in his response to Jung's interest in spiritualistic phenomena. They are as well part of a concerted attempt to exercise the strictest control over his own imaginative inclinations.[46] Jones has furnished examples of Freud's superstitiousness which began as a young man and persisted through his life.[47] The following is an instance Freud himself gives in "Gradiva" (1907), a work he wrote apparently to please Jung:

> It must be remembered...that the belief in spirits and ghosts and the return of the dead,...is far from having disappeared among educated people, and that many who are sensible in other repects find it possible to combine spiritualism with reason. A man who has grown rational and skeptical...may for a moment return to a belief in spirits under the combined impact of strong emotion and perplexity.[48]

Freud clearly associated belief in spirits with a confused state in which reason had temporarily abated. This obviously implies that reason and Spiritualism cannot coexist without one taking an inferior position to the other. In the same work Freud went on to describe a doctor who saw a dead patient come into his consulting room. The doctor responded, according to Freud, "So after all it's true that the dead can come back to life."[49] It turned out that the person who had entered the room was the dead person's sister; the doctor was Freud himself. He concluded:

> The fact, finally, is familiar to every psychiatrist that in severe cases of chronic delusions (in paranoia) the most extreme examples occur of ingeniously elaborated and well-supported absurdities.[50]

It would seem that Freud would side with the mature Kant in viewing such beliefs as ranging from mildly to severely psychiatric.

Freud, like Kant, held that incidental superstitions would be an indication of minor psychiatric instability, whereas grandiose beliefs in a spirit world were a sign of madness.

Freud's psychiatric evaluation of spiritualistic phenomena would present great difficulties for Jung. While he might have been prepared to accept Freud's view that such beliefs were purely psychological, he would find great difficulty in seeing them as entirely pathological. In addition, Jung would find problematical Freud's insistence that the psychological etiology was always repressed sexuality.

In June 1907, Jung went to Paris. He had been in contact with Flournoy in Geneva and intended to go to see Janet in Paris.[51] In July, Freud wrote revealing his concern and relief about Jung's attraction to the French school of psychology. In his letter to Jung he stated:

> I was very glad to hear that you are back...and am delighted with your impressions of your trip. You can imagine that I should have been very sorry if your Vienna complex had been obliged to share the available cathexis with a Paris complex. Luckily, ...nothing of the sort happened, you gained the impression that the days of the great Charcot are past and that the new life of psychiatry is with us, between Zürich and Vienna. So we have emerged safe and sound from a first danger.[52]

If Jung's inclination to accept the theories about human psychology proposed by the French school of psychology was for Freud the first danger, his attraction to spiritualistic phenomena or what Freud called "the Occult," was the second. For the time being Jung was prepared "for a bit of historical mysticism!"[53] This he outlined as follows:

> *Vienna* has produced 3 anthropological-medical reformers: Mesmer, Gall [founder of phrenology], Freud.... Freud... went unrecognized. Mesmer and Gall then moved to Paris.
>
> Mesmer's views remained confined to Paris until *Lavater* [clergyman, mystic and founder of physiognomy] of *Zürich* imported them into Germany, at first *Bremen*. Hypnotism revived in France and was imported into Germany by *Forel* of *Zürich*. Forel's first pupil of many years' standing is *Delbrück* of *Bremen*....

> *Freud* first met with clinical recognition in *Zürich*. The
> first *German* asylum to recognize Freud was *Bremen*....
> Apart from Delbrück the only German assistant at the
> Burghölzli...is Dr. Abraham of *Bremen*.[54]

This peculiar "bit of historical mysticism" is of interest for the following reasons: (1) Jung tried to justify his distancing himself from
the French school of psychology by finding a mythical pattern, (2)
he identified himself with other Swiss who mediated significant
medical influences, and (3) he granted Abraham an important status in the spread of Freud's teachings.[55] Abraham, as I shall
demonstrate shortly, was also aware of the differences between
Vienna and Zurich. It may be that this is the real reason why Abraham is given a role in Jung's "historical mysticism."
    In January 1908, Jung wrote to Freud that he was treating a
case of severe hysteria. Jung mentioned that his patient was a
twenty-six-year-old female who had:

> transference dreams...in the most miraculous way, many of
> them are of somnambulistic clarity. Naturally everything
> fits in with your theory. The early sexual history is not yet
> clear, since from the 13th year everything is shrouded in ret-
> rograde amnesic darkness phosphorescently lit up only by
> the dreams. The twilight states are similar to those in the
> case I first published ("Occult Phenomena"). The patient
> plays to perfection and with positively thrilling dramatic
> beauty the personality that is her dream ideal.[56]

This case is remarkably similar in many details to Jung's cousin,
Helly Preiswerk, the medium. Helly was thirteen at the time the
séances began and at the date of this letter would also have been,
as was Jung's patient, twenty-six years old. Jung went on to mention that this patient longed for her lover's child and displayed
symptoms that suited Freud's theory.[57] It is likely that Jung's memory of his cousin, which had not subsided, may have been at the
back of his interest in this particular case.[58]
    To return to the correspondence, Freud replied to Jung's letter:

> If you were here, I am sure we should have the most inter-
> esting things to tell each other about what can be learned
> from our cases—I am working on eleven of them at the
> moment.[59]

A week later, on January 22, 1908, Jung wrote to Freud in a tone that may suggest he was slightly defensive about the case he out-lined earlier:

> We would all like, just for once, to hear a lecture from you—something quite ordinary—in which you might present one of your cases; we all want to learn from you....Perhaps you would be kind enough to tell us something *systematic about your wide experience of hysteria.*[60]

Freud's views on hysteria were of particular interest to Jung because he had delivered a lecture, "The Freudian Theory of Hysteria," before the First International Congress of Psychiatry and Neurology the previous September, which left him with a "senti-ment d'incomplétude!"[61] This "sentiment" may not have been due to his lack of understanding Freud's position toward hysteria. Rather, Jung's own feeling was that he could not tolerate reducing all psy-chological disorders to repressed sexuality and not consider their purposiveness which could render them therapeutic and not merely pathological. This is evident in a letter Jung wrote to Freud a month later:

> Autoerotism, as an overcompensation of conflicts with real-ity, is largely teleological. This conception has afforded me some valuable insights. The hysteric, besides repressing reality, makes repeated attempts to link up with it again, the paranoiac forgoes even this and is only intent on keep-ing up his libido defenses. Hence the fixation of the com-plexes. The patients do not, as in hysteria, risk the leap into suitable new situations by linking up with reality, but work for decades at defending themselves against the com-plex by inner compensations. The paranoiac always seeks inner solutions, the hysteric outer ones, probably, and often quite obviously, because in paranoia the complex becomes an absolutely sovereign and incontrovertible fact, whereas in hysteria it is always a bit of a comedy, with one part of the personality playing the role of a mere spectator. But this wealth of psychic reality could hardly be expressed in a mere 9 theses.[62]

The letter indicates that Jung was seriously concerned about the distinction between hysteria and paranoia or dementia praecox. He had noted as early as his dissertation that the complex can have a purposeful intentionality. Once again the idea seems to have taken a hold of him with great force. This emphasis on Jung's part suggests a certain difference with Freud's view. This difference was something that Abraham had noted and which he thought was rooted in Jung's religious preoccupation, and especially his preoccupation with Spiritualism.

Karl Abraham (1877–1925) had studied psychiatry in Berlin and was on the staff of the Burghölzli from 1904 to 1907 as an assistant to Bleuler.[63] He had worked with Jung while he was there and began corresponding with Freud shortly before he resigned.[64] Jung expressed jealously when he heard of Abraham's correspondence with Freud and suspected him of being a bit of an opportunist, lacking in empathy, and with an affinity for bureaucracy.[65] When Freud finally met Abraham he thought him "more congenial" than Jung's report and added, "He told me a good deal about Bleuler, in whom he is evidently much interested as a psychoanalytic problem."[66] Jung wrote to Freud self-consciously about his feelings towards Abraham:

> my description of our colleague Abraham was, after all, too black....however, the "self-preservation complex" of our colleague towards me has certainly played its part. At any rate he seems to have been more forthcoming with you than with me. This difference may account for our different impressions. It is just as well that A. has told you a good deal about Bleuler, thus making up for my negligence.[67]

Freud attempted to soothe Jung's injured feelings by explaining to him that Abraham "is prevented from unbending by preoccupations that I understand only too well: the fact of being a Jew and concern over his future."[68]

Jung suspected that Abraham was in fact using a number of his ideas, only serving them up as though they were his own, and with the modifications necessary to bring them more in line with Freud's views.[69] This irritated Jung because it tended to cast doubt on him.[70] Moreover, it was difficult for Jung to dismiss Abraham's implicit allegations about the tendencies in Zurich when the would-be accuser had himself spent a number of years there and had the ear of Freud. Up to this point Abraham had been cautious and reserved, and gradually developed a close relationship with Freud, though he never achieved the level of intimacy of either Jung or Sandor Ferenczi. It was becoming evident to Freud, Jung, and

Abraham that differences of opinion were emerging. Jung expressed a need to talk to Freud personally.[71] One of his own letters to Freud, he felt, had "an oddly dry tone."[72]

The Salzburg Congress of Psychoanalysis, held on April 27, 1908, provided Freud and Jung with the opportunity to meet and talk. If we cannot be a party to those conversations, we do have some idea of the polarization that was occurring from the papers that were given. Freud's paper, known among analysts as "The Man with the Rats" was a veritable *tour de force* lasting, according to Jones, five hours.[73] In it Freud recounted the case history of a young man suffering from an obsessive neurosis, which he traced to infantile sexuality. Freud differentiated obsessive neurosis from hysteria by maintaining that in the latter, repression took the form of "amnesia of the important complexes," whereas in the former, "retention of the complex in consciousness, but with a dissociation of its affect" was the rule.[74] As I have already mentioned, Freud, the year before, had linked obsessive neurosis with religion in a paper he gave before the Vienna Society, at which Jung was present. From the specifics of the case Freud described at Salzburg, he made a number of generalizations to which Jung would later react. He observed that obsessional patients were inordinately fearful of their thoughts—or more particularly their wishes—coming true in reality, and part of them believed that they had the power to bring this about.[75] Freud named this belief the "Omnipotence of Thoughts."[76] Freud linked to this another general feature, which Jones has summarized as follows:

> [Obsessionals] believe, for instance, that if they think of someone and meet him soon after that there is an inherent connection between the two facts. Freud related this tendency to the characteristic dissociation mentioned above that breaks the connection between two thoughts so as to blot out their significance. The "endopsychic perception," as he termed it, of the repressed connection becomes projected into the outer world, where significant connections are believed to be perceived in purely accidental occurrences. This feature, so highly developed in this particular neurosis [the Rat Man], throws light on the nature and genesis of *superstition* in general.[77]

Karl Abraham, picking up hints dropped by Freud, also delivered a paper at the Salzburg Congress entitled, "The Psycho-Sex-

ual Differences Between Hysteria and Dementia Praecox" (1908).[78]
Freud had earlier ventured the opinion that the difference between
neurosis and dementia praecox was simply that the latter had
become fixed at a much earlier period of "autoerotism," to which
the individual regressed in the course of the illness.[79] In a disarm-
ing gesture, Freud later made reference to the fiction that the ideas
he presented were Abraham's, and stated that he was obliged to
plagiarize them for his essay on Schreber.[80] But less than three
months later, in a letter (March 3, 1911) to Abraham, Freud
remarked, referring to his nemesis Wilhelm Fleiss: "Do not forget
that it was through him that both of us came to understand the
secret of paranoia ('The Psycho-Sexual Differences')."[81]

The last paper on the day program at the Salzburg Congress
was Jung's "On Dementia Praecox." In it he argued:

> The depotentiation of the association process or *abaisse-*
> *ment du niveau mental*, which consequently has a down-
> right dreamlike quality, seems to indicate that a
> pathogenic agent contributes to dementia praecox which is
> absent in, say, hysteria. The characteristics of the *abaisse-*
> *ment* were assigned to the pathogenic agent, which was
> construed as organically conditioned and likened to a
> symptom of poisoning (e.g., paranoid states in chronic poi-
> soning).[82]

Jung thus ignored Freud's suggestions, along with his conclusion,
that the "'dementia' in this disease was due, not to any destruction
of intellectual capacities, but to a massive blocking of the feeling
process...."[83] Jones, who was present when the paper was given,
interpreted Jung's position on dementia praecox to be: "the disease
was an organic condition of the brain produced by a hypothetical
'psycho-toxin.'"[84] In maintaining this position Jung allied himself
with his chief, Bleuler. Nor would he ever entirely relinquish the
explanation for dementia praecox/schizophrenia which he put forward in 1908.[85]

Immediately after the congress, Jung wrote to Freud, "I am in
two minds as to whether I should apply a business or an emotional
yardstick to the Salzburg Congress."[86] On the subject of dementia
praecox he stated:

> I now realize (actually I have always realized) what an end-
> less amount of excavation is still needed in order to dig up

anything and present it with certainty. Unfortunately there was no physical and psychological opportunity in Salzburg for discussing my particular case.... Meanwhile...it has become easier, too, for Bleuler made marked progress in Salzburg, so that he is even beginning to doubt that there are organic primary symptoms in Dem. pr., as he had always asserted without qualification earlier.... Only harder work can bring me more clarity. Maybe I have done too little analytical work on Dem. praec. these last nine months, with the result that the impressive material has become too much of an imposition on me. The chief obstacle is my pupils.... They get ahead at my expense, while I stand still. This knowledge weighed heavily on me in Salzburg.[87]

Jung's letter indicates that he was rather subdued by the events of the Salzburg Congress. The weakening of defenses that he attributed to Bleuler, obviously characterized his own feelings as well. Nevertheless, the Jewish contingent that had accompanied Freud from Vienna had deep suspicions that Jung, the Gentile, was poising himself for a break from the psychoanalytic camp.[88] "Hate has a keen eye," Jones later remarked, quoting a German proverb.[89] For the present Freud was willing to allow Jung some room to reconsider his views in the hope that he would in time commit himself to Freud's explanatory model of the sexual etiology of psychological disorders. Freud was even willing to oblige Jung by claiming on his behalf that Bleuler, whom he experienced as a rather uncanny character, was responsible for any rumors that Zurich was drifting from the psychoanalytic camp.[90] His chief opponent in this course of action was Karl Abraham.

Freud, in a letter (May 3, 1908) to Abraham, attributed Jung's sensitiveness to his vacillation and pleaded:

Please be tolerant and do not forget that it is really easier for you than it is for Jung to follow my ideas,...you are closer to my intellectual constitution because of racial kinship, while he as a Christian and a pastor's son finds his way to me only against great inner resistances.[91]

Abraham felt he was justified in taking a stand against Zurich.[92] He replied that his animosity toward Jung and Bleuler was based on their having turned "aside from the theory of sexuality" and picking up on Freud's remark on racial kinship he added:

I freely admit that I find it easier to go along with you
rather than with Jung. I, too, have always felt this intellectual kinship. After all, our Talmudic way of thinking cannot disappear just like that.[93]

Freud wrote Abraham that he deplored the quarrel that was
going on between him and Jung.[94] Abraham responded in a letter
(July 16, 1908) in which he insisted that the tension was not personal but ideological:

My brief reference to Zürich in my last letter did not refer
to my personal disagreement with Jung, but to the general
attitude at present adopted in Zürich....
The matter goes deeper. Jung's behaviour to me is, after
all, only a symptom. I believe all the gentlemen from Vienna
had the impression at Salzburg that not much more could be
expected from Zürich. I had news from a reliable source
about the latest developments, and it was under the impact
of this that I wrote to you last time. I do not wish to worry
you with details. But the sudden fading-out of the Freudian
evenings, so well attended until April, is striking. Jung
seems to be reverting to his former spiritualistic inclinations. But please keep this between ourselves. However, if
Jung gives up for this reason and for the sake of his career,
then we can no longer count on the Burghölzli.... [Bleuler] is
a very complex personality, a mass of reaction formations.
His external simplicity and often exaggerated modesty
cover strong grandiose tendencies.... My remark referred to
these matters and not to my personal affairs.[95]

Freud responded immediately stating:

I shall write to you about Burghölzli more fully next time; I
am thinking of going to Zürich at the end of September; I
think a great deal more favourably about Jung, but not
about Bleuler. On the whole it is easier for us Jews, as we
lack the mystical element.[96]

Making good his promise, Freud wrote a letter (July 23, 1908) to
Abraham. In it he expressed his consternation over the difficulties
that had surfaced in the conflict between Jung and Abraham. He
also added:

I prefer not to share your unfavorable prognosis in regard to the co-operation of Burghölzli. The dropping of the evening discussions struck me too; but I do not know whether it is final. Bleuler I surrender to you; at Salzburg he struck me as very odd.... But Jung is a different matter,...he writes to me about his chief—just as you did, and in fact in the same words. Moreover, he can hardly back out, he could not repudiate his past even if he wanted to.[97]

It is interesting to note that Freud, in order to exonerate Jung, chose to blame Bleuler for having influenced him. In the light of the emphasis Jung placed, as Bleuler did, on a "psycho-toxin" cause in his Salzburg paper on dementia praecox, Freud would seem to have hit the mark. But, to borrow Abraham's phrase, "the matter goes deeper": Freud, in a letter (June 21, 1908) to Jung a month before, wrote:

I see...that your views have once again come much closer to mine. I wasn't worried though. At one time, yes, before our last meeting. But just seeing you in Salzburg, though there was hardly a chance of talking to you, I knew that our views would soon be reconciled, that you had not, as I had feared, been alienated from me by some inner development deriving from the relationship with your father and the beliefs of the Church but merely by the influence of your chief. I must own, I was not entirely pleased with Bleuler, he sometimes made me feel rather creepy, but after a while I felt sure that I would not lose you to *him*.[98]

While Freud stated that his fear Jung's religious upbringing and tie to his pastor father might have prevented him from accepting the psycho-sexual theory was now unwarranted, it never seemed to have occurred to him that other religious and parental influences might have been at work, driving Jung in his own direction.[99] Freud, disregarding Abraham's clue about Jung's "former spiritualistic inclinations," pointed to Bleuler, whom he thought uncanny, as the culprit. The solution, Freud now concluded, was to separate Jung from his surrogate father, Bleuler. Then Jung would be his.

In September Freud went to stay with Jung at the Burghölzli. Over the course of four days they had several conversations and Freud disclosed to Jung the doubts and rumors he had heard from Abraham. In the end they parted, having to Freud's satisfaction reconciled their differences.[100] When Freud arrived in Vienna he wrote to Abraham:

> I could not write to you from Zürich; I was never alone until late at night; we spent up to eight hours a day walking and talking.

After clearing up some business matters Freud added:

> Now to the chief thing. I am glad to say that you were only partly right, that is to say, only about Bleuler. As for Jung, he has overcome his vacillation, adheres unreservedly to the cause, and also will continue to work energetically on the dementia praecox question on our lines. That is highly gratifying to me, and I hope it will be pleasing to you also. But nothing will come of Bleuler, his defection is imminent, and his relations with Jung are strained to the breaking-point. Jung is giving up his position as physician, but remains head of the laboratory and will work completely independently of Bleuler.

And on the subject of the rumors Abraham had heard about Jung and his "former spiritualistic inclinations," Freud wrote a little more vaguely:

> He spoke only in hints, but I was able to conclude that he thinks you have had ideas about him put into your head by others that do not correspond to reality, and regrets it.[101]

Abraham replied to Freud encouraging him in his optimism about Jung, but not unreservedly:

> I am very pleased indeed that the unpleasant situation has been brought to an end. You may rest assured that in my correspondence with Jung I shall not refer in any way to what is past. Admittedly, I see some things at the Burghöl-zli differently from you. In three years of daily contact one gains insight into a great deal.[102]

Freud felt caught between Jung and Abraham, perhaps seeing in each attributes he himself possessed. His unfulfilled wish, which he now felt was within reach, he expressed in an earlier letter to

Abraham: "Why cannot I harness Jung and you together, your precision and his *élan*?"[103]

Freud, in his first letter after his visit to Zurich, addressed Jung as "My dear friend and heir."[104] In the letter Freud reiterated the incorrectness of Jung's distinction between the source of hysteria and the source of dementia praecox.[105] He had also thrust increasing responsibility upon Jung by encouraging him to organize and act as editor of the *Jahrbuch für psychoanalytische und psychopathologische Forschungen.*[106]

At the end of March 1909, Jung resigned his position at Burghölzli and then went to Vienna for a second time to visit Freud.[107] He took the opportunity to raise the topic of spiritualistic phenomena. Freud, to his surprise, responded by dismissing such questions as nonsensical. Jung later described what immediately followed:

> While Freud was going on this way, I had a curious sensation. It was as if my diaphragm were made of iron and were becoming red-hot—a glowing vault. And at that moment there was such a loud report in the bookcase, which stood right next to us, that we both started up in alarm, fearing the thing was going to topple over on us. I said to Freud: "There, that is an example of a so-called catalytic exteriorization phenomenon."
>
> "Oh come," he exclaimed. "That is sheer bosh."
>
> "It is not," I replied. "You are mistaken, Herr Professor. And to prove my point I now predict that in a moment there will be another such loud report!" Sure enough, no sooner had I said the words than the same detonation went off in the bookcase.[108]

Jones mentioned this incident in his biography of Freud, stating that Jung:

> regaled Freud one evening with astonishing stories of his experiences, and also displayed his powers as a poltergeist by making various articles in the room rattle on the furniture. Freud admitted having been very much impressed by this feat and tried to imitate it after Jung's departure.[109]

When Jung returned to Zurich he started a letter to Freud which he was able to complete only ten days later. After offering his apologies to him for not writing sooner, Jung wrote:

Since Vienna all scientific work has been out of the question. But in my practice I have accomplished much. At the moment a madly interesting case is stretching me on the rack. Some of the symptoms come suspiciously close to the organic borderline (brain tumour?), yet they all hover over a dimly divined psychogenic depth, so that in analysing them all one's misgivings are forgotten. First-rate spiritualistic phenomena occur in this case, though so far only one in my presence. Altogether it makes a very peculiar impression.

Jung went on to add:

When I left Vienna I was afflicted with some *sentiments d'incomplétude* because of the last evening I spent with you. It seemed to me that my spookery struck you as altogether too stupid and perhaps unpleasant because of the Fliess analogy. (Insanity!) Just recently, however, the impression I had of the last-named patient smote me with renewed force.... I had the feeling that under it all there must be some quite special complex, a universal one having to do with the prospective tendencies in man. If there is a "psychanalysis" there must also be a "psychosynthesis" which creates future events according to the same laws.... The leap towards psychosynthesis proceeds via the person of my patient, whose unconscious is right now preparing, apparently with nothing to stop it, a new stereotype into which everything from outside, as it were, fits in conformity with the complex. (Hence the idea of the objective effect of the prospective tendency!)[110]

The poltergeist incident in Vienna troubled Freud, and Jung's statement that it aroused in him a certain mistrust is probably, and quite understandably, true.[111] Freud, in his reply to Jung's letter, admitted that he was impressed by his stories and experiment with the furniture, but he seemed to have tried to seek a rational explanation for what happened and dismissed the "poltergeist business" by observing that in his rooms the floorboards constantly creaked. Moreover, he added:

My credulity...vanished with the magic of your personal presence; once again, for some inward reasons that I can't put my finger on, it strikes me as quite unlikely that such phenomena should exist.... I...warn my dear son to keep a cool head, for it is better not to understand something than make such great sacrifices to understanding. I also shake my wise head over psychosynthesis.[112]

That Freud mentioned "psychosynthesis" negatively suggests once again that he detected the tendency in Jung to seek for some sort of unifying perspective. It is also an obvious comment on the fact that Jung did not find this in Freud's theory of sexuality.

Jung wrote to Freud a month later, on May 12, 1909, that he had "not gone over to any system yet and shall also guard against putting my trust in those spooks."[113] The "poltergeist business" was not mentioned again directly and Freud and Jung temporarily turned their attention to other matters.

Herman Nunberg, a psychoanalyst who studied the word association method under Jung at Burghölzli, also recalled Jung's preoccupation with the "poltergeist business."

When I used to work with him [Jung] in his study,...it sometimes happened that he would suddenly call my attention to a cracking in the shelves of his library. "Do you hear?" he would exclaim, as if he were hearing uncanny noises, as if he were hearing ghosts.[114]

This description is remarkably similar to the scene that transpired in Freud's study. Nunberg went on to add:

In Zurich we knew that, as a young psychiatrist in Basel, Jung had been interested in occultism, and I therefore did not attribute much significance to his exclamation....

Jung had previously sent his essay on occult phenomena to Bleuler; after reading it, Bleuler had had Jung come from Basel to Burghölzli and made him his assistant.[115]

It seems quite clear that Jung was preoccupied with spiritualistic phenomena during this period. Nunberg's conclusions are that Jung's ghost experiences and his psychology represent "a delusional system that has been put into a rational framework."[116] The rational part of Freud, at least, would have agreed.

During the initial period of the exchanges with Freud over the correct interpretation of the distinction between various psychiatric disorders, Jung had become involved in an intimate relationship with a highly disturbed, but equally gifted, young female patient, Sabina Spielrein. Her case and her relationship with Jung had a direct bearing on both the question of the etiology of psychiatric disorders and the interpretation of spiritualistic phenomena. In an earlier letter (October 23, 1906), Jung mentioned her case to Freud and that he was attempting to treat her psychoanalytically.[117] His treatment was successful and he presented her case in his paper "The Freudian Theory of Hysteria."[118] The latter presentation, it might be recalled, left him with a "sentiment d'incomplétude!"[119] While at first his patient, so embroiled did Jung's relationship with Sabina Spielrein become that it began to threaten both his professional status and his marriage. In the spring of 1909 it also came to Freud's attention.

Jung, in a letter (March 7, 1909) to Freud mentioned:

> a woman patient, whom years ago I pulled out of a very sticky neurosis with unstinting effort, has violated my confidence and my friendship in the most mortifying way imaginable. She has kicked up a vile scandal solely because I denied myself the pleasure of giving her a child.... But you know how it is—the devil can use even the best of things for the fabrication of filth.... [U]ntil now I had a totally inadequate idea of my polygamous components despite all self-analysis. Now I know where and how the devil can be laid by the heels.[120]

Freud replied to Jung two days later that he had already received news of Jung's patient who had been introducing herself as Jung's mistress. He had "presumed that the situation was quite different and that the only possible explanation was a neurosis."[121] He also pointed out to Jung that "you definitely lapse into the theological style in relating this experience."[122] Jung opened his letter of reply to Freud with a curious declaration of faithfulness:

> I must answer you at once. Your kind words have relieved and comforted me. You may rest assured, not only now but for the future, that nothing Fliess-like is going to happen.... Except for moments of infatuation my affection is lasting and reliable. It's just that for the past fortnight the devil has been tormenting me in the shape of neurotic ingratitude. But I shall not be unfaithful to psychoanalysis on that account. On the contrary, I am learning from it how to do better in the future. You mustn't take on about my "theological style," I just felt that way. Now and then, I admit,

the devil does strike a chill into my—on the whole—blame-
less heart.... I've never really had a mistress and am the
most innocent of spouses.... I simply cannot imagine who it
might have been. I don't think it is the same lady.[123]

In fact it turned out to be the same lady, as Jung knew only too well!

In Jung's letter it is evident that his disclaimers about
unfaithfulness to psychoanalysis are curiously mixed up with both
Freud and his relationship with Sabina Spielrein. The reasons are
evidently bound up in the strategic role that Spielrein played as
liaison in the crucial issues that would eventually divide Jung and
Freud, as John Kerr has recently pointed out.[124] Nevertheless, at
this early stage such an argument is too anachronistic to be
entirely persuasive. There is another factor that explains the origins of Jung's curious mix of feelings in the letter, and it is not
Jung or Freud who pointed it out but Sabina Spielrein herself. She
did this in her exchange with Freud, to which I shall now turn.

On May 30, 1909 Sabina Spielrein wrote to Freud requesting
to see him.[125] Four days later Freud wrote to Jung and enclosed
Spielrein's letter.[126] In his letter to Jung he stated: "Weird! What is
she? A busybody, a chatterbox, or a paranoiac?" He also added,
"Your Russian...probably has some utopian dream of a world-
saving therapy and feels that the work isn't getting on fast
enough."[127] Jung next fired off a telegram to Freud which is missing, but it can be inferred that in it he attempted to clarify his relationship to Sabina Spielrein.[128] In a follow-up letter Jung accused
Spielrein of trying to create a scandal by "spreading a rumour that
I shall soon get a divorce from my wife and marry a certain girl student, which has thrown not a few of my colleagues into a flutter."[129]
Jung also added the following:

> On top of that, naturally, an amiable complex had to throw
> an outsize monkey-wrench into the works. As I have indi-
> cated before, my first visit to Vienna had a *very* long uncon-
> scious aftermath, first the compulsive infatuation in
> Abbazia, then the Jewess popped up in another form, in the
> shape of my patient. Now of course the whole bag of tricks
> lies there quite clearly before my eyes.[130]

Freud seemed to have overlooked the hint Jung was dropping
about his own personal complexes and instead wrote to him suggesting that he had been taken in quite badly by his patient.[131] He also
informed him that he had written directly to Spielrein.[132] Jung's

reaction was to agree with Freud's reprimand and state: "it is too stupid that I of all people, your "son and heir," should squander your heritage so heedlessly."[133] Freud in turn consoled Jung by entreating him not to "go too far in the direction of contrition and reaction."[134]

On June 20, 1909, Sabina Spielrein wrote another letter to Freud. In it she stated that she had spoken to Jung, who promised a full disclosure to Freud.[135] She also alluded to the fact that Jung had developed an affection for Freud's daughter, Mathilde.[136] She explained this affection to Freud as a betrayal of himself because "he was looking to you for support, that he wanted your love and therefore in his own defense grasped at the first plausible thing." But in reality, Spielrein added, "the roots of his [Jung's] love for me must be sought somewhere else entirely."[137] Setting the stage for her reader's curiosity, Spielrein completed her disclosure by introducing the subject of his dissertation, Helene Preiswerk, the medium:

> One might think I was jealous [of Freud's daughter], but then I would have to be jealous of Frl. S. W. [Helene Preiswerk]! After all, love is always transferred from one object to another.... It is important that you realize that I was hostile only toward you, and long before I heard anything about your daughter. In conversation and also in a letter Dr. Jung identifies me with his mother.... In the course of an analysis it turned out that so-and-so many years ago Dr. Jung had been fond of a dark-haired hysterical girl called S. W., who always described herself as Jewish (but in reality was not).... Now just listen, Prof. Freud, and tell me if this is not interesting: Dr. Jung and I were very good at reading each other's minds. But suddenly he gets terribly worked up, gives me his diary,...that I should open it at random.... I open it—and lo and behold! it was the very passage where S. W. appeared to Dr. Jung one night in a white garment.... [H]e then described this girl in his dissertation.... This girl was deeply rooted in him, and she was my prototype.... [H]e would sometimes turn reflective when I said something to him; such and such a woman had spoken in just this way, etc. And it was always this girl![138]

The day after Spielrein wrote her letter, June 21, 1909, Jung himself wrote to Freud in language reminiscent of an earlier and somewhat defensive letter on the subject of Abraham:

I have good news to report of my Spielrein affair. I took too black a view of things. After breaking up with her I was almost certain of her revenge.[139]

Jung reported to Freud in the letter that he had settled matters with Spielrein after she had come to see him two days earlier. He added:

I nevertheless deplore the sins I have committed, for I am largely to blame for the high-flying hopes of my former patient.... I discussed with her the problem of the child, imagining that I was talking theoretically, but naturally Eros was lurking in the background. Thus I imputed all the other wishes and hopes entirely to my patient without seeing the same thing in myself. When the situation had become so tense that the continued preservation of the relationship could be rounded out only by sexual acts, I defended myself in a manner that cannot be justified morally. Caught in my delusion that I was the victim of the sexual wiles of my patient, I wrote to her mother that I was not the gratifier of her daughter's sexual desires.... my action was a piece of knavery which I very reluctantly confess to you as my father.[140]

Freud, after receiving Jung's letter, wrote a pleasant and apologetic letter to Sabina Spielrein stating "the lapse has to be blamed on the man and not the woman."[141] Six days later, on June 30, 1909, he wrote to Jung: "Yours would have reconciled me to greater misdeeds on your part; perhaps I am already too biased in your favour."[142] Freud added that he had written to Spielrein and received yet another letter from her which he described as "Amazingly awkward...hard to read and hard to understand."[143] Nevertheless, Freud concluded, "the matter has ended in a manner satisfactory to all."[144]

Whether Freud chose to ignore Jung's earlier hints, and Spielrein's disclosures, or simply found them otiose, the fact remains that an important series of entangled associations passed before him in the letters he received from Jung and Spielrein. Jung's hint about the Jewess referred back to the figure of Ivenes, whom he encountered in the séances he conducted with his cousin, Helene Preiswerk. This fact is confirmed in Spielrein's letter of June 20 to Freud. Moreover, Spielrein remarks clearly emphasized the importance of Helene Preiswerk and Jung's mother for an understanding of his personal psychology. Even Jung's pleading to his father, in the guise of Freud, harks back to this earlier period of his life and the tension he experienced between Christianity and Spiritualism. Freud seemed to have overlooked these items and therefore missed the extent to which Jung's letter of June 21 was a recapitulation of the difficulties he underwent in his emotional relationship with his cousin, the medium. Freud also missed the source of the influence which he rather insistently sought in Jung's theological forebears and then in the uncanniness of Bleuler.

In August 1909 Jung and Freud traveled to the United States to lecture at Clark University. While he was there, Jung took the opportunity to speak with William James. James was invited to discuss his researches on spiritualistic phenomena and, in particular, his study of the famous medium, Mrs. Piper.[145] Jung recalled years later:

> I spent two delightful evenings with William James alone and I was tremendously impressed by the clearness of his mind and the complete absence of intellectual prejudices....
>
> I was also interested in parapsychology and my discussions with William James were chiefly about this subject and about the psychology of religious experience.[146]

And in another letter Jung wrote of his meeting with James:

> We talked mostly about his experiments with Mrs. Piper, which are well enough known, and did not speak of his philosophy at all. I was particularly interested to see what his attitude was to so-called "occult phenomena...." He... answered my questions and interjections as though speaking to an equal.... Aside from Theodore Flournoy he was the only outstanding mind with whom I could conduct an uncomplicated conversation.[147]

As I have already pointed out in a previous chapter, Flournoy was the author of an important psychological study of a medium, a work on which Jung modeled his dissertation. He was also a close friend of William James. In a letter (September 28, 1909) to Flournoy, most of which is about psychical research, James wrote of his encounter with Jung and Freud at Clark University:

> I went...to see what Freud was like, and met also Yung
> [Jung] of Zurich, who professed great esteem for you, and
> made a very pleasant impression. I hope that Freud and his
> pupils will push their ideas to their utmost limits, so that we
> may learn what they are. They can't fail to throw light on
> human nature, but I confess that he [Freud] made on me
> personally the impression of a man obsessed by fixed
> ideas.[148]

The exchange which Jung had with William James is additional
evidence that he maintained a continued interest in spiritualistic
phenomena and sought a means by which to properly understand
its psychological significance.

There is another incident that occurred at the Clark University Conference that may indicate the tension between Freud and
Jung over the latter's interest in spiritualistic phenomena. Stanley
Hall, then president of Clark University, and a distinguished psychologist, had observed a girl claiming to have spiritualistic powers. Hall mentioned this to Freud and Jung and they asked to see
her. Apparently the following transpired:

> in a short interview with her they at once diagnosed the
> true nature of it all, and to my surprise she frankly con-
> fessed that her chief motive from the first had been to win
> the love of her adored one....The erotic motivation was
> obvious and the German savants saw little further to inter-
> est them in the case, and I was a trifle mortified that now
> the purpose so long hidden from us was so conscious and so
> openly confessed. They suspected a possible incipient
> dementia praecox.[149]

While it is distinctly possible the girl had erotic designs on Hall
from the beginning, it could well be that Freud sought, for Jung's
benefit, to uncover the erotic component of her Spiritualism and
thereby explain all of it in terms of her sexuality. It is also possible
that Jung agreed with much of Freud's analysis, as Hall implied.
On the other hand, considering Jung's conversation with James, it
is more likely that Jung was of two minds about spiritualistic phenomena. With James he may have leaned toward believing that
such phenomena indicated some possible transpersonal reality
and, at the same time, agreed with Freud that sexuality may have
been an important factor. Discussing such matters with Freud,

Jung probably tried to influence him to consider the possibility of an intermediate position which he, however, had not yet worked out. Freud's earlier mention of Jung's interest in psychosynthesis perhaps points to this as does the "poltergeist incident" in Freud's apartment. In addition so does Freud's curiosity about occultism, a curiosity that did not originate in his encounter with Jung but that was certainly strengthened because of it.

Ernest Jones has surveyed Freud's interest in the occult and expressed the view that the central problem of occultism "though presenting itself in endlessly varied guises, is whether thoughts or spiritual beings can exist in space with no ascertainable connection with a corporeal body."[150] Furthermore, Jones pointed out, the decline of traditional religion had contributed to an interest in Spiritualism among the general population and, in some cases, even among scientists.[151] Freud himself, we are informed, "was always very skeptical about the spiritistic performance of mediums, although he often thought they might possess special telepathic powers."[152] The history of Freud's views on the occult is not only intrinsically interesting but can also be directly related to his relationship with Jung.[153]

When Freud returned from the United States to Europe in the autumn of 1909 he travelled to Berlin with Sandor Ferenczi, a Hungarian psychoanalyst. They had gone there to see a medium, Frau Seidler, to conduct séances with her. Freud was disturbed by the fact that some of the phenomena he observed suggested the possibility of thought transference. He concluded that the medium possessed a "physiological gift" but denied "this implied accepting a belief in occultism."[154] Freud wrote a long letter to Ferenczi in which he stated, "I am afraid you have begun to discover something big, but there will be great difficulties in the way of making use of it."[155] In addition, Freud spoke quietly of the matter to others but, as Jones wrote, "he swore Ferenczi to absolute silence."[156]

Ferenczi had long been interested in the subject of spiritualistic phenomena. As early as 1899 he had written on Spiritualism, calling for a scientific investigation of the subject:

> It is quite possible that the greater part of spiritistic phenomena is based on the...simple or multiple split in mental functioning, one function alone being focused in the mirror of consciousness, while the rest is carried on automatically and unconsciously....

The arguments based on authorities mean little. The thing to do is to find a scientist or committee of scientists to take charge of this field, to expose the fraud, to enlighten the self-deceived and to enrich psychology with the new discoveries that would result.[157]

As Jones has remarked about such an early interest: "in this respect he resembled Jung."[158] After returning from the Clark Conference most of the letters exchanged between Freud and Ferenczi were taken up with the subject of spiritualistic phenomena.[159] Ferenczi maintained an interest in mediumistic phenomena and continued to send Freud reports on his observations.[160] Freud was obviously hesitant but becoming seriously interested in the subject.[161]

Jung, like Freud and Ferenczi, also attended séances after he returned from the United States. In a letter to William James, Theodore Flournoy mentioned that Jung was present at a number of séances conducted, in the late winter of 1910, with the medium Carancini.[162] Jung also stated that he met Freud in Vienna, during which time a conversation about spiritualistic phenomena took place.[163] Jung vividly recalled this conversation years later when he recorded it in his autobiography:

> Freud said to me, "My dear Jung, promise me never to abandon the sexual theory. That is the most essential thing of all. You see, we must make a dogma of it, an unshakable bulwark." He said that to me with great emotion, in the tone of a father saying, "And promise me this one thing, my dear son: that you will go to Church every Sunday." In some astonishment I asked him, "A bulwark—against what?" To which he replied, "Against the black tide of mud"—and here he hesitated for a moment, then added—"of occultism."[164]

By way of comment Jung added:

> This was the thing that struck at the heart of our friendship. I knew that I would never be able to accept such an attitude. What Freud seemed to mean by "occultism" was virtually everything that philosophy and religion, including the rising contemporary science of parapsychology, had learned about the psyche.[165]

If this incident took place, it clearly demonstrates the mounting tension between Freud and Jung.

Jung's feeling that Freud, by abrogating "occultism," was throwing out philosophy and religion, as well as parapsychology, is revealing.[166] Jung's own inclinations are evident in his insistence in pursuing these very subjects. As much as Freud bade him otherwise, he certainly would have been unwilling to surrender this whole territory of human knowledge and experience to Freud's sexual theory. In fact, Jung inclined instead to want to baptize psychoanalysis and turn *it* into a religion. This was made plain in a letter (February 11, 1910) Jung wrote to Freud in which he "abreacted" at length. In it he referred to the possibility of psychoanalysis joining an ethical and cultural movement:

> If a coalition is to have any ethical significance it should never be an artificial one but must be nourished by the deep instincts of the race. Somewhat like Christian Science, Islam, Buddhism. Religion can be replaced only by religion....
>
> The ethical problem of sexual freedom really is enormous.... But 2000 years of Christianity can only be replaced by something equivalent....I imagine a far finer and more comprehensive task for psychoanalysis than alliance with an ethical fraternity. I think we must give it time to infiltrate into people from many centres, to revivify among intellectuals a feeling for symbol and myth.[167]

Freud's response was simply, "you mustn't regard me as the founder of a religion."[168] Jung in turn replied that he was immersed in mythology, and even his dreams were filled with symbolism. He also stated:

> My last letter was naturally another of those rampages of fantasy I indulge in from time to time. This time unfortunately it hit you, which was probably the intention.[169]

In his next letter, Jung attempted to clarify his ideas by distinguishing between two types of thinking: (1) logical, or thinking in words that is directed outwards and (2) analogical, or fantasy thinking that is wordless, emotionally toned, pictorial, and inner directed. The former is conscious thought; the latter, unconscious.[170] Little more is said about this distinction, but the idea surfaced in the first part of *Symbols of Transformation,* which would be published the following year.[171] In a letter (April 17, 1910) to Freud, Jung mentioned that the distinguished German psychiatrist Emil Kraepelin had accused "us of being mystics and spiritualists (Bleuler is a mystic too!!)."[172] That Jung should have presented this item to Freud as though he were surprised at the accusation is revealing. It is quite evident that Jung fostered more than medical ambitions for psychoanalysis throughout this period. Moreover, he seemed to have developed a reputation for these interests among his professional colleagues. Presumably Freud would have been disconcerted by the nature of the accusation.

Freud had kept his own inquiries about spiritualistic phenomena from being made public though he did have a discussion on the subject, as reported in the 1910 minutes of the Vienna Psychoanalytic Society.[173] Indeed, it is reported that Ferenczi had even brought a medium to one of the meetings of the Vienna Society.[174] Freud even accepted an invitation to become a corresponding member of the Society for Psychical Research.[175] But he would not venture to publish on the subject. Instead, he finally decided to leave it to Jung and Ferenczi to continue their explorations of this field.

During the same period, Jung was buried in the mythological and religious literature which would eventually form the documentation for *Symbols of Transformation.* The ideas that he advanced in this work had their origin in his student lectures and medical dissertation as well as in his disagreements with Freud. The first of these disagreements emerged at the end of 1909. Freud had sent Jung the proofs of his Salzburg paper, "Rat Man." Jung responded that he found it a subtle and ingenious work.[176] Freud replied to Jung, overjoyed with his praise.[177] But, the tone of the exchange on the subject became considerably less cordial. Two months later, Jung wrote a letter (December 14, 1909) to Freud in which he took issue with Freud's understanding of the libido and the use of the phrase "omnipotence of thoughts."[178] Jung also wrote Ferenczi soon after, on Christmas Day, complaining that Freud's "Rat Man" was hard to understand as well as mentioning that he was uncomfortable with the "symptom of *omnipotence.*"[179] These issues were to absorb and exasperate both Freud and Jung beyond the endurance of either of them.

Jung's differences with Freud on the subject of the libido he and Freud would argue out on the basis of data drawn from religion, mythology and occultism. What Jung thought he uncovered in these realms reinforced his beliefs and threatened Freud's conception of psychoanalysis, the kingdom Jung was slated to inherit. Freud had kept abreast of Jung's researches, in the hope that they would inevitably lead him back to the psychosexual theory. To Freud's dismay, it was becoming increasingly obvious that this hope was unlikely to come to pass. Evidence for this can be found in Jung's own notions of the nature of the libido, which were expressed in an early draft of *Symbols of Transformation,* to which Freud responded with caution.[180] Freud's concerns can also be seen in a letter (August 10, 1910) in which he chastised Jung for shirking his duties:

> As it is, the first months of your reign, my dear son and successor, have not turned out brilliantly. Sometimes I have the impression that you yourself have not taken your functions seriously enough and have not yet begun to act in a manner appropriate to your new dignity.[181]

At the time that Freud wrote the above remarks to Jung he was on vacation and at last able to make a detailed study of a work which he had put off reading, Schreber's *Memoirs of My Nervous Illness* (1903).[182] On his way back to Vienna, Freud formulated the outline of the essay he would author in response to his reading.[183] He completed it in mid-December 1910.[184]

The significance of Freud's essay on Schreber, "Psychoanalytic Notes on an Autobiographical Account of a Case of Paranoia (Dementia Paranoides)," is that in it he advanced ideas he only touched upon in his earlier writings and hints such as those picked up by Abraham for his Salzburg paper.[185] The most important of these ideas was to argue that psychosis was amenable to psychoanalytic investigation, which revealed a direct connection between repressed homosexuality and paranoia, the chief symptom of psychotic dementia praecox.[186] Yet, Freud stated in a letter (December 18, 1910) to Jung:

> I am unable to judge its objective worth as was possible with earlier papers, because in working on it I have had to fight off complexes within myself (Fliess).[187]

Indeed, as I pointed out earlier, Freud claimed that it was through Fliess that he "came to understand the secret of paranoia."[188] Even though Freud lit on the Fliess analogy a year and a half earlier during Jung's poltergeist demonstrations in his study, he now resisted any attempt to associate Fliess with Jung; instead he displaced his ill feelings onto Bleuler and Adler.[189] Freud's uneasiness, it turned out, was not without foundation, because it emerged later that his Schreber essay, "had its fateful associations."[190] As Ernest Jones also remarked, it "proved to be the starting point of the differences between Freud and Jung."[191]

Freud and Jung met in Munich at the end of December 1910.[192] Ostensibly, the meeting was called to iron out the differences between Freud and Zurich, and in particular Bleuler, whom Freud met privately before Jung arrived.[193] In anticipation, Jung had written Freud the week before:

> I am greatly looking forward to Munich, where the Schreber will play a not unimportant role. I hope my hands won't be empty either, though unfortunately I cannot bring my manuscript along with me. For one thing it has still to be copied out, and for another it is only the first half. The earlier lecture I sent you has been vastly expanded. Moreover the second half...has proved to be so rich...that I haven't yet been able to put everything in order.... I can publish the second half only in the summer.... It seems to me, however, that this time I have hit the mark.... Too much shouldn't be revealed yet.[194]

After the Munich meetings, Freud wrote to Ferenczi of Bleuler:

> I came to a complete understanding with him and achieved a good personal relationship. After all he is only a poor devil like ourselves and in need of a little love, a fact which perhaps has been neglected in certain quarters that matter to him.[195]

On the subject of Jung, Freud added:

> He was magnificent and did me a power of good. I opened my heart to him, about the Adler affair, my own difficulties and my worry over what to do about the matter of telepathy...I am more than ever convinced that he is the man of the future.[196]

In Munich, Freud had spoken to Jung about Ferenczi's experiments with the occult and the conclusions he drew from them. In the course of the conversation Jung admitted to Freud that he too had conducted experiments that demonstrated to his satisfaction the reality of telepathy. Freud urged Jung to communicate with Ferenczi with the possibility of collaborating.[197] While he was in Munich Freud also intended to visit an astrologer, Frau Arnold, whose talents lay in her ability to predict the future on the basis of astrological data. For some reason Freud could not recall her name and never ended up seeing her.[198] Ernest Jones informs his readers that "It was by no means the only time that Freud had made use of an unconscious parapraxis to interfere with his investigation of occultism."[199] Nevertheless, Freud's powers of criticism and caution gained the upper hand, and, echoing the statement Jung claimed he made about "the black tide of mud of occultism," he wrote to Ferenczi about Jung's researches:

> His own investigations have carried him far into the realm of mythology, which he wants to open up with the key of the libido theory. However agreeable all that may be I nevertheless bade him return in good time to the neuroses. There is the motherland where we have first to fortify our dominion against everything and everybody.[200]

One of Freud's first steps in the building of the fortification was taken in a small essay, "Formulations on the Two Principles of Mental Functioning," which he completed at the end of January 1911.[201] It only superficially resembled Jung's earlier formulation on two kinds of thinking, to which I have already referred. Actually, as Jones pointed out, it harks back, as did the Schreber essay, to Freud's "Fliess period," during which he tentatively formulated a distinction between the primary process and secondary process of mental functioning.[202] Now, Freud turned these into the "pleasure principle" and the "reality principle." Thus characterizing unconscious mental processes chiefly in terms of the former, the "pleasure principle," he safely undermined any attempt to endow them with supranormal characteristics.

During the same month that Freud completed his essay on "Two Principles," he sent Ferenczi what he considered the best example of telepathy he had come upon.[203] This fired up Ferenczi and he took to experimenting with people in public streetcars![204] Jung, if more discreet than Ferenczi, was no less enthusiastic and wrote to Freud in the spring:

Besides the psychology of religion and mythology, the "manifest forms of unconscious fantasies" are eating me alive. I have made remarkable discoveries....

Occultism is another field we shall have to conquer.... There are strange and wondrous things in these lands of darkness. Please don't worry about my wanderings in these infinitudes. I shall return laden with rich booty for our knowledge of the human psyche. For a while longer I must...fathom the secrets that lie hidden in the abysses of the unconscious.[205]

After Freud received Jung's letter he wrote to Ferenczi:

Jung writes to me that we must conquer the field of occultism and asks for my agreeing to his leading a crusade....I can see that you two are not to be held back. At least go forward in collaboration with each other; it is a dangerous expedition and I cannot accompany you.[206]

Freud also wrote to Jung the next day:

I am aware that you are driven by innermost inclination to the study of the occult and I am sure you will return home richly laden. I cannot argue with that, it is always right to go where your impulses lead. You will be accused of mysticism.... Just don't stay in the tropical colonies too long; you must reign at home.[207]

A month later Jung wrote to Freud about a dementia praecox case he was working on and in which he uncovered "a tremendous unconscious fantasy system."[208] From his observations of this case, Jung concluded:

It seems that in Dem. praec. you have at all costs to bring to light the inner world produced by the introversion of libido, which in paranoiacs suddenly appears in distorted form as a delusional system (Schreber).... It seems that introversion leads not only, as in hysteria, to a recrudescence of infantile memories but also to a loosening up of the historical layers of the unconscious, thus giving rise to perilous formations which come to light only in exceptional cases.[209]

He also informed Freud that he had taken up astrology and was quite impressed by the remarkable correspondence between horoscopes and biographical details. From this most recent excursion into "tropical colonies" Jung drew the following conclusions:

> I dare say that we shall one day discover in astrology a good deal of knowledge that has been intuitively projected into the heavens. For instance, it appears that the signs of the zodiac are character pictures, in other words libido symbols which depict the typical qualities of the libido at a given moment.[210]

Freud replied to Jung in a letter (June 15, 1911) in which he responded to "the mysterious matters you mention."[211]

> In matters of occultism I have grown humble since the great lessons Ferenczi's experiences gave me. I promise to believe anything that can be made to look reasonable. I shall not do so gladly, that you know. But my hubris has been shattered. I should be glad to know that you are in harmony with F[erenczi] when one of you decides to take the dangerous step into publication.

While Freud was encouraging, he nevertheless introduced a caveat against the conclusions Jung seemed to be drawing from his studies:

> I am very much interested in what you tell me about the system of ucs. fantasies in a case of D. pr. These constructions are known to me from hysteria and obsessional neurosis; they are nothing other than carefully cultivated daydreams.... the symptoms spring not directly from the memories but from the fantasies built on them.... these fantasies provide the closest link between hysteria and the paranoids.... On the role of fantasies—your introversion of the libido—I am mulling over a few fundamental ideas.[212]

This difficulty over the interpretation of unconscious fantasy brought to the surface their different understanding of the nature of the libido. What had at first been tentative assertions on Jung's part, and which had only made Freud impatient, now threatened to emerge as the key element in a larger psychological system. It was becoming clear that Jung's views on unconscious fantasy and the nature of the libido were directly related to his researches into what Freud called "occultism." In Munich, Freud had attempted to harness Jung's interest in occultism by urging him to collaborate with Ferenczi, but nothing came of this.[213] Both Ferenczi and Freud became increasingly hesitant about committing themselves prematurely to the investigation of telepathic and similar phenomena.[214] In addition, Ferenczi became entangled with some disreputable mediums and in the end he did not venture to publish on the subject.[215]

In August 1911, Freud received his copy of the *Jahrbuch* in which were published "Two Principles" and the "Schreber Case," as well as part 1 of Jung's *Symbols of Transformation*.[216] On the same day Freud wrote a letter (August 20, 1911) to Jung in which he made the following cryptic remarks:

> I have been working in a field where you will be surprised to meet me. I have unearthed strange and uncanny things and will almost feel obliged *not* to discuss them with you. But you are too shrewd not to guess what I am up to when I add that I am dying to read your "Transformations and Symb. of the Lib."[217]

Jung replied to Freud, finding his remarks somewhat quizzical:

> your letter has got me on tenderhooks because, for all my "shrewdness," I can't quite make out what is going on so enigmatically behind the scenes. Together with my wife I have tried to unriddle your words, and we have reached surmises which, for the time being at any rate, I would rather keep to myself. I can only hope that your embargo on discussion will be lifted during your stay here. I, too, have the feeling that...we are on the threshold of something really sensational,...the reincarnation of ancient wisdom in the shape of psychoanalysis. I daren't say too much,...let my "Transf. and Symb. of the Lib." unleash your associations and/or fantasies: I am sure you will hit upon strange things if you do.[218]

When Freud received Jung's letter he wrote back:

> I am glad to release you as well as your dear wife, well known to me as a solver of riddles, from the darkness by informing you that my work in these last few weeks has

dealt with the same theme as yours, to wit, the origin of religion.... But since I can see from a first reading of your article in the *Jahrbuch*...that my conclusions are known to you, I find, much to my relief, that there is no need for secrecy. So you too are aware that the Oedipus complex is at the root of religious feeling. Bravo! What evidence I have to contribute can be told in five minutes.[219]

Two weeks later Freud went to stay with Jung in Küsnacht on his way to the Third Psychoanalytic Congress, held on September 21–22, in Weimar.[220] While he was there Freud did not mention Jung's essay, but his silence left Jung's wife the impression that he was disturbed by some of its contents.[221] At the congress, Freud gave a short paper, "Postscript to the Analysis of Schreber," in which he drew a parallel between paranoia and mythology by introducing the primitive idea of Totemism.[222] In Freud's view the totem, an animal or object, symbolized the origin of a primitive tribe, and therefore stood, in the light of psychoanalysis, as a representation of the father. On the basis of this assertion he drew a conclusion which was at the heart of a work in progress, "Totem and Taboo":

> We have here arrived at the consideration of matters which, as it seems to me, may make it possible to arrive at a psycho-analytic explanation of the origins of religion.[223]

At the close of his paper Freud, in a very characteristic gesture, made reference to Jung:

> This short postscript to my analysis of a paranoid patient may serve to show that Jung had excellent grounds for his assertion that the mythopoeic forces of mankind are not extinct, but that to this day they give rise in the neuroses to the same psychical products as in the remotest past ages.

Yet, he went on to add:

> I should like to take up a suggestion that I myself made some time ago, and add that the same holds good of the forces that construct religions. And I am of the opinion that the time will soon be ripe for us to make an extension of a thesis which has long been asserted by psycho-analysts, and to complete what has hitherto had only an individual and ontogenetic application by the addition of its anthropologi-

cal counterpart, which is to be conceived phylogenetically. 'In dreams and in neuroses...we come once more upon the *child....*' 'And we come upon the *savage* too.'[224]

The earlier "suggestion" that Freud made reference to is none other than his first excursion into the psychology of religion, "Obsessive Actions and Religious Practices." It is also the first paper Jung heard Freud deliver. The hint Freud dropped about the origin of religion in "Postscript to the Analysis of Schreber" he would elaborate on in considerable detail in "Totem and Taboo."[225]

Jung also delivered a paper at Weimar entitled "Contributions on Symbolism."[226] The following is a report of its contents:

> Starting from the contrast that exists between hysterical fantasies and those of dementia praecox...in order to understand the latter, historical parallels must be adduced, because in dementia praecox the patient suffers from the reminiscences of mankind. In contrast to hysteria, his language uses ancient images of universal validity, even though at first glance they seem incomprehensible to us.[227]

From these opening remarks Jung next turned to a case of a female neurotic "to illustrate how a recent fantasy can be documented and elucidated by historical material."[228] She had a fantasy in which the man she loved was strung up by his genitals. Jung concluded:

> This fantasy, when taken together with corresponding ethnological traditions and mythological parallels of the sacrifice of the god of spring by hanging or flaying, signifies a sacrifice of sexuality which one hangs on to and cannot get rid of and which in ancient cults was offered to the Great Mother as a sacrifice of the phallus.[229]

The two papers stand in stark contrast to one another. Yet, remarkably enough, Freud and Jung were perceived by some to be on the best of terms in Weimar.[230] This was not a perception shared by Jung's wife, who was also there.[231] Shortly after the Congress, Emma Jung wrote Ferenczi expressing her concern over the growing estrangement between her husband and Freud. She attributed this state of affairs to Freud's reluctance to shed his authority for friendship, and she also sensed Freud's disapproval of part 1 of Jung's *Symbols of Transformation*. Ferenczi, in a letter (October 19,

1911) to Freud, enclosed Emma Jung's letter.[232] In his letter he surmised that Freud's reserve, which Emma Jung had detected, was the result of "the profound after-effects of the Breuer-Fliess experiences."[233] He also thought Emma Jung sensed that Freud had become alarmed because of Jung's preoccupation with occultism and his work on the libido.[234] Nevertheless, Ferenczi wanted to write Emma Jung that her concerns were unfounded and that she should communicate with Freud directly, and he wrote to Freud seeking his approval for this course of action.[235]

Freud responded to Ferenczi's letter advising him to go ahead but specifically requested him *not* to mention "occultism or libido."[236] Ferenczi curiously misread Freud's instructions, sent Emma Jung a letter in which he mentioned the subjects occultism and libido, and then, realizing what he had done, he anxiously wrote to Freud:

> You can imagine my unpleasant surprise when now *naturally* after sending the letter to Frau Jung, I reread your letter and noticed that...I had mistakenly read to *strike* [*streichen*], for *to touch upon* [*streifen*]![237]

It was too late, Ferenczi wrote apologetically, "I touched on occultism and libido transformation."[238] In subsequent letters to Freud, Emma Jung raised her concerns with him and even ventured to address Freud on the subject of his personal life and his relationship with his children, in the hope that this would make him understand the nature of the father/son conflict he had with her husband.[239]

Freud, in a letter (November 12, 1911) to Jung, decided to forego his silence and comment on part 1 of *Symbols of Transformation*. He called it "the best thing" Jung had written.[240] In addition to a few critical remarks Freud wrote:

> it is a torment to me to think, when I conceive an idea... that I may be...appropriating something that might just as well have been acquired by you.... Why in God's name did I allow myself to follow you into this field?[241]

Jung responded, thanking Freud for his letter, and added:

> However, the outlook for me is very gloomy if you too get into the psychology of religion. You are a dangerous rival—if one has to speak of rivalry. Yet I think it has to be this way,

for a natural development cannot be halted, nor should one try to halt it. Our personal differences will make our work different. You dig up the precious stones, but I...proceed from the outside to the inside and from the whole to the part. I would find it too upsetting to let large tracts of human knowledge lie there neglected. And because of the difference in our working methods we shall undoubtedly meet from time to time in unexpected places.... It is difficult only at first to accustom oneself to this thought. Later one comes to accept it.[242]

The somewhat romanticized picture which Jung painted of his differences with Freud would turn out to be more accurate than either of them realized at the time. The letters that Freud and Jung exchanged over the next year document the increasingly tragic breakdown of their collaboration and friendship. The subject of the nature of the libido became the focal point of their disagreement. For Freud, libido would remain primarily psychosexual in nature; for Jung, it would be understood in a more neutral sense as psychic energy, unattached to its manifest content. Yet, Jung's ambitions involved more than transcending the restrictions with which Freud circumscribed his empirical observation. As Jung plainly wrote Freud in the late winter of 1912: "I have opinions which are not yours about the ultimate truths of psychoanalysis."[243]

Jung completed part 2 of *Symbols of Transformation* in the spring of 1912.[244] Jones read the proofs of Jung's essay and sent a report of its contents to Freud in September. When Freud finally read the full text of part 2 he wrote to Jones that he knew "the very page where Jung went wrong (p. 174); having discovered that he lost further interest."[245] The next letter Freud addressed to Jung was headed with the more formal "Dear Dr. Jung" instead of his usual "Dear Friend"![246]

Freud published his his own excursion into the psychology of religion, "Totem and Taboo," in installments during the course of 1912 and 1913. In a letter (May 13, 1913) to Ferenczi he commented: "In the dispute with Zurich it comes at the right time to divide us as an acid does a salt."[247] But evidence of the coming division had been obvious for some time and remained only to be formalized. In January 1913 Freud had already proposed in a letter to Jung that they abandon their personal relations altogether.[248] Jung concurred.[249] The rest of their letters over the course of the following year were taken up with business matters until things became impossible for both men. The subjects that had divided them, occultism and the nature of the libido, were never really broached again.

The previous discussion illuminates the role Jung played in Freud's attraction to "the Occult." It would seem that Jung, like Ferenczi, drew Freud into concerning himself and psychoanalysis with the subject of occultism. Jung himself was by far the more serious student of the subject and avoided much of the superstitiousness that sometimes characterized Ferenczi and even Freud. Jung, in contrast to Freud, was thoroughly at home with the literature of spiritualistic phenomena or occultism. He explored the field in order to establish that the psychological processes involved indicated not only pathology but an intelligible purposive intentionality within the psyche. Moreover, Jung viewed as positive proof the fact that these psychological processes were identical to the patterns and symbols in world mythology and religion. He attempted a preliminary demonstration of this in *Symbols of Transformation* (1911–12).

In spite of his differences with Jung, Freud continued to express an interest in occultism, but like Ferenczi he would not take the vital step of "belief" in his publications. In private, however, it was a rather different matter and Freud appears to have been much more ambiguous. Jones characterized Freud's attitude as follows:

> we find throughout an exquisite oscillation between skepticism and credulity so striking that it is possible to quote just as many pieces of evidence in support of his doubt concerning occult beliefs as of his adherence to them.[250]

Some years later Freud even tried to play the part of the medium at a séance, with some success.[251] But his interest in occultism alarmed some of his followers. For the benefit of the future of psychoanalysis, Freud felt it necessary to treat the subject with the utmost caution. He would only state: "I have no opinion on the matter; I know nothing about it."[252] Freud could not admit that belief in such things as telepathy would, in itself, undermine science, but he was unwilling to take the decisive step of saying so publicly. In a letter from 1921, which came to light only in 1953, replying to a request to become an editor of a periodical devoted to the study of occultism, he wrote:

> I am not one of those who dismiss *a priori* the study of so-called occult psychic phenomena as unscientific, discreditable or even as dangerous. If I were at the beginning

rather than at the end of a scientific career, as I am today, I might possibly choose just this field of research, in spite of all difficulties.

I must ask you nevertheless to refrain from mentioning my name in connection with your venture, and this for several reasons.

First, because in the sphere of the occult I am a complete layman and newcomer and have no...authority in this connection.

Second, because I have good reason to be interested in sharply demarcating psychoanalysis (which has nothing occult about it) from this as yet unexplored sphere of knowledge, and in not offering any occasion for misunderstanding in this respect.

Finally, because I cannot rid myself of certain skeptical materialistic prejudices which I would bring with me into the study of the occult. Thus I am utterly incapable of considering the "survival of the personality" after death even as a scientific possibility, and I feel no different about the "idroplasma."[253]

Eight years later, Freud incorrectly denied that he had even written the remarkable statements with which he began this letter.[254] Perhaps he realized that the systematic exploration of "occult psychic phenomena" would seriously affect psychoanalytic theory. He had, after all, seen the direction Jung had taken during the intervening years and how he drastically modified psychoanalysis to incorporate such concepts as the collective unconscious, archetypes, and so on. Furthermore, there were the eccentricities of Ferenczi that, according to Ernest Jones, led him to believe he was being successfully psychoanalysed telepathically from across the Atlantic by an ex-patient of his—a woman whom Freud called "Ferenczi's evil genius."[255]

Jones gives an account of Freud's private attitude toward spiritualistic phenomena which will complete the background against which Jung's experiences and ideas were formed. Jones records that:

In the years before the Great War, I had several talks with Freud on occultism and kindred topics. He was fond, especially after midnight, of regaling me with strange or uncanny experiences with patients, characteristically

about misfortunes or deaths supervening many years after
a wish or prediction. He...was evidentally impressed by
their more mysterious aspects. When I would protest at
some of the taller stories Freud was wont to reply..."There
are more things in heaven and earth than are dreamed of
in your philosophy."...When they were concerned with
clairvoyant visions...or visitations from departed spirits, I
ventured to reprove him for his inclination to accept occult
beliefs on flimsy evidence. His reply was: "I don't like it at
all myself, but there is some truth in it.".... I then asked him
where such beliefs could halt: if one could believe in mental
processes floating in the air, one could go on to a belief in
angels. He closed the discussion...with the remark: "Quite
so, even *der liebe Gott* [the good God]." This was said in a
jocular tone...and with a quizzical look as if he were
pleased at shocking me. But there was something search-
ing also in the glance, and I went away not entirely happy
lest there be some more serious undertone as well.[256]

If this description of Freud is accurate, it would seem only
natural that he would be drawn to Jung. During his psychoanalyti-
cal period, Jung's preoccupation with spiritualistic phenomena had
not abated in the least. Freud was certainly aware of Jung's attraction to this field and to some extent developed an interest in it himself. What disturbed Freud most, and Jones's account suggests this
tendency could be found in Freud himself, was that the attraction
to such phenomena, at bottom, was religious in nature. Years later
Freud himself clearly expressed such suspicions:

If we accept the truth of what, according to the occultists'
information, still occurs today, we must also believe in the
authenticity of the reports which have come down to us
from ancient times. And we must then reflect that the tradition and sacred books of all peoples are brimful of similar
marvelous tales and that the religions base their claim to
credibility on precisely such miraculous events and find
proof in them of the operation of superhuman powers. That
being so, it will be hard for us to avoid a suspicion that the
interest in occultism is in fact a religious one and that one
of the secret motives of the occultist movement is to come to
the help of religion, threatened as it is by the advance of
scientific thought. And with the discovery of this motive

our distrust must increase and our disinclination to embark on the examination of these supposedly occult phenomena.[257]

In the end, Freud was not prepared to seriously and publicly consider the data of spiritualistic phenomena, or what he called "occultism," as raw material upon which to build a psychology. Such phenomena, Freud thought, might hold great promise, but the trade-off in public shame and intellectual confusion was too costly.

Jung, on the other hand, had long experience with spiritualistic phenomena and understood its pathology. He also recognized that in such phenomena was to be found direct evidence of the primal unconscious. These same data at times occurred in hysterical, and especially in psychotic individuals. Moreover, the religious and mythological literature of the world also contained similar material. How all these factors could be brought together was for Jung the crucial question. In the course of addressing himself to this question it became increasingly clear to Jung that he was moving away from Freud and from psychoanalysis.[258]

Notes

1. *MDR*, 111–12. There is a woodcut of the Burghölzli in Jaffé, *Word and Image*, 37.

2. Aubrey Lewis, "Jung's Early Work," *Journal of Analytical Psychology* 2 (1957): 119–20.

3. Ellenberger, *Discovery*, 286–87.

4. *MDR*, 112–13.

5. Lewis, 120 et seq. Jung's writings on these subjects can be found in three volumes of his *Collected Works: Psychiaatric Studies* (vol. 1); *Experimental Researches* (vol. 2); and *The Psychogenesis of Mental Disease* (vol. 3). It would be no exaggeration to state that these are probably the least read of Jung's writings.

6. Ellenberger, *Discovery*, 692–93.

7. Ibid.

8. Ibid.

9. Ibid.

10. John R. Haule, "Archetype and Integration: Exploring the Janetian Roots of Analytical Psychology," 253–267; Witzig, 131–48.

11. Wehr, 82.

12. John R. Haule, "From Somnambulism to the Archetypes: The French Roots of Jung's Split with Freud," 635–59.

13. Ellenberger, *Discovery*, 694.

14. Ibid.

15. C. G. Jung, "On Spiritualistic Phenomena" (1905), in *The Symbolic Life*, 293–308.

16. Ibid., 293.

17. Ibid., 294, 299.

18. Ibid., 301.

19. Ibid., 301, 304.

20. Ibid., 304.

21. Ibid., 301–302.

22. Ibid., 302–303.

23. Ibid., 304–305.

24. Ibid., 306–307.

25. Ibid., 308.

26. Von Franz, *C. G. Jung: His Myth in Our Time*, 55.

27. Ibid., 56. Presumably with one of the mediums Jung referred to in his Basel lecture on Spiritualism.

28. Sigmund Freud, "Preface to the Translation of Bernheim's *Suggestion*" (1888) in *Pre-Psycho-Analytic Publications and Unpublished Drafts*, 73–85.

29. *MDR*, 94. The copy is in Jung library; see *Katalog*, 10.

30. Jung, "Sigmund Freud: *On Dreams*" (1901), in *The Symbolic Life*, 361–68.

31. Steele, 184.

32. Ellenberger, *Discovery*, 694.

33. Jung, "The Psychology of Dementia Praecox" (1907), in *The Psychogenesis of Mental Disease*, 3–4.

34. Paul Stepansky, "The Empiricist as Rebel: Jung, Freud, and the Burdens of Discipleship," *Journal of the History of the Behavioral Sciences* 12 (1976): 216–39.

35. These form part of Jung's *Studies in Word Association* (1904–09); see *The Freud/Jung Letters*, 24, 3.

36. *MDR*, 149.

37. Herman Nunberg and Ernst Federn, eds., *Minutes of the Vienna Psychoanalytic Society*, vol. 1 (New York: International Universities Press, 1962), 128 n. 2, 142 n. 4, 144; *The Freud/Jung Letters*, 24, 42 n. 2.

38. Sigmund Freud, "Obsessive Actions and Religious Practices" (1907), in *Standard Edition*, vol. 9, *Jensen's 'Gradiva' and Other Works* (London: The Hogarth Press, 1959), 117–27.

39. Ibid., 126–27.

40. *The Freud/Jung Letters*, 25.

41. Ibid., 26.

42. *MDR*, 149.

43. Ibid., 149–50. I might point out that Freud viewed "any expression of spirituality" as a somewhat vaguely defined field of human experience, and he did not draw hard distinctions between religion and what he called "occultism." By the latter, he understood the whole gamut of spiritualistic phenomena, though he did isolate for special consideration the phenomenon of telepathy. The distinction Jones makes (vol. 3, 349–74, 375–407), between religion and occultism in his survey of these topics in Freud's life and thought is not without value, even though Jones's lack of sympathy for these subjects, or his downright ignorance of them, is, at times, rather disconcerting, e.g. (vol. 3, 350), when he calls the *Torah* "a book of Jewish philosophy rather than of religion."

44. *MDR*, 149.

45. Jung's papers on psychoanalysis are in *Freud and Psychoanalysis*.

46. Jones, vol. 2, 33.

47. Jones, vol. 3, 379 et seq.

48. Sigmund Freud, "Delusions and Dreams in Jensen's *Gradiva*" (1907), in *Standard Edition*, vol. 9, *Jensen's 'Gradiva' and Other Works* (London: The Hogarth Press, 1959), 71. The editorial comment, ibid., 4, links the work to Jung.

49. Ibid., 71.

50. Ibid., 71–72.

51. *The Freud/Jung Letters*, 62 et seq.

52. Ibid., 68.

53. Ibid., 73.

54. Ibid., 73–74.

55. Jung's "bit of historical mysticism" is pat, except for the fact that Freud's views did not, at first, receive the same reception in Paris as did those of Mesmer and Gall. This was largely due to the tension between the Freudian claim to originality and previous psychological investigations (e.g., those of Janet) which would seem to undercut the uniqueness of some of Freud's early theories; see Ellenberger, *Discovery*, 538–40. On a more personal level, the word association tests to which Jung anonymously submitted himself in 1907 indicate Vienna/Paris was an emotionally toned association for him as were Goethe, philosophy, and father/death; see William McGuire, "Jung's Complex Reactions (1907): Word Association Experiments Performed by Binswanger," *Spring* (1984): 3, 17; 5, 12, 23; 10; 14, respectively. Presumably, Jung lived in the tension between knowing that Freud's theories were part of a much broader world of psychological investigation and his need to idealize Freud. In this he was not alone; see Frank J. Sulloway, *Freud, Biologist of the Mind* (New York: Basic Books, 1979), 445–95, on Freud and "The Myth of the Hero."

56. *The Freud/Jung Letters*, 107–8. Jung also mentioned this case in a letter to Abraham, the day after he wrote to Freud; see Jung, *Letters 1: 1905–1950*, 5.

57. *The Freud/Jung Letters*, 108.

58. I will return to the subject of Jung's cousin, the medium.

59. *The Freud/Jung Letters*, 109.

60. Ibid., 111.

61. Ibid.; Jung, "The Freudian Theory of Hysteria" (1908), in *Freud and Psychoanalysis*, 10–24.

62. *The Freud/Jung Letters*, 124.

63. Ibid., 74 n. 7.

64. Sigmund Freud, *A Psycho-Analytic Dialogue: The Letters of Sigmund Freud and Karl Abraham 1907–1926*, ed. Hilda C. Abraham and Ernst L. Freud (New York: Basic Books, 1965) (hereafter *The Freud/Abraham Letters*).

65. *The Freud/Jung Letters*, 78.

66. Ibid., 105.

67. Ibid., 106.

68. Ibid., 109. Similar ideas were touched upon by Freud and Abraham is an exchange of letters three months earlier, see *The Freud/Abraham Letters*, 8–9.

69. *The Freud/Jung Letters*, 78, 79, 93, 103, 134.

70. Ibid., 137–39.

71. Ibid., 133, 138.

72. Ibid., 139.

73. Jones, vol. 2, 41–42, 262–68. According to Abraham, Freud's paper took two hours to deliver; see *The Freud/Abraham Letters*, 146. The paper was published, in a revised form, as Sigmund Freud, "Notes Upon a Case of Obsessional Neurosis" (1909) in *Standard Edition*, vol. 10, *Two Case Histories ('Little Hans' and the 'Rat Man')*, (London: The Hogarth Press, 1955), 153–318.

74. Jones, vol. 2, 264.

75. Ibid., 266.

76. Ibid.

77. Ibid. It is not hard to see in these comments a critique of observations that Jung would later enshrine as a precept in "Synchronicity: An Acausal Connecting Principle," in *The Structure and Dynamics of the Psyche*, 419–519. I will return to this essay in the concluding chapter.

78. Karl Abraham, "The Psycho-Sexual Differences Between Hysteria and Dementia Praecox" (1908), in *Selected Papers of Karl Abraham* (London: The Hogarth Press, 1948), 64–79.

79. Jones, vol. 2, 46–47.

80. *The Freud/Abraham Letters*, 97. For the Schreber case, Sigmund Freud, "Psycho-Analytic Notes on an Autobiographical Account of a Case of Paranoia (Dementia Paranoides)" (1911–12) in *The Case of Schreber: Papers on Technique and Other Works*, 9–82.

81. *The Freud/Abraham Letters*, 103. As Jones, vol. 2, 47 n. 37, pointed out, Freud had come upon this idea in his exchange with Fleiss in 1899; see Sigmund Freud, *The Origins of Psycho-Analysis, Letters to Wilhelm Fliess, Drafts and Notes: 1887–1902*, ed. Marie Bonaparte, Anna Freud, and Ernst Kris (New York: Basic Books, 1954), 303–4.

82. C. G. Jung, "On Dementia Praecox" (1908), in *The Symbolic Life*, 335. This is the abstract of the paper "On Dementia Praecox," no copies of which have survived.

83. Jones, vol. 2, 47.

84. Ibid.

85. See C. G. Jung, "Schizophrenia" (1958), in *The Psychogenesis of Mental Diseases*, 263–64, where in a paper he sent to the second International Congress for Psychiatry held in Zurich, in 1957, he mentioned his early views on dementia praecox and came down on the side of "psychogenic causation." But in a letter of clarification, ibid., 272, to a Symposium on Chemical Concepts of Psychosis, at the same congress, he advocated a dual causation, emotional and chemical.

86. *The Freud/Jung Letters*, 143.

87. Ibid., 144.

88. Jones, vol. 2, 44.

89. Ibid.

90. Ibid., 138.

91. *The Freud/Abraham Letters*, 34.

92. Abraham had snubbed Jung and Bleuler by failing to mention their work on dementia praecox in his Salzburg paper, see Jones, vol. 2, 46 et seq. Jung, in turn, felt Abraham had stolen some of his ideas from him; see *The Freud/Jung Letters*, 149.

93. *The Freud/Abraham Letters*, 36. This remark does not necessarily imply any "religiosity" on Abraham's part. His father had been a teacher of religion, who for financial reasons had to enter business but remained a devout Jew. Despite this traditional Jewish background, Abraham himself repudiated all religious belief, see Edward Glover, "Abraham, Karl," in Ludwig Eidelberg, ed., *Encyclopedia of Psychoanalysis* (New York: The Free Press, 1968), 3–4. Jones, vol. 2, 159, described Abraham as devoid of any inclination toward rash or speculative thinking!

94. *The Freud/Abraham Letters*, 43.

95. Ibid., 44–45.

96. Ibid., 46.

97. Ibid., 47.

98. *The Freud/Jung Letters*, 158.

99. Jung, in a late letter (May 7, 1956), stated of Freud's misguided suspicions: "Naturally he assumed that my more positive ideas about religion and its importance for our psychological life were nothing but an outcrop of my unrealized resistances against my clergyman father, whereas in reality my problem and my personal prejudice were never centered in my father but most emphatically in my mother," Jung, *Letters 2: 1951–1961*, 296.

100. *The Freud/Jung Letters*, 171; Jones, vol. 2, 50–53.

101. *The Freud/Abraham Letters*, 51–52.

102. Ibid., 53.

103. Ibid., 47; also Freud's remarks in ibid., 54.

104. *The Freud/Jung Letters*, 172.

105. Ibid., 172–73.

106. Ibid., 207.The journal appeared in March 1909.

107. Ibid., 214–15.

108. *MDR*, 155.

109. Jones, vol. 3, 383–84.

110. *The Freud/Jung Letters*, 215, 216–17.

111. *MDR*, 156.

112. *The Freud/Jung Letters*, 218–19. For psychosynthesis see ibid., 91; and C. G. Jung, "Abstracts of the Psychological Works of Swiss Authors" (1910), in *The Symbolic Life*, 398–99.

113. *The Freud/Jung Letters*, 220.

114. Herman Nunberg, *Memoirs: Recollections, Ideas, Reflections.* (New York: The Psychoanalytic Research and Development Fund, 1969), 109.

115. Ibid., 116. Bennet, *Meetings With Jung*, 110–11, reports a conversation in which Jung mentioned that an incident similar to the one he experienced with Freud occurred with Bleuler. According to Jung, Bleuler at first said "it was all nonsense; but twenty years later he became a spiritualist and had many experiences of this kind."

116. Nunberg, 112.

117. *The Freud/Jung Letters*, 7, where Jung called Spielrein a hysteric.

118. Jung, "The Freudian Theory of Hysteria," 20–22, where he categorized Spielrein as a hysteric-psychotic. Aldo Carotenuto, *A Secret Symmetry: Sabina Spielrein between Jung and Freud* (New York: Pantheon Books, 1984), 140–41, states that Spielrein was a patient at Burghölzli in 1904–5 and probably an outpatient for a time afterward. At the later stage of her treatment, she also studied medicine and psychiatry at the University of Zurich, graduating in 1911 with a dissertation on schizophrenia.

119. *The Freud/Jung Letters*, 111. See also McGuire, "Jung's Complex Reactions (1907)," 2–5, for the presence of his relationship with Spielrein in the association-tests he underwent; and Spielrein's own comments in Carotenuto, 102.

120. *The Freud/Jung Letters*, 207.

121. Ibid., 210.

122. Ibid., 211.

123. Ibid., 211–12.

124. John Kerr, "Beyond the Pleasure Principle and Back Again: Freud, Jung, and Sabina Spielrein," in Paul E. Stepansky, *Freud: Appraisals and Reappraisals*, vol. 3, (Hillsdale, N.J.: The Analytic Press, 1988), 3–79.

125. Carotenuto, 91.

126. *The Freud/Jung Letters*, 226.

127. Ibid., 226.

128. Ibid., 228.

129. Ibid., 228–29.

130. Ibid., 229.

131. Ibid., 230.

132. Ibid. For Freud's letter to Spielrein see Carotenuto, 113.

133. *The Freud/Jung Letters*, 232.

134. Ibid., 235.

135. Carotenuto, 104.

136. Ibid.

137. Ibid.

138. Ibid., 104–5.

139. *The Freud/Jung Letters*, 236.

140. Ibid.

141. Carotenuto, 115.

142. *The Freud/Jung Letters*, 238.

143. Ibid.

144. Ibid.

145. Jung, *Letters 1: 1905–1950*, 531.

146. Ibid.

147. Jung, *Letters 2: 1951–1961*, 452. Eugene Taylor, "C. G. Jung and the Boston Psychopathologists, 1902–1912," in E. Mark Stern, ed., *Carl Jung and Soul Psychology* (New York: The Haworth Press, 1986), 140, points out that James' annotated copy of Jung's dissertation, *On the Psychology and Pathology of So-Called Occult Phenomena*, is in Houghton Library, Harvard University. He thinks it likely that Jung gave it to James at the time of their meeting in 1909, and adds (140 n.3), "Jung's interest in the occult at once divided him from Freud and more closely allied him with the Boston psychopathologists [Adolf Meyer, James Putnam, and William James].... He continually differed with Freud over psychic events, believing himself capable of eliciting the phenomena, even in Freud's presence. Indeed, the occult for Jung was not a peripheral problem beyond science, but rather at the very heart of his psychology, for the psychic dimension of personality represented not the merely diabolical element within each one of us, but also unconscious creative ferment—the personality in transition, not for mere social adaptation, but for the forging of character—the achievement of the unique spiritual destiny of each individual."

148. William James, *The Letters of William James and Theodore Flournoy*, ed. Robert C. Le Clair (Madison: The University of Wisconsin Press, 1966), 224 (hereafter *The James/Flournoy Letters*). Flournoy was familiar with Jung's dissertation, having given it a very positive review in *Archives de Psychologie* 2 (1903): 85–86.

149. G. Stanley Hall, "A Medium in the Bud," *The American Journal of Psychology* 29 (1918): 156. It is interesting to note that Hall's encounter with Spiritualism was rather extensive. He had been a spiritualist when he was younger and maintained a continuous, if critical, interest in the subject; see Moore, 153.

150. Jones, vol. 3, 375–76.

151. Ibid., 376–77.

152. Ibid., 378.

153. Ibid., 378–83, on the various forms of superstition to which Freud was susceptible as well as the emergence in him of an interest in "thought transference."

154. Ibid., 385.

155. Ibid.

156. Ibid. Even though Freud and Ferenczi visited Abraham during their stay in Berlin, there is no mention of their "experiments" with the medium in Freud's letters to Abraham; see Jones, vol. 2, 65. Abraham, in a letter (November 10, 1909) to Freud, did state, "I shall probably have to give evidence concerning a spiritualist medium, about whose unmasking there was a great deal in the press," *The Freud/Abraham Letters*, 81–82. Freud, however, did make mention of his "project" with Ferenczi in a letter to Jung, *The Freud/Jung Letters*, 255.

157. Sandor Ferenczi, "Spiritism" (1899) *The Psychoanalytic Review* 50 (1963): 144.

158. Jones, vol. 3, 384. Michael Bálint, Ferenczi's literary editor, claims that the latter's interest in spiritualistic phenomena went back to his early youth; see Nandor Fodor, "Sandor Ferenczi's Psychic Adventures," *International Journal of Parapsychology* 3 (1961), 52.

159. Jones, vol. 3, 384. The complete correspondence between Freud and Ferenczi consists of approximately twenty-five hundred letters, according to Paul Roazen, *Freud and His Followers* (New York: Alfred A. Knopf, 1975), 359. Until recently they had been withheld, but following the death of Anna Freud in 1982, the heirs of the Freud estate decided to allow their full publication; see Ilse Grubrich-Simitis, "Six Letters of Sigmund Freud and Sándor Ferenczi on the Interrelationship of Psychoanalytic Theory and Technique," *International Review of Psycho-Analysis* 13 (1986): 259. Presumably these letters when published will shed some light on Freud's and Ferenczi's interests in "Occultism" because, as Jones, vol. 3, 384, points out, "A good deal of their correspondence over the years is taken up with discussions of various aspects of the subject."

160. Jones, vol. 3, 384 et seq.

161. Ibid., 386–87.

162. *The James/Flournoy Letters*, 228.

163. *MDR*, 150, gives the date as 1910; Jones, vol. 2, 140, states Jung was in Vienna on April 19, 1910. McGuire in *The Freud/Jung Letters*, 216 n. 4, claims there is no evidence Jung visited Freud in Vienna after March 1909, and suggests this conversation may have taken place during that visit. Jung's reference *MDR*, 153, to "that second conversation" would seem

to suggest he had merely confused 1910 and 1909. If the conversation did take place prior to the Clark conference, it would indeed underline Freud's concerns about uncovering for Jung the sexual etiology of spiritualistic phenomena evident in the analysis of Hall's medium.

164. *MDR*, 150.

165. Ibid., 150–51.

166. It would seem that Jung, like Freud, associated all of these areas, not always making any hard distinctions between them.

167. *The Freud/Jung Letters*, 293–94.

168. Ibid., 295.

169. Ibid., 296.

170. Ibid., 298–99.

171. Jung, *Symbols of Transformation*, 7–33.

172. *The Freud/Jung Letters*, 308.

173. Nunberg and Federn, *Minutes of the Vienna Psychoanalytic Society*, vol. 2, 422.

174. Roazen, 233, citing an interview with Edoardo Weiss.

175. *The Freud/Jung Letters*, 396.

176. Ibid., 251.

177. Ibid., 254.

178. Ibid., 274–76.

179. Jung, *Letters 1: 1905–1950*, 14.

180. See Freud's comments in *The Freud/Jung Letters*, 332–35.

181. Ibid., 343.

182. Ibid., 311; Jones, vol. 2, 268. Jung, in *Symbols of Transformation*, 300 n. 65, claimed that he brought Schreber's work to the attention of Freud.

183. *The Freud/Jung Letters*, 353.

184. Ibid., 379.

185. Jones, vol. 2, 268.

186. Ibid., 270.

187. *The Freud/Jung Letters*, 380.

188. *The Freud/Abraham Letters*, 103.

189. *The Freud/Jung Letters*, 216, 219, 376, 382.

190. Jones, vol. 2, 269.

191. Ibid., 268.

192. *The Freud/Jung Letters*, 384.

193. Ibid., 378 et seq.

194. Ibid., 378.

195. Jones, vol. 2, 140, citing Freud's letter (December 29, 1910) to Ferenczi.

196. Ibid.

197. Jones, vol. 3, 387.

198. Ibid., 385–87.

199. Ibid., 387.

200. Jones, vol. 2, 140, citing Freud's letter (December 29, 1910) to Ferenczi.

201. Jones, vol. 2, 312. Sigmund Freud, "Formulations on the Two Principles of Mental Functioning" (1911), in *The Case of Schreber Papers on Technique and Other Works*, 218–26.

202. Jones, vol. 2, 312–13.

203. Jones, vol. 3, 387. Freud later included this example in "Dreams and Telepathy" (1922) in *Standard Edition,* vol. 18, *Beyond the Pleasure Principle: Group Psychology and Other Works* (London: The Hogarth Press, 1955), 209 et seq.

204. Jones, vol. 3, 387.

205. *The Freud/Jung Letters*, 421.

206. Ibid., 421 n.6, citing Freud's letter (May 11, 1911) to Ferenczi.

207. *The Freud/Jung Letters*, 422.

208. Ibid., 426.

209. Ibid., 426–27.

210. Ibid., 427.

211. Ibid., 428.

212. Ibid., 429–30.

213. Jones, vol. 3, 387 et seq.

214. Ibid.

215. Ibid., 388–89.

216. *The Freud/Jung Letters*, 438, 565.

217. Ibid., 438.

218. Ibid., 439.

219. Ibid., 441.

220. Ibid., 443.

221. Ibid., 452.

222. Ibid., 575; Sigmund Freud, "Psycho-Analytic Notes on an Auto-biographical Account of a Case of Paranoia (Dementia Paranoides)," 81.

223. Ibid.

224. Ibid., 82.

225. Sigmund Freud, "Totem and Taboo" (1913), in *Standard Edition*, vol 13, *Totem and Taboo and Other Works* (London: The Hogarth Press, 1955), 1–161.

226. *The Freud/Jung Letters*, 575. Jung's paper has not survived except as an abstract; see C. G. Jung, "Contributions to Symbolism," in *The Symbolic Life*, 446.

227. Ibid.

228. Ibid.

229. Ibid.

230. Jones, vol. 2, 86.

231. She is included in the group photograph of the Weimar Congress; see *The Freud/Jung Letters*, plate 6 facing page 444.

232. Donn, 137, citing Ferenczi's letter (October 19, 1911) to Freud, Sigmund Freud Collection, Accession number 19042. Library of Congress, Washington, D.C.

233. Ibid.

234. Ibid.

235. Ibid., 137–38.

236. Donn, 138, citing Ferenczi's letter (October 23, 1911) to Freud. Sigmund Freud Collection, Accession number 19042.

237. Ibid.

238. Ibid.

239. *The Freud/Jung Letters,* 452–53; 455–56.

240. Ibid., 459.

241. Ibid.

242. Ibid., 460.

243. Ibid., 491.

244. Ibid., 502.

245. Jones, vol. 2, 143. Emma Jung had sent Freud an offprint of Jung's essay; see *The Freud/Jung Letters,* 514.

246. Ibid., 517.

247. Jones, vol. 2, 354, citing Freud's letter (May 13, 1913) to Ferenczi.

248. *The Freud/Jung Letters,* 539.

249. Ibid., 540.

250. Jones, vol. 3, 375.

251. Ibid., 393. Anna Freud and Ferenczi were the other participants.

252. Ibid., 404.

253. Sigmund Freud, *Letters of Sigmund Freud,* ed. Ernst L. Freud (New York: Basic Books, 1960), 334.

254. Jones, vol. 3, 392.

255. Ibid., 407.

256. Ibid., 381.

257. Sigmund Freud, "New Introductory Lectures on Psycho-Analysis" (1933), in *Standard Edition*, vol. 22, *New Introductory Lectures on Psycho-Analysis and Other Works* (London: The Hogarth Press, 1964), 34.

258. *MDR*, 166–67.

Part 4

Analytical Psychology and Metapsychology

Chapter 7

Spiritualism and the Emergence of
Jung's Psychology

Jung's break with Freud was not the result of any one act or event. Its course can be traced in the correspondence between the two men. The central antagonism to which all the minor ones became attached was the conflict over the precise understanding of the term *libido*. In the end Jung could no longer accept the assumptions about the psychosexual nature of the libido that were essential to remain a Freudian. This placed Jung in a terrible dilemma, and the time after his "psychoanalytic period" was a difficult one for him. It was, in his own words, "a period of inner uncertainty.... It would be no exaggeration to call it a state of disorientation."[1] For some time Jung "felt totally suspended in mid-air."[2] In desperation he even wondered if in Christianity he could find the meaning and security he needed. But to no avail.[3] In fact, it has even been claimed that Jung became so unstable that he found it necessary to undergo psychiatric treatment during this period.[4]

In keeping with Jung's views on the nature of opposites and the tendency of one opposite to run into the other, it is interesting to note some of the factors that tended to cluster together at the high point of Jung's Freudianism and which marked his descent into an uncertain underworld when he broke with Freud. In volume 2 of the *Jahrbuch* (August 1910), Jung published a series of abstracts of psychological works by Swiss authors, including one of his dissertation, *On the Psychology and Pathology of So-Called Occult Phenomena*. In the abstract Jung completely disregarded his own earlier comments on the significance of spirits as indicators of future personality development and capitulated to a Freudian reading, which he expressed as follows:

> Besides clinical and psychological discussions on the nature of hysterical somnambulism, this work contains detailed

observations on a case of spiritualistic mediumship. The splitting of the personality derives from its infantile tendencies and the fantasy systems are found to be rooted in sexual wish-deliria.[5]

Jung also included among the abstracts one of Flournoy's study of mediumship which had served as the model for his own dissertation. In it he commended Flournoy's work as "extremely important," adding that he "comes very close to certain of Freud's views, though no use could be made of his more recent discoveries."[6] Which of Flournoy's "recent discoveries" Jung had in mind he did not say. But within two years Jung would take the opposite view of at least one of Flournoy's discoveries, that of "creative imagination," an example of which he published in the account of the fantasies of a young woman called Miss Frank Miller.[7] These fantasies served Jung as the catalyst for organizing the enormous amount of material on mythology and religion which made up *Symbols of Transformation*.[8]

Little is known about the author of the fantasies, Miss Frank Miller. Jung reported that she had been under the care of Flournoy, and, following a brief sojourn in Europe, she returned to the United States where she began to suffer from schizophrenia.[9] During the First World War Jung stated that he heard from an American physician who was treating her that she had become "entirely deranged."[10] According to Jung, Flournoy confirmed that his analysis of her fantasies in *Symbols of Transformation* had "hit off the young woman's mentality very well."[11] In addition, her American physician had written to him, Jung stated, "to say that my exposition of the case was so exhaustive that even personal acquaintance with the patient had not taught him 'one iota more' about her mentality."[12] There are also one or two items about Miss Miller that can be added to what Jung reported about her and that help one to better understand why he chose her fantasies as the skeleton upon which to hang the almost excessive amount of data he presented in *Symbols of Transformation*.

James Hyslop, a noted American psychical researcher and former professor of logic and ethics, published an English version of the fantasies translated by Miss Miller herself, to which he added a prefatory note.[13] In it Hyslop stated:

> Miss Miller was at one time a student under me in the department of philosophy when I was at Columbia Univer-

sity and is now employed in a private school as a teacher and lecturer. She has been an intelligent student of the phenomena with which the Society [American Society for Psychical Research] is occupied, and her relation to all the work done under me exhibited the same intellectual appreciation of psychological problems.

Hyslop went on to remark on the significance of Miss Miller's fantasies:

> The paper is especially interesting and important as illustrating those mental functions which at least simulate personalities independent of the normal consciousness and it is...an example of those phenomena which many who are little acquainted with the complexities of psychic research mistake for such foreign personalities.... They are most important in estimating the nature and limitations of the supernormal, and perhaps...may throw light on the conditions which affect the development of supernormal experiences and the influences which disturb and distort the passage of foreign thoughts.[14]

In Hyslop's remarks, it is evident that he was concerned to draw a distinction between normal and pathological forms of multiple personality and the possibility of supernormal manifestations by spirit entities. Behind this distinction lies the fact that Hyslop deeply believed that communication between the living and the dead was possible.[15] Jung wrote of him:

> I once discussed the proof of identity for a long time with a friend of William James, Professor Hyslop in New York. He admitted that, all things considered, all these metapsychic phenomena could be explained better by the hypothesis of spirits than by the qualities and peculiarities of the unconscious. And here, on the basis of my own experience, I am bound to concede he is right. In each individual case I must of necessity be skeptical, but in the long run I have to admit that the spirit hypothesis yields better results in practice than any other.[16]

Jung's recollection of his conversation with Hyslop took place late in his life (1946), when he was in the midst of reformulating his own views on the subject of Spiritualism.[17] At the beginning of the second decade of this century he was more concerned with developing a clearly psychological view of spiritualistic phenomena.[18]

Theodore Flournoy, in his introduction to the Miller fantasies, provided the following description of the woman behind the name Miss Frank Miller:

> The author of these observations is a young American woman, who studied for a semester at our [Geneva] university and who to-day pursues a brilliant career as a writer and lecturer in the United States. Naturally given to introspection and of very alert intelligence, she shows at the same time an impressionability and a vivacity of emotional reaction which would easily border on excess, were they not checked by a good dose of strong will and self-mastery. Miss Miller thus combines in a most happy way something of the peculiar temperament which...authors designate by almost synonymous names of "automatist," "medium," "sensitive," etc., and all the advantages of a critical mind which is not satisfied with appearances; thanks to which fact she can interest herself in cases of Spiritism, without becoming the prey of it.... And her intention,...has been precisely to make clear the phenomena of subconscious imagination which unfold themselves to mediums...that she has observed in the fastnesses of her own mind.[19]

Flournoy's description of Miss Miller made no mention of her being a patient as Jung implied. Instead, Miss Miller is presented as an exceptional young woman with all the talents to be a medium but with sufficient intelligence to recognize her fantasies originated in her own mind. Indeed, Flournoy speculated that she "would have made an excellent medium and especially a medium for incarnation."[20] And, he also added:

> As a spiritualistic medium, Miss Miller would certainly be the reincarnation of some princess of historic or pre-historic antiquity...and she would not have failed to furnish us with interesting revelations....[21]

Nevertheless, Flournoy concluded, "the firmness of her reason counterbalancing the inclination of her temperament...always kept her from being wrecked on the flowery slopes of occult philosophy."[22] In the end, instead of fantastic revelations, Miss Miller provided "fragments of sane psychological observations."[23]

As is evident from Flournoy's comments, his own inclination was to link spiritualistic phenomena with the psychology of the medium as he did in his major work, *From India to the Planet Mars*. At the same time, Flournoy did not doubt the existence of telepathy and clairvoyance. He even believed in the survival of the soul. But, his Kantianism prevented him from favoring the belief in the experimental communication between the living and the dead.[24] Flournoy's developed interest in mediumistic phenomena and a carefully cultivated psychological perspective must have proved a happy combination for Miss Miller, who, according to Flournoy's biographer, was one of his students.[25] And her own psychological analysis of her fantasies may have been framed under his influence.[26]

Flournoy's influence also extended to Jung and went beyond the theoretical formulations on the subject of mediumistic phenomena, which influenced his dissertation. In his autobiography Jung referred to Flournoy as "my revered and fatherly friend."[27] In the Swiss edition of the same work is included an appendix in which Jung made plain the significance of Flournoy during the time of his difficulties with Freud. Jung stated that he saw Flournoy regularly when he became aware of the limitations of Freud's views.[28] Indeed, it was Flournoy who clarified for Jung the nature of Freud's antireligious positivism and onesidedness and who, in conversations on somnambulism, parapsychology, and the psychology of religion, was in complete agreement with Jung and encouraged his research.[29] Flournoy also attended the Fourth Psychoanalytic Congress in Munich, in 1913, in support of Jung and came to fill the vacuum in Jung's life created by Freud's absence.[30] Most of all Jung was impressed by Flournoy's capacity for objectivity and for not loosing sight of the whole.[31] More specifically Jung was attracted to Flournoy's ideas on "creative imagination" and this led quite naturally to his taking an interest in the Miller fantasies Flournoy had published and to use them as the *point de départ* of his own *Symbols of Transformation*.[32] In fact, when Jung wrote the latter work he stated that he had consulted Flournoy "for a thorough analysis."[33] After the work was published in book form, in 1912, Flournoy gave it a laudatory review.[34]

In addition to Flournoy's fatherly influence there is a further reason why Jung was drawn to the Miller fantasies. As in the case of his cousin Helene Preiswerk, the medium, he also shared with Miss Miller the talent for constructing elaborate hypnogogic fantasies. As Jung frankly stated in his 1925 seminar:

I saw in Miss Miller a person who, like myself, had had mythological fantasies, fantasies and dreams of a thoroughly impersonal character...as well as the fact that they must come from the lower "cellars,"... This then is the way the book grew up.[35]

And, Jung added, reflecting on the development of this realization in himself:

When one writes such a book, one has the idea that one is writing about certain objective material, and in my case I thought I was merely handling the Miller fantasies with a certain point of view together with the attendant mythological material. It took me...several years to see that it, the *Psychology of the Unconscious* [*Symbols of Transformation*], can be taken as myself and that an analysis of it leads inevitably into an analysis of my own unconscious processes.[36]

It might seem unusual that Jung, a psychoanalytically conscious psychiatrist, took so long to see past the temptation to perceive only similarities between himself and Miss Miller. Later he did admit the difficulty he had in acknowledging the fact that in analyzing the Miller fantasies he was, inadvertently, trying to analyze himself. The reasons for his difficulty he explained as follows, alluding to the two forms of thinking, intellectual and fantastical, he had outlined at the beginning of *Symbols of Transformation*:

I took Miss Miller's fantasies as such an autonomous form of [fantastical] thinking, but I did not realize that she stood for that form of thinking in myself. She took over my fantasy.... In other words, she became an anima figure, a carrier of an inferior function of which I was very little conscious.[37]

Seemingly forgetting his own childhood inclinations, and fastening on to his hard-won intellectual freedom which resulted from his encounter with philosophy and psychiatry, Jung went on to add:

I was in my consciousness an active thinker accustomed to subjecting my thoughts to the most rigorous sort of direction, and therefore fantasizing was a mental process that was directly repellent to me. As a form of thinking I held it to be altogether impure, a sort of incestuous intercourse, thoroughly immoral from an intellectual point of view.... it was against all the intellectual ideals I had developed for myself, and so great was my resistance to it, that I could only admit the fact in myself through the process of project- ing my material into Miss Miller's. Or, to put it even more strongly, passive thinking seemed to me such a weak and perverted thing that I could only handle it through a dis- eased woman.[38]

In the light of the material that has been presented in previ- ous chapters, Jung's realization of his unconscious identification with Miss Miller appears as a further variation on the theme of "the medium," whose earlier prefigurations can be found in Sabina Spielrein, Helly Preiswerk, and his mother. The dilemma that Jung personally faced in part 2 of *Symbols of Transformation*, as his thinking encountered the regressive images of incestuous sexu- ality that began to surface, was to find a way to free these same experiences from the tyranny of Freudian interpretation. As Jung himself phrased it:

How is it possible then to get across from the sexual, for example, to the spiritual, not only from the scientific stand- point, but as a phenomenon in the individual? Sexuality and spirituality are pairs of opposites that need each other. How is the process that leads from the sexual stage to the spiritual stage brought about.[39]

The only way to accomplish the transition, Jung felt, was to adhere to ideals, to assume the role of the hero. But to follow the path of the hero was not without its problems. As Jung remarked:

Man comes then into conflict with the unconscious, and this struggle is that of winning free from his unconscious, his mother. His unconscious...forms images of perfect people but when he tries to realize these hero types, another trend in the unconscious is aroused,...to destroy the image. So is developed the terrible mother, the devouring dragon, the dangers of rebirth, etc. At the same time the appearance of the hero ideal means the strengthening of the hopes of man. It gives man the notion that he can reorganize the

lines of his life if the mother will allow it. This can't be done
by a literal rebirth, so it is accomplished by a transformation process, or psychological rebirth. But this is not to be
done without serious battle with the mother. The
paramount question becomes, Will the mother allow the
hero to be born? And then, What can be done to satisfy the
mother so that she will allow it?[40]

According to Jung, the hero is both cursed and blessed by the
mother because she is in fact of dual nature: stifling and impeding,
nourishing and encouraging.[41] There is only one way out of this
deadlock, Jung stated:

> A sacrifice must be done in order to cut the hero away from
> the power of the unconscious and give him his individual
> autonomy. He has to pay himself off and contrive to fill the
> vacuum left in the unconscious. What is to be sacrificed?
> According to mythology, it is childhood, the veil of Maya,
> past ideals.[42]

Symbols of Transformation signaled the beginning of Jung's
journey into his own past, into the early years of his childhood.
This journey was initiated by his unconscious identification with
the fantasies of Miss Frank Miller. But, Jung refused to accept the
terminal insight that accompanied a psychoanalytic understanding
of the regression to childhood that was present in the Miller fantasies and that he was now compelled to undergo in himself.
Regression, according to Jung, was not the end of the matter, as he
pointed out in the revision of a work he first delivered before an
audience at Fordham University at the time of the completion of
part 2 of *Symbols of Transformation:*

> It would, in general, be a great mistake to deny any teleo-
> logical value to the apparently pathological fantasies of a
> neurotic. They are, as a matter of fact, the first beginnings
> of spiritualization, the first groping attempts to find new
> ways of adapting. His retreat to the infantile level does not
> mean only regression and stagnation, but also the possibil-
> ity of discovering a new lifeplan. Regression is thus in very
> truth the basic condition for the act of creation. Once again
> I must refer you to my oft-cited book *Symbols of Transfor-
> mation.*[43]

Late in life, in the preface Jung wrote for the 1952 edition of *Symbols of Transformation*, he stated of the experience of spiritualization:

> the man who thinks he can live without myth, or outside it, is an exception. He is like one uprooted, having no true link either with the past, or with the ancestral life which continues within him.... [He] lives a life of his own, sunk in a subjective mania of his own devising, which he believes to be the newly discovered truth.... The psyche is not of today; its ancestry goes back many millions of years.[44]

And in this same preface, he wrote of the beginnings of his own self-analysis:

> I suspected that myth had a meaning which I was sure to miss if I lived outside it in the haze of my own speculations. I was driven to ask myself..."What is the myth you are living?..." I did not know that I was living a myth, and even if I had known it, I would not have known what sort of myth was ordering my life without my knowledge. So, in the most natural way, I took it upon myself to get to know "my" myth.... I simply had to know what unconscious or preconscious myth was forming me, from what rhizome I sprang. This resolve led me to devote many years of my life to investigating the subjective contents which are the products of unconscious processes.... Here I discovered, bit by bit, the connecting links that I should have known about before if I was to join up the fragments of my book.[45]

From 1912 to 1920, Jung pursued his inner images. These years, he maintained, were the most important in his life. The later elaborations, he claimed, only supplemented and clarified the images and material that burst forth. At this juncture in his life, we find Jung undergoing a process of radical introversion and he became intensely preoccupied with dreams and waking fantasies which, at times, severely threatened the stability of his own consciousness.

If we turn to Jung's own inner life in 1912, we can see the first outlines of the direction he was taking. He was no longer living the Christian myth, as he realized, and this led him to an impasse.[46] Instead, the myth that was ordering his life seemed to be associated with the dead. The first signs of a break came in a dream Jung had in which a dove transformed itself into a little girl and told him, "Only in the first hours of the night can I transform myself into a human being, while the male dove is busy with the twelve dead."[47] Jung found this perplexing.

At about the same time, a fantasy kept returning to him in which "there was something dead present, but it was also still alive."[48] This came to a climax in a dream in which Jung was walking down a lane with a long row of tombs. At the first tomb at which he stopped, he saw a dead mummified man from the 1830s. Suddenly, he observed, the man moved and came to life. Jung continued to walk down the row until he found himself in the twelfth century and again the same thing was repeated. None of the dead were in fact dead; they all, without exception, showed signs of being alive.[49] Jung interpreted this to mean that the contents of the unconscious were not dead but alive, and he was moved to go over the details of his life, paying special attention to the early years. Of this he said, "I thought there might be something in my past which I could not see and which might possibly be the cause of the disturbance."[50] Though the dead, as Jung claimed, pressed upon him from within, he still felt he could credibly interpret this psychologically and identify the dead with contents of the unconscious.

Jung next resigned himself to "acting out" his early life and played at the building games of his childhood. He built a village and, when the church was completed, he found a stone for the altar. At that moment, he recalled the phallus dream of early childhood.[51] The significance of this should not be overlooked. The phallus clearly represented what Jung later called the "Self." That it should take the place of Christ on the altar is not surprising in the light of Jung's later ideas, most clearly stated in his book *Aion*. Toward the end of 1913, Jung had a series of visions of great destruction that he later associated with World War I, which began the following August. Of this he said, "I had to try to understand what had happened and to what extent my own experience coincided with that of mankind in general."[52]

From this point onward, a string of fantasies broke forth and on December 12, 1913, Jung resolved to sink into them. The outcome was as follows:

> I let myself drop...and I plunged down into dark depths. I could not fend off a feeling of panic . But then...I landed on my feet in a soft, sticky mass.... Before me was the entrance

to a dark cave, in which stood a dwarf with a leathery skin.... I squeezed past him...and waded...through icy water to the other end of the cave where...I saw a glowing red crystal. I grasped the stone, lifted it.... I saw that there was running water. In it a corpse floated by, a youth with blond hair and a wound in the head. He was followed by a gigantic black scarab and then by a red, newborn sun...but then a fluid welled out. It was blood.... the blood continued to spurt.... At last it ceased, and the vision came to an end.[53]

Jung recognized this vision as referring to the hero of the solar myth which, in a following dream, he identified with Siegfried. He interpreted this to mean he had to dispense with the hero myth and after some effort was able to do so.[54]

Shortly afterwards Jung had another fantasy/vision which, once again, involved the dead. The following is a description of this experience:

I had the feeling that I was in the land of the dead. The atmosphere was that of the other world.... I caught sight of two figures, an old man with a white beard and a beautiful young girl. I summoned up my courage and approached them as though they were real people.... The old man explained that he was Elijah, and that gave me a shock. But the girl staggered me even more, for she called herself Salome! She was blind.... They had a black serpent living with them.... Elijah and I had a long conversation which, however, I did not understand.[55]

Out of the Elijah figure emerged one whom Jung called Philemon. So startlingly real was this figure that Jung recalled, "I went walking up and down the garden with him, and to me he was what the Indians call a guru."[56] Jung almost hinted that Philemon actually existed as a historical figure. When a cultivated Indian told him that certain persons had spirits as gurus, he stated, "At that moment I thought of Philemon."[57] Philemon seems to have had some sort of objective existence for Jung because he stated of him:

Philemon represented a force which was not myself.... I held conversations with him, and he said things which I had not consciously thought. For I observed clearly that it was he who spoke, not I. He said I treated thoughts as if I generated them myself, but in his view thoughts were like animals in the forest, or people in a room...and added, "If you should see people in a room, you would not think that you had made those people, or that you were responsible for them." It was he who taught me psychic objectivity, the reality of the psyche.[58]

Elijah, the biblical figure out of which Philemon evolved, must have been familiar to Jung as a child growing up in the church. He is chiefly known to Christians as the prophet who was miraculously taken up to heaven and who was to return to precede the Messiah.[59] In the New Testament Elijah is identified with John the Baptist, whom the Christian church looks upon as the harbinger of the Messiah, Jesus.[60] It was at the request of Salome that John was beheaded.[61] This may explain why the female figure in Jung's dream was named Salome.[62] I shall say more about this female figure shortly.

In the meantime it should be pointed out that Elijah and Philemon share a number of characteristics. Elijah was the true and faithful prophet in the Old Testament account of his activities.[63] Philemon in contrast hails from classical antiquity. He and his companion Baucis were also faithful, in this case to the gods of classical mythology.[64] This same Philemon also turns up in Goethe's *Faust,* which is probably the source from which Jung took the name.[65] Jung gives the following summary of the story of Philemon, Baucis, and Faust:

> In his blind urge for superhuman power, Faust brought about the murder of Philemon and Baucis. Who are these two humble old people? When the world had become godless and no longer offered a hospitable retreat to the divine strangers Jupiter and Mercury, it was Philemon and Baucis who received the superhuman guests. And when Baucis was about to sacrifice her last goose for them, the metamorphosis came to pass: the gods made themselves known, the humble cottage was changed into a temple, and the old couple became immortal servitors at the shrine.[66]

Jung himself felt he had identified with the Faust figure when he was young. During the period of his life from 1912 to 1920, he sought to "dis-identify" himself from the Faustian spirit.[67] This struggle to free himself was given concrete expression in the figure of Philemon. In the 1920s when Jung built his tower at Bollingen, he inscribed over the gate *Philemonis Sacrum—Fausti Poenitentia.*[68]

Jung described his Philemon as an elderly bearded man with the horns of a bull, wings of a kingfisher, and carrying in his hands a bunch of four keys.[69] Furthermore, Philemon had a lame foot.[70] Jung made a number of paintings of this figure, one of which he put on the wall of his sleeping chamber in his country house in Bollingen.[71] It should be pointed out that this Elijah/Philemon figure seems to be entangled with Jung's father and Freud. Of the first it might be said that there are clear biblical and religious associations—Jung's father was an Old Testament scholar and clergyman. Moreover, Jung's memory of his father is of:

> a sufferer stricken with an Amfortas wound, a "fisher king" whose wound would not heal.... I as a "dumb" Parsifal was the witness of this sickness during the years of my boyhood, and, like Parsifal, speech failed me. I had only inklings.... He regarded his suffering as a personal affliction for which you might ask a doctor's advice; he did not see it as the suffering of the Christian in general.... "There are eunuchs who have made themselves eunuchs for the sake of the kingdom of heaven. He who is able to receive this, let him receive it" (Matthew 19:11f.). Blind acceptance never leads to a solution; at best it leads only to a standstill and is paid for heavily in the next generation.[72]

Jung's father was a lame fisher-king. Philemon was lame and had "king-fisher" wings. Von Franz clarifies Jung's allusion to his father's Amfortas wound when, referring to the Grail legend, she states:

> Amfortas suffers from a wound which cannot be healed; he cannot recover and hand over the authority to Parzifal.... His wound is in the thigh, or the genital region, undoubtedly an allusion to the problem of sexuality, unsolved in Christendom.[73]

This explanation of the "Amfortas wound" as a euphemism for sexual problems may also explain the reason Jung quoted the biblical passage about eunuchs. Together these suggest that Jung's father had some difficulty with sexuality in his marriage which, in turn, had a negative impact upon his son.

In order to further clarify the relation between Jung's father and the Philemon figure, it is necessary to examine the dreams Jung referred to in his memoirs immediately prior to his remarks about his father's Amfortas wound. Jung explained that during this period (1940s) he was preoccupied with the theme of the *coniunctio*.[74] He claimed the researches that reflected this preoccupation were heralded by dreams.[75] In one dream that clearly reflects the enduring influence of the parental conflict Jung experienced in his early life, he recorded:

> I dreamed...that my house had a large wing which I had never visited.... I came to a big double door.... I found myself in a room.... This was my father's workroom. However, he was not there. On shelves...stood hundreds of bottles containing every imaginable sort of fish....
>
> As I stood there...I noticed a curtain which bellied out.... Suddenly Hans, a young man from the country, appeared.... I saw an expression of terror on his face. He said only, "Yes, there is something. It's haunted in there!"
>
> Then I myself went, and found a door which led to my mother's room. There was no one in it. The atmosphere was uncanny.... I knew that this was the room where my mother, who in reality had long been dead, was visited, and that she had set up these beds for visiting spirits to sleep. They were spirits who came in pairs, ghostly married couples...who spent the night or even the day there.[76]

Jung went on to describe a lobby outside his mother's room which reflected worldliness, in sharp contrast to "the fish laboratory and the hanging pavilions for spirits."[77] He interpreted the dream as indicating he had an unfinished task connected with the "cure of souls" which remained with his parents—that is to say in the unconscious.[78] The fish, according to Jung, were a symbol for Christian souls because his father was a pastor or a fisher-of-men. His mother quite obviously is represented as a spiritualist. Jung stressed that the room for spirits represented a concern for the *coniunctio*, while the fish laboratory indicated Christ, who is himself the fish.[79] He scarcely even considered that this dream preserved the traumatic memory of the parental and religious conflict he experienced in his early life. Instead, he preferred to read the dream in much more symbolical terms. This penchant of Jung's to interpret dreams as highly symbolical is evident in two other dreams that occurred at the time. The significance of these dreams is that they provide us an insight into how the highly personal and highly symbolical are entangled with one another in Jung's own mind.

In a letter (December 19, 1947) to Father Victor White, Jung wrote:

> Last night I dreamt of at least 3 Catholic priests who were quite friendly and one of them had a remarkable library. I was the whole time under a sort of military order and I had to sleep in the barracks. There was a scarcity of beds, so that two men had to share one bed. My partner had already gone to bed. The bed was very clean, white, and fresh and he was a most venerable looking, very old man with white locks and a long flowing white beard. He offered me graciously one half of the bed and I woke up when I was just slipping into it.[80]

Immediately following this, betraying his penchant for the highly symbolical, Jung remarked:

> I must say that up to now I have handled the problem of Christ strictly on the level with the dogma, which is the leading thread through the maze of "my" unthought thoughts.[81]

Shortly afterwards Jung wrote, "What I am 'distrait' about is depicted in that [the above] letter."[82]

In another letter to Father White, Jung attempted to clarify his dream and perhaps why he was "distrait." He began with a comment on one of Father White's dreams:

> The emphasis on the anima means of course the totality of man: male plus female = conscious plus unconscious. Whatever the unconscious and whatever the S. Spir. [Holy Spirit] is, the unconscious realm of the psyche is the place where the living Spirit that is more than man manifests itself.

And then he added, referring to the previous dream:

> Something similar happened in my dream, of which, unfortunately, I have given you the mere outlines. While I stood before the bed of the Old Man, I thought and felt: *Indignus sum Domine* [I am not worthy, Lord]. I know Him very well: He was my "guru" more than 30 years ago, a real ghostly guru—but that is a long and—I am afraid—exceedingly strange story.[83]

After referring to the figure of Philemon, Jung stated:

> Soon after this particular dream, I had another one contin-
> uing a subject alluded to in the former dream, viz. the fig-
> ure of the priest, the head of the library. His carriage and
> the fact that he unexpectedly had a short grey beard
> reminded me strongly of my own father.[84]

In these two dreams Jung's father is connected to the Philemon figure. Whether or not these two figures are identical is not clear. In
the first dream, Philemon is identified as having a long beard; in
the second dream, the figure Jung associated with his father had a
short beard.

   In the long, detailed dream which followed, Jung felt a fore-
shadowing of ideas to which he had "the greatest inner resistances."[85] These ideas he enshrined in the most subjective of all of
his works, *Answer to Job* (1952). Jung gave the following description of the dream:

> It started with my paying a visit to my long-deceased
> father. He was living in the country.... I saw a house in the
> style of the eighteenth century, very roomy, with several
> rather large outbuildings.... it seemed that many great per-
> sonages...had stopped there. Furthermore, several had
> died and their sarcophagi were in a crypt belonging to the
> house. My father guarded these as custodian.
>
>   He was...not only the custodian but also a distinguished
> scholar.[86]

At this stage of the dream Jung reported that he was with a fellow
psychiatrist and his son. All three of them were listening to Jung's
father interpret Old Testament texts in a very learned manner. So
learned, in fact, that no one could follow him.[87] Jung continued,

> Then the scene changed. My father and I were in front of
> the house.... We heard loud thumps.... my father indicated
> to me that the place was haunted.[88]

At this point it is important to include a few details Jung added to the
description of the dream, in a letter to Father White, where he stated:

> I was...very much preoccupied by a peculiar question which
> had been raised at the beginning of the dream: "How is it

possible that my mother celebrates her 70th birthday in this year 1948 while I am reaching my 74th year?" My father is going to answer it and he takes me up with him to the first floor of [his house].... Coming out on the 1st floor, we find ourselves in a (circular) gallery, from which a small bridge leads to an isolated cuplike platform in the center of the room.... From the platform a narrow staircase, almost a ladder, leads up to a small door high up in the wall. I know this is *his* room. The moment we enter the bridge, I fall on my knees, completely overcome by the sudden understanding that my father is going to lead me into the "supreme presence."[89]

Jung added that the first platform reminded him of the hall of audience of Akbar the Great in Fatehpur-Sikri, which was used to discuss religion and philosophy with representatives of every creed.[90] The upper room by contrast was not only his father's room but the solitary chamber where Uriah, the biblical King David's general, lived.[91] Lastly, when Jung knelt he bowed but refused to touch his head to the ground.[92]

Remarkably, Jung interpreted this dream along the lines of his previous interpretation: his father represented the unconscious working out of the intricate symbolism of the fish, Christ and the God-image. The one personal remark he made was that the Uriah figure, whom the biblical King David had sent to his death so he could take his wife Bathsheba, signified the death of his own wife.[93] As for his mother, and the problems of the discrepancy between their ages—in the dream he was seventy-four and she was seventy—he stated:

My mother = anima is younger than myself. When I was 3 years old I had my first anima-experience, the woman that was *not* my mother. It means a lot that escapes me for the time being.[94]

Jung's ingenious interpretation is not entirely convincing, but his reference to the early period in his life bears some consideration. If we follow Jung's clue and examine certain crucial events of the third/fourth year of his own early life there are a number of details that are strikingly similar to those that are recorded in these dreams.

In 1879, when Jung was three or four years old, his parents

moved to Klein-Hüningen, near Basel.[95] The eighteenth-century
house they occupied had been the residence of a wealthy patrician
family.[96] The Jung family remained in this house until the death of
Jung's father in 1896.[97] The description of this house fits the
description of Jung's father's house in his last dream. Shortly after
moving to the house Jung's parents slept apart; he slept in his
father's room.[98] It is quite evident that Jung's parents' marriage
was breaking down. Furthermore, he recorded:

> All sorts of things were happening at night, things incom-
> prehensible and alarming.... From the door to my mother's
> room came frightening influences. At night Mother was
> strange and mysterious. One night I saw coming from her
> door a faintly luminous, indefinite figure whose head
> detached...and floated along in front of it.[99]

This matches the description of Jung's first dream of his mother's
separate room. Like he did with the priest in his dream, Jung may
well have shared a bed with his father in *his* room.

Why Jung should have viewed his father as a learned librarian
in one of the dreams is not clear. His library was modest though he
did complete his Ph.D. in philology.[100] One volume in the library
which did fascinate Jung was an old illustrated children's book
which contained accounts of Eastern religion. Jung returned again
and again to this volume.[101] He associated the illustrations of Eastern religion with his powerful phallus dream.[102] This association is
significant because the dream Jung had of the platform on the first
floor of his father's house reminded him of Akbar's hall of audience
where the world religions were debated. Furthermore, the description of this platform and the phallus dream have certain features in
common. Both had a platform with a throne in the center, one in a
basin resting on a huge column, the other enthroning a huge phallus, one accessible by a bridge, the other by a red carpet.[103]

One of the obvious differences in the dreams when they are
compared is that in the dream of the hall of audience Jung's father
is present, while in the phallus dream it is his mother who is
there.[104] Moreover, in the latter dream Jung's mother is ruthless
and aggressive, whereas in the former dream Jung's father is supportive but somewhat passive. Another contrast is that the phallus
is underground while the hall of audience is suspended on a column
above ground. The former evokes sexual associations, the latter
spiritual associations. If the dreams are looked at in developmental

terms, Jung's threatening mother has been replaced by his more passive father, who now acts as his guide. In the second dream the phallus has, as it were, grown out of the ground to produce the hall of audience for religious discussion. Both dreams had staircases, but the one feature in the hall of audience dream that is somewhat incomprehensible is the additional staircase leading up to another room.[105] According to Jung, this room housed the divine presence. At the same time this was both his father's and Uriah's room.[106]

Jung's explanation of the significance of this room is somewhat opaque. He claimed the figure of Uriah, who was sacrificed by King David so he could take his pregnant wife Bathsheba, was a prefiguration of Christ, whom God also sacrificed.[107] Jung identified Uriah and his father presumably because he felt God (David) expected service and obedience from his father (Uriah), which prevented him having an adequate relationship with his wife (Bathsheba). In the end God (David) took Jung's mother (Bathsheba) for himself. Jung enmeshed himself even further in this network of associations when he stated:

> Only later did I understand what this allusion to Uriah signified: not only was I forced to speak publicly, and very much to my detriment, about the ambivalence of the God-image in the Old Testament; but also, my wife would be taken from me by death.[108]

It is quite clear from these remarks that Jung also identified himself with his father and with Uriah. Therefore, he, presumably, saw himself as a Christ figure. What this suggests is that the upper chamber of Jung's dream was not only the room of the divine presence, Uriah's, and his father's room, but also *his* room. In this dream, as in his childhood, Jung shared his father's room. The Philemon figure he shared a bed with in the earlier dream he described to Father White also seems to have been identified with his father. As I mentioned previously, Jung hung a painting of Philemon in *his room*, in his tower in Bollingen. Exactly what the link is between the phallus dream, the lame Philemon, Jung's father and his Amfortas wound, the dream of the hall of audience, Uriah, and the upper room, eludes precise reconstruction. However, there are certain additional details that can be drawn into the picture, and these have mainly to do with Jung's relationship with Freud.

Ludwig Binswanger reports that when he and Jung visited

Freud for the first time in 1907 the discussion centered on dream interpretation. Freud questioned Jung about his dreams and concluded that one in particular indicated Jung wished to dethrone him.[109] In a dream Jung reports took place in Vienna, Freud appeared to Jung "as a *very, very frail old man*."[110] In a similar dream which Jung claimed took place a few years later, he dreamt of Freud as an elderly Austrian customs official:

> He walked past, somewhat stooped, without paying any attention to me.... and someone informed me that the old man was not really there, but was the ghost of a customs official who had died years ago. "He is one of those who still couldn't die properly."[111]

Jung interpreted the ghostly character of the figure as "an allusion to Freud's potential immortality."[112] At the same time he denied any death wish toward Freud and generally concluded the dream indicated he should take a more critical attitude to psychoanalytic claims. The one admission that Jung did make was that he saw Freud as the person "upon whom I projected the father, and at the time of the dream this projection was still far from eliminated."[113]

The extent to which Jung associated Freud with "father" is evident in the correspondence between the two men. Jung's father had died in 1896 leaving his son, then only twenty, with a number of unresolved conflicts. I briefly touched on these conflicts in chapter 2 and need only mention that the religious factor was clearly the most important element reported by Jung himself. That Jung was able to transfer the father figure onto Freud may at first seem odd, given that Pastor Paul Jung and Sigmund Freud were so very different. On the surface Jung appears not to have found it necessary to account for the differences between these two men. Yet, at a deeper level, there was an important and disturbing reason behind Jung's attachment to Freud as father. This reason will emerge in what follows and will lead to the figure of Philemon who is, at least in part, a conflation of the phallus dream, Jung's father, and Freud.

Jung utilized religious language very early in his letters to Freud. Exactly one year (August 11, 1907) after Freud's first letter to him we find Jung stating:

> With your help I have come to see pretty deeply into things, but I am still far from seeing them *clearly*. Nevertheless, I have the feeling of having made considerable inner progress

since I got to know you personally; it seems to me that one can never quite understand your science unless one knows you in the flesh. Where so much still remains dark to us outsiders only faith can help; but the best and most effective faith is knowledge of your personality.[114]

Jung went on to write to Freud about psychoanalysis as the fruit of the tree of paradise, which when eaten makes one "become clairvoyant."[115] He clearly appreciated sharing this new faith with Freud and even requested that he send him a photograph—"a long cherished and constantly repressed wish"—not as Freud used to look but as he did when he first met him. In other words as a man in his fifties.[116] Jung ended the letter with the plea:

> Would you have the great kindness to grant this wish of mine sometime? I would be ever so grateful because again and again I feel the want of your picture.[117]

Freud complied with Jung's request.[118]

Shortly after, on October 28, 1907, Jung wrote Freud a revealing letter in which he made the following confession:

> Actually—and I confess this to you with a struggle—I have a boundless admiration for you both as a man and a researcher, and I bear you no conscious grudge. So the self-preservation complex does not come from there; it is rather that my veneration for you has something of the character of a "religious" crush. Though it does not really bother me, I still feel it is disgusting and ridiculous because of its undeniable erotic undertone. This abominable feeling comes from the fact that as a boy I was the victim of a sexual assault by a man I once worshipped. Even in Vienna the remarks of the ladies ("enfin seuls," etc.) sickened me, although the reason for it was not clear to me at the time.[119]

This latter remark referred to a comment "alone at last" that was apparently made in March 1907 by Mrs. Freud and Mrs. Jung when their husbands first met and withdrew into Freud's study to be together. Jung continued his disquieting disclosure and added:

> This feeling, which I still have not quite got rid of, hampers me considerably. Another manifestation of it is that I find

psychological insight makes relations with colleagues who have a strong transference to me downright disgusting. *I therefore fear your confidence.* I also fear the same reaction from you when I speak of my intimate affairs. Consequently, I skirt round such things as much as possible, for, to my feeling at any rate, every intimate relationship turns out after a while to be sentimental and banal or exhibitionistic, as with my chief, whose confidences are offensive.

I think I owe you this explanation. I would rather not have said it.[120]

Erik Erikson has commented on this letter and underscored the disturbing nature of Jung's confession:

Jung makes further remarkable confessions induced, no doubt, by the vortex of associations aroused by the new, the psychoanalytic, kind of confessional. At any rate, the German words for "I was the victim" are *Ich bin unterlegen*—literally, "layed under," that is, I submitted. It is probable that a true transference played into the panicky reaction to being privated with the great man. Furthermore, it is said that Jung as a boy for many years shared his father's bedroom.[121]

It seems evident that Jung associated certain religious feelings and phallic sexuality with "the father" though we do not know for certain who victimized Jung sexually as a young boy. Nevertheless, Jung's added reference to his chief, Eugene Bleuler, would support Erikson's analysis. Bleuler seems to have served Jung as an interim father figure. He came into contact with Bleuler shortly after his father's death in 1896. Bleuler, like Jung's father, was somewhat of a self-effacing Christian.[122] By the early winter of 1908 Jung felt that a number of factors coincided to change his relationship with Bleuler. Of these he stated:

I feel that the conjunction of the birth of a son with the rationalization of the father complex is an extremely important turning-point in my life, not least because I am now extricating myself from the social father-relationship as well. It doesn't grieve me. Bleuler has delusions of homosexual persecution in his dreams and is beginning to boast of his intensified heterosexual fantasies. The tie on his side seems to be the stronger.[123]

Jung resigned from the Burghölzli at the end of March 1909. He thereby severed certain ties with its director, Eugene Bleuler. Immediately afterward Jung journeyed to Vienna to see Freud.[124] It was during the latter visit that the famous poltergeist incident involving Freud's bookcase occurred.[125] I have described this incident in a previous chapter and need only add that Jung commented on it in a letter to Freud:

> That last evening with you has, most happily, freed me inwardly from the oppressive sense of your paternal authority. My unconscious celebrated this impression with a great dream which has preoccupied me for some days and which I have just finished analysing. I hope I am now rid of all unnecessary encumbrances. Your cause must and will prosper, so my pregnancy fantasies tell me.[126]

Freud replied in a now famous letter,

> It is strange that on the very same evening when I formally adopted you as eldest son and anointed you—*in partibus infidelium* [in the lands of the unbelievers]—as my successor and crown price, you should have divested me of my paternal dignity, which divesting seems to have given you as much pleasure as I, on the contrary, derived from the investiture of your person.[127]

Erikson has commented on this passage:

> Here, the words "divested" and "investiture" are in German *entkleidet* and *Einkleidung*, that is, "disrobed" and "clothing" and thus imply a more primitive mode of exposing a kind of nakedness.[128]

Through the twists and turns of their correspondence it is evident, as I demonstrated previously, that Jung demanded of Freud that he assume a religious mantle. Jung's insistence came to a head in the winter of 1910. He invited Freud to consider the possibility that psychoanalysis could be the new religion to replace all the old ones.[129] This if course would make Freud the founder of a new religion. Freud respectfully, but firmly, declined the honor.[130] Jung, in a letter which followed, revealed a dream in which his wife's arm had been chopped off. He related this to a finger he had injured. Both of these dreams Jung interpreted as phallic.[131] He also admitted his father-complex expressed itself in his resistance to Freud.[132] Jung ended his letter with the following observations:

> Homosexuality would be a tremendous advantage.... It would also be excellently suited to large agglomerations of males.... Because of our shortsightedness we fail to recognize the biological services rendered by homosexual seducers. Actually they should be credited with something of the sanctity of monks.[133]

Freud's reply is missing.[134] Nevertheless, we can construe from Jung's next letter that Freud found Jung's remarks disturbing. Jung wrote:

> I was very perturbed by your letter—all sorts of misunderstandings seem to be in the air. How could you have been so mistaken in me? I don't follow. I can't say any more about it now, because writing is a bad business and all too often one misses the right note.[135]

Freud replied to Jung that he was "merely irritated...that you have not yet disposed of the resistances arising from your father-complex."[136]

Following this exchange the question of the nature of the libido surfaced and became the focus of the conflict between Freud and Jung. On a personal level their relationship progressively deteriorated, finally coming to an end in 1913. Freud, as I concluded in a previous chapter, would not subscribe to Jung's need to incorporate spiritual elements into psychoanalysis. Jung, as I also indicated, seemed willing—indeed determined—to argue for a psychic substrate that was transpersonal and therefore transsexual. For his thinking to reach the latter stage, it had to go through a number of conceptual transformations that eventually disengaged the psychological data from Freud's sexual literalism. The phallus would become a symbol of the creative potential of the undiscovered Self; his father would also represent some part of the Self, as would Freud.

Jung emerged from this process of "deliteralizing" with the rudimentary features of his later psychology. What is remarkable is that Jung was able to chart a path through the emotionally distraught years of his childhood. These years of his early life left wounds and memories of parental discord, a terrifying huge phallus, and deep confusion about gender identity, all entangled in the most profoundly felt religious conflict. Jung, of course, did not make the journey to maturity alone: his father in the guise of Philemon was with him. Freud too was Philemon. In fact, it has been noted how much Philemon and Freud looked alike.[137]

Jung was unable to heal the memory of his father's faltering spirituality by uncovering its sexual etiology. Indeed, there is very little evidence that he ever systematically attempted this sort of reductionistic analysis. This is the case in spite of the clearly suggested sexual difficulties his father had. Furthermore, Jung never seemed to have attempted any systematic form of a Freudian analysis of himself and his experiences. Instead, he moved the discussion of such matters as human sexuality from a literal and concrete to a symbolic and spiritual level of interpretation.[138] Jung's own specific emotional entanglement with his father, with Bleuler, and then with Freud was resolved and transformed into an encounter with the father in general. The initial stage of Jung's direct encounter with "the father" as symbol is embodied in his relationship with the ghostly figure of Philemon. Eventually he was able to integrate this figure.[139] Later in life (1946) he even referred to himself as "the limping messenger," that is, Philemon.[140] The last stage of Jung's encounter with "the father" is evident in his most vehement, and most subjective work, *Answer to Job*.[141] In this work the object of Jung's attention is the ultimate in paternal figures, the Judeo-Christian God, the Father.

The importance of the figure of Philemon following Jung's break with Freud can hardly be overstated. In the final analysis Philemon, while being a conflation of Jung's father, Bleuler, Freud, and Flournoy, transcends them all by being a winged creature—a spirit-being. For Jung personally Philemon replaced the father figure of his early life by personifying the spirit. In Jung's psychology Philemon serves as the prototype of the archetype of the Self. Jung later called the Self "a transcendental postulate which, although justifiable psychologically, does not allow of scientific proof."[142] He also stated of the Self,

> The beginnings of our whole psychic life seem to be inextricably rooted in this point, and all our highest and ultimate purposes seem to be striving towards it.[143]

And, according to Jung, "It might equally well be called the 'God within us.'"[144]

The blind Salome of Jung's fantasy/vision that accompanied
Elijah out of whom Philemon evolved, also had its human counter-
parts. Jung's Salome is prefigured in his cousin Helene Preiswerk
and Sabina Spielrein, but finds its clearest expression in the person
of Jung's lifelong companion, Antonia (Toni) Wolff (1888–1953).[145]
Jung first mentioned Toni Wolff in a letter (August 29, 1911) to
Freud describing her as "a remarkable intellect with an excellent
feeling for religion and philosophy."[146] She had come to Jung sometime before as a seriously depressed and disoriented young woman
who had lost her father, the head of an old Zurich family.[147] As part
of his treatment Jung introduced her to the material he was assem-
bling for *Symbols of Transformation*. This had a positive effect upon
her, and she did some research for him and became interested
enough to attend the Weimer Psychoanalytic Congress in 1911.[148]
What transpired afterwards is not entirely clear, as it appears that
Jung sought to secure the relative anonymity of his relationship
with Toni Wolff, and his surviving family and followers have done
likewise.[149] The few details that do emerge suggest that it was not
very long before Jung and Toni Wolff exceeded the bounds of a doc-
tor/patient relationship and became intimate.[150] What proved decisive in Jung's decision to become involved with Toni Wolff was his
alleged need to deflect his eros from his daughters, and in particular
his eldest, Agathe, with whom, as we have seen, he identified.[151]

As with Helene Preiswerk, Sabina Spielrein, and Miss Frank
Miller, what attracted Jung to Toni Wolff was that they were in
certain respects remarkably alike.[152] In other words Jung saw in
Toni Wolff traits of himself; in particular he shared with Toni Wolff
the tendency toward dissociation. Toni Wolff stood in sharp contrast to Jung's wife Emma, and in the later language of analytical
psychology each might be considered a representative of a certain
type of woman. Emma stood for the "married mother" type and
Toni Wolff for the "friend and concubine" type, otherwise known as
the "hetaira type."[153] The latter type, Jung informed a female correspondent, as *femme inspiratrice*, "are not meant to bear physical
children, but they are those that give rebirth to a man in a spiritual
sense."[154] In fact, Jung's distinction of these two types had been
developed further by Toni Wolff herself in a paper she delivered
before the Psychological Club in 1934, in Zurich. In it she added
two additional types which she termed the "amazon type" and the
"mediumistic type."[155]

As Jung's mistress, Toni Wolff clearly demonstrated that she
was of the "hetaira type," yet there is evidence that she could be

classified as a "mediumistic type" as well, and this may have been an even more important reason for Jung's attraction to her. Indeed, it was as the latter type that Toni Wolff was usually perceived by those who knew her. As one of her early analysands described her:

> She had very changeable looks, as so many intuitives do, and could sometimes look beautiful and sometime quite plain. Her extraordinary brilliant eyes—mystic's eyes— were always expressive. To me she fitted perfectly the "medium" type of her own writing. Also I am sure "hetaira" too, though that was not the side of her that I knew.[156]

Even toward the end of her life Toni Wolff gave the same impression which one person described as follows:

> Toni Wolff's appearance at the [C. G. Jung] Institute…was that of a ghost-like figure, gaunt, haughty and forbidding…. The icy impression she conveyed made most of us ponder how she could ever have been a "femme fatale" or "femme inspiratrice" to anybody, least of all C. G. Jung.[157]

Indeed, in the opinion of another early member of Jung's circle, Toni Wolff "almost as a medium, helped Jung see his images and talk with them."[158] One of Toni Wolff's later students concurred, stating, "she mediated Jung's mind and intuitive ideas directly, for she had been part of their creation from the unconscious."[159]

Toni Wolff, in her description of the mediumistic type, offered the following observations which could be taken, at least in part, as autobiographical:

> The mediumistic type is concerned with the *unconscious* contents of its time…. the differentiated type today encounters certain difficulties in its attempt to realize and express itself…. the mediumistic type…possesses less ego consciousness than the other, it is the one that most easily loses. It carries and personifies the unconscious of other people or of its epoch…. Similarly, if this type is affected by the unconscious of a person closely related, the contents of the relationship are not personal, but impersonal and unconscious.[160]

In her conclusion of the descriptions of the four types of women, Toni Wolff listed what she called "the archetypal forms of human *relationships*" found in the types:

> Thus formulated, the mother type would correspond to
> the...wife, the hetaira to that of the lover, the Amazon to
> that of the sister, and the mediumistic type to that of the
> daughter.[161]

The difference in age between Jung and Toni Wolff was thirteen years, yet, as Barbara Hannah has remarked, "anyone who
knew them both well, and often saw them together, would agree
that, while he seemed the prototype of the wise old man, she had a
quality of eternal youth."[162] In other words the relationship between
Jung and Toni Wolff had the characteristics of a father/daughter
relationship. And, as Toni Wolff has remarked:

> We know that the spiritual side of women is formed by the
> spiritual attitude of the father. The mediumistic type
> therefore not infrequently represents the unconscious,
> impersonal side of the masculine anima, as so often hap-
> pens between father and daughter.[163]

For Jung, the anima was the "soul image," the personification of
the feminine in men.[164]

In Jung's earlier fantasy the anima was undoubtedly
expressed in the figure of Salome and carried a definite erotic component. Another characteristic of Jung's Salome was that she was
blind.[165] It is interesting to note that Toni Wolff was considered to
suffer from a certain psychological blindness and never herself
practiced the introverted Jungian method of active imagination.
This fact baffled one of Jung's close followers who further reported:

> But I soon found out that not only had she no ability to do
> active imagination, she had not the slightest wish...to
> experience the unconscious at first hand. She had no doubt
> whatever of its objective existence, but no inclination to go
> into it herself.... I have never seen anyone else in the least
> like her in this respect.[166]

In Jung's language of explanation, Toni Wolff experienced the
unconscious through him, and presumably, in part, the same held
true for Jung himself. On this matter, and its connection with the
journey toward individuation, Jung wrote that an individual has
two choices: either they enter the unconscious directly, which
means a guilt-ridden break from God and the world which is somehow redressed in a person's soul:

Or it may go another way: in order to expiate the guilt, he gives his supreme good, his love, not to the soul but to a human being who stands for his soul, and from this human being it goes to God and through this human being it comes back to the lover, but only so long as this human being stands for his soul. Thus enriched, the lover begins to give to his soul the good he has received, and he will receive it again from God, in so far as he is destined to climb so high that he can stand in solitude before God and before mankind.[167]

Jung concluded by attempting to reconcile these two apparently dissimilar ways:

if a man's libido goes to the unconscious, the less it goes to a human being; if it goes to a human being, the less it goes to the unconscious. But if it goes to a human being, and it is a true love, then it is the same as if the libido went direct to the unconscious, so very much is the other person a representative of the unconscious, though only if the other person is truly loved.

Only then does love give him the quality of a mediator, which otherwise and in himself he would not possess.[168]

If Jung was willing to admit that woman as "daughter" could be the spiritual companion of man as "father," he would always view this companionship as more than tinged by eros.[169] It was the prerogative of the masculine to be spiritual, and if a woman demonstrated such inclinations it was the masculine (animus/ logos) in her that was at work.[170] In Toni Wolff's description of the mediumistic type, with whom she can be identified, she mentioned that the appearance of this type can be associated historically with the emerging suffragettes (Amazon type) who were the feminists of the nineteenth century.[171] She went on to add:

The suffragettes were identified with the intellect and the mediumistic types with the unconscious psyche. This identification took concrete form as the former tended to play the part of men and the latter that of spirits.

The differentiated mediumistic type is generally less easy to detect than the Amazon since it less frequently appears in public. In private life, however, it is manifested in the woman who assists a man to realize his unconscious ideas, either by making him conscious of them or else by personifying and living out in reality what is constellated in his personal unconscious, often to such an extent that too much of his outside life is mistaken for her own. This is a frequent danger in the erotic zone; if, for instance, a man has an unconscious erotic problem, a mediumistic woman can be affected by it and instead of regarding it as an objective problem she will identify herself with it and thus become involved in it by mistake.[172]

Presumably, the insights Toni Wolff offered in her description of the difficulties experienced by the mediumistic type arose out of her own experiences with Jung. As Barbara Hannah described it:

Toni also overcame the besetting sin of so many single women, the desire somehow to destroy the marriage and marry the man herself. Toni told me once it had cost her more than anything in her life to learn that she must *not* give way to this almost universal feminine instinct. It was characteristic of Toni to learn *facts* slowly—she was an intuitive type.... She also realized later that Jung's unswerving loyalty to his marriage gave her more than she could possibly have had without it.[173]

It is difficult to know to what extent Jung appreciated the depth of Toni Wolff's sacrifice and her achievements. Their relationship did endure for several decades and established itself into a weekly routine. Like his maternal grandfather, Samuel Preiswerk, who held weekly séances with the spirit of his first wife, Jung and Toni Wolff spent Wednesdays together.[174] Later in life, these Wednesdays settled into sedate sessions of afternoon tea in Jung's library or garden.[175] Jung did not always look forward to these sessions and, at times, insisted that others be present.[176] Toni Wolff's last years were overshadowed by crippling arthritis, excessive smoking and drinking, and the loneliness caused by Jung's diminished attentions.[177] Her sudden death on March 20, 1953, and the rumored uncertainty surrounding its cause, has led to the suggestion that she, like Helene Preiswerk years before, died of a broken heart.[178] Jung did not attend her funeral.[179]

When Jung received news of Toni Wolff's death he was dismayed that he had not received any warnings, nor could he decipher the event in past dreams. As he remarked in a letter of May 28, 1953, "Nobody who was close to her had any warning dreams...only people who knew her superficially."[180] One of the latter individuals, Irene Champernowne, had actually managed to get rather close to Toni Wolff, and she has recorded the details in a fascinating memoir which has recently been published.[181] Irene Champernowne had met Jung in 1936, and worked as an assistant to the prominent British Jungian, Dr. Godwin Baynes, until his death in 1943.[182] Beginning in 1946 she went to Zurich regularly, eventually becoming an analysand of Toni Wolff.[183] From 1949 to 1951 she was deeply preoccupied with the issue of "women and the spirit."[184] On November 5, 1950 she had a rather unusual dream which she later painted. In the dream she is supporting a lame Toni Wolff, and together they stand on the edge of the world. An enormous disc approached them covered with white cloaked figures all around its rim. The two stand in awe "in that unearthly cosmic space, their position untenable except at the moment of vision."[185]

The significance of Irene Champernowne's dream was brought home to her and Toni Wolff almost two and a half years later. The two were going over some material in an analytic session when Toni Wolff became violently ill. Irene Champernowne moved to help Toni Wolff and in an uncanny moment the latter recalled the figures in the dream.[186] In a telephone conversation that evening Toni Wolff insisted on explaining the impact of some of the material Irene Champernowne had left her: "It is impersonal, all impersonal," Toni Wolff stated, adding, "It is a diamond, a hexagram."[187] They agreed to meet the next day but this was not to be, as that night Toni Wolff died.[188]

When Irene Champernowne received the news about Toni Wolff's death the next day, she decided to call Jung. He invited her to see him that afternoon, and together with Emma Jung they spoke about her material and Toni Wolff's death. Emma Jung felt strongly that both the dream material and Toni Wolff's psychological work had some importance for women in general.[189] Jung had seen Toni Wolff on their last Wednesday together only two days before.[190] The suddenness of her death and the fact that he had received no warning, seemed to have put him into a state of shock. He once remarked that he would be forever grateful to Toni Wolff for the help she had given him during the fateful period following his break with Freud.[191] Now she had gone, and only a dream on Easter Eve in which she appeared young and beautiful in a colorful dress, with the blue of the kingfisher most obvious, gave him any respite.[192] Philemon too had the kingfisher's color in his wings, and it can be surmised that Jung interpreted the dream as a sign of Toni Wolff's spiritual attainment. Yet, in a curious way, Jung at this time seemed not to have realized that Toni Wolff had a life and achievements independent of him; an independence she had won at considerable cost.

In 1958 when Jung published his book on flying saucers he used Irene Champernowne's painting of the dream of the two women, one lame, the other supporting her, and the approaching disc encircled by cloaked figures as the frontpiece.[193] In the text he analysed the picture as follows:

> It obviously represents a borderline situation.... Out beyond is cosmic space...or the beyond may be the land of the dead or the unconscious. The first possibility suggests a space-ship...the second, angels of some kind or departed spirits, who come to earth in order to fetch a soul. This would refer to X [Toni Wolff], who was already in need of "support," as she was ill. Her health really did give grounds for anxiety, and in fact she died about two years after the dream.... The third possibility, that the beyond is the unconscious, points to a personification of the latter, namely the animus in his characteristic plurality; the festive white robes of the crew suggest the idea of a marital union of opposites. The symbolism...also applies to death as a final realization of wholeness. The dreamer's view that the dream gave warning of the death of her friend may therefore be right.[194]

After a brief digression Jung concluded:

> In a borderline situation such as our dream depicts we may expect something extraordinary...though in reality it has always been inherent in such situations: The ship of death approaches with a corona of departed spirits, the deceased joins their company, and the multitudinous dead take the soul with them.[195]

Perhaps by this time Jung had developed a greater appreciation for Toni Wolff's own achievements. On March 18, 1958, exactly five years after he had last seen her, Jung wrote to the publisher Daniel Brody:

I feel the need to recommend the collected papers of Toni Wolff to your attention. As president of the Psychological Club in Zurich for many years, she had a unique opportunity to get to know the ambience of analytical psychology from all sides as well as a host of its representatives from practically all the nations of Europe and all Anglo-Saxon countries. Her circle of friends and acquaintances extended over continents and, as an assiduous correspondent, she maintained the liveliest contacts with them all her life. Her activity as a practicing psychologist, however, left her little time for literary work, only a small part of which has been printed and become known to a wider public. All her papers have been collected in this volume. They are distinguished not only by their intellectual content but by the fact that the author had personally experienced the development of analytical psychology from the fateful year 1912 right up to the recent past and was thus in a position to record her reactions and sympathetic interest from the first. Her papers therefore have a documentary value. Even those who did not know the author personally will glean from them an impression of the versatility and depth of her spiritual personality. I am sure that her collected papers will be welcome not only by the numerous friends who mourn her death but by many other people who are interested in the problems of analytical psychology.[196]

In the same year, 1958, the American Jungian Joseph Henderson visited Jung for the last time at his home in Küsnacht. The conversation turned to the subject of Jung's book on UFOs and the visit ended by Jung showing Henderson a stone carving he had made in his garden in memory of Toni Wolff. On the stone were four sets of Chinese characters arranged vertically. They read beginning with the uppermost one:

Toni Wolff
Lotus
Nun
Mysterious[197]

While Philemon, modelled on Jung's father and Freud, was certainly the prototype of Jung's archetype of the Self, Salome, beginning in the darkness of his mother's personality, prefigured in Helene Preiswerk and incarnated in Toni Wolff, was the prototype of Jung's archetype of the anima. In the latter instance, there is little discrepancy between the real and the ideal; in the former instance this is not the case. In the end, reality and symbol did meet: Jung became Philemon.

Following Jung's break with Freud there were, in addition to Philemon and Salome, other figures that came to Jung, but they were of lesser significance.[198] This flood of figures culminated in a final revelation of spirits that was to rival and even surpass those of his eccentric grandfather, the Reverend Samuel Preiswerk. Like his clerical relatives, Jung was also to become a writer of sermons; unlike them, he was to direct his sermons to the dead and not the living. As a prelude to his experience of the spirits, Jung had a fantasy that he had lost his soul:

> This was a significant event: the soul, the anima, establishes the relationship to the unconscious. In a certain sense this is also a relationship to the collectivity of the dead; for the unconscious corresponds to the mythic land of the dead, the land of the ancestors.... therefore,...the soul vanishing...means that it has withdrawn into the unconscious or into the land of the dead.... Like a medium, it gives the dead a chance to manifest themselves.[199]

What was to subsequently occur in Jung's life, in 1916, was one of the more unusual experiences he had had to date. It was also, in a way, the culmination of Jung's ongoing dialogue with Spiritualism that he had been engaged in for some time. The following is Jung's description of what occurred:

> Around five o'clock...on Sunday the front doorbell began ringing frantically.... there was no one in sight. I was sitting near the doorbell, and not only heard it but saw it moving.... The atmosphere was thick, believe me!... The whole house was filled as if there were a crowd present, crammed full of spirits. They were packed deep right up to the door, and the air was so thick it was scarcely possible to breathe. As for myself, I was all a-quiver with the question: "For God's sake, what in the world is this?" Then they cried out in chorus, "We have come back from Jerusalem where we found not what we sought." That is the beginning of the *Septem Sermones.*
>
> Then it began to flow out of me, and in the course of

three evenings the thing was written. As soon as I took up
the pen, the whole ghostly assemblage evaporated. The
room quieted and the atmosphere cleared. The haunting
was over.[200]

"The experience," Jung went on to say, "has to be taken for what it
was, or as it seems to have been."[201]

In *Septem Sermones ad Mortuos,* as James Heisig has pointed
out, are to be found cast in exotic gnostic language, virtually all of
Jung's later developed ideas.[202] In these sermons, Jung felt that he
was forced from within to express to the dead what might have
been said by his spirit guide, Philemon.[203] In the first sermon, he
taught the spirits about the nature of absolute reality, which is the
paradoxical state of nothingness and fullness at the same time and
of which "there is no profit in thinking upon."[204] This is clearly the
equivalent of Kant's noumenal. The sermon's real concern was to
point out that humans, when true to themselves, follow their own
being and strive towards distinctiveness or the phenomenal. This
striving Jung called the *Principium Individuationis,* the same term
he used in his later psychology and interpreted to mean a coming to
a state of self-realization.[205] The second sermon addressed itself to
the knowledge of god. Here Jung stated that god and devil are
effective opposites but that above them is the supreme god who
himself is effectiveness and stands behind both god and devil. At
the end of this sermon we are informed that "The dead now raised
a great tumult, for they were Christians."[206]

Sermon 3 began with the dead Christians crying: "Speak further unto us concerning the supreme god."[207] Jung then spoke of the
dualistic nature of god, which he named Abraxas, stating: "Abraxas
begetteth truth and lying, good and evil, light and darkness, in the
same word and in the same act."[208] After hearing of this god of gods
we are told "the dead howled and raged, for they were unper-
fected."[209] We may see a connection between Abraxas and the functioning unconscious, which of itself is neither good nor evil, but the
impersonal source of all values.[210]

Sermon 4 addressed itself to the question of "gods and devils"
who seemed to be less powerful images of Abraxas himself and
were called by Jung "god-devils." There are four of them: the god-
sun, Eros, the Tree of Life, and the devil. Later in the sermon Jung,
after enumerating the four principal gods, stated: "woe unto you,
who replace these incompatible many by a single god."[211] The gods
too, it would seem, strive towards their own distinctiveness. In this

sermon there is also the following revealing statement: "For redemption's sake I teach you the rejected truth, for the sake of which I was rejected."[212]

Sermon 5 began with "The dead mocked and cried: Teach us, fool, of the church and holy communion."[213] Jung taught that the world of the gods was expressed in spirituality and sexuality, which are respectively personified as the Celestial Mother and Phallos, or the earthly father, both superhuman daemons. Communion is necessary because humans are weak, but "communion in everything is dismemberment and dissolution.... In singleness the one man shall be superior to the others, that every man may come to himself and avoid slavery."[214] The relation between what is said here and Jung's notion of individuation is obvious.

Sermon 6 was a continuation of the discourse on spirituality and sexuality as daemons to which humans are subject and from which they must differentiate themselves. The sermon ended: "With disdainful glance the dead spake: Cease this talk of gods and daemons and souls. At bottom this hath long been known to us."[215]

Sermon 7 opened with the dead having returned saying, "There is yet one matter we forgot to mention. Teach us about man."[216] "Man," Jung taught the spirits, "is a gateway, through which from the outer world of gods, daemons, and souls ye pass into the inner world; out of the greater into the smaller world."[217] Each human has one single Star. "This is the one god of this one man. This is his world, his pleroma, his divinity."[218] Here again, we meet Jung's archetype of the Self.

The *Septem Sermones ad Mortuos* marked the final point from which Jung emerged as the destined individual he sensed he potentially was as a young child. He believed he had discovered profound truths that lie in the depths of the human psyche. He certainly must have felt he had now passed the test of his own process of individuation and reentered the world as the later Jung, destined to be a teacher and healer of some importance. In his experience the dead confirmed this for they submitted to be taught by him. In these seven sermons, he taught them about the nature of reality, the supreme god, gods and devils, the church, spirituality and sexuality, and lastly about human beings. But, in a sense, the entire message was about human beings, their world, their dreams, and their destinies. There is a distinct gnostic flavor to the sermons, for Jung was communicating knowledge, not faith. Further, we find in them the good and evil god, as well as other typical notions that we have already seen in his early thoughts and experiences. There is, indeed, a deep connection between these sermons and the series of spiritualistic events that had taken place since Jung's childhood.

The sermons also express the ever existing tension between Jung's "maternal" Spiritualism and his "paternal" Christianity because, as we are informed at the end of the second sermon on the knowledge of god, the dead were Christians. It was they who had gone to Jerusalem and had not found what they were looking for. These dead, the sermons relate, finally realized that their Christianity was empty of meaning and turned instead to Zurich to be taught a new and transformed Christianity in which the Self replaces Christ, the Collective Unconscious replaces God, and where the goal of life is not the *Imitatio Christi* but the *Principium Individuationis*. Jung had now come into his own. It was not the dead who instructed him, it was he who instructed the dead. As he wrote later:

> Quite early I had learned that it was necessary for me to instruct the figures of the unconscious, or that other group which is often indistinguishable from them, the "spirits of the departed."[219]

In *Septem Sermones ad Mortuos* Jung revealed to the host of Christian spirits the basic program from which was to emerge his own school of psychology. Later in a more cautiously presented fashion, couched in guarded psychological language, Jung would make his program public.

It is evident that Jung, as a consequence of turning from Freud, expanded his psychological thinking to incorporate transpersonal and collective factors as, ultimately, the reality behind personal and subjective experiences. Jung recognized these collective factors, which he later termed "archetypes," as identical with the universal human belief in spirits. Yet, even then he was unwilling to publicly grant the identification between the collective factors and spirits as any indication that spirits may exist in themselves. In a lecture before the British Society for Psychical Research that he delivered in London in 1919, he stated:

> I for one am certainly convinced that they [spirits] are exteriorizations [of unconscious complexes]. I have repeatedly observed the telepathic effects of unconscious complexes, and also a number of parapsychic phenomena. But in all this I see no proof whatever of the existence of real spirits,

and until such proof is forthcoming I must regard this whole territory as an appendix of psychology.[220]

In spite of such public assertions about the psychological explanation of belief in spirits, there are indications that Jung privately held such a view had certain limitations. This is evident in an unusual experience Jung underwent, possibly during the very summer he delivered his lecture before the British Society for Psychical Research. While Jung was busy lecturing in London, a cottage in the country had been rented for him to use on the weekends.[221] Over the course of a number of nights while in this cottage, Jung became unusually apprehensive about the atmosphere in the room in which he stayed. At night the room was stuffy and had an unpleasant odour, next Jung heard the sound of dripping water and then creaking noises. When he lit a candle or in the first light of dawn all of these smells and sounds disappeared.[222]

Jung subjected himself and the other guests of the cottage to psychological probing but he could not account for these unusual occurrences.[223] When the noises increased he began to seriously consider that the cottage was haunted.[224] According to Jung, two servant girls from the village confirmed to him that this was in fact well known by the locals.[225] During one of the last weekends Jung spent in the cottage the following occurred:

> it was a beautiful moonlight night, with no wind; in the room there were rustlings, creakings, and bangings; from outside, blows rained on the walls. I had the feeling there was something near me, and opened my eyes. There, beside me on the pillow, I saw the head of an old woman, and the right eye, wide open, glared at me. The left half of the face was missing below the eye. The sight of it was so sudden and unexpected that I leapt out of bed with one bound, lit the candle, and spent the rest of the night in an armchair. The next day I moved into the adjoining room, where I slept splendidly and was no longer disturbed during this or the following weekend.[226]

Jung told another doctor staying with him that he was convinced the house was haunted. The doctor dismissed this explanation with amused skepticism.[227] Annoyed by his reaction Jung challenged the doctor to spend a night in the room. He agreed. While alone one weekend the doctor decided he would sleep downstairs.

Even then, according to Jung, he became so distraught by the inexplicable noises that he went outside the cottage to spend the rest of the night in the garden. The doctor reported all of this to Jung including the fact that the cottage had to be torn down shortly afterwards because no one would buy or rent it.[228]

Jung would later publicly modify his claim that the phenomenon of spirits should be considered exclusively an appendix of psychology.[229] The source of this modification is already implicit in Jung's formal notion of the transpersonal psyche and its contents, the archetypes. If by 1919, in spite of his own experiences, Jung still maintained publicly that the spirits remained split-off portions of the psyche, the psyche now had roots in the collective unconscious, something akin to a would-soul. It is this fact which complicates any attempt to isolate Jung's beliefs about the exact status of the spirits. The question is not whether Jung thought there was anything more to the phenomenon of spirits than something purely psychological, but rather his precise understanding of the term *psychological*.

Privately, Jung kept abreast of the literature on parapsychological research and attended a number of séances in the 1920s and 1930s during which he witnessed materializations and other phenomena.[230] For the next two and a half decades Jung would remain publicly reserved about the phenomenon of spirits.[231] He continued to analyze such phenomena within the prescribed limits set by Kant and Schopenhauer, and aptly echoed by his friend and associate H. G. Baynes when he stated:

> What we cannot determine is whether the spirit-world, which appears to be inhabited by the spirits of those who have died, is an aspect of this vast hinterland of the psyche, or whether it can be regarded as existing independently. All we know is that the spirits of the dead can become part of our experience only by means of our conscious psychic envelope, and just because of this inevitable condition it is practically impossible to determine whether they exist independently of the psyche, or whether they live because the living give them life.[232]

In the 1940s, in a number of essays which I will examine in the following chapter, Jung offered a comprehensive theory of the nature of the psyche. In these essays he sharpened his understanding of the psychological by defining it against a posited trans-psychic reality. Focusing initially on the phenomenology of the archetype, he was moved to consider the possibility that archetypes have a trans-psychic source. As I will demonstrate, he speculated that archetypes were rooted in a trans-psychic reality that was on the one end matter, and on the other end spirit. The implications of this argument for the independent status of spirits are ambiguous but extremely suggestive. In the following chapter it will become clear that even late in life Jung's interests and writings betray a longing to prove the truth of his early experiences, though even his genius could not place that truth beyond the reach of doubt.

Notes

1. *MDR*, 170.

2. Ibid.

3. Ibid., 171.

4. François Roustang in *Dire Mastery: Discipleship from Freud to Lacan*, trans. Ned Lukacher (Baltimore, Md.: The John Hopkins University Press, 1976), 54, suggests this is what the unpublished correspondence between Bleuler and Freud indicates. Franz Alexander and Sheldon T. Selesnick, in "Freud-Bleuler Correspondence," *Archives of General Psychiatry* 12 (1965): 1–9, make no mention of Jung having undergone psychiatric treatment.

5. C. G. Jung, "Abstracts of the Psychological Works of Swiss Authors" (1910), in *The Symbolic Life*, 403.

6. Ibid., 401–2.

7. Miss Frank Miller, "Quelque faits de l'imagination créatrice subconsciente." Introduction by Theodore Flournoy, *Archives de psychologie* 5 (1906): 36–51. Recently it has come to light that Miss Frank Miller was actually the woman's name and not a pseudonym; see Sonu Shamdasani, "A Woman Called Frank," *Spring* (1990): 31.

8. *MDR*, 162–63.

9. Jung, *Symbols of Transformation*, xxviii; *Analytical Psychology*, 28. In 1909 Miss Miller was admitted to Danvers State Hospital in Massachussets. She was diagnosed as suffering from "Psychopathic personality, with hypomanic traits." She was described as "unstable," "erotic," "vain," and from a "bad" family. The prognosis for Miss Miller's hypomania was considered "good," while the prognosis for her psychopathic personality was said to be "very bad."; Shamdasani, 31, citing Danvers Hospital Records, case no. 14852, year no. 1321 (1909), 4.

10. Jung, *Analytical Psychology*, 28; *Symbols of Transformation*, xxviii. What was the eventual outcome of Miss Miller's condition is not entirely clear. Danvers State Hospital records indicate she was discharged a week after her admission into the custody of an aunt. She was described as being "clear" and "unclouded." Her own assessment of her condition was that she suffered from nervous exhaustion, and her aunt promised to take her to a private sanatorium for a rest; Shamdasani, 31–32, citing Danvers Hospital Record, 16, 5 and 19.

11. Jung, *Symbols of Transformation*, xxviii.

12. Ibid. Miss Miller's physician at Danvers State Hospital was Dr. E. Katzenellenbogen who, in a letter (December 17, 1955) to Jung, recalled having confirmed Jung's "intuitive analysis"; Shamdasani, 30. Katzenellenbogen may have been acquainted with Jung's early work through Dr. Charles Ricksher, who was Assistant Physician at Danvers State Hospital. Ricksher had been a colleague of Jung's at the Burghölzli and co-authored a paper with him; see Charles Ricksher and C. G. Jung, "Further Investigations on the Galvanic Phenomenon and Respiration in Normal and Insane Individuals," (1907–08) in *Experimental Researches*, 554–80. The psychiatrist who admitted Miss Miller to Danvers State Hospital, it turns out, was none other than Charles Ricksher; see Shamdasani, 32. It is also likely that Katzenellenbogen met Jung at Clark University in 1909; see the group photograph of the Psychology Conference at Clark University in George E. Gifford, Jr., ed., *Psychoanalysis, Psychotherapy and the New England Medical Scene, 1894–1944* (New York: Science History Publications, 1978) plate 5, page 89.

13. Miss Frank Miller, "Some Instances of Subconscious Creative Imagination." Prefatory note by James H. Hyslop and introduction by Theodore Flournoy, *Journal of the American Society for Psychical Research* 1 (1907): 287–308.

14. Ibid., 287–88.

15. Fodor, *Encyclopedia of Psychic Science*, s.v. "Hyslop, James Hervey," 180.

16. Jung, *Letters: 1906–1950*, 431. It is not exactly clear when the conversation between Jung and Hyslop took place, but it must have been during one of Jung's early trips to the United States. McGuire suggests that Jung's election to the American Society for Psychical Research in 1907 was "probably sponsored" by Hyslop; see *The Freud/Jung Letters*, 96 n. 4.

17. I will return to this in the concluding chapter.

18. Hyslop seemed to have been rather critical of Jung's early views and considered them a form of psychoanalytic reductionism with sexuality as the centerpiece; see his review of *Symbols of Transformation*, then pub-

lished in English under the title *Psychology of the Unconscious,* in *Journal of the American Society for Psychical Research* 13 (1919): 44–47. Even though Hyslop may have misunderstood Jung's argument, his differences with Jung at that time were undoubtedly influenced by the latter's association with Freud. For Hyslop's views on reductionism in general see his "Kant and Spiritualism," *Journal of the American Society for Psychical Research,* 14 (1920): 226–31.

19. Miller, "Some Instances of Subconscious Creative Imagination," 288–89.

20. Ibid., 289.

21. Ibid., 289–90.

22. Ibid., 290.

23. Ibid.

24. Fodor, *Encyclopedia of Psychic Science,* s.v. "Flournoy, Theodore," 141–42. Ed. Claparède, "Théodore Flournoy: sa vie et son oeuvre 1854–1920," *Archives de Psychologie* 18 (1923): 10 et seq., has indicated how deeply influenced Flournoy was by Kant.

25. Ibid., 71 n. 1.

26. Compare Flournoy's remarks with those of Miss Miller; Miller, "Some Instances of Subconscious Creative Imagination," 288–93, 293–96.

27. *MDR,* 162.

28. C. G. Jung, *Erinnerungen, Träume, Gedanken,* 378.

29. Ibid.

30. Ibid.

31. Ibid., 379.

32. Ibid.

33. Ibid.

34. Theodore Flournoy, "Review of Dr. C. G. Jung, *Wandlungen und Symbole der Libido,*" *Archives de Psychologie* 13 (1913): 195–99.

35. Jung, *Analytical Psychology,* 24.

36. Ibid., 27.

37. Ibid.

38. Ibid., 27–28.

39. Ibid., 29.

40. Ibid.

41. Ibid., 30.

42. Ibid.

43. C. G. Jung, "The Theory of Psychoanalysis" (1913, rev. 1955), in *Freud and Psychoanalysis*, 180.

44. Jung, *Symbols of Transformation*, xxiv.

45. Ibid., xxiv–xxv.

46. *MDR*, 171.

47. Ibid., 172. This dream as well as several others *by the same dreamer* are given as case-history examples of the archetype of the anima in C. G. Jung, "The Psychological Aspect of the Kore" (1941, rev. 1951), in *The Archetypes and the Collective Unconscious*, 200–3. It is interesting to note that a few of the other dreams reported involve spirits. In a slightly different version of the dream, which Jung described in conversation, he associated the little girl with his daughter, Agathe, with whom he shared mediumistic abilities; see Bennet, *Meetings with Jung*, 75.

48. *MDR*, 172. Von Franz, *C. G. Jung: His Myth in Our Time*, 105, has remarked of this period of Jung's life, "Jung's report of his experiences after separating from Freud strikes one as being an astonishing parallel to this form of primeval experience of the spirit-world, that is, of the unconscious."

49. *MDR*, 172–73.

50. Ibid., 173.

51. Ibid., 173–74.

52. Ibid., 176.

53. Ibid., 179.

54. Ibid., 179 et seq.

55. Ibid., 181.

56. Ibid., 183.

57. Ibid., 184; C. G. Jung, "The Phenomenology of the Spirit in Fairytales" (1945, rev. 1948) in *The Archetypes and the Collective Unconscious*, 216 n. 11.

58. *MDR*, 183.

59. 2 Kings 2:11, Mal. 4:5. Jung himself gave a long list of legends, stories, and associations that have become attached to the figure of Elijah; see C. G. Jung, "Letter to Père Bruno" (1953) in *The Symbolic Life*, 673–78.

60. Matt. 17: 10–13.

61. Matt. 14: 1–12. The New Testament does not identify the dancer as Salome, but Josephus does in *Antiquities*, 18.5.4.

62. The figure of the biblical Salome was a compelling and also exceedingly popular image at the turn of the century and became the subject of plays, operas, and art; see Helen Grace Zagona, *The Legend of Salome* (Geneva: Droz, 1960); Cecil Roth, "Salome," in *Encyclopedia Judaica*, vol. 14, ed. Cecil Roth (Jerusalem: Keter, 1972), 689–90; and Bram Dijkstra, *Idols of Perversity* (New York: Oxford University Press, 1986), 352–401. The dark and enticing image of Salome as "the priestess of the severed head" with all of its associations of religion and sexuality in *fin-de-siècle* Europe are a more likely source of Jung's Salome than Lou Andreas-Salomé, as suggested by Stanley Leavy in "A Footnote to Jung's 'Memories,'" *The Psychoanalytic Quarterly* 33 (1964): 567–74. For Jung and Lou Andreas-Salomé, see Karl M. Abenheimer, "Lou Andreas-Salomé's Main Contribution to Psycho-Analysis," *Spring* (1971): 33–34.

63. 1 Kings 17 et seq.

64. Ovid, *Metamorphoses*, 8, 611–726.

65. Goethe, *Faust*, pt. 2, act 5.

66. C. G. Jung, *Collected Works*, vol. 12, *Psychology and Alchemy* (1944, rev. 1952), 2nd ed. (Princeton, N.J. Princeton University Press, 1968), 480.

67. Jung, *Letters 1: 1906–1950*, 49, 309–10; see also Wolfgang Giegerich, "Hospitality Toward the Gods in an Ungodly Age: Philemon-Faust-Jung," *Spring* (1984): 61–75.

68. Shrine of Philemon—Repentance of Faust; *MDR*, 235 n. 5.

69. Ibid., 182–83.

70. Ibid., 185.

71. There is a photograph of one painting in Mary Louise von Franz, "The Process of Individuation," in C. G. Jung, ed., *Man and His Symbols* (New York: Doubleday, 1964), 198; another in *The Sunday Times* (London), November 28, 1975; and another in Jaffé, *Word and Image*, 67. Wehr, 183–84, mentions having seen a painting of Philemon in Bollingen.

72. *MDR*, 215.

73. Von Franz, *C. G. Jung: His Myth in Our Time*, 274.

74. Jung's preoccupation with the theme of the coniunctio culminated in the publication of his *Collected Works*, vol. 14, *Mysterium Coniunctionis* (1955–56), 2nd ed. (Princeton, N.J. Princeton University Press, 1970).

75. *MDR*, 213.

76. Ibid., 213–14.

77. Ibid., 214.

78. Ibid.

79. Ibid.

80. Jung, *Letters 1: 1906–1950*, 481. This letter is to the Catholic priest Victor White, with whom Jung had an intimate friendship. The dream itself is linked to the one Jung reported in *MDR*, 217 et seq., immediately after the remark about his father's Amfortas wound; see Jung, *Letters 1: 1906–1950*, 491 n. 12.

81. Ibid., 481.

82. Ibid., 482.

83. Ibid., 490–91.

84. Ibid., 491.

85. *MDR*, 216.

86. Ibid., 217.

87. Ibid., 217–18.

88. Ibid., 218.

89. Jung, *Letters 1: 1906–1950*, 491.

90. Ibid., 491–92.

91. *MDR*, 219; 2 Sam. 11.

92. *MDR*, 219.

93. Ibid., 219–20.

94. Jung, *Letters 1: 1906–1950*, 493.

95. *MDR*, 15.

96. Ibid.; Brome, 36. There is a drawing of the house in Jaffé, *Word and Image*, 16.

97. Ibid., 14.

98. *MDR*, 18.

99. Ibid.

100. Ibid., 56, 76.

101. Ibid., 17.

102. Ibid. Jung had, with uncertainty, placed his phallus dream when he was between three and four years old and living in Laufen, ibid., 11. If the dream occurred when he was four years old it would have taken place in Klein-Hüningen, ibid., 15. It is interesting to note that the cupola on the rectory or church building in Klein-Hüningen is distinctly phallic looking, according to a nineteenth-century drawing reproduced in Jaffé, *Word and Image*, 16.

103. Compare *MDR*, 11–13 and 218–19.

104. Ibid.

105. Ibid., 219.

106. Ibid., Jung, *Letters 1: 1906–1950*, 491.

107. *MDR*, 219. Uriah, according to Israelite army practice, observed the taboo which forbade sexual intercourse to warriors consecrated for battle; see 1 Sam. 21: 4–5. He therefore could not have been made (as David would have wished) to appear as the father of Bathsheba's child; see 2 Sam. 11.

108. *MDR*, 219–20.

109. Ludwig Binswanger, "My First Three Visits with Freud in Vienna (1957)," in Hendrik M. Ruitenbeek, ed., *Freud as We Knew Him* (Detroit: Wayne State University Press, 1973), 361.

110. *The Freud/Jung Letters*, 96. Bennet, *Meetings with Jung*, 65, reports that Jung also remarked late in life (August 31, 1956) that he had the following dream when he visited Freud in Vienna the first time: "He was in the ghetto in Prague and it was narrow, twisted and low ceilinged, with staircases hanging down. He thought, 'How in hell can people live in such a place?'"

111. *MDR*, 163.

112. Ibid., 164.

113. Ibid., 163.

114. *The Freud/Jung Letters*, 30.

115. Ibid., 56.

116. Ibid., 86. Jung's father was fifty-three years old when he died in 1896.

117. Ibid.

118. Ibid., 88.

119. Ibid., 95.

120. Ibid.

121. Erik H. Erikson, "Themes of Adulthood in the Freud-Jung Correspondence," in Neil J. Smelser and Erik H. Erikson, eds., *Themes of Work and Love in Adulthood* (Cambridge, Mass.: Harvard University Press, 1980), 55.

122. *The Freud/Jung Letters*, 123. At the beginning of this letter (February 20, 1908) Jung asked Freud to look on their relationship as "that of father and son," ibid., 122. In an earlier letter Jung called Bleuler a "pseudo-personality," ibid., 97.

123. Ibid., 188–89.

124. Ibid, 215.

125. *MDR*, 155–56.

126. *The Freud/Jung Letters*, 217.

127. Ibid., 218.

128. Erikson, "Themes of Adulthood in the Freud-Jung Correspondence," 56.

129. *The Freud/Jung Letters*, 294.

130. Ibid., 295.

131. Ibid., 296.

132. Ibid., 297.

133. Ibid., 298.

134. Ibid., 298 n. 1.

135. Ibid., 298.

136. Ibid., 300.

137. Samuel Rosenberg in *Why Freud Fainted* (New York: The Bobbs-Merrill Co., 1978), 41, writes:

> I asked myself, "What did Philemon *really* signify to Jung? What did he look like?" I turned the pages of Jung's memoirs, found the "painting" he had made of Philemon—and saw that it was an unmistakable portrait of Sigmund Freud. Others to whom I showed the image and asked, "Who does this look like?" all answered at once—"Sigmund Freud."

138. The first signs of this are evident in part 2 of *Symbols of Transformation*, which Jung was writing at the latter stages of his relationship with Freud.

139. *MDR*, 185. Flournoy seems to have served as a transitional father figure between Freud and Philemon.

140. Jung, *Letters 1: 1906–1950*, 417.

141. C. G. Jung, *Answer to Job* (1952), in *Psychology and Religion*, 357–470.

142. C. G. Jung, "The Relations between the Ego and the Unconscious" (1916, rev. 1935), in *Two Essays on Analytical Psychology*, 240.

143. Ibid., 238.

144. Ibid.

145. Hannah, 117, clearly associates Toni Wolff and Salome.

146. *The Freud/Jung Letters*, 440.

147. Various dates are given of Toni Wolff's first consultations with Jung: 1909 by Stern, 135, and Wehr, 143; 1910 by Brome, 129; and 1911 by Hannah, 103–4.

148. Hannah, 104. There is a group photograph of the Weimer Congress reproduced in *The Freud/Jung Letters*, plate 6 facing page 444.

149. Jung apparently destroyed their correspondence; Jung, *Letters 1: 1906–1950*, xi. His published remarks about Toni Wolff are notably detached; see C. G. Jung, "Introduction to Toni Wolff's *Studies in Jungian Psychology*" (1959), in *Civilization in Transition*, 469–76; nor is she mentioned in *MDR*. Hannah, 7, comments on the Jung family's disapproval of revealing the private life of the man. Gerhard Adler mentions "a very private memorial booklet" in honor of Toni Wolff, which has never been published, in his "Memory of Toni Wolff," in Ferne Jensen and Sidney Mullen, eds., *C. G. Jung, Emma Jung and Toni Wolff: A Collection of Remembrances* (San Francisco: The Analytical Psychology Club of San Francisco, 1982), 1.

150. Toni Wolff is reported to have stated "that she had gone for consultation but that very quickly the relationship had changed"; see Tina Keller, "Beginnings of Active Imagination: Analysis with C. G. Jung and Toni Wolff, 1915–1928," *Spring* (1982): 288.

151. Hannah, 119; Brome, 170; Suzanne Percheron, "Memory of C. G. Jung," in Jensen and Mullen, 60.

152. Brome, 226. Jung is reported to have commented that Toni Wolff was the same psychological type as himself, i.e.,thinking-intuitive; see Irene Champernowne, *A Memoir of Toni Wolff* (San Francisco: C. G. Jung Institute of San Francisco, 1980), 8.

153. Jung, *Letters 2: 1951–1961*, 454–55.

154. Ibid., 455.

155. Toni Wolff, "A few Thoughts on the Process of Individuation in Women" (1934), *Spring* (1941): 90.

156. Helena Henderson, "Toni Wolff," in Jensen and Mullen, 31.

157. Peter C. Lynn, "C. G. Jung, Emma Jung, and Toni Wolff," in Jensen and Mullen, 42.

158. Keller, 288.

159. Champernowne, 6.

160. Wolff, 100–1.

161. Ibid., 102.

162. Hannah, 117.

163. Wolff, 103.

164. C. G. Jung, "Concerning the Archetypes, with Special Reference to the Anima Concept" (1936, rev. 1954), in *The Archetypes and the Collective Unconscious*, 54–72.

165. *MDR*, 181.

166. Hannah, 119. According to von Franz, "Very split people and people threatened by a latent psychosis generally cannot do active imagination at all," M.-L. von Franz, "On Active Imagination," in Ian F. Baker, ed., *Methods of Treatment in Analytical Psychology* (Fellback: Bonz, 1980), 91.

167. C. G. Jung, "Adaptation, Individuation, Collectivity" (1916), in *The Symbolic Life*, 453–54.

168. Ibid., 454.

169. See Jung's remarks on the unconscious incestuous relationship between father and daughter in his "Psychological Aspects of the Mother Archetype," (1938, rev. 1954) in *The Archetypes and the Collective Unconscious*, 88.

170. Ibid., 94–97.

171. Wolff, 101.

172. Ibid.

173. Hannah, 120.

174. Brome, 24.

175. Glin Bennet, "Domestic Life With C. G. Jung: Tape Recorded Conversations with Ruth Bailey," 182.

176. Brome, 257.

177. Ibid., 258; Stern, 141.

178. Brome, 258, which, however, has the year wrong; Stern, 141.

179. Brome, 258.

180. C. G. Jung, *Letters 2: 1951–1961*, 118.

181. Champernowne.

182. Ibid., 8.

183. Ibid., 8 et seq.

184. Ibid., 8.

185. Ibid., 10.

186. Ibid., 48–49.

187. Ibid., 50.

188. Ibid., 50–51.

189. Ibid., 51–52.

190. Jung, *Letters 2: 1951–1961*, 118.

191. Hannah, 120.

192. Ibid., 313.

193. Champernowne, 52. The painting of the dream is reproduced in

C. G. Jung, *Flying Saucers: A Modern Myth of Things Seen in the Sky* (1958), in *Civilization in Transition*, plate 1 facing page 404.

194. Ibid., 368–69.

195. Ibid., 372.

196. Jung, *Letters 2: 1951–1961*, 424–25.

197. Joseph L. Henderson's foreword to Champernowne, 3–4.

198. *MDR*, 183–84.

199. Ibid., 191.

200. Ibid., 190–91.

201. Ibid., 191.

202. James Heisig, "The VII Sermones: Play and Theory," 206–18.

203. *MDR*, 190.

204. Ibid., 380.

205. Ibid., 395 et seq. Schopenhauer, in *The World as Will and Representation*, used this term extensively.

206. *MDR*, 383.

207. Ibid.

208. Ibid, 383–84.

209. Ibid., 385.

210. Heisig, "The VII Sumones: Play and Theory," 212.

211. *MDR*, 385.

212. Ibid., 386.

213. Ibid.

214. Ibid., 388.

215. Ibid., 389.

216. Ibid.

217. Ibid.

218. Ibid.

219. Ibid., 306. Jung made clear the significance of his experience when he wrote, ibid, 192, "These conversations with the dead formed a kind of prelude to what I had to communicate to the world about the unconscious: a kind of pattern of order and interpretation of its general contents."

220. C. G. Jung, "The Psychological Foundations of Belief in Spirits," in *The Structure and Dynamics of the Psyche*, 318.

221. In Jung's "Contribution to Moser: *Spuk: Irrglaube Oder Wahrglaube?*" (1950), in *The Symbolic Life*, 320, he stated that he was invited to give a series of lectures in the summer of 1920, in London. In fact it was in the previous year (1919) that Jung lectured in London before various societies where he delivered the following lectures: "Instinct and the Unconscious," in *The Structure of Dynamics of the Psyche*, 129–38; "The Psychological Foundations of Belief in Spirits," in ibid, 301–18; and "On the Problem of Psychogenesis in Mental Diseases," in, *The Psychogenesis of Mental Disease*, 211–25. Jung did visit England in the summer of 1920, but this was to conduct a seminar at Sennen Cove, Cornwall. While he was there he apparently shared a boarding house with a dozen other people. This seminar has not survived; see Hannah, 141.

222. Jung's "Contribution to Moser: *Spuk: Irrglaube Oder Wahrglaube?*" 321–22.

223. Ibid.

224. Ibid., 323.

225. Ibid.

226. Ibid., 324.

227. Ibid.

228. Ibid., 324–25.

229. It may be that Jung's experience of the haunted cottage had something to do with his public change of mind. As von Franz has written in *Jung: His Myth in Our Time*, 58, "Although in this early period Jung regarded 'spirits' as 'only' psychic complexes, he changed his position in his later work. It is difficult to see how a 'place-bound' spook, for example, could have been evoked through a person's complexes." I shall document this shift in Jung's thinking in more detail in the next chapter.

230. Jaffé, *From the Life and Work of C. G. Jung*, 10, reports: "In the early twenties Jung, together with Count Albert Schrenk-Notzing and Professor Eugen Bleuler, carried out a series of experiments with the Austrian medium, Rudi Schneider, at the Burghölzli. They witnessed materializations, psychokinetic and other phenomena. Jung conducted similar experi-

ments with the medium O. Schl. [Oscar Schlag]." The latter experiments took place in Zurich in the house of Professor Rudolph Bernoulli; see Jung, *Letters 2: 1951–1961*, 627–28. The Schneider Journal for the séance in Zurich on June 21, 1925 contains, in Jung's hand, the signature "C. G. Jung Psychoanalyst"; see Anita Gregory, *The Strange Case of Rudi Schneider* (Metuchen, N.Y.: The Scarecrow Press, 1985), 73 fig. 8, 74. According to Fodor, *Freud, Jung and Occultism*, 122–23, who had it on the authority of Dr. Gerda Walther, Schrenk-Notzing's research secretary: "Jung had only attended one series of three sittings in 1925 in Zurich at the house of Dr. Rudolph Bernouilly, a friend of Bleuler and Jung. Of these sittings the first and third were blanks, in the second, however, telekinetic phenomena and the materialization of human limbs were observed." Fodor also mentioned the Otto Schlag séance which followed in 1931, during which a sample of ectoplasm was secured. Bennet, *Meetings with Jung*, 96–97, records that Jung mentioned a similar event. See also Jung, *Letters 1: 1906–1950*, 511.

231. Jung's reticence extended to other matters parapsychological as well. Fodor, *Freud, Jung and Occultism*, 123, cites Dr. Gerda Walther as having written the following: "Jung was much impressed by these [the Schlag] sittings. He once embraced Schlag when suddenly Schlag's jacket dematerialized…. Jung said he was quite convinced of the genuineness of the phenomena he witnessed. When I asked him, why didn't he publish this verdict, he said that he had so many important things to say—which were only accepted very reluctantly. When they would be 'swallowed', the time for writing about these phenomena will be at hand."

232. H. G. Baynes, "The Ghost as a Psychic Phenomenon" (1936), in *Analytical Psychology and the English Mind* (London: Methuen & Co., 1950), 167.

Chapter 8

Conclusion: Archetypes and Spirits

In the preceding pages I have attempted to demonstrate that the experiences, beliefs, and ideas that are broadly characteristic of Spiritualism in the nineteenth century were a significant influence in the early life of C. G. Jung. Moreover, I have also suggested that, as a consequence, Spiritualism should be regarded as one of the important contributing factors to the foundations upon which Jung erected his psychology. To conclude, I would like to briefly recapitulate my argument and make a number of suggestions about the significance of these data for an understanding of Jung's concept of the "archetype." In addition, I will also offer a few general observations on the role of religious influences in Jung's psychological understanding of religion.

In chapter 1, I sketched the social and medical history of the interrelation of mesmerism, hypnotism, and Spiritualism in the nineteenth century. The phenomena that emerged from the mesmeric, hypnotic, and mediumistic trance indicated certain mental processes that escaped conscious control and even suggested abnormal states of mind. These abnormal states manifested as personalities. On a popular level the existence of these personalities were often interpreted as evidence of communication with a spirit world. The beliefs and ideas attached to such phenomena were loosely gathered under the designation "Spiritualism." The medical view, as represented by neurology and psychiatry, recognized the autonomy of these secondary personalities, but preferred to relate them to the personalities of the mediums and to interpret their existence as evidence of dissociation and psychopathology. It is at this point that Jung, as a young psychiatrist, entered the debate. For certain personal and professional reasons, the vital question for Jung became: Are such autonomous psychical processes as found in spiritualistic phenomena necessarily always pathological? When Jung later provided a negative answer to this question, he moved away from an exclusively psychiatric view of such phenomena to create a general psychology. In addition, this was to have a major impact on his psychological understanding of religious experience. It is my contention that the background of this question and Jung's answer lies in the intertwining of mesmerism, hypnotism, and Spiritualism in the nineteenth century.

In chapter 2, I demonstrated that there is a great deal of evidence for the influence of Spiritualism in Jung's early life and that this came chiefly through his mother and her side of the family. Several members of Jung's maternal side of the family exhibited personality characteristics of dissociation identical with those found in mediums. The beliefs that arose out of the experiences of Jung's maternal relatives are clearly the loose knit of ideas known as Spiritualism. Jung seems to have had a predisposition to the same type of experiences and to have shared in the popular religious beliefs to which these pointed.

On Jung's paternal side the direct religious influences were much more doubtful and precarious. The Reverend Paul Jung, the psychiatrist's father, was a man who was at pains to separate religious belief from experience. The consequences for Jung were to put him into severe tension with his father and the Christian religion. The sense of isolation and inadequacy that resulted seems to have driven Jung to try to mythologize his paternal ancestry by granting it a status and significance it did not possess. In doing this, Jung also attempted to compensate for the overwhelming influence of his maternal side of the family. I have maintained that this resulted in creating in Jung a crisis, trapping him between two powerful influences, both parental and religious. This experience so colored Jung's early life that it seems to have largely determined what little he had to say about the general psychology of children.

In chapter 3, I uncovered the philosophical basis of Jung's intellectual response to spiritualistic experiences and beliefs. Initially, this response was precipitated by the death of Jung's father and the discovery of the literature of Spiritualism. Gradually, it was Jung's own developing mind that caused him to seek out a more sophisticated philosophical understanding of Spiritualism. His explorations of the questions raised by spiritualistic experiences led him to the writings of Kant and Schopenhauer on the subject of Spiritualism. Kant's little-known writings on Spiritualism were preliminary attempts to found a method of organizing knowledge and experience in terms of certain basic categories of understanding. These investigations that Kant made of Spiritualism were published during his precritical period—that is before his *Critique of Pure Reason* in 1781. In this chapter I have demonstrated that Kant's precritical studies of Spiritualism, and the interpretation that Schopenhauer offered of them, are the early sources of Jung's so-called Kantianism and the philosophical foundation upon which he built his psychology of spiritualistic experience.

Kant, in his writings on Spiritualism, made a distinction between (1) phenomenal reality, which can be apprehended by the senses as determined by the *a priori* categories of time and space and (2) the noumenal, or things as they are in themselves. Phenomena are the result of a sensory process, noumena are not. It follows that human knowledge is possible only within the limits of phenomenal reality; the noumena remains inaccessible to human reason. The former contains objects of knowledge; the latter objects of belief, such as spirits.

Schopenhauer interpreted Kant's examination of the belief in spirits as an attempt to separate spirits from phenomenal reality and not as a denial of their existence. Furthermore, Schopenhauer argued that a person could experience an image or spirit arising out of the noumenal only through an inner course by which it would enter the phenomenal world to be conditioned by all that characterizes this world. He concluded that this process is so subjective and so entangled in the sensory faculties that it would assume the characteristics of the person through whom this occurred. Schopenhauer does not deny the possibility of spirits influencing living persons, but surmised they could do so only through a person's neuropsychological faculties. This would make it exceedingly difficult to separate the living from the dead. In chapter 3, I have stressed the importance of these ideas as they were later appropriated by Jung.

In chapter 4, I examined Jung's *Zofingia Lectures* which he gave as a student in the late 1890s. These lectures indicate (1) that Jung subjected Spiritualism to a philosophical analysis drawing upon Kant and Schopenhauer and (2) that he was moving from philosophy to psychiatry in order to develop a clearer understanding of the psychological nature of spiritualistic phenomena. It is evident in Jung's student lectures that under the influence of Kant and Schopenhauer, he came to situate the source of spiritualistic phenomena within the individual. Moreover, he accepted the limitations to which these phenomena would be subjected when they entered phenomenal reality. For Jung, this amounted to a shift in perspective from a metaphysical to a psychological understanding of Spiritualism. Nevertheless, there are indications that, on the personal level, this formal intellectual change did not reconcile the deep division and instability Jung experienced since childhood; it did, though, allow him to place this division within himself.

In chapter 5, I considered Jung's medical dissertation, which is a psychiatric analysis of a medium. The dissertation marks the end of Jung's university studies and launched him into a career as a psychiatrist. In it Jung attempted to address the question I formulated on his behalf in the chapter 1, namely: are such autonomous psychical processes as found in spiritualistic phenomena necessarily always pathological? In his dissertation, Jung argued they are not; he maintained this on the basis of his careful examination of the medium's communications during several séances. Jung did not, however, reveal the extent to which he was personally involved in the data he was subjecting to a psychiatric analysis.

The personal dimension of Jung's life emerges once again when, as I have shown, it is evident that the séances were conducted in Jung's own home, the medium was his cousin, and the participants, members of his own family. In addition, a number of the spirits with which the medium was allegedly in communication were none other than Jung's ancestors. Moreover, Jung's cousin, the medium, had personality characteristics typical of mediums and which Jung himself shared, namely the tendency toward severe dissociation. I have, therefore, suggested that there are signs of self-analysis in Jung's dissertation which should not be overlooked. I have also suggested that unresolved sexual feelings between Jung and his cousin, the medium, became an important factor influencing the way he interpreted his data. Jung's interpretation that the chief spirit in the séances can be understood as a subconscious personality embodying the medium's future development seems sound enough, but the sexual fantasies and dynamic are only half-explained. Jung appears to have had difficulty incorporating the sexual element of the séances into his analyses. I have argued that this problem may have been a factor in Jung's attraction to Freud's theories.

In chapter 6, I focused on Jung's relationships with Freud in the light of the former's preoccupation with spiritualistic phenomena. I have argued that the conflict that arose between Freud and Jung over the correct interpretation of such phenomena was an important factor in the subsequent break between them. Initially, Freud's theories provided Jung with a more scientifically credible and secure psychological understanding of the human psyche. I have also suggested that the significance of the psychosexual nature of Freud's theory should not be overlooked, given the difficulties that arose for Jung with the sexual data in his dissertation. An additional point I have made in this chapter is the extent to which Freud himself became involved in the study of spiritualistic phenomena. In the end, Freud thought the investigation of spiritualistic or what he called "occult" phenomena might hold great promise but the trade-off in public shame and intellectual confusion was too costly. In contrast, Jung, unlike Freud, was prepared to consider the data of spiritualistic phenomena as raw material upon which to build a psychology.

In chapter 7, I have examined the place of spiritualistic phenomena in Jung's life during the period from 1912 to 1920 and the extent to which these were entangled with the past and with people with whom he became emotionally involved, most notably Sigmund Freud and Toni Wolff. During this time Jung underwent a number of powerful experiences which were accompanied by unusual and bizarre phenomena. The most important of these experiences culminated in the haunting of Jung's house by a chorus of spirits and the subsequent composition of *Septem Sermones ad Mortuos* (1916). These sermons not only express the ever-existing tension Jung experienced between his maternal Spiritualism and paternal Christianity, but also embody, in exotic gnostic language, virtually all of Jung's later ideas: the problem of opposites, the archetypes, individuation, and so on.

In constructing his model of the psyche out of the experiences he had, Jung felt it necessary to address the subject of belief in the existence of spirits. In "The Psychological Foundations of Belief in Spirits" (1919), Jung subsumed spirits under the category of psychological complexes and he maintained that this was the most a scientific, or thinking, mode of analysis could demonstrate. At the same time, Jung qualified his analysis by suggesting that feeling, in contrast to thinking, may arrive at a different conviction.

Jung's own conviction was that (1) scientifically, spirits are demonstrable evidence of the autonomy of unconscious complexes and are therefore psychologically real and (2) from the point of view of feelings and subliminal perceptions, the independent existence of spirits may be an object of belief. This distinction between these two modes of understanding what spirits are mirrors the division that is perceptible in Jung himself: (1) his psychological understanding of spirits as unconscious complexes and (2) his own expe-

riences of the reality of spirits. We have in this tension the continued evidence of the split Jung himself testified to in his memoirs
between personality No. 1 and personality No. 2. Personality No. 1
is clearly perceivable in Jung as a professional psychiatrist; personality No. 2 is kept in the background and emerges only in his memoirs in the record of the powerful experiences he underwent during
the course of his life. The rationalization for this division Jung
believed he uncovered in the Kantian distinction between phenomena and noumena. Like Kant, Jung maintained that the distinction
between objects of knowledge and objects of belief was essential for
a clear understanding of reality. And, like Kant in his more unbut-
toned moments, Jung voiced his beliefs. Indeed, there are indications that Jung went even further and hinted that objects of belief
in themselves may even become objects of knowledge. This latter
point I will address in what follows by briefly examining Jung's
concept of the archetype.

Jung, in "A Review of the Complex Theory," stated:

> The universal belief in spirits is a direct expression of the
> complex structure of the unconscious. Complexes are in
> truth the living units of the unconscious psyche, and it is
> only through them that we are able to deduce its existence
> and its constitution.... The *via regia* to the unconscious...is
> not the dream...but the complex, which is the architect of
> dreams and of symptoms.[1]

The specificity and autonomy of the complex, as Jung expressed it
in this statement, is a further clarification of a concept that began
as the observed phenomenon of feeling-toned groups of representations in the unconscious.[2] The latter idea, which Jung first
expressed in *Studies in Word Association*, gave way to a more mul-
tifarious notion of the complexes as "psychic agencies whose deepest nature is still unfathomed."[3]

This development from a particularized and subjectively
determined idea of the complex to viewing it as a more impersonal
and universal phenomenon of the unconscious, testifies to the
emergence of an important concept in Jung's thought. He himself
expressed this as follows:

> Certain complexes arise on account of painful or distressing
> experiences in a person's life, experiences of an emotional
> nature which leave lasting psychic wounds behind them....

All these produce unconscious complexes of a personal nature.... A great many autonomous complexes arise in this way. But there are others that come from quite a different source. While the first source is easily understood, since it concerns the outward life everyone can see, this other source is obscure and difficult to understand because it has to do with perceptions or impressions of the collective unconscious.... At bottom they [these complexes] are irrational contents of which the individual has never been conscious before.[4]

In this passage it is quite clear that Jung has in mind two kinds of complexes: (1) split-off portions of consciousness that resulted from repression or some other factor and can be related to the individual in a personal way and (2) autonomous psychical entities which have never been in consciousness previously and are related to the individual in a more impersonal and collective way. For the former Jung retained the term "complex"; for the latter he searched out a new term calling it in 1912 "primordial image," in 1917 "dominants of the collective unconscious," and finally in 1919 he settled on "archetype."[5] At this time Jung defined archetypes as "*a priori*, inborn forms of 'intuition'...the...determinants of all psychic processes."[6]

Jung went on to refine his concept of the archetype in his later writings by introducing the distinction between the archetype as such and the archetype as represented.[7] This latter distinction is part of a far-reaching discussion on the nature of the archetype which represents Jung's most mature and formal thinking on the subject. I am, of course, referring to Jung's wide-ranging essay "On the Nature of the Psyche."[8] In what follows I will outline the contents of this essay and indicate its significance for an understanding of the implications of the influence of Spiritualism on Jung's psychology.

At the outset of his discussion in "On the Nature of the Psyche," Jung castigated experimental psychology for denying the significance of such concepts as the unconscious or unconscious processes.[9] This denial, he claimed, along with certain philosophical ideas, restricted human psychology to the realm of individual or collective consciousness.[10] In Western philosophy, according to Jung, this is evident in the victory of Hegel over Kant, where philosophical reason in the guise of the human spirit replaces God.[11]

In Jung's view, the psychiatric evidence of the dissociability of the psyche was simple proof that human psychology consists of more than consciousness. In fact, he argued, conscious contents themselves are also partly unconscious, that is, they are never completely known.[12] Moreover, conscious contents can become lost to consciousness and therefore unconscious. Jung also claimed that there are unconscious contents that can enter consciousness for the first time.[13] But, what chiefly interested him in this essay is the psychopathological phenomenon of secondary personalities. By the latter Jung meant contents that are not part of normal consciousness but which, nevertheless, possess a power and intentionality of their own and therefore manifest a consciousness within the unconscious. He divided these phenomena into two groups as follows:

> in the one case, there is an originally conscious content that became subliminal because it was repressed on account of its incompatible nature: in the other case, the secondary subject consists essentially in a process that never entered into consciousness at all because no possibilities exist there of apperceiving it.[14]

This distinction, as I have already mentioned, is the one Jung made between complex and archetype. He also maintained that these secondary personalities have an indirect effect on consciousness, which manifests symbolically.[15] In addition, he stated,

> In the majority of cases they are not repressed contents, but simply contents that are *not yet conscious*...like the demons and gods of the primitives.... This state is neither pathological nor in any way peculiar; it is on the contrary the original norm, whereas the psychic wholeness comprehended in the unity of consciousness is an ideal goal that has never yet been reached.[16]

Jung, at this time, introduced a further distinction into his concept of the archetype. He characterized the archetype as it is in itself by the term "psychoid"; the archetype as manifest in consciousness he called the "archetypal image."[17] The term "psychoid" indicated the irrepresentible nature of the archetype. Jung claimed that he had uncovered evidence that suggested the psyche was on the one hand rooted in matter and on the other in spirit.[18] As Jung himself stated:

Just as, in its lower reaches, the psyche loses itself in the organic-material substrate, so in its upper reaches it resolves itself into a "spiritual" form about which we know as little as we do about the functional basis of instinct.[19]

In the final analysis Jung theorized that the archetypes as psychoid are transcendent realities and therefore transpsychic. By contrast, the archetypes as expressed in archetypal images are psychic, being conditioned by the medium through which they manifested, namely the psyche. Jung has described this new development in his thinking as follows:

> In my previous writings I have always treated archetypal phenomena as psychic, because the material to be expounded or investigated was concerned solely with ideas and images. The psychoid nature of the archetype...does not contradict these earlier formulations....
> ...the archetype, describes a field which exhibits none of the peculiarities of the physiological and yet, in the last analysis, can no longer be regarded as psychic, although it manifests itself psychically.... Since their essential being is unconscious to us, and still they are experienced as spontaneous agencies, there is probably no alternative now but to describe their nature, in accordance with their chiefest effect, as "spirit...." If so, the position of the archetype would be located beyond the psychic sphere, analogous to the position of physiological instinct, which...with its psychoid nature, forms the bridge to matter in general.[20]

These formulations clearly moved Jung beyond the limits of empirical science and involved his psychology in metapsychological questions that are fundamentally religious in nature. The ideas that he presented are also remarkably like the speculations of Kant and Schopenhauer on the possible relation between the world of spirits and the world of human beings, which I outlined in chapter 3. Kant had inferred that spirits might be able to communicate to humans through their souls in a symbolic way, much in the manner Jung suggests archetypes manifest in human consciousness symbolically.[21] Initially, Kant speculated about such possibilities, but in his later writings, he became critical of those who would take the world of appearances to be a collection of symbols sustaining a hidden world.[22] He charged them with engaging in fantasy. Fantasy, Kant asserted, was either superstition or madness.[23] The consequences of indulging in fantasy, according to Kant, were to threaten the walls dividing noumena from phenomena; fantasy was both dangerous and corrupting.[24]

Jung would diverge from Kant on the value of fantasy. In fact Jung claimed that it was through fantasy that he was able to uncover the existence of the archetypes.[25] Of this he wrote,

> I...took up a dream-image or association of the patient's, and...set him the task of elaborating...by giving free rein to his fantasy.... The result of this technique was a vast number of complicated designs...I was able to recognize...I was witnessing the spontaneous manifestation of an unconscious process...to which I later gave the name "individuation process.".....
>
> The chaotic assortment of images that at first confronted me reduced itself...to certain well-defined themes and formal elements, which repeated themselves in identical or analogous form with the most varied individuals.[26]

Jung observed that this form of directed fantasy, which he termed "active imagination," reduced the intensity of the unconscious, making further progress possible.[27] In fact, to some extent, active imagination replaced dream analysis in Jung's psychology.[28] What characterized active imagination was that the individual participated consciously in integrating unconscious contents. This technique also allowed Jung to observe that these contents had a particular quality, which he described as follows:

> the archetypes have, when they appear, a distinctly numinous character which can only be described as "spiritual...." Consequently this phenomenon is of the utmost significance for the psychology of religion.... It not infrequently happens that the archetype appears in the form of a *spirit* in dreams or fantasy-products, or even comports itself like a ghost. There is a mystical aura about its numinosity, and it has a corresponding effect upon the emotions. It mobilizes philosophical and religious convictions in the very people who deemed themselves miles above any such fits of weakness.[29]

Jung placed great importance on the method of active imagination. He maintained that:

By means of "active imagination" we are put in a position of advantage, for we can then make the discovery of the archetype without sinking back into the instinctual sphere, which would only lead to blank unconsciousness or, worse still, to some kind of intellectual substitute for instinct.[30]

According to Jung, it was the spiritual characteristic of the archetypes as experienced by consciousness that prevented a person from slipping into the unconsciousness of instinctual life. This observation also drove Jung to speculate that the archetype in itself was transpsychic and derived from some transcendental source.[31] This source, he maintained, is inaccessible to human understanding because human knowledge is determined by the *a priori* conditions of time, space, and causality. Nevertheless, Jung concluded, there were phenomena, mainly of a parapsychological nature, which indicated a relativization of time, space and causality. Swedenborg's parapsychological knowledge of the fire in Stockholm, which I cited in chapter 3, is an example of such an event to which Jung himself referred.[32] Jung claimed that a careful observation of such phenomena indicated an arrangement of events on the basis of meaning. That two events could occur simultaneously with no causal connection and yet be related by meaning, Jung termed "synchronicity." He speculated that there was an inner, acausal association between such events and the constellation of an archetype. On the basis of such occurrences Jung ventured the opinion that there was a dimension of the human psyche which existed outside of the bounds of time, space, and causality.[33] In the light of such ideas Jung concluded "that psyche and matter are two different aspects of one and the same thing."[34] With such a hypothesis Jung comes very close to saying that objects of belief may even become objects of knowledge.

With these ideas of Jung's in mind and considering the topic under study, I would like to outline Jung's later views about the reality of spirits. As I pointed out in the previous chapter Jung, in his lecture "The Psychological Foundations of Belief in Spirits" (1919), had subsumed spirits under the category of complexes, albeit those complexes of the archetypal kind. In this lecture Jung stated:

I for one am certainly convinced that they [spirits] are exteriorizations [of unconscious complexes]. I have repeatedly observed the telepathic effects of unconscious complexes, and also a number of parapsychic phenomena. But in all of this I see no proof whatever of the existence of real spirits, and until such proof is forthcoming I must regard this whole territory as an appendix of psychology.[35]

This clearly represents the cautious Jung who, in the light of his own experiences, seemed preoccupied with presenting himself as the scientific empiricist.

The later Jung was somewhat less hesitant, and we find in the 1948 revision of his lecture the following footnote to the above remark:

After collecting psychological experiences from many people and many countries for fifty years, I no longer feel as certain as I did in 1919, when I wrote this sentence. To put it bluntly, I doubt whether an exclusively psychological approach can do justice to the phenomena in question. Not only the findings of parapsychology, but my own theoretical reflections, outlined in "On the Nature of the Psyche," have led me to certain postulates which touch on the realm of nuclear physics and the conception of the space-time continuum. This opens up the whole question of the transpsychic reality immediately underlying the psyche.[36]

Exactly how one could differentiate a spirit from an archetype Jung did not make clear, as is evident in some of his late remarks. In a letter (July 10, 1946) on the subject of a book on Spiritualism featuring a woman spirit, he wrote:

I am inclined to assume that she is more probably a spirit than an archetype, although she presumably represents both at the same time. Altogether, it seems to me that spirits tend increasingly to coalesce with archetypes. For archetypes can behave exactly like real spirits, so that communications like Betty's could just as well come from an indubitably genuine archetype.[37]

And in a recent article, Marie Louise von Franz has revealed that Jung interpreted certain dreams of the dead as actual visits of the dead to the dreamer.[38] Indeed, in his own autobiography he seems to have done precisely the same and even speculated in detail about the conditions of the afterlife.[39]

Two late dreams in particular indicate the train of Jung's thought on the subject. In the first dream (1944) Jung dreamed he had come upon a Yogi who had his face. The implication was clear to him: the Yogi was in meditation dreaming out Jung's life. In the second dream (1958) Jung came upon a UFO which he found had a projector. To his surprise the projector was projecting him.[40] In both dreams the suggestion is that Jung's life is the dream and the transpersonal world the reality. This seems to have been the direction in which Jung's psychology was moving. Indeed, it could be argued that Jung's preoccupation with the spiritual, and more specifically with spirits, was lifelong and naturally expressed itself in such views. Jung commented on this idea of a twofold existence in a late letter of May 30, 1960:

> We may therefore expect postmortal phenomena to occur which must be regarded as authentic. Nothing can be ascertained about existence outside time. The comparative rarity of such phenomena suggests at all events that the forms of existence inside and outside time are so sharply divided that crossing this boundary presents the greatest difficulties. But this does not exclude the possibility that there is an existence outside time which runs parallel with existence inside time. Yes, we ourselves may simultaneously exist in both worlds, and occasionally we do have intimations of a twofold existence. But what is outside time is, according to our understanding, outside change. It possesses relative eternity.[41]

In the foregoing I have tried to indicate how the influence of Spiritualism is evident in Jung's notion of the archetype. Though he identified himself as an empirical scientist, Jung seems in his later formulations on the nature of the archetype to have moved beyond the borders of science as traditionally understood. He obviously recognized this when he wrote:

> I fancied I was working along the best scientific lines, establishing facts, observing, classifying, describing causal and functional relations, only to discover in the end that I had involved myself in a net of reflections which extend far beyond natural science and ramify into the fields of philosophy, theology, comparative religion.... This transgression, as inevitable as it was suspect, has caused me no little

worry. Quite apart from my personal incompetence in these fields, it seemed to me that my reflections were suspect also in principle, because I am profoundly convinced that the "personal equation" has a telling effect upon the results of psychological observation.[42]

To conclude, I would like to make a few remarks about the significance of religious experience in the formation of Jung's psychological theory by focusing on the subject matter of this study. I have shown—fairly conclusively I think—that Jung, during his early life, came under the influence of certain experiences and beliefs that are characteristic of Spiritualism. Spiritualism later provided him with a religious framework within which he could fit his extraordinary experiences. While he ventured into philosophy and then psychiatry in order to more adequately account for such experiences, these approaches did not completely satisfy him. When Jung moved to create a general psychology he sought to incorporate such religious experiences into psychological molds which he termed "archetypes," that would do justice to what he called their "numinous," or spiritual, content. As a consequence he developed a unique psychology which, while it situated the experience of the numinous within the psyche, it did not reduce the numinous to some other causal factor. By attempting to found such a psychology Jung sought to bring religion and science together in the psyche itself and thereby heal a long-standing schism and in turn heal himself.

Notes

1. C. G. Jung, "A Review of the Complex Theory" (1934, rev. 1948), in *The Structure and Dynamics of the Psyche*, 101. Jung's psychology is sometimes called "complex psychology," indicating the importance he gave to this concept. See the brief review of the meaning of "complex" and other designations for Jung's psychological theories, in James Hillman, *Loose Ends* (Zurich: Spring Publications, 1975), 138 et seq.

2. The history of this development is briefly presented in Jolande Jacobi, *Complex/Archetype/Symbol* (Princeton, N.J.: Princeton University Press, 1959), 6–30.

3. Jung, "A Review of the Complex Theory," 104.

4. Jung, "The Psychological Foundations of Belief in Spirits," 313–14.

5. Respectively in *Symbols of Transformation, Two Essays in Analytical Psychology,* and "Instinct and the Unconscious"; see the survey in Jacobi, 33–35.

6. C. G. Jung, "Instinct and the Unconscious" (1919), in *The Structure and Dynamics of The Psyche,* 133.

7. Jung, "On the Nature of the Psyche," 213.

8. Jung's essay "On the Nature of the Psyche" was originally delivered as an Eranos lecture in 1946 and entitled "The Spirit of Psychology." It was subsequently revised and augmented in 1954; see ibid., 159 n. 1.

9. Ibid., 163.

10. Ibid., 167 et seq.

11. Ibid., 169–70.

12. Ibid., 173–74.

13. Ibid., 174–75.

14. Ibid.

15. Ibid., 175.

16. Ibid.

17. Ibid., 213.

18. Ibid., 180 et seq.

19. Ibid., 183.

20. Ibid., 215–16; also *MDR,* 351–52.

21. Broad, 137.

22. Butts, 86.

23. Ibid.; and the sources cited.

24. Ibid., 71 n. 8.

25. Jung, "On the Nature of the Psyche," 202.

26. Ibid., 202–03.

27. Ibid., 202. The history of the development of active imagination in Jung's thought is briefly documented in R. F. C. Hull, "Bibliographical Notes on Active Imagination in the Works of C. G. Jung," *Spring* (1971): 115–20. See also Elie G. Humbert, "Active Imagination According to Jung," in Papadopoulos and Saayman, 89–108; Keller, 279–94; Barbara Hannah,

Encounters with the Soul: Active Imagination as Developed by C. G. Jung (Santa Monica: Sigo Press, 1981). On the differences between Jung's active imagination and other imaginative techniques, see M. L. von Franz, "On Active Imagination," 88–99.

28. Jung, "On the Nature of the Psyche," 204.

29. Ibid., 205–6.

30. Ibid., 211.

31. Ibid., 212–13.

32. Ibid.; Jung, "Synchronicity: An Acausal Connecting Principle," 481.

33. Ibid., 505–19.

34. Jung, "On the Nature of the Psyche," 215.

35. Jung, "The Psychological Foundations of Belief in Spirits," 318.

36. Ibid. Von Franz makes very clear the impact of Jung's publicly revised views when she states in *Jung: His Myth in Our Time,* 58–59, "Although in this early period [1919] Jung regard 'spirits' as 'only' psychic complexes, he changed his position in his later work. It is difficult to see how a 'place-bound' spook, for example, could have been evoked through a person's complexes. Jung finally expressed a certain doubt, therefore, as to whether an exclusively psychological method could explain such phenomena, for somewhere deep in the ground of being, the psyche and the microphysical conceptions of the space-time continuum meet, or at least are connected."

37. Jung, *Letters: 1906–1950,* 432, commenting on the figure Betty in Stewart Edward White's *The Unobstructed Universe* (1940). See also C. G. Jung, "Psychology and Spiritualism" (1948), in *The Symbolic Life,* 312–16, which is a preface to the German edition of the book in question.

38. Marie Louise von Franz, "Archetypes Surrounding Death," *Quadrant* 12, (1979): 5–23. Von Franz also demonstrates the ambiguity and the difficulty of the Jungian view when she states in her *On Dreams and Death* (Boston: Shambhala, 1987) xiv, "For me, the mixture of reality and fantasy in spiritualism is something very difficult to sort out. This has been discouraging, even though I do not doubt the genuineness of certain parapsychological phenomena. For this reason I have confined myself to an occasional reference to the *archetypal symbolism* of these phenomena, without discussing the question of their 'reality'. For the only certainty is that most parapsychological events follow certain archetypal patterns, which can be understood and interpreted psychologically. I cannot conclude, however, whether it is really the dead who respond in spiritualistic

séances, or just the complexes of the living participants, or the activated contents of the collective unconscious." In spite of this she adds, ibid., xv, "Nevertheless, I 'believe' that the dead do manifest themselves occasionally in parapsychological events, although for the time being this does not seem to me to be unequivocally provable."

39. *MDR*, 299–326.

40. Ibid., 323.

41. Jung, *Letters 2: 1951–1961*, 561.

42. Jung, "On the Nature of the Psyche," 216.

Bibliography

Abenheimer, Karl M. "Lou Andreas-Salomé's Main Contribution to Psycho-Analysis." *Spring* (1971): 22–37.

Abraham, Karl. "The Psycho-Sexual Differences Between Hysteria and Dementia Praecox." 1908. In *Selected Papers of Karl Abraham*. Trans. Douglas Bryan and Alix Strachey. London: The Hogarth Press, 1948. 64–79.

Adler, Gerhard. "The Memoirs of C. G. Jung." *Spring* (1964): 139–46.

————. "Review of *Memories, Dreams, and Reflections*, by C. G. Jung." *Journal of Analytical Psychology* 8 (1963): 173–75.

————. "Memory of Toni Wolff." In *C. G. Jung, Emma Jung and Toni Wolff: A Collection of Remembrances*. Ed. Ferne Jensen and Sidney Mullen. San Francisco: The Analytical Psychology Club of San Francisco, 1982. 1.

Alexander, Franz, and Sheldon T. Selesnick. "Freud-Bleuler Correspondence." *Archives of General Psychiatry* 12 (1965): 1–9.

Astor, James. "A Conversation with Dr. Michael Fordham." *Journal of Child Psychotherapy* 14 (1988): 3–11.

Aziz, Robert. *C. G. Jung's Psychology of Religion and Synchronicity*. Albany: State University of New York Press, 1990.

Bakan, David. *Sigmund Freud and the Jewish Mystical Tradition*. Princeton, N.J.: Van Nostrand, 1958.

Barbour, John D. "Character and Characterization in Religious Autobiography." *Journal of the American Academy of Religion* 55 (1987): 307–27.

Barrow, Logie. *Independent Spirits: Spiritualism and English Plebians, 1850–1910*. London: Routledge & Kegan Paul, 1986.

Baudouin, Charles. *L'Oeuvre de jung*. Paris: Payot, 1963.

Baynes, H. G. "The Ghost as a Psychic Phenomenon." 1936. In *Analytical*

Psychology and the English Mind. London: Methuen & Co., 1950. 154–67.

Beard, George M. "The Psychology of Spiritism." *The North American Review* 129 (1879): 65–80.

Bednarowski, Mary Farrell. "Outside the Mainstream: Women's Religion and Women Religious Leaders in Nineteenth-Century America." *Journal of the American Academy of Religion* 48 (1980): 207–31.

Bennet, E. A. *C. G. Jung.* London: Barrie and Rockliff, 1961.

———. *Meetings with Jung.* London: The Anchor Press, 1982.

Bennet, Glin. "Domestic Life with C. G. Jung: Taperecorded Conversations with Ruth Bailey." *Spring* (1986): 177–89.

Berry, Thomas E. *Spiritualism in Tzarist Society and Literature.* Baltimore, Md.: Edgar Allen Poe Society, 1985.

Binswanger, Ludwig. "My First Three Visits with Freud in Vienna (1957)." In *Freud as We Knew Him.* Ed. Hendrik M. Ruitenbeek. Detroit: Wayne State University Press, 1973. 360–68.

Boor, Myron, and Philip M. Coons. "A Comprehensive Bibliography of Literature Pertaining to Multiple Personality." *Psychological Reports* 53 (1983): 295–310.

Boring, Edwin G. *A History of Experimental Psychology.* New York: Appleton-Century-Crofts, 1957.

Brenner, E. M. "Gnosticism and Psychology: Jung's *Septem Sermones ad Mortuos.*" *Journal of Analytical Psychology* 35 (1990): 397–419.

Brent, T. David. "Jung's Debt to Kant: The Transcendental Method and the Structure of Jung's Psychology." Ph.D. dissertation. University of Chicago, 1977.

Broad, C. D. "Immanuel Kant and Psychical Research." In *Religion, Philosophy and Psychical Research.* London: Routledge & Kegan Paul, 1953. 116–55.

Brome, Vincent. *Jung: Man and Myth.* London: Macmillan, 1978.

Brown, Edward M. "Neurology and Spiritualism in the 1870s." *Bulletin of the History of Medicine* 57 (1983): 563–77.

Bruun, Geoffrey. *Nineteenth-Century European Civilization 1815–1914.* London: Oxford University Press, 1959.

Buber, Martin. *Eclipse of God.* New York: Harper & Row, 1952.

Buranelli, Vincent. *The Wizard from Vienna: Franz Anton Mesmer.* New York: Coward, McCann & Geohegan, 1975.

Butts, Robert E. *Kant and the Double Government Methodology.* Dordrecht: D. Reidel, 1984.

Carotenuto, Aldo. *A Secret Symmetry: Sabina Spielrein between Jung and Freud.* New York: Pantheon Books, 1984.

Cassirer, Ernst. *Kant's Life and Thought.* Trans. James Haden. New Haven: Yale University Press, 1981.

Chadwick, Owen. *The Secularization of the European Mind in the Nineteenth Century.* Cambridge: Cambridge University Press, 1975.

Champernowne, Irene. *A Memoir of Toni Wolff.* San Francisco: C. G. Jung Institute of San Francisco, 1980.

Charcot, Jean-Martin. "The Faith-Cure." *The New Review* 6 (1893): 18–31.

————. "Spiritualism and Hysteria." In *Clinical Lectures on Diseases of the Nervous System,* vol. 3. Trans. Thomas Savill. London: The New Sydenham Society, 1889. 198–206.

Chertok, Leon. "Relation and Influence." *American Journal of Clinical Hypnosis* 29 (1986): 13–22.

Claparède, Ed. "Théodore Flournoy: sa vie et son oeuvre 1854–1920." *Archives de Psychologie* 18 (1923): 1–125.

Copleston, Frederick. *History of Philosophy,* vol. 6, pt. 1, *The French Enlightenment to Kant.* New York: Image Books, 1960.

————. *A History of Philosophy,* vol. 6 pt. 2, *Kant.* New York: Image Books, 1960.

Coward, Harold. *Jung and Eastern Thought.* Albany: State University of New York Press, 1985.

Creelan, Paul. "Watson as Mythmaker: The Millenarian Sources of Watson's Behaviorism." *Journal for the Scientific Study of Religion* 24 (1985): 194–216.

Cross, Whitney R. *The Burned-Over District: The Social and Intellectual History of Enthusiastic Religion in Western New York, 1800–1850.* Ithaca: Cornell University Press, 1950.

Dain, Norman. *Concepts of Insanity in the United States, 1789–1865.* New Brunswick, N.J.: Rutgers University Press, 1964.

Darnton, Robert. "Mesmer, Franz Anton." In *Dictionary of Scientific Biog-*

raphy, vol. 9. Ed. Charles Coulston Gillispie. New York: Charles Scribner's Sons, 1974. 325–28.

—. *Mesmerism and the End of the Enlightenment in France.* Cambridge, Mass.: Harvard University Press, 1968.

Delp, Robert W. "Andrew Jackson Davis: Prophet of American Spiritualism." *The Journal of American History* 59 (1967): 43–56.

Dijkstra, Bram. *Idols of Perversity.* New York: Oxford University Press, 1986.

Donn, Linda. *Freud and Jung: Years of Friendship, Years of Loss.* New York: Charles Scribner's Sons, 1988.

Drinka, George Frederick. *The Birth of Neurosis.* New York: Simon and Schuster, 1984.

Eissler, K. R. *Psychologische Aspekte Des Briefwechsels Zwischen Freud und Jung.* Stuttgart: Fromann Holzboog, 1982.

Elder, George R. "Phallus." In *The Encyclopedia of Religion,* vol. 11. Ed. Mircea Eliade. New York: Macmillan, 1987. 263–69.

Eliade, Mircea, and Joseph M. Kitagawa, eds. *The History of Religions: Essays in Methodology.* Chicago: The University of Chicago Press, 1959.

Ellenberger, Henri F. "Carl Gustav Jung: His Historical Setting." In *Historical Explorations in Medicine and Psychiatry.* Ed. Hertha Riese. New York: Springer, 1978. 142–49.

—. *The Discovery of the Unconscious.* New York: Basic Books, 1970.

Erikson, Erik H. *Insight and Responsibility.* New York: W. W. Norton, 1964.

—. "Themes of Adulthood in the Freud-Jung Correspondence." In *Themes of Work and Love in Adulthood.* Ed. Neil J. Smelser and Erik H. Erikson. Cambridge, Mass.: Harvard University Press, 1980. 43–74.

—. *Young Man Luther.* London: Faber and Faber, 1958.

Ferenczi, Sandor. "Spiritism." (1899) *The Psychoanalytic Review* 50 (1963): 139–44.

Flammarion, Camille. *Mysterious Psychic Forces.* Boston: Small, Maynard and Co., 1909.

Florovsky, George. *Ways of Russian Theology,* vol. I. Belmont, Mass.: Norland Press, 1979.

Flournoy, Theodore. *From India to the Planet Mars.* (1900) Reprint, New Hyde Park, New York: University Books, 1963.

———. "Review of Dr. C. G. Jung, *Wandlungen und Symbole der Libido.*" *Archives de Psychologie* 13 (1913): 195–99.

———. "Review of Dr. C. G. Jung, *Zur Psychologie und Pathologie sogenannter occulter Phänomene.*" *Archives de Psychologie* 2 (1903): 85–86.

———. *Spiritism and Psychology.* New York: Harper & Brothers, 1911.

Fodor, Nandor. *Encyclopedia of Psychic Science.* (1934) Reprint, New Hyde Park, New York: University Books, 1966.

———. *Freud, Jung and Occultism.* New Hyde Park, N.Y.: University Books, 1971.

———. "Jung's Sermons to the Dead." *The Psychoanalytic Review* 51 (1964): 74–78.

———. "Sandor Ferenczi's Psychic Adventures." *International Journal of Parapsychology* 3 (1961): 49–63.

Fordham, Michael. *Children as Individuals.* New York: G. P. Putnam's Sons, 1970.

———. "Maturation of a Child Within the Family." *Journal of Analytical Psychology* 22 (1977): 91–105.

———. "Memories and Thoughts about C. G. Jung." *Journal of Analytical Psychology* 20 (1975): 102–13.

———. "Primary Self, Primary Narcissism and Related Concepts." *Journal of Analytical Psychology* 16 (1971): 168–87.

Franz, Marie-Louise von. "Archetypes Surrounding Death." *Quadrant* 12 (1979): 5–23.

———. *C. G. Jung: His Myth in Our Time.* London: Hodder and Stroughton, 1975.

———. Introduction to *The Zofingia Lectures.* In C. G. Jung, *Collected Works,* Suppl. vol. A, *The Zofingia Lectures,* Princeton, N.J.: Princeton University Press, 1983. xiii – xxv.

———. "The Library of C. G. Jung," *Spring* (1970): 190–95.

———. "On Active Imagination." In *Methods of Treatment in Analytical Psychology.* Ed. Ian F. Baker.Fellbach: Bonz, 1980. 88–99.

———. *On Dreams and Death.* Boston: Shambala, 1987.

————. "The Process of Individuation." In *Man and His Symbols*. Ed., C. G. Jung. New York: Doubleday, 1964. 158–229.

Freud, Sigmund. "Delusions and Dreams in Jensen's *Gradiva*" (1907) In *Standard Edition*, vol. 9, *Jensen's 'Gradiva' and Other Works*. London: The Hogarth Press, 1959. 7–93.

————. "Dreams and Telepathy." (1922) In *Standard Edition*, vol. 18, *Beyond the Pleasure Principle Group Psychology and Other Works*. London: The Hogarth Press, 1955. 197–220.

————. "Formulations on the Two Principles of Mental Functioning." (1911) In *Standard Edition*, vol. 12, *The Case of Schreber Papers on Technique and Other Works*. London: The Hogarth Press, 1958. 218–26.

————. *The Freud/Jung Letters*. Ed. William McGuire. Trans. Ralph Manheim and R. F. C. Hull. Princeton, N.J.: Princeton University Press, 1974.

————. *Letters of Sigmund Freud*. Ed. Ernst L. Freud. Trans. Tania and James Stern. New York: Basic Books, 1960.

————. *The Letters of Sigmund Freud to Eduard Silberstein 1871–1881*. Ed. Walter Boehlich. Trans. Arnold J. Pomerans. Cambridge Mass.: Harvard University Press, 1990.

————. "New Introductory Lectures on Psycho-Analysis." (1933) In *Standard Edition*, vol. 22, *New Introductory Lectures on Psycho-Analysis and Other Works*. London: The Hogarth Press, 1964. 5–182.

————. "A Note on the Unconscious in Psycho-Analysis" (1912) *Standard Edition*, vol. 12, *The Case of Schreber Papers on Technique and Other Works*. London: The Hogarth Press, 1958. 257–66

————. "Notes Upon a Case of Obsessional Neurosis." (1909) In *Standard Edition*, vol. 10, *Two Case Histories ('Little Hans' and The 'Rat Man')*. London: The Hogarth Press, 1955. 155–318.

————. "Obsessive Actions and Religious Practices." (1907) In *Standard Edition*, vol. 9, *Jensen's 'Gradiva' and Other Works*. London: The Hogarth Press, 1959. 117–27.

————. *The Origins of Psycho-analysis: Letters to Wilhelm Fliess, Drafts and Notes: 1887–1902*. Ed. Marie Bonaparte, Anna Freud, and Ernst Kris. Trans. Eric Mosbacher and James Strachey. New York: Basic Books, 1954.

————. "Papers on Hypnotism and Suggestion" (1888–92) In *Standard Edition*, vol. 1, *Pre-Psycho-Analytic Publications and Unpublished Drafts*. London: The Hogarth Press, 1966. 63–128.

————. "Preface to the Translation of Bernheim's *Suggestion.*" (1888) In *Standard Edition*, vol. 1, *Pre-Psycho-Analytic Publications and Unpublished Drafts.* London: the Hogarth Press, 1966. 73–85.

————. *A Psycho-Analytic Dialogue: The Letters of Sigmund Freud and Karl Abraham 1907–1926.* Ed. Hilda C. Abraham and Ernst L. Freud. Trans. Bernard Marsh and Hilda C. Abraham. New York: Basic Books, 1965.

————. "Psycho-Analytic Notes on an Autobiographical Account of a Case of Paranoia (Demetia Paranoides)." (1911–12) In *Standard Edition*, vol. 12, *The Case of Schreber Papers on Technique and Other Works.* London: The Hogarth Press, 1958. 9–82.

————. *The Standard Edition of the Complete Psychological Works of Sigmund Freud.* 24 vols. English translation edited by James Strachey. In collaboration with Anna Freud. Assisted by Alex Strachey, Alan Tyson and Angela Richards. London: The Hogarth Press, 1953–74.

————. "Totem and Taboo." (1913) In *Standard Edition*, vol. 13, *Totem and Taboo and Other Works.* London: The Hogarth Press, 1955. 1–161.

Friedenthal, Richard. *Goethe: His Life and Times.* London: Weidenfeld and Nicholson, 1963.

Fromm, Erich. "C. G. Jung: Prophet of the Unconscious." *Scientific American* 209 (1963): 283–90.

Fuller, Robert C. *Mesmerism and the American Cure of Souls.* Philadelphia: University of Pennsylvania Press, 1982.

Gardiner, Patrick. *Schopenhauer.* Harmondsworth, Middlesex: Penguin, 1963.

Gauld, Alan. *The Founders of Psychical Research.* New York: Schocken, 1968.

Gay, Peter. *A Godless Jew.* New Haven: Yale University Press, 1987.

Gedo, John E. *Portraits of the Artist.* New York: The Guildford Press, 1983.

Gerber, William. "Philosophical Dictionaries and Encyclopedias." In *The Encyclopedia of Philosophy*, vol. 6. Ed. Paul Edwards. New York: Macmillan, 1967. 170–99.

Giegerich, Wolfgang. "Hospitality Toward the Gods in an Ungodly Age: Philemon-Faust-Jung." *Spring* (1984): 61–75.

Gifford, Jr., George E., ed. *Psychoanalysis, Psychotherapy and the New England Medical Scene, 1894–1944.* New York: Science History Publications, 1978.

Gilmore, William J. *Psychohistorical Inquiry: A Comprehensive Research Bibliography.* New York: Garland, 1984.

Glaser, Hermann, ed. *The German Mind of the 19th Century.* New York: Continuum, 1981.

Glover, Edward. "Abraham, Karl." In *Encyclopedia of Psychoanalysis.* Ed. Ludwig Eidelberg. New York: The Free Press, 1968. 1–8.

Goldenberg, Naomi R. "Looking at Jung Looking at Himself: A Psychoanalytic Rereading of *Memories, Dreams, Reflections.*" In *Returning Words to Flesh: Feminism, Psychoanalysis and the Resurrection of the Body.* Boston: Beacon Press, 1990. 116–45.

Goldfarb, Russel M., and Clare R. *Spiritualism and Nineteenth-Century Letters.* Rutherford, N.J.: Fairleigh Dickinson University Press, 1978.

Goldstein, Jan. *Console and Classify: The French Psychiatric Profession in the Nineteenth Century.* Cambridge: Cambridge University Press, 1987.

———. "The Hysteria Diagnosis and the Politics of Anticlericalism in Late Nineteenth-Century France." *Journal of Modern History* 54 (1982): 209–39.

Goodheart, William B. "C. G. Jung's First 'Patient'." *Journal of Analytical Psychology* 29 (1984): 1–34.

———. "Letter to the Editors." *International Journal of Psycho-Analysis* 70 (1989): 545–49.

——— et al. "Comments." *Spring* (1985): 161–85.

Gormley, William J. *Medical Hypnosis: Historical Introduction to Its Morality in the Light of Papal, Theological and Medical Teaching.* Washington, D. C.: Catholic University of America Press, 1961.

Gravitz, Melvin A., and Manuel I. Gerton. "Freud and Hypnosis: Report of Post-Rejection Use." *Journal of the History of the Behavioral Sciences* 17 (1981): 68–74.

———. "Polgar as Freud's Hypnotist? Contrary Evidence." *The American Journal of Clinical Hypnosis* 24 (1982): 272–76.

Gregory, Anita. *The Strange Case of Rudi Schneider.* Metuchen, N.Y.: The Scarecrow Press, 1985.

Grubrich-Simitis, Ilse. "Six Letters of Sigmund Freud and Sándor Ferenczi on the Interrelationship of Psychoanalytic Theory and Technique." *International Review of Psycho-Analysis* 13 (1986): 259–77.

Guillain, George S. *J. M. Charcot 1825–1893: His Life and Work.* Ed. and trans. Pearce Bailey. New York: Paul B. Hoeber, 1959.

Hall, G. Stanley. "A Medium in the Bud." *The American Journal of Psychology* 29 (1918): 144–58.

Hannah, Barbara. *Encounters with the Soul: Active Imagination as Developed by C. G. Jung.* Santa Monica: Sigo Press, 1981.

———. *Jung: His Life and Work.* New York: G. P. Putnam's Sons, 1976.

Harms, Ernest. "Review of *Memories, Dreams, and Reflections.*" *American Journal of Psychotherapy* 19 (1965): 153.

Harris, Ruth. "Murder Under Hypnosis." *Psychological Medicine* 15 (1985): 477–505.

Haule, John R. "Archetype and Integration: Exploring the Janetian Roots of Analytical Psychology." *Journal of Analytical Psychology* 28 (1983): 253–67.

———. "From Somnambulism to the Archetypes: The French Roots of Jung's Split with Freud." *The Psychoanalytic Review* 71 (1984): 635–59.

Hawthorn, Jeremy. *Multiple Personality and the Disintegration of Literary Character.* London: Edward Arnold, 1983.

Heisig, James. *Imago Dei.* Lewisburg, Pa.: Bucknell University Press, 1979.

———. "Jung and Theology: A Bibliographical Essay." *Spring* (1973): 204–55.

———. "The VII Sermones: Play and Theory." *Spring* (1972): 206–18.

Henderson, Helena. "Toni Wolff." In *C. G. Jung, Emma Jung and Toni Wolff: A Collection of Remembrances.* Ed. Ferne Jensen and Sidney Mullen. San Francisco: The Analytical Psychology Club of San Francisco, 1982. 31.

Hillman, James. *Loose Ends.* Zurich: Spring Publications, 1975.

———. "Some Early Background to Jung's Ideas: Notes on *C. G. Jung's Medium* by Stephanie Zumstein-Preiswerk." *Spring* (1976): 123–36.

———, and Paul Kugler. "The Autonomous Psyche: A Communication to Goodheart from the Bi-Personal Field of Paul Kugler and James Hillman." *Spring* (1985): 141–61.

Hillman, Robert G. "A Scientific Study of Mystery: The Role of the Medical and Popular Press in the Nancy-Salpêtrière Controversy on Hypnotism." *Bulletin of the History of Medicine* 39 (1965): 163–82.

Hobdell, Roger. "A Bibliography of the Writings of Michael Fordham." *Journal of Analytical Psychology* 31 (1986): 307–15.

Hoeller, Stephan A. *The Gnostic Jung and the Seven Sermons to the Dead.* Wheaton, Ill.: The Theosophical Publishing House, 1982.

Hogenson, George B. *Jung's Struggle with Freud.* Notre Dame: University of Notre Dame Press, 1983.

Homans, Peter. *Jung in Context.* Chicago: The University of Chicago Press, 1979.

Hubback, Judith. "VII Sermones Ad Mortuos." *Journal of Analytical Psychology* 11 (1966): 95–111.

Hughes, H. Stuart. *Consciousness and Society.* Rev. ed. New York: Vintage Books, 1977.

Hull, R. F. C. "Bibliographical Notes on Active Imagination in the Works of C. G. Jung." *Spring* (1971): 115–20.

Humbert, Elie G. "Active Imagination According to C. G. Jung." In *Jung in Modern Perspective.* Ed. Renos K. Papadopoulos and Graham S. Saayman. Hounslow, Middlesex: Wildwood House, 1984. 89–108.

Hyslop, James H. "Kant and Spiritualism." *Journal of the American Society for Psychical Research* 14 (1920): 226–31.

———. "Review of *Psychology of the Unconscious* by C. G. Jung." *Journal of the American Society for Psychical Research* 13 (1919): 44–47.

Isaacs, Ernest. "The Fox Sisters and American Spiritualism." In *The Occult in America: New Historical Perspectives.* Ed. Howard Kerr and Charles L. Crow. Urbana: University of Illinois Press, 1983. 79–110.

Jacobi, Jolande. *Complex/Archetype/Symbol.* Princeton, N.J.: Princeton University Press, 1959.

Jaffé, Aniela. *C. G. Jung: Word and Image.* Princeton, N.J.: Princeton University Press, 1979.

———. "Details about C. G. Jung's Family." *Spring* (1984): 35–43.

———. *From the Life and Work of C. G. Jung.* London: Hodder and Stroughton, 1971.

———. *The Myth of Meaning.* New York: G. P. Putnam's Sons, 1971.

James, William. *Essays on Psychical Research.* Cambridge, Mass.: Harvard University Press, 1986.

————. *The Letters of William James and Theodore Flournoy.* Ed. Robert C. Le Clair. Madison: The University of Wisconsin Press, 1966.

Jarret, James L. "Schopenhauer and Jung." *Spring* (1981): 193– 204.

Johnson, Paul E. *A Shopkeeper's Millenium: Society and Revivals in Rochester, New York, 1815–1837.* New York: Hill and Wang, 1978.

Jones, Ernest. *The Life and Work of Sigmund Freud.* 3 Vols. New York: Basic Books, 1953–57.

Jonsson, Inge. "Swedenborg, Emanuel." In *The Encyclopedia of Philosophy,* vol. 8. Ed. Paul Edwards. New York: Macmillan, 1967. 48–51.

Judah, J. Stillson. *The History and Philosophy of the Metaphysical Movements in America.* Philadelphia: The Westminster Press, 1967.

Jung, C. G. "Abstracts of the Psychological Works of Swiss Authors" (1910) In *Collected Works,* vol. 18, *The Symbolic Life.* Princeton, N.J.: Princeton University Press, 1976. 398–421.

————. "Adaptation, Individuation, Collectivity." (1916) In *Collected Works,* vol. 18, *The Symbolic Life.* Princeton, N.J.: Princeton University Press, 1976. 449–54.

————. *Analytical Psychology* (1925) Ed. William McGuire. Princeton, N.J.: Princeton University Press, 1989.

————. *Answer to Job* (1952) In *Collected Works,* vol. 11, *Psychology and Religion.* 2nd ed. Princeton, N.J.: Princeton University Press, 1969. 357–470.

————. *C. G. Jung Bibliothek: Katalog.* Kusnacht-Zurich: 1967.

————. *The Collected Works of C. G. Jung.* 21 Vols. Edited by Herbert Read, Michael Fordham, Gerhard Adler. Executive editor William McGuire. Translated by R. F. C. Hull, Leopold Stein, Diana Riviere, Jan van Heurck. Princeton, N.J.: Princeton University Press, 1953–83.

————. *Collected Works,* vol. 1, *Psychiatric Studies* (1902–06) 2nd ed. Princeton, N.J.: Princeton University Press, 1970.

————. *Collected Works,* vol. 2, *Experimental Researches* (1905–37) 2nd ed. Princeton, N.J.: Princeton University Press, 1973.

————. *Collected Works,* vol. 3, *The Psychogenesis of Mental Disease.* New York: Pantheon Books, 1960.

————. *Collected Works,* vol. 4, *Freud and Psychoanalysis* (1906–31) Princeton, N.J.: Princeton University Press, 1961.

———. *Collected Works*, vol. 5, *Symbols of Transformation* (1912, rev. 1952) 2nd ed. Princeton, N.J.: Princeton University Press, 1967.

———. *Collected Works*, vol. 6, *Psychological Types* (1921) Princeton, N.J.: Princeton University Press, 1971.

———. *Collected Works*, vol. 7, *Two Essays on Analytical Psychology.* (1917/1916 rev. 1943/1935) 2nd. ed. Princeton, N.J.: Princeton Univeristy Press, 1966.

———. *Collected Works*, vol. 9i, *The Archetypes and the Collective Unconscious.* (1936–54) 2nd ed. Princeton, N.J.: Princeton University Press, 1969.

———. *Collected Works*, vol. 9ii, *Aion* (1951) 2nd ed. Princeton, N.J.: Princeton University Press, 1968.

———. *Collected Works*, vol. 11, *Psychology and Religion.* (1928–54) 2nd. ed. Princeton, N.J.: Princeton University Press, 1969.

———. *Collected Works*, vol. 12, *Psychology and Alchemy.* (1944, rev. 1952) 2nd ed. Princeton, N.J.: Princeton University Press, 1968.

———. *Collected Works*, vol. 14, *Mysterium Coniunctionis.* (1955–56) 2nd ed. Princeton, N.J.: Princeton University Press, 1970.

———. *Collected Works*, vol. 17, *The Development of Personality.* (1909–42). New York: Pantheon Books, 1954.

———. *Collected Works*, vol. 19, *General Bibliography.* Compiled by Lisa Ress. Princeton, N.J.: Princeton University Press, 1979.

———. "Concerning the Archetypes, with Special Reference to the Anima Concept." (1936, rev. 1954) In *Collected Works*, vol. 9i, *The Archetypes and The Collective Unconscious.* 2nd ed. Princeton, N.J.: Princeton University Press, 1969. 54–72.

———. "Contribution to Moser: *Spuk: Irrglaube Oder Wahrglaube?*" (1950) In *Collected Works*, vol. 18, *The Symbolic Life.* Princeton, N.J.: Princeton University Press, 1976. 320–26.

———. "Contributions to Symbolism." (1911) In *Collected Works*, vol. 18, *The Symbolic Life.* Princeton, N.J.: Princeton University Press, 1976. 446.

———. *Dream Analysis.* (1928–30). Ed. William McGuire. Princeton, N.J.: Princeton University Press, 1984.

———. *Erinnerungen, Träume, Gedanken.* Recorded and edited by Aniela Jaffé. Zurich: Rascher, 1961.

———. *Flying Saucers: A Modern Myth of Things Seen in the Skies.* (1958). In *Collected Works,* vol. 10, *Civilization in Transition.* 2nd ed. Princeton, N.J.: Princeton University Press, 1970. 309–433.

———. "Freud and Jung: Contrasts." (1929) In *Collected Works,* vol. 4, *Freud and Psychoanalysis.* Princeton, N.J.: Princeton University Press, 1961. 333–40.

———. "The Freudian Theory of Hysteria." (1908) In *Collected Works,* vol. 4, *Freud and Psychoanalysis.* Princeton, N.J.: Princeton University Press, 1961. 10–24.

———. "The Gifted Child." (1942) In *Collected Works,* vol. 17, *The Development of the Personality.* New York: Pantheon Books, 1954. 135–45.

———. "Instinct and the Unconscious." (1919) In *Collected Works,* vol. 8, *The Structure and Dynamics of the Psyche.* 2nd ed. Princeton, N.J.: Princeton University Press, 1969. 129–138.

———. "Introduction to Toni Wolff's '*Studies in Jungian Psychology*'." (1959) In *Collected Works,* vol. 10, *Civilization in Transition.* 2nd ed. Princeton, N.J.: Princeton University Press, 1970. 469–76.

———. "Introduction to Wickes's '*Analyse Der Kinderseele*'." (1931) In *Collected Works,* vol. 17, *The Development of Personality.* New York: Pantheon Books, 1954. 39–46.

———. "Letter to Père Bruno." (1953) In *Collected Works,* vol. 18, *The Symbolic Life.* Princeton, N.J.: Princeton University Press, 1976. 673–78.

———. *Letters: 1906–1961.* Ed. Gerhard Adler and Aniela Jaffé. Trans. R. F. C. Hull. 2 vols. Princeton, N.J.: Princeton University Press, 1973–1975.

———. *Memories, Dreams, Reflections.* Recorded and edited by Aniela Jaffé. Trans. Richard and Clara Winston. New York: Vintage Books, 1973.

———. "Mind and Earth." (1927, rev. 1931) In *Collected Works,* vol. 10, *Civilization in Transition.* 2nd ed. Princeton, N.J.: Princeton University Press, 1970. 29–49.

———. *Nietzsche's Zarathustra.* (1934–39). Ed. James L. Jarret. 2 vols. Princeton, N.J.: Princeton University Press, 1988.

———. "On Dementia Praecox." (1908) In *Collected Works,* vol. 18, *The Symbolic Life.* Princeton, N.J.: Princeton University Press, 1976. 335.

———. "On Spiritualistic Phenomena." (1905) In *Collected Works,* vol. 18,

The Symbolic Life. Princeton, N.J.: Princeton University Press, 1976. 293–308.

———. "On the Nature of the Psyche." (1947, rev. 1954). In *Collected Works*, vol. 8, *The Structure and Dynamics of the Psyche*. 2nd ed. Princeton, N.J.: Princeton University Press, 1969. 159–234.

———. "On the Problem of Psychogenesis in Mental Disease." (1919) In *Collected Works*, vol. 3, *The Psychogenesis of Mental Disease*. New York: Pantheon Books, 1960. 211–25.

———. *On the Psychology and Pathology of So-Called Occult Phenomena*. (1902) *Collected Works*, vol. 1, *Psychiatric Studies*. 2nd ed. Princeton, N.J.: Princeton University Press, 1970. 3–88.

———. "On the Psychology of the Unconscious." (1917 rev. 1943) In *Collected Works*, vol. 7, *Two Essays on Analytical Psychology*. 2nd ed. Princeton, N.J.: Princeton University Press, 1966. 3–119.

———. "The Phenomenology of the Spirit in Fairytales." (1945 rev. 1948) In *Collected Works*, vol. 9i, *The Archetypes and the Collective Unconscious*. 2nd ed. Princeton, N.J.: Princeton University Press, 1969. 207–54.

———. "Psychic Conflicts in a Child." (1909, rev. 1946) In *Collected Works*, vol. 17, *The Development of Personality*. New York: Pantheon Books, 1954. 1–35.

———. "The Psychological Aspect of the Kore." (1941, rev. 1951) In *Collected Works*, vol. 9i, *The Archetypes and the Collective Unconscious*. 2nd ed. Princeton, N.J.: Princeton University Press, 1969. 182–203.

———. "Psychological Aspects of the Mother Archetype." (1938, rev. 1954) In *Collected Works*, vol. 9i, *The Archetypes and the Collective Unconscious*. 2nd ed. Princeton, N.J.: Princeton University Press, 1969. 75–110.

———. "The Psychological Foundations of Belief in Spirits." (1919, rev. 1948) In *Collected Works*, vol. 8, *The Structure and Dynamics of the Psyche*. 2nd ed. Princeton, N.J.: Princeton University Press, 1969. 301–18.

———. "Psychology and Spiritualism." (1948) In *Collected Works*, vol. 18, *The Symbolic Life*. Princeton, N.J.: Princeton University Press, 1976. 312–16.

———. *The Psychology of Dementia Praecox*. (1907) In *Collected Works*, vol. 3, *The Psychogenesis of Mental Disease*. New York: Pantheon Books, 1960. 1–151.

―――. "A Rejoinder to Dr. Bally." (1934) In *Collected Works*, vol. 10, *Civilization in Transition*. 2nd ed. Princeton, N.J.: Princeton University Press, 1970. 535–44.

―――. "The Relations Between the Ego and the Unconscious." (1916, rev. 1935) In *Collected Works*, vol. 7, *Two Essays on Analytical Psychology*. 2nd ed. Princeton, N.J.: Princeton University Press, 1966. 123–241.

―――. "Religion and Psychology. A Reply to Martin Buber." (1952) In *Collected Works*, vol. 18, *The Symbolic Life*. Princeton, N.J.: Princeton University Press, 1976. 663–70.

―――. "A Review of the Complex Theory." (1934, rev. 1948) In *Collected Works*, vol. 8, *The Structure and Dynamics of the Psyche*. 2nd ed. Princeton, N.J.: Princeton University Press, 1969. 92–104.

―――. "Schizophrenia." (1958) In *Collected Works*, vol. 3, *The Psychogenisis of Mental Disease*. New York: Pantheon Books, 1960. 256–72.

―――. "A Seminar with C. G. Jung: Comments on a Child's Dream." (1936–37). *Spring* (1974): 200–23.

―――. "Sigmund Freud: *'On Dreams'*." (1901) In *Collected Works*, vol. 18, *The Symbolic Life*. Princeton, N.J.: Princeton University Press, 1976. 361–368.

―――. *Studies in Word Association*. (1904–09). In *Collected Works*, vol. 2, *Experimental Researches*. Princeton, N.J.: Princeton University Press, 1973. 3–479.

―――. "Synchronicity: An Acausal Connecting Principle." (1952, rev. 1955) In *Collected Works*, vol. 8, *The Structure and Dynamics of the Psyche*. 2nd ed. Princeton, N.J.: Princeton University Press, 1969. 419–519.

―――. *The Tavistock Lectures*. (1935) In *Collected Works*, vol. 18, *The Symbolic Life*. Princeton, N.J.: Princeton University Press, 1976. 1–182.

―――. *The Theory of Psychoanalysis*. (1913, rev. ed. 1955) In *Collected Works*, vol. 4, *Freud and Psychoanalysis*. Princeton, N.J.: Princeton University Press, 1961. 83–226.

―――. *The Zofingia Lectures*. (1896–99) *Collected Works, Supplementary Vol. A*. Princeton, N.J.: Princeton University Press, 1983.

Kant, Immanuel. *Anthropology From a Pragmatic Point of View*. (1798) Trans. Victor Lyle Dowdell. Rev. and ed. Hans H. Rudnick. Carbondale, Ill.: Southern Illinois University Press, 1978.

————. *Dreams of a Spirit-Seer and Other Related Writings*. Trans. by John Manolesco. New York: Vantage Press, 1969.

————. *Universal Natural History and Theory of the Heavens*. (1755) Trans. by Stanley L. Jaki. Edinburgh: Scottish Academic Press, 1981.

Kaplan, Fred. *Dickens and Mesmerism: The Hidden Springs of Fiction*. Princeton, N.J.: Princeton University Press, 1975.

Keller, Tina. "Beginnings of Active Imagination: Analysis with C. G. Jung and Toni Wolff, 1915–1928." *Spring* (1982): 279–94.

Kerr, Howard. *Mediums, and Spirit-Rappers, and Roaring Radicals*. Urbana, Ill.: University of Illinois Press, 1972.

Kerr, John. "Beyond the Pleasure Principle and Back Again: Freud, Jung, and Sabina Spielrein." In *Freud: Appraisals and Reappraisals*, vol. 3. Ed. Paul E. Stepansky. Hillsdale, N.J.: The Analytic Press, 1988. 3–79.

————. "The *Devil's Elixirs*, Jung's 'Theology' and the Dissolution of Freud's 'Poisoning Complex.'" *Psychoanalytic Review* 75 (1988): 1–33.

Klein, Dennis B. *Jewish Origins of the Psychoanalytic Movement*. Chicago: University of Chicago Press, 1985.

Koss, Joan D. "Symbolic Transformations in Traditional Healing Rituals." *Journal of Analytical Psychology* 31 (1986): 341–55.

Kottler, Malcolm Jay. "Alfred Russel Wallace, the Origin of Man, and Spiritualism." *Isis* 65 (1974): 145–92.

Lapponi, Joseph. *Hypnotism and Spiritualism: A Critical and Medical Study*. 2nd ed. New York: Longmans, Green, and Co., 1907.

Leavy, Stanley A. "A Footnote to Jung's 'Memories.'" *The Psychoanalytic Quarterly* 33 (1964): 567–74.

Lewis, Aubrey. "Jung's Early Work." *Journal of Analytical Psychology* 2 (1957): 119–36.

Lindroth, Sten. "Swedenborg, Emanuel." In *Dictionary of Scientific Biography*, vol. 13. Ed. Charles Coulston Gillispie. New York: Scribner's, 1974. 178–81.

Looser, Guenther. "Jung's Childhood Prayer." *Spring* (1966): 76–80.

Ludwig, Arnold M. "Hyponosis in Fiction." *The International Journal of Clinical and Experimental Hypnosis* 11 (1963): 71–80.

Lynn, Peter C. "C. G. Jung, Emma Jung, and Toni Wolff." In *C. G. Jung,*

Emma Jung and Toni Wolff: A Collection of Remembrances. Ed. Ferne Jensen and Sidney Mullen. San Francisco: The Analytical Psychology Club of San Francisco, 1982. 41–42.

Marshall, Marilyn E., and Russell A. Wendt. "Wilhelm Wundt, Spiritism, and the Assumptions of Science." In *Wundt Studies: A Centennial Collection.* Ed. W. G. Bringmann and R. D. Tweney. Toronto: C. J. Hogrefe, 1980. 158–75.

McClendon, James Wm. *Biography as Theology.* Nashville: Abingdon, 1974.

McConkey, Kevin M., and Campbell Perry. "Benjamin Franklin and Mesmerism." *The International Journal of Clinical and Experimental Hypnosis* 33 (1985): 122–30.

McGrath, William. "How Jewish was Freud?" *The New York Reveiw of Books.* Dec. 5, 1991. 27–31.

McGuire, William. "Jung's Complex Reactions (1907): Word Association Experiments Performed by Binswanger." *Spring* (1984): 1–34.

Mearns, James. "Preiswerk, Samuel." In *A Dictionary of Hymology,* vol. 2 (rev. 1907). Ed. J. Julian. Reprint, New York: Dover, 1957. 907–8.

Meier, C. A. *The Psychology of C. G. Jung,* vol. 1, *The Unconscious in its Empirical Manifestations.* Boston: Sigo Press, 1984.

Mesmer, Franz Anton. *Mesmerism: A Translation of the Original Scientific and Medical Writings of F. A. Mesmer.* Ed. George Block. Los Altos, California: William Kaufmann, 1980.

Messent, Peter B., ed. *Literature of the Occult: A Collection of Critical Essays.* Englewood Cliffs, N.J.: Prentice-Hall, 1981.

Micale, Mark S. "The Salpêtrière in the Age of Charcot: An Institutional Perspective on Medical History in the Late Nineteenth Century." *Journal of Contemporary History* 20 (1985): 703–31.

Miller, Miss Frank. "Quelques faits de l'imagination créatrice subconsciente." Introduction by Theodore Flournoy. *Archives de psychologie* 5 (1906): 36–51.

———. "Some Instances of Subconscious Creative Imagination." Prefatory note by James H. Hyslop and introduction by Theodore Flournoy. *Journal of the American Society for Psychical Research* 1 (1907): 287–308.

Miller, Justin. "Interpretations of Freud's Jewishness 1924–1974." *Journal of the History of the Behavioral Sciences* 17 (1981): 357–74.

320   *Bibliography*

Moore, R. Laurence. *In Search of White Crows.* New York: Oxford University Press, 1977.

Moreau, Christian. *Freud et l'occultisme.* Toulouse: Edouard Privat, 1976.

Moser, Liselotte. "Germany." In *Abnormal Hypnotic Phenomena,* vol. 2. Ed. Eric J. Dingwall. London: J & A Churchill, 1967. 103–99.

Nagy, Marilyn. "Self and Freedom in Jung's Lecture on Ritschl." *Journal of Analytical Psychology* 35 (1990): 443–57.

Neill, Stephen. *The Interpretation of the New Testament* 1861–1961. London: Oxford University Press, 1964.

Nelson, Geoffrey K. *Spiritualism and Society.* London: Routledge & Kegan Paul, 1969.

Noel, David C. "Veiled Kabir: C. G. Jung's Phallic Self-Image." *Spring* (1974): 224–42.

Noll, R. "Multiple Personality, Dissociation, and C. G. Jung's Complex Theory." *Journal of Analytical Psychology* 34 (1989): 353–70.

Nunberg, Herman. *Memoirs: Recollections, Ideas, Reflections.* New York: The Psychoanalytic Research and Development Fund, 1969.

———, and Ernst Federn, eds. *Minutes of the Vienna Psychoanalytic Society,* vols. 1–2. New York: International Universities Press, 1962–67.

Oeri, Albert. "Some Youthful Memories of C. G. Jung." *Spring* (1970): 182–89.

Oppenheim, Janet. *The Other World: Spiritualism and Psychical Research in England 1850–1914.* Cambridge: Cambridge University Press, 1985.

Owen, A. R. G. *Hysteria, Hypnosis and Healing: The Work of J.-M. Charcot.* London: Dennis Dobson: 1971.

Owen, Alex. *The Darkened Room: Women, Power and Spiritualism in Late Victorian England.* Philadelphia: University of Pennsylvania Press, 1990.

Pace, Edward A. "Spiritism." In *The Catholic Encyclopedia,* vol. 14. Ed. Charles G. Herbermann. New York: Robert Appleton, 1907–14. 221.

Palfreman, Jon. "Between Skepticism and Credulity: A Study of Victorian Scientific Attitudes to Modern Spiritualism." In *On the Margins of Science: The Social Construction of Rejected Knowledge.* Ed. Roy Wallis. Sociological Review Monograph no. 27. Keele, Staffordshire: University of Keele Press, 1979. 201–36.

Pals, Daniel. "Reductionism and Belief: An Appraisal of Recent Attacks on the Doctrine of Irreducible Religion." *Journal of Religion* 66 (1986): 18–36.

Pattie, Frank A. "Mesmer's Medical Dissertation and its Debt to Mead's *De Imperio Solis ac Lunae.*" *Journal of the History of Medicine and Allied Sciences* 11 (1956): 275–87.

Peat, F. David. *Synchronicity: The Bridge Between Matter and Mind.* Toronto: Bantam Books, 1987.

Percheron, Suzanne. "Memory of C. G. Jung." In *C. G. Jung, Emma Jung and Toni Wolff: A Collection of Remembrances.* Ed. Ferne Jensen and Sidney Mullen. San Francisco: The Analytical Psychology Club of San Francisco, 1982. 51–70.

Pick, B. "Preiswerk, Samuel, Dr." In *Cyclopedia of Biblical, Theological and Ecclesiastical Literature,* vol. 8. Ed. John M'Clintock and James Strong. Harper and Brothers, 1879. 505.

Plaut, A. "Letter to the Editors." *International Journal of Psycho-Analysis* 69 (1988): 552–53.

Podmore, Frank. *Modern Spiritualism.* 2 vols. London: Methuen & Co., 1902.

Post, Laurens van der. *Jung and the Story of Our Time.* New York: Pantheon Books, 1975.

Quen, Jacques M. ed. *Split Minds/Split Brains: Historical and Current Perspectives.* New York: New York University Press, 1986.

Quispel, Gilles. "C. G. Jung und die Gnosis." *Eranos Jahrbuch* (1968): 277–98.

Reynolds, Frank E., and Donald Capps, eds. *The Biographical Process: Studies in the History and Psychology of Religion.* The Hague: Mouton, 1976.

Richardson, Alan. *History: Sacred and Profane.* London: S. C. M. Press, 1964.

Ricketts, Mac Linsott. "The Nature and Extent of Eliade's 'Jungianism'." *Union Seminary Quarterly Review* 25 (1970): 211–34.

Ricksher, Charles, and C. G. Jung, "Further Investigations on the Galvanic Phenomenon and Respiration in Normal and Insane Individuals." (1907–08). In C. G. Jung, *Collected Works,* vol. 2, *Experimental Researches.* Princeton, N.J.: Princeton University Press, 1973. 554–80.

Roazen, Paul. *Freud and His Followers.* New York: Alfred A. Knopf, 1975.

Robbins, Rossell Hope. "The Rochester Rappings." *Dalhousie Review* 45 (1965): 153–64.

Robert, Marthe. *From Oedipus to Moses.* New York: Doubleday, 1976.

Rosenberg, Samuel. *Why Freud Fainted.* New York: The Bobbs-Merrill Co., 1978.

Roth, Cecil. "Salome." In *Encyclopedia Judaica,* vol. 14. Ed. Cecil Roth. Jerusalem: Keter, 1972. 689–90.

Roustang, François. *Dire Mastery: Discipleship from Freud to Lacan.* Trans. Ned Lukacher. Baltimore, Md.: The Johns Hopkins University Press, 1976.

Runyan, William McKinley. "The Psychobiography Debate: An Analytical Review." *Review of Personality and Social Psychology* 3 (1982): 225–53.

Schaefer, Francis J. "Gassner, Johann Joseph." In *The Catholic Encyclopedia,* vol. 6. Ed. Charles G. Herbermann. New York: Robert Appleton, 1907–14. 392.

Scharfstein, Ben-Ami. *The Philosophers: Their Lives and the Nature of Their Thought.* New York: Oxford University Press, 1980.

Schneck, Jerome M. "Freud's 'Medical Hypnotist.'" *The American Journal of Clinical Hypnosis* 19 (1976): 80–81.

———. "Jean-Martin Charcot and the History of Experimental Hypnosis." *Journal of the History of Medicine and Allied Sciencies* 16 (1961): 297–305.

Schopenhauer, Arthur. "Essay on Spirit Seeing." (1851) In *Parerga and Paralipomena,* vol. 1. Trans. E. F. J. Payne. Oxford: The Clarendon Press, 1974. 227–309.

———. *The World as Will and Representation,* 2 vols. (1819, 3rd ed. 1859). Trans. E. F. J. Payne. Indian Hills, Colorado: The Falcon's Wing Press, 1958.

Schultz, Duane. *Intimate Friends, Dangerous Rivals.* Los Angeles: Jeremy P. Tarcher, 1990.

Schweitzer, Albert. *The Quest of the Historical Jesus.* (1906) London: A. & C. Black, 1964.

Shamdasani, Sonu. "A Woman Called Frank." *Spring* 50 (1980): 26–56.

Sharpe, Eric J. *Comparative Religion: A History.* London: Duckworth, 1975.

Shortt, S. E. D. "Physicians and Psychics: The Anglo-American Medical Response to Spiritualism, 1870–1890." *Journal of the History of Medicine and Allied Sciences* 39 (1984): 339–55.

Skultans, V. *Intimacy and Ritual: A Study of Spiritualism, Mediums and Groups.* London: Routledge & Kegan Paul, 1974.

Smart. Ninian. *Concept and Empathy.* Ed. Donald Wiebe. New York: New York University Press, 1986.

Smith-Rosenberg, Carroll. "The Hysterical Woman: Sex Roles and Role Conflict in 19th-Century America." *Social Research* 39 (1972): 652–78.

Spiegelman, J. Marvin. "Psychology and the Occult." *Spring* (1976): 104–22.

Steele, Robert S. *Freud and Jung: Conflicts of Interpretation.* London: Routledge & Kegan Paul, 1982.

Steiner, Gustav. "Erinnerungen an Carl Gustav Jung." *Basler Stadtbuch* (1965): 117–63.

Stepansky, Paul. "The Empiricist as Rebel: Jung, Freud, and the Burdens of Discipleship." *Journal of the History of the Behavioral Sciences* 12 (1976): 216–39.

Stern, Paul J. *C. G. Jung: The Haunted Prophet.* New York: George Braziller, 1976.

Stolorow, Robert D. and George E. Atwood. *Faces in a Cloud: Subjectivity in Personality Theory.* New York: Jason Aronson, 1979.

Sulloway, Frank J. *Freud, Biologist of the Mind.* New York: Basic Books, 1979.

The Sunday Times (London), 28 November 1975.

Sutton, Geoffrey. "Electric Medicine and Mesmerism." *Isis* 72 (1981): 375–92.

Taylor, Eugene. "C. G. Jung and the Boston Psychopathologists 1902–1912." In *Carl Jung and Soul Psychology.* Ed. E. Mark Stern. New York: The Haworth Press, 1986. 131–44.

———. "William James and C. G. Jung." *Spring* (1980): 157–68.

Tomlinson, J. C., and W. Haymaker. "Jean-Martin Charcot (1825–1893)." *American Medical Association Archives of Neurology and Psychiatry* 77 (1957): 44–48.

Tomlinson, Wallace K., and J. John Perret. "Mesmerism in New Orleans:

1845–1861." *The American Journal of Clinical Hypnosis* 18 (1975): 1–5.

Turner, Frank M. "The Victorian Conflict between Science and Religion: A Professional Dimension." *Isis* 69 (1978): 356–76.

Tymms, Ralf. *Doubles in Literary Psychology.* Cambridge: Bowes & Bowes, 1949.

Veith, Ilza. *Hysteria: The History of a Disease.* Chicago: University of Chicago Press, 1965.

Vitz, Paul. *Sigmund Freud's Christian Unconscious.* New York: The Guildford Press, 1988.

Vogt, Gregory M. "The Kugler/Hillman/Goodheart Drama." *Spring* (1986): 156–61.

Voogd, Stephanie de. "C. G. Jung: Psychologist of the Future 'Philosopher' of the Past." *Spring* (1977): 175–82.

———. "Fantasy Versus Fiction: Jung's Kantianism Appraised." In *Jung in Modern Perspective.* Ed. Renos K. Papadopoulos and Graham Saayman. Hounslow, Middlesex: Wildwood House, 1984. 204–28.

Waardenburg, Jacques, ed. *Classical Approaches to the Study of Religion.* 2 vols. The Hague: Mouton, 1973–74.

Wallace, Erwin R. "Freud's Mysticism and its Psychodynamic Determinants." *Bulletin of the Menninger Clinic* 42 (1978): 203–22.

Wallerstein, Robert S. "One Psychoanalysis or Many?" *International Journal of Psycho-Analysis* 69 (1988): 5–21.

Walsh, Anthony A. "A Note on the Origin of 'Modern' Spiritualism." *Journal of the History of Medicine and Allied Sciences* 28 (1973): 167–71.

Walsh, W. H. "Kant, Immanuel." In *The Encyclopedia of Philosophy,* vol. 4. Ed. Paul Edwards. New York: Macmillan, 1967. 305–24.

Webb, James. *The Occult Establishment.* La Salle, Ill.: Open Court, 1976.

———. *The Occult Underground.* La Salle, Ill.: Open Court, 1974.

Wehr, Gerhard. *Jung: A Biography.* Boston: Shambala, 1987.

Welch, Claude, ed. *God and Incarnation in Mid-Nineteenth Century German Theology.* New York: Oxford University Press, 1965.

———. *Protestant Thought in the Nineteenth Century.* 2 vols. New Haven: Yale University Press, 1972–85.

Wester, William C. "The Phreno-Magnetic Society of Cincinnati—1842."

The American Journal of Clinical Hypnosis 18 (1976): 277–81.

Whaling, Frank, ed. *Contemporary Approaches to the Study of Religion.* 2 vols. Berlin: Mouton, 1983–85.

White, Andrew D. *A History of the Warfare of Science with Theology in Christendom.* (1896). New York: George Braziller, 1955.

Whitmont, Edward C. "Prefatory Remarks to Jung's 'Reply to Buber.'" *Spring* (1973): 188–95.

Wickes, Frances G. *The Inner World of Childhood.* New York: Appleton-Century-Crofts, 1927.

Williams, J. P. "Psychical Research and Psychiatry in Late Victorian Britain: Trance as Escasty or Trance as Insanity." In *The Anatomy of Madness: Essays in the History of Psychiatry,* vol. 1, *People and Ideas.* Ed. W. F. Bynum, Roy Porter, and Michael Shepherd. London: Tavistock Publications, 1985. 233–54.

Windholz, George. "Pavlov's Religious Orientation." *Journal for the Scientific Study of Religion* 25 (1986): 320–27.

Winnicott, D. W. "Review of *Memories, Dreams, Reflections.*" *The International Journal of Psycho-Analysis* 45 (1964): 450–55.

Witzig, James S. "Theodore Flournoy—A Friend Indeed." *Journal of Analytical Psychology* 27 (1982): 131–48.

Wolf, Ernest S. "Review of *Psychologische Aspekte Des Briefwechsels Zwischen Freud und Jung.* By K. R. Eissler." *The Psychoanalytic Quarterly* 53 (1984): 450–54.

Wolff, Toni. "A Few Thoughts on the Process of Individuation in Women" (1934). *Spring* (1941): 81–103.

Wolff-Windegg, Philip. "C. G. Jung—Bachofen, Burckhardt, and Basel." *Spring* (1976): 137–47.

Wulff, David M. "Psychological Approaches." In *Contemporary Approaches to the Study of Religion,* vol. 2, *The Social Sciences.* Ed. Frank Whaling. Berlin: Mouton, 1985. 21–88.

———. Wulff, David M. *Psychology of Religion: Classic and Contemporary Views.* New York: John Wiley & Sons, 1991.

Wundt, Wilhelm. "Spiritualism as a Scientific Question." *The Popular Science Monthly* (1879): 577–93.

Zagona, Helen Grace. *The Legend of Salome.* Geneva: Droz, 1960.

Zangwill, O. L. "Freud on Hypnosis." In *The Oxford Companion to the*

Mind. Ed. Richard L. Gregory. New York: Oxford University Press, 1987. 275–76.

Zumstein-Preiswerk, Stephanie. *C. G. Jungs Medium.* Munich: Kindler Verlag, 1975.

Index